Communications in Computer and Information Science 2643

Series Editors

Rationale

The CCIS series is devoted to the publication of proceedings of computer science conferences. Its aim is to efficiently disseminate original research results in informatics in printed and electronic form. While the focus is on publication of peer-reviewed full papers presenting mature work, inclusion of reviewed short papers reporting on work in progress is welcome, too. Besides globally relevant meetings with internationally representative program committees guaranteeing a strict peer-reviewing and paper selection process, conferences run by societies or of high regional or national relevance are also considered for publication.

Topics

The topical scope of CCIS spans the entire spectrum of informatics ranging from foundational topics in the theory of computing to information and communications science and technology and a broad variety of interdisciplinary application fields.

Information for Volume Editors and Authors

Publication in CCIS is free of charge. No royalties are paid, however, we offer registered conference participants temporary free access to the online version of the conference proceedings on SpringerLink (http://link.springer.com) by means of an http referrer from the conference website and/or a number of complimentary printed copies, as specified in the official acceptance email of the event.

CCIS proceedings can be published in time for distribution at conferences or as post-proceedings, and delivered in the form of printed books and/or electronically as USBs and/or e-content licenses for accessing proceedings at SpringerLink. Furthermore, CCIS proceedings are included in the CCIS electronic book series hosted in the SpringerLink digital library at http://link.springer.com/bookseries/7899. Conferences publishing in CCIS are allowed to use Online Conference Service (OCS) for managing the whole proceedings lifecycle (from submission and reviewing to preparing for publication) free of charge.

Publication process

The language of publication is exclusively English. Authors publishing in CCIS have to sign the Springer CCIS copyright transfer form, however, they are free to use their material published in CCIS for substantially changed, more elaborate subsequent publications elsewhere. For the preparation of the camera-ready papers/files, authors have to strictly adhere to the Springer CCIS Authors' Instructions and are strongly encouraged to use the CCIS LaTeX style files or templates.

Abstracting/Indexing

CCIS is abstracted/indexed in DBLP, Google Scholar, EI-Compendex, Mathematical Reviews, SCImago, Scopus. CCIS volumes are also submitted for the inclusion in ISI Proceedings.

How to start

To start the evaluation of your proposal for inclusion in the CCIS series, please send an e-mail to ccis@springer.com.

Kean Wah Lee · Lung Hsiang Wong
Editors

Intelligent Technology for Educational Applications

Second International Conference, ITEA 2025
Bangkok, Thailand, May 19–21, 2025
Proceedings

Springer

Editors
Kean Wah Lee
University of Nottingham Malaysia
Semenyih, Malaysia

Lung Hsiang Wong
National Institute of Education Nanyang
Technological University
Singapore, Singapore

ISSN 1865-0929 ISSN 1865-0937 (electronic)
Communications in Computer and Information Science
ISBN 978-981-95-2010-7 ISBN 978-981-95-2011-4 (eBook)
https://doi.org/10.1007/978-981-95-2011-4

This Springer imprint is published by the registered company Springer Nature Singapore Pte Ltd.
The registered company address is: 152 Beach Road, #21-01/04 Gateway East, Singapore 189721, Singapore

Preface

Welcome to the proceedings of the 2nd International Conference on Intelligent Technology for Educational Applications (ITEA 2025).

Education is a dynamic, evolving field, and technology has long been instrumental in transforming the sector to meet the ever-changing needs of students. In today's interconnected and fast-paced world, the importance and complexity of education have reached unprecedented levels. Now more than ever, it is essential to critically analyze the relationship between education and technology, understand the fundamental principles of effective learning, and harness the latest innovations to enhance both learning efficiency and educational effectiveness.

ITEA 2025 served as a platform for sharing groundbreaking ideas and state-of-the-art technologies among educators, researchers, and industry professionals from across the globe. The conference encouraged the exchange of the latest innovations and practical experiences in the realm of intelligent educational technologies, providing a space for insightful discussions and collaborative learning.

ITEA 2025 received 88 full-paper submissions from 25 countries. Each submission underwent a rigorous single-blind peer review process with an average of three reviews, ensuring that only the highest-quality research would be included. After a thorough screening process, 34 papers were accepted, resulting in an acceptance rate of 38.6%. These selected papers represent cutting-edge research, innovative applications, and forward-thinking perspectives that highlight the transformative potential of intelligent technologies in education.

We extend our deepest gratitude to the organizing committee, reviewers, authors, and participants whose collective efforts made ITEA 2025 a resounding success. We hope that the diverse range of pioneering research presented in these proceedings will inspire new ideas and further advance the development of intelligent educational technologies, fostering continuous growth in this vital field.

June 2025

Kean Wah Lee
Lung Hsiang Wong

Organization

General Chair

Siti Hajar Halili	Universiti Malaya, Malaysia

Program Committee Chairs

Kean Wah Lee	University of Nottingham Malaysia, Malaysia
Lung Hsiang Wong	Nanyang Technological University, Singapore

Program Committee Co-chair

Noor Maizura Mohamad Noor	Universiti Malaysia Terengganu, Malaysia

Technical Program Committee Chairs

Li Liu	Chongqing University, China
Celio Goncalo Marques	Polytechnic Institute of Tomar, Portugal

Publicity Chair

Feifei Han	Australian Catholic University, Australia

Program Committee

Ali Soltani Sharif Abadi	Warsaw University of Technology, Poland
Maged Ali	University of Essex, UK
Fernando Almeida	ISPGAYA & INESC TEC, Portugal
Rashed Isam Ashqar	Al Zaytona University of Science & Technology, Palestine
Ernie Avila	Polytechnic University of the Philippines, Philippines
Emil Brajkovic	University of Mostar, Bosnia and Herzegovina

Anna Tanova	Peter the Great St. Petersburg Polytechnic University, Russia
Veronica Vasconcelos	Polytechnic Institute of Coimbra, Portugal
Vladyslav Velychko	Donbas State Pedagogical University, Ukraine
Fernando Vera	Red Internacional de Investigadores en Educación, Chile
Gang Wang	Xi'an Jiaotong University, China
Yi-Shun Wang	National Changhua University of Education, Taiwan
Liang Zhang	University of Memphis, USA

Contents

AI-Driven Personalized Learning and Adaptive Systems

Markov Chain Monte Carlo Methods for Dynamic Student Assessment

Aled Williams(✉)

Department of Computer Science, Royal Holloway University of London, London, UK
aled.williams@rhul.ac.uk

Abstract. In this paper we explore an application of Markov Chain Monte Carlo (MCMC) methods to the field of educational assessment. The aim of our approach is to dynamically evaluate student understanding and adaptively tailor question difficulty and topic coverage in real-time. In particular, our model employs a variant of a classical algorithm to decide on question transitions, optimising the assessment process to balance exploration of the student's knowledge base and exploitation of known learning gaps. The model not only adjusts the sequence of questions based on previous responses, but also integrates student-reported confidence levels to refine the estimation of their understanding.

Keywords: Markov Chain Monte Carlo · Dynamic assessment · Student understanding · Educational testing · Adaptive learning · Formative assessment

1 Introduction

Classroom assessment practices have long employed methods such as teacher-devised tests, school-level performance systems, and national standardised examinations [16]. These varied practices underscore the power of assessment as an educational tool. The Assessment Reform Group affirms that "assessment is one of the most powerful educational tools for promoting effective learning ... [that] must be used in the right way" [15, pp. 2]. OFSTED similarly highlights the critical role of effective assessment in motivating learning [31]. However, as noted in [16], poorly designed assessments can harm student motivation, reinforcing the need to align assessments with learning goals.

Chambers and Timlin [9, pp. 119] note that assessment supports both teachers and students by identifying progress and areas for improvement. This paper proposes a Markov Chain Monte Carlo (MCMC) framework for educational assessment, with emphasis on assessment for learning (AfL) over assessment of learning (AoL). After reviewing necessary preliminaries, Sect. 2 presents the proposed methodology, while Sect. 3 explores various proposal distributions.

Earl and Katz define AoL as "strategies designed to confirm what students know" and to "demonstrate whether or not they have met curriculum outcomes or the goals of their individualized programs" [10, pp. 55]. In contrast, Black et

K. W. Lee and L. H. Wong (Eds.): ITEA 2025, CCIS 2643, pp. 3–14, 2026.
https://doi.org/10.1007/978-981-95-2011-4_1

al. describe AfL as "any assessment for which the priority in its design and practice is to serve the purpose of promoting students' learning" [5, pp. 10]. Boaler elaborates that AfL is rooted in ensuring students understand their learning objectives, current standing, and the steps needed to achieve mastery [7, Ch. 4].

In practice, AoL refers to summative assessments that provide a snapshot of attainment, typically as a grade. AfL is formative, aiming to enhance ongoing learning through feedback and reflection. Black et al. [5] note that AoL can also serve formative purposes when its results inform teaching strategies—an approach known as "formative assessment." This becomes most effective when the feedback benefits both teachers and students, supporting self- and peer-assessment, and shaping learning activities [5].

Boaler identifies three purposes of AfL: clarifying learning goals, understanding progress, and offering actionable guidance [7, Ch. 4]. OFSTED also stresses assessment's role in not just evaluating attainment, but improving teaching practices [31]. Effective assessment, they note, involves continual monitoring, encourages student reflection on strengths and weaknesses, and provides constructive feedback [31].

Sadler discusses forms of feedback such as grades, marks, and qualitative comments, emphasising that effective feedback should focus on individual progress rather than peer comparison [35]. Performance should be evaluated relative to a student's own development. Suurtamm, Koch, and Arden extend this view by framing assessment as a social practice that offers continuous insights to guide both learning and teaching [38].

The Assessment Reform Group advises that feedback should help students identify their next learning steps and how to achieve them [16]. Feedback must be constructive and informative, guiding improvement. Suurtamm et al. further advocate that teachers support students in developing self-assessment skills and in acting on feedback [38], a point echoed by the Group [16], who recommend helping students understand the assessment criteria to better evaluate and improve their own work.

The Group also cautions against using grades or comparisons to judge student work, as this can hinder engagement with assessment [16]. To promote meaningful learning, teachers are encouraged to avoid grades and reduce opportunities for superficial comparison.

While traditional assessment methods—both AoL and AfL—remain essential to shaping educational outcomes, there is increasing interest in dynamic and adaptive approaches that better address the complexities of individual learning. Dynamic assessment, for example, integrates instruction and evaluation, offering a more responsive measure of student development.

In line with these advancements, computational methods, such as Markov Chain Monte Carlo (MCMC) methods, offer promising avenues for enhancing the precision and adaptability of assessments. These techniques model learning as a probabilistic, iterative process—particularly suited to capturing student progress in mathematical sciences. This paper explores the role of MCMC and related methods in supporting more personalised and effective assessment strategies.

Maqsood et al. [27] demonstrated the application of mixture Markov models to predict student (dis)engagement patterns. Leung [23] discussed the theoretical foundations of dynamic assessment, aligning it with Vygotskian principles and highlighting its potential to replace static testing with interactive, learning-centred approaches. Wu, Kuo, and Wang [41] developed a computerised adaptive test with immediate feedback for primary mathematics, showing improved learning outcomes. Suarsa et al. [37] used Markov Chains to analyse grade transitions in a statistics course, linking outcomes to prerequisite knowledge. Jeltova et al. [19] demonstrated how dynamic assessment can uncover deeper insights into students' cognitive processes and learning potential.

Grupur, Pankaj, Jai, and Rudraraju [17] developed a tool combining concept maps and Markov chains to assess student understanding of complex topics through the structure and depth of their knowledge representation. Nandakumar et al. [30] proposed a Markov chainâĂŞbased adaptive e-assessment strategy, improving reliability and personalisation by classifying student performance across varying difficulty levels. Bosco [8] used Markov chain models to analyse response dynamics in psychological testing, capturing sequential dependencies that reveal underlying cognitive processes. Yuan [43] applied Markov chains to evaluate teaching quality, offering objective, adaptive classroom measures.

In AI-enhanced education, Wei, Wang, and Conlon [40] introduced a parallel MCMC algorithm for Bayesian dynamic item response models, significantly accelerating computation for large, longitudinal datasets. Lim [25] proposed an AI integration framework for technology education to foster problem-solving and individualised learning. Zhai and Nehm [44] explored AI's role in formative assessment, focusing on feedback quality and bias mitigation. Gligorea et al. [14] reviewed AI-powered adaptive learning systems, highlighting their potential to personalise education and improve outcomes, while noting integration challenges.

Recent studies further explore AI's role in personalised learning. Jeon and Lee [21] examined the complementary functions of large language models like ChatGPT alongside teachers, emphasising AI's support role in content delivery, evaluation, and conversation. Ayeni et al. [3] reviewed AI-driven tools for personalised education, noting both their transformative potential and associated ethical concerns. Messer et al. [28] surveyed automated grading and feedback tools in programming education, highlighting their consistency and limitations across diverse coding paradigms.

Atwal and Quides [2] introduced a dynamic, answer-dependent multiple-choice framework using an R-based workflow to streamline grading in high-enrollment courses, enabling nuanced assessment and fostering inclusivity. Mohd Al Hamad et al. [1] reviewed STEM innovations, emphasising technology integration, project-based learning, and interdisciplinary strategies to enhance outcomes. Onesi-Ozigagun et al. [32] examined AI's role in personalised learning, adaptive teaching, and administrative optimisation, contributing to more efficient educational ecosystems.

Further, Vale and Barbosa [39] explored active learning in mathematics, showing how hands-on strategies promote understanding and engagement among pre-service teachers. Engelbrecht and Borba [11] reviewed the rapid adoption of digital tools in mathematics education, including the impact of AI and COVID-19 on teaching practices. Jeon [20] demonstrated that chatbot-assisted dynamic assessment (CA-DA) improves vocabulary acquisition and diagnostic insight in language learning. Luzano [26] assessed AI's role in mathematics education, identifying both risks—such as bias and data privacy—and opportunities like personalised learning. Bahena et al. [4] advocated for equity through formative and project-based assessments in mathematics. Fahad Mon et al. [12] reviewed reinforcement learning (RL) in education, highlighting its potential through Markov decision processes and deep RL networks.

Yang and Wang [42] explored AI's potential to improve learning outcomes in under-resourced STEM contexts. Park and Kwon [33] demonstrated that AI education in South Korean middle schools boosted student interest and aspirations. Lim [24] proposed a learning style model for AI-based problem-solving, focusing on cognitive, creative, and interactive development. Shminan and Othman [36] introduced a dynamic assessment framework using affective and profile data to personalise learning via decision tree analysis. Käser et al. [22] used Dynamic Bayesian Networks to model student skills, significantly improving predictive accuracy.

2 Methodology

2.1 Definitions

A sequence of random variables $X_0, X_1, X_2, \ldots$ taking values in the (finite) state space $\{1, 2, \ldots, M\}$ is called a *Markov chain* if for all $n \geq 0$, we have

$$P\{X_{n+1} = j \mid X_n = i, X_{n-1} = i_{n-1}, \ldots, X_0 = i_0\} = P\{X_{n+1} = j \mid X_n = i\}.$$

The quantity $P\{X_{n+1} = j \mid X_n = i\}$ is called the *transition probability* from state i to state j. Note that a Markov chain is called homogeneous (or time-homogeneous) when the transition probabilities are fixed for all $n \in \mathbb{Z}_{\geq 0}$. Let $Q = (q_{ij})$ denote the $M \times M$ transition matrix of the chain, i.e. let $q_{ij} = P\{X_{n+1} = j \mid X_n = i\}$ be the transition probability from state i to state j for each i and j.

A Markov chain with transition matrix Q is *irreducible* if for any two states i and j, it is possible to go from i to j in a finite number of steps (with strictly positive probability). State i of a Markov chain is recurrent if starting from i, the probability that the chain will eventually return to i is 1. If instead there is a nonzero probability that from state i the chain will never return to i, then state i is called transient. It should be noted that in an irreducible Markov chain with a finite state space, all states are recurrent (see e.g. [6, Ch. 11]).

A row vector $\boldsymbol{s} = (s_1, s_2, \ldots, s_M)$ such that $s_i \geq 0$ and $\sum_i s_i = 1$ is a stationary distribution for a Markov chain with transition matrix Q if

$$\sum_i s_i q_{ij} = s_j$$

holds for all j, i.e. if $\boldsymbol{s}Q = \boldsymbol{s}$. Note that the above equation represents that the total probability of moving into each state j equals the probability of being in state j. It is known in consequence to the Perron-Frobenius theorem [13,34] that any irreducible Markov chain has a unique stationary distribution.

2.2 Model Description

The MCMC model that will be the basis of our approach is the Metropolis-Hastings algorithm [18,29] This allows us to start with any irreducible Markov chain on the state space of interest and modify this into a new Markov chain that has the desired stationary distribution. The algorithm selectively proposes moves from the original chain, accepting or rejecting them based on a carefully defined acceptance probability. This ensures convergence to the target distribution. We now outline the Metropolis-Hastings algorithm.

Let $\boldsymbol{s} = (s_1, s_2, \ldots, s_M)$ be a desired stationary distribution on the state space $\{1, 2, \ldots, M\}$. Suppose without loss of generality that $s_i > 0$ for all i. Note that if not, then we can simply delete any states i with $s_i = 0$ from the state space. Suppose that $P = (p_{ij})$ is the transition matrix for a Markov chain on the state space $\{1, 2, \ldots, M\}$. The matrix P corresponds to a Markov chain we can simulate but which lacks the desired stationary distribution.

The Metropolis-Hastings algorithm modifies P in order to construct a Markov chain $X_0, X_1, X_2, \ldots$ with stationary distribution $\boldsymbol{s}$. To begin we pick X_0 either randomly or deterministically. Suppose that the new chain is currently at X_n for $n \geq 0$. Then:

Step 1: *If $X_n = i$, then we propose a new state j using the transition probabilities in the i -th row of the transition matrix P.*

Step 2: *Compute the acceptance probability* $a_{ij} = \min\left(\frac{s_j p_{ji}}{s_i p_{ij}}, 1\right)$.

Step 3: *Generate a random number $U \sim U(0,1)$. If $U < a_{ij}$, set (accept) $X_{n+1} = j$. Otherwise, set (reject) $X_{n+1} = i$.*

In particular, the algorithm uses the original transition probabilities p_{ij} to propose where to go next, before accepting the proposal with probability a_{ij}, where the chain remains in its current state in the event of a rejection. It should be noted that p_{ij} appearing the denominator of the acceptance probability a_{ij} will never be 0 when the algorithm is run. This follows immediately since if $p_{ij} = 0$, then the original chain would never propose going from i to j.

2.3 State Space and Transition Mechanisms

In our model, the state space comprises potential questions, each characterised by attributes such as difficulty and topic relevance. The Metropolis-Hastings algorithm navigates this space to adaptively select the next question, aiming to assess understanding efficiently while minimising question fatigue.

The process begins with either a random or strategically chosen initial question, informed by prior assessments or expected ability. From there, new questions are proposed using a predefined proposal distribution, which may consider factors like difficulty similarity, relevance to past errors, or gaps in topic coverage. These distributions are discussed in Sect. 3.

The core of the algorithm lies in evaluating whether to transition to a proposed question. This is determined by an acceptance probability, reflecting how informative the new question is likely to be. If accepted, the new question is posed; if rejected, the current question is retained. This ensures the sequence of questions is both adaptive and informative, optimising the assessment process.

2.4 Incorporation of Confidence Levels

To further enhance the adaptive nature of the assessment process, we incorporate student-reported confidence levels into the decision-making framework of the Metropolis-Hastings algorithm. The confidence level, denoted by γ_n at step n, is a normalised value within the interval $[0, 1]$, where 1 represents the highest level of confidence and 0 represents the lowest. This confidence factor allows the transition mechanism to dynamically adjust its behavior based on the student's self-assessed certainty in their responses.

The transition probability from state (question) i to state j at step n is adjusted to yield

$$q_{ij}^{(n)} = \gamma_n \cdot q_{ij} + (1 - \gamma_n) \cdot \tilde{q}_{ij},$$

where q_{ij} is the base transition probability derived from the predefined proposal distribution, reflecting the likelihood of moving from question i to question j without considering confidence, $\tilde{q}_{ij}$ represents an alternative transition probability that is influenced by the student's confidence level. For instance, if the student reports high confidence, $\tilde{q}_{ij}$ could be weighted to favour transitions to more challenging questions. Conversely, low confidence would adjust $\tilde{q}_{ij}$ to favour transitions to questions that reinforce more foundational knowledge.

This adjustment modifies the acceptance probability $a_{ij}^{(n)}$ used in the Metropolis-Hastings algorithm to accept or reject a proposed question, namely

$$a_{ij}^{(n)} = \min\left(\frac{s_j q_{ji}^{(n)}}{s_i q_{ij}^{(n)}}, 1\right),$$

where $q_{ji}^{(n)}$ denotes the adjusted transition probability in the reverse direction, which incorporates confidence at step n by construction.

It should be emphasised that by incorporating confidence levels into both the transition and acceptance probabilities, the assessment process becomes more personalised and responsive. A student who consistently reports low confidence in their correct answers may benefit from additional reinforcement, while a student with high confidence and correct answers can be challenged with more difficult questions. This dynamic adjustment aims to both accurately assess the student's current knowledge and encourage optimal learning progression by aligning the difficulty of questions with the student's self-assessed readiness.

3 Proposal Distributions

3.1 Normal Distribution Centered on Current Estimate of Ability

The most simple and intuitive centres a normal distribution on the current student's ability level estimate. This approach assumes that the next best question to ask is likely close in difficulty to the student's current estimated ability. The mean of the distribution would be the current ability estimate and the standard deviation could be adjusted based on how quickly one would want the assessment to explore the state space (i.e. the range of questions). More precisely, the mathematical representation is

$$Q\left(x' \mid x\right) = \frac{1}{\sqrt{2\pi\sigma^2}} e^{-\frac{(x'-\theta)^2}{2\sigma^2}},$$

where x denotes the current state (question), x' is the proposed state (question), θ is the mean of the distribution (current estimate of a student's ability) and σ is the standard deviation (spread of question difficulties around θ), respectively. The decision to move from x to x' is made based on the likelihood of x' providing more informative data about the student's ability compared to staying at x.

3.2 Categorical Distribution Based on Knowledge Gaps

If student performance data across different topics is available, then another approach would be to use a categorical distribution, where the probability of selecting a question from a particular topic is inversely proportional to the student's performance in that topic. This approach assigns higher probabilities to topics where the student has previously shown weaker understanding, targeting areas that need reinforcement, which may potentially improve learning outcomes. More precisely, the the mathematical representation is

$$P(\text{topic } i) = \frac{w_i}{\sum_{j=1}^{n} w_j},$$

where w_i denotes the weight assigned to topic i, which is determined inversely by the student's performance in that topic. It should be noted that if a student demonstrates weakness in a specific area (e.g. via lower performance scores), then the corresponding w_i increases, thereby increasing the probability of selecting questions from that topic. Further, it should be emphasised that the above formulation is used to determine the probability of selecting a topic i rather than a specific question with that topic. Thus, an additional mechanism or set of criteria would typically be used to choose a specific question within the selected topic. This could be another probabilistic model, a simple random selection, or a more sophisticated method that considers factors like question difficulty, relevance to given learning objectives or previous exposure to similar questions.

3.3 Adaptive Step-Size Normal Distribution

An extension of the first approach would be to adapt the underlying spread of the normal distribution dynamically based on the student's responses. If for example a student answers several questions correctly and with high confidence, the model could then increase the standard deviation to allow for broader exploration of more challenging questions. In particular, in this case the standard deviation would be adjusted based on the variability in the student's recent performance scores and/or confidence levels. This approach could intuitively encourage a more exploratory or conservative question selection strategy as needed. More precisely, the mathematical representation is

$$\sigma = \sigma_0 + c \cdot (\bar{c} - \tau),$$

where σ_0 denotes the base standard deviation (level of variability in question difficulty), c is a scaling factor that determines how sensitively σ should respond to changes in the student's confidence levels, $\bar{c} = \frac{1}{n}\sum_{i=1}^{n} c_i$ is the average confidence given by the student (where $c_1, c_2, \ldots, c_n$ denotes the reported confidence level for the first n questions) and τ is a predefined confidence level that acts as a benchmark, respectively. If the average confidence exceeds this predefined threshold, then this indicates that the student is generally more confident, suggesting readiness for more challenging questions. If instead that student's average confidence falls below this threshold, it may indicate a need for reinforcement of foundational concepts. Other natural options for $\bar{c}$ include recent-response averages, which may better reflect current confidence.

3.4 Beta Distribution Adjusted for Confidence Levels

An alternative would be to instead utilise a beta distribution to model the selection probabilities based on both student performance and their self-reported confidence level. The parameters of the beta distribution could in such case be adjusted based on aggregated confidence levels where, for example, higher confidence and consistent correct answers could skew the distribution to propose more challenging questions. More precisely, the mathematical representation is

$$P(x) = \frac{x^{\alpha-1}(1-x)^{\beta-1}}{B(\alpha, \beta)},$$

where $B(\alpha, \beta)$ is the beta function (which normalises the distribution) and the (positive) shape parameters α and β could be functions of the confidence levels, with higher confidence leading to a more aggressive questioning strategy. Note that when a student expresses high confidence in their correct responses, it suggests not only understanding but also assurance in their knowledge. This may lead to increasing α, which can be interpreted as accumulating "successes" in the student's ability estimation. This adjustment increases the probability mass towards higher levels of performance, suggesting the student is ready for more challenging questions. Conversely, low confidence, especially if associated with incorrect answers, might lead to an increase in β, indicating more "failures". This shifts the distribution to reflect a higher probability of lower performance levels, indicating that the student may need reinforcement in foundational concepts or easier questions. One potential approach to adjusting these parameters would be

$$\alpha = \alpha_0 + k \cdot \gamma \cdot n_c$$
$$\beta = \beta_0 + k \cdot (1 - \gamma) \cdot n_i ,$$

where α_0 is the initial value of α, k is a scaling factor adjusting the impact of confidence and correctness, γ represents the confidence factor, n_c is the number of correct responses, β_0 is the initial value of β and n_i is the number of incorrect responses, respectively. Note that the confidence factor γ represents how confident the student is in their answer, where a higher value significantly influences α, whereas a lower value impacts β to a greater extent. The confidence factor could change dynamically each time a student answers a question.

3.5 Hybrid Distribution Combining Multiple Criteria

It is additionally possible to combine different aspects such as difficulty level, topic relevance and confidence into a hybrid model. This method would involve parameters from multiple distributions, possibly requiring more complex computation, but while providing a tailored approach to question selection. For instance, it would be possible to use a normal distribution while overlaying a categorical layer for topic selection based on knowledge gaps. The mathematical representation is

$$P(x) = \lambda_1 N(\theta, \sigma^2) + \lambda_2 \sum_{i=1}^{n} p_i \delta(x - x_i),$$

where $N(\theta, \sigma^2)$ is a normal distribution centered around the student's current estimated ability level θ , with a standard deviation σ that controls the range of difficulties for the proposed questions, λ_i for $i \in \{1, 2\}$ is a weighting factor that determines the influence of the i-th distribution in the overall hybrid model, and $\delta(x - x_i)$ is the Dirac delta function with "spike" at x_i. These specific questions are chosen based on their relevance to the student's identified knowledge gaps, as determined by a categorical distribution p_i, which reflects the probability of selecting topic (or question) i where the student has shown weakness or requires reinforcement.

The combination of these distributions allows for both a highly flexible and adaptive approach. In particular, the normal distribution component enables the system to explore a range of difficulties around the student's current estimated ability, promoting a comprehensive assessment of the student's capabilities. The categorical distribution embedded in the Dirac delta function allows the probabilistic system to precisely target areas where the student needs improvement, ensuring that key concepts are reinforced. Further, by adjusting the weights λ_i, the system can dynamically balance between exploring new areas of difficulty and focusing on consolidating knowledge in critical areas.

4 Conclusion

This study demonstrates the potential of Markov Chain Monte Carlo methods for dynamic student assessment, offering an adaptive framework that integrates real-time feedback and confidence levels to tailor question selection. By employing diverse proposal distributions, the model effectively balances exploration of student knowledge with reinforcement of learning gaps.

Future work should explore the scalability of this approach in large-scale, computationally constrained settings. This would be particularly interesting within diverse educational settings where computational efficiency is paramount to drawing conclusions in "reasonable" time. Moreover, the integration of more sophisticated machine learning techniques, such as reinforcement learning, could enhance the adaptability and precision of the model. Another promising area for exploration is the inclusion of multimodal data, such as behavioural and emotional cues, to further refine the assessment's responsiveness to individual student needs. Empirical comparisons with traditional assessment methods could clarify practical benefits and support broader implementation.

Disclosure of Interests. The authors have no competing interests to declare that are relevant to the content of this article.

References

1. Al Hamad, N.M., et al.: A review on the innovative approaches to stem education. Int. J. Sci. Res. Arch. **11**(1), 244–252 (2024)
2. Atwal, H.K., Quides, K.W.: Dynamic answer-dependent multiple-choice questions and holistic assessment analysis in high-enrollment courses. J. Microbiol. Biol. Educ., e00047–24 (2024)
3. Ayeni, O.O., Al Hamad, N.M., Chisom, O.N., Osawaru, B., Adewusi, O.E.: Ai in education: a review of personalized learning and educational technology. GSC Adv. Res. Rev. **18**(2), 261–271 (2024)
4. Bahena, R., et al.: From method to equity: rethinking mathematics assessment policies in education. Excellencia: Int. Multi. J. Educ. (2994-9521) **2**(1), 121–132 (2024)
5. Black, P., Harrison, C., Lee, C., Marshall, B., Wiliam, D.: Working inside the black box: assessment for learning in the classroom. Phi Delta Kappan **86**(1), 9–21 (2004). https://doi.org/10.1177/003172170408600105
6. Blitzstein, J.K., Hwang, J.: Introduction to probability. CRC Press, Taylor & Francis Group (2015)
7. Boaler, J.: The elephant in the classroom: helping children learn and love maths. Souvenir Press, London (2015)
8. Bosco, A.: Markov chain models for inspecting response dynamics in psychological testing. arXiv:2403.17982 (2024)
9. Chambers, P., Timlin, R.: Teaching mathematics in the secondary school, 2nd edn. Sage Publications, London (2013)
10. Earl, L., Katz, S.: Rethinking classroom assessment with purpose in mind. Manitoba Education, Citizenship and Youth (2006)

11. Engelbrecht, J., Borba, M.C.: Recent developments in using digital technology in mathematics education. ZDM-Math. Educ. **56**(2), 281–292 (2024)
12. Fahad Mon, B., Wasfi, A., Hayajneh, M., Slim, A., Abu Ali, N.: Reinforcement learning in education: a literature review. Informatics **10**(3), 74 (2023)
13. Frobenius, G.: Über matrizen aus nicht negativen elementen. Königliche Akademie der Wissenschaften Berlin, pp. 456–477 (1912)
14. Gligorea, I.: Adaptive learning using artificial intelligence in e-learning: a literature review. Educ. Sci. **13**(12), 1216 (2023)
15. Group, A.R.: Assessment for learning: beyond the black box. Qualifications and Curriculum Authority (1999)
16. Group, A.R.: Testing, motivation and learning. University of Cambrdige, Faculty of Eduction (2002)
17. Gurupur, V.P., Jain, G.P., Rudraraju, R.: Evaluating student learning using concept maps and Markov chains. Expert Syst. Appl. **42**(7), 3306–3314 (2015)
18. Hastings, W.K.: Monte Carlo sampling methods using Markov chains and their applications. Biometrika **57**(1), 97–109 (1970)
19. Jeltova, I.: Making instruction and assessment responsive to diverse students' progress: Group-administered dynamic assessment in teaching mathematics. J. Learn. Disabil. **44**(4), 381–395 (2011)
20. Jeon, J.: Chatbot-assisted dynamic assessment (ca-da) for l2 vocabulary learning and diagnosis. Comput. Assist. Lang. Learn. **36**(7), 1338–1364 (2023)
21. Jeon, J., Lee, S.: Large language models in education: a focus on the complementary relationship between human teachers and ChatGPT. Educ. Inf. Technol. **28**(12), 15873–15892 (2023)
22. Käser, T., Klingler, S., Schwing, A.G., Gross, M.: Dynamic Bayesian networks for student modeling. IEEE Trans. Learn. Technol. **10**(4), 450–462 (2017)
23. Leung, C.: Dynamic assessment: assessment for and as teaching? Lang. Assess. Q. **4**(3), 257–278 (2007)
24. Lim, M.: Learning style for AI convergence in technology education. J. Hum. centric Sci. Technol. Innov. **1**(2), 1–8 (2021)
25. Lim, M.: Developing a framework for the integration of artificial intelligence in technology education: enhancing learning and innovation. Tehnički glasnik **18**(2), 229–233 (2024)
26. Luzano, J.: Assessment in mathematics education in the sphere of artificial intelligence: a systematic review on its threats and opportunities. Int. J. Acad. Multi. Res. **8**(2), 100–104 (2024)
27. Maqsood, R., Ceravolo, P., Romero, C., Ventura, S.: Modeling and predicting students' engagement behaviors using mixture Markov models. Knowl. Inf. Syst. **64**(5), 1349–1384 (2022)
28. Messer, M., Brown, N.C., Kölling, M., Shi, M.: Automated grading and feedback tools for programming education: a systematic review. ACM Trans. Comput. Educ. **24**(1), 1–43 (2024)
29. Metropolis, N., Rosenbluth, A.W., Rosenbluth, M.N., Teller, A.H., Teller, E.: Equation of state calculations by fast computing machines. J. Chem. Phys. **21**(6), 1087–1092 (1953)
30. Nandakumar, G.S., Thangasamy, S., Geetha, V., Haridoss, V.: A Markovian model for adaptive e-assessment. WSEAS Trans. Comput. **15**, 179–188 (2016)
31. Office for Standards in Education (OFSTED): Good assessment practice in mathematics. HMI 1477, OFSTED, London (2003)

32. Onesi-Ozigagun, O., Ololade, Y.J., Eyo-Udo, N.L., Ogundipe, D.O.: Revolutionizing education through AI: a comprehensive review of enhancing learning experiences. Int. J. Appl. Res. Soc. Sci. **6**(4), 589–607 (2024)
33. Park, W., Kwon, H.: Implementing artificial intelligence education for middle school technology education in republic of Korea. Int. J. Technol. Des. Educ. **34**(1), 109–135 (2024)
34. Perron, O.: Zur theorie der matrices. Math. Ann. **64**(2), 248–263 (1907)
35. Sadler, D.R.: Formative assessment: revisiting the territory. Assess. Educ. Principles Policy Prac. **5**(1), 77–84 (1998). https://doi.org/10.1080/0969595980050104
36. Shminan, A.S., Othman, M.K.: Dynamic student assessment to advocate personalized learning plan. In: 2015 International Conference on Information Technology Systems and Innovation (ICITSI), pp. 1–6. IEEE (2015)
37. Suarsa, I.P.E., et al.: Determining the probability of changing grades from the mathematical statistics ii prerequisites course using the Markov chain process. Int. J. Educ. Lit. **3**(2), 37–43 (2024)
38. Suurtamm, C., Koch, M., Arden, A.: Teachers' assessment practices in mathematics: classrooms in the context of reform. Assess. Educ. Principles Policy Pract. **17**(4), 399–417 (2010). https://doi.org/10.1080/0969594X.2010.497469
39. Vale, I., Barbosa, A.: Active learning strategies for an effective mathematics teaching and learning. Eur. J. Sci. Math. Educ. **11**(3), 573–588 (2023)
40. Wei, Z., Wang, X., Conlon, E.M.: Parallel Markov chain monte Carlo for Bayesian dynamic item response models in educational testing. Statistics **6**(1), 420–433 (2017)
41. Wu, H.M., Kuo, B.C., Wang, S.C.: Computerized dynamic adaptive tests with immediately individualized feedback for primary school mathematics learning. J. Educ. Technol. Soc. **20**(1), 61–72 (2017)
42. Yang, X., Wang, S.: The exploration of high quality education in scientific and technological innovation based on artificial intelligence. Comput. Sci. Math. Forum **8**(1) (2023)
43. Yuan, T.: Algorithm of classroom teaching quality evaluation based on Markov chain. Complexity **2021**(1), 9943865 (2021)
44. Zhai, X., Nehm, R.H.: AI and formative assessment: the train has left the station. J. Res. Sci. Teach. **60**(6), 1390–1398 (2023)

An Embedded Generative AI Agent for Personalised Documentation in Early Childhood Education

Wenjun Liu[1], Chenwei Liang[1,2], Shiyu Sun[1,2], and Shengjun Ma[2(✉)]

[1] Universiti Teknologi Malaysia, Johor Bahru, Malaysia
liu@graduate.utm.my

[2] School of Tech, New Zealand Skills and Education College (NZSE), Auckland, New Zealand
eric@nzse.ac.nz, shengjun.ma@ieee.org

Abstract. Generative AI has been increasingly explored across various domains, including education. However, its application in early childhood education (ECE) for assisting teachers' administrative tasks remains limited. In this study, an embedded generative AI agent is developed and deployed on the Jetson Orin Nano platform, integrated with a touchscreen interface and an onboard camera for data input. Log generation is performed entirely on-device through simple user inputs and real-time image analysis, enabling automated creation of personalised child activity logs. The system's effectiveness is evaluated in terms of accuracy and efficiency. In addition, data privacy concerns associated with collecting children's behavioural data are addressed, offering insights into the practical deployment of embedded AI agents in ECE environments.

Keywords: Embedded AI System · Early Childhood Education · Jetson Orin Nano Super · Generative AI

1 Introduction

Early childhood education (ECE) practitioners manage classroom activities and document children's development and behaviour. Personalised child activity logs are usually created manually, which increases the workload of practitioners and can lead to errors in documentation [22]. Accurate records are essential for tracking children's progress and supporting communication with families [20]. Although some digital tools have been introduced to assist practitioners, their use in ECE remains limited due to privacy concerns and the complexity of classroom environments. Most existing research focuses on AI applications for improving children's learning outcomes [1], while fewer studies explore the use of AI to support practitioners with administrative tasks [24].

To address these challenges, localised processing through embedded AI systems offers a practical solution. Embedded AI allows data to be processed directly on the device, reducing reliance on cloud services and improving data privacy [9]. In educational settings, embedded AI has been applied to tasks such as learning analytics and assessment [4]. However, its potential for automating routine documentation in ECE has not been

K. W. Lee and L. H. Wong (Eds.): ITEA 2025, CCIS 2643, pp. 15–27, 2026.
https://doi.org/10.1007/978-981-95-2011-4_2

fully explored. AI agents have been investigated for providing educational support [16], but their role in assisting practitioners with administrative work remains limited [17].

This study develops an embedded generative AI agent to support practitioners in ECE by automating the creation of personalised child activity logs. The system is implemented on the Jetson Orin Nano platform, which integrates a touchscreen interface and an onboard camera. Log generation is performed on the device using simple user inputs and image analysis. This design reduces the workload of practitioners, improves data accuracy, and addresses privacy concerns.

2 Related Work

In recent years, artificial intelligence (AI) technology has been continuously improving. AI is increasingly used in education, agriculture, healthcare, transportation, and other fields [23]. In the field of education, AI has been used in higher education [3]. Such as assessment, prediction, AI assistant, intelligent tutoring system (ITS), and managing student learning. In addition, generative AI (GenAI) such as large language models (LLMs) and multimodal models have emerged on a large scale. They play a huge role in developing courses and providing course tutoring [2].

Although GenAI technology has been initially applied in higher education. However, its implementation in early childhood education is still relatively limited. In terms of providing auxiliary support for early childhood educators (teachers, managers), related research is still in its infancy.

2.1 Application of AI in Early Childhood Education

In recent years, the application of artificial intelligence technology in early childhood education scenarios have gradually attracted the attention of researchers. Related work includes using artificial intelligence as a learning partner [27]. Using artificial intelligence to improve children's creativity and computational thinking skills [26]. Artificial intelligence literacy is also a major direction of artificial intelligence in early childhood education scenarios [25]. However, existing research often focuses on how to help children learn. Research on auxiliary systems for professional groups such as kindergarten teachers and educators are scarce.

Yue et al. [30] designed an intelligent system to depict children's psychological states. The system used video clips and emotional data from kindergarten classrooms to achieve the goal. Huijnen et al. [10] proposed that intelligent robots can be used as a valuable tool for educating autistic children. They also outlined the research on various artificial intelligence robots. Ismail et al. [12] introduced seven different intelligent robot systems and analyzed their applications in improving the social interaction of autistic children.

Although these studies are all aimed at improving children's education, most of them focus on children themselves. There is a lack of support for educators' daily document tasks. Especially in the field of text generation, the design of using generative AI technology to assist teachers in generating standardized and structured records of children's activities is still exceedingly rare. How to combine children's behavioral characteristics to generate educational logs that can help children grow is still a blank in current research.

2.2 Jetson Edge GPU on GenAI

Generative AI models (such as LLaMA and GPT) usually require strong computing power. Due to the large scale of generative models, most GenAI applications are currently deployed in the cloud [31]. In addition, it relies on expensive A100-class data center GPUs, which have extremely high deployment costs [13].

The NVIDIA Jetson platform was developed to provide embedded computing solutions for edge artificial intelligence (Edge AI) applications. Now, this platform has been widely used in fields such as robotics, computer vision, Internet of Things (IoT), and automation [28, 18]. The platform supports the deployment of complex AI models in resource-constrained environments, enabling localized data processing and real-time response [11]. In recent years, NVIDIA Jetson series edge devices, as a low-power, low-cost inference platform, have gradually become an important direction for lightweight deployment of large models.

Some studies have tried to run recognition models and LLM on Jetson Orin. For example, Pham et al. used NVIDIA JETSON NANO to realize artificial intelligence and IoT face recognition [19]. Hashemi integrates Qt and LLMs on the NVIDIA Jetson development board for controlling a patient-assisting robot arm [8]. Sourav et al. used Jetson Orin Nano to deploy downstream models to demonstrate the practicality of the framework in resource-constrained environments [14]. However, there is currently no research specifically targeting early childhood education scenarios, combining Jetson Edge with GenAI to develop an edge intelligence generation system for teachers or education managers.

2.3 GenAI Privacy Concerns

With the widespread application of large language models in sensitive fields such as education, medical care, and justice, privacy protection issues are becoming increasingly important. Many existing GenAI systems (such as ChatGPT and Claude) rely on cloud deployment. After receiving personal or sensitive information entered by the user, the model needs to upload it to a remote server, which poses a risk of leakage. Maanak et al. found that malicious users can exploit GPT vulnerabilities to bypass the ethical constraints of the model and steal malicious information [7]. Aurora discussed the data security and privacy issues faced by generative AI [29].

Therefore, local deployment of Gen AI has become a new option. Dobur et al. [5]. Developed a locally deployed knowledge base system based on large language models (LLMs). The system is deployed locally to respond to user queries in a timely manner. The system also allows users to query in natural language through natural language processing technology. Through these designs, the system improves the organization's information acquisition efficiency. Beauden John proposed a novel edge computing architecture [21]. Studies have shown that traditional cloud-centric models face high latency, bandwidth limitations and privacy issues when processing GenAI tasks. However, in the field of early childhood education, locally deployed GenAI applications are still in a blank stage. Children's photos, activity records, etc. in educational scenarios involve highly confidential information. Localized deployment of GenAI can reduce the risk of leakage of this confidential information.

3 Research Design

The proposed portable edge AI platform integrates meticulously selected hard-ware components and sophisticated software algorithms to deliver robust real- time inference capabilities. Specifically, the hardware design combines a Jetson Orin Nano computational core, DC-DC voltage regulation, precise motor control via EasyDriver, and intuitive interaction through an HDMI touch interface, ensuring reliable mobile performance. Concurrently, the software architecture employs Meta's LLaMA 3.2-vision model, fine-tuned through Low-Rank Adaptation (LoRA). This architecture incorporates a dynamically updated knowledge base and leverages Chain-of-Thought (CoT) reasoning to generate personalized, contextually relevant children's activity logs. The seamless integration of these hardware and software components results in a cohesive and adaptive framework, optimized for efficient and precise edge AI applications.

3.1 Hardware Design

The hardware components for this portable edge AI device were meticulously selected to optimize computational performance, energy efficiency, and mechanical precision within a compact and mobile framework. Central to this selection is the Jetson Orin Nano, chosen specifically for its GPU accelerated processing capabilities, enabling efficient realtime AI inference and data processing while maintaining minimal power consumption. To further capitalize on Orin's computational potential, an EasyDriver stepper motor controller was integrated, facilitating precise mechanical control through direct GPIO pin interaction. This ensures accurate step and direction commands critical for actuator-driven applications, such as robotics and precise positioning systems.

The fundamental operational principle of a boost converter involves two main switching phases:

- **Phase 1 (Switch ON):** The inductor stores energy directly from the battery.
- **Phase 2 (Switch OFF):** Stored energy in the inductor is transferred to the output through a diode, increasing the output voltage.

Assuming ideal conditions, the relationship between the output voltage Vout, input voltage Vin, and duty cycle D can be described as:

$$V_{out} = \frac{V_{in}}{1 - D} \tag{1}$$

Rearranging Eq. 1 to solve for the duty cycle D gives:

$$D = 1 - \frac{V_{in}}{V_{out}} \tag{2}$$

For our application, stepping up from the 3.7 V battery to 12 V yields a duty cycle:

$$D = 1 - \frac{3.7\ V}{12\ V} \approx 0.6917 \tag{3}$$

As illustrated in Fig. 1, the integration of hardware components strictly follows professional engineering standards, emphasizing electrical stability, safety, and operational reliability. In comparison, theoretical calculations offer initial guidance for system design. Still, practical deployment scenarios require addressing real-world factors, including switching losses within the boost converter transistor, the output capacitor's equivalent series resistance (ESR), and the diode's forward voltage drop.

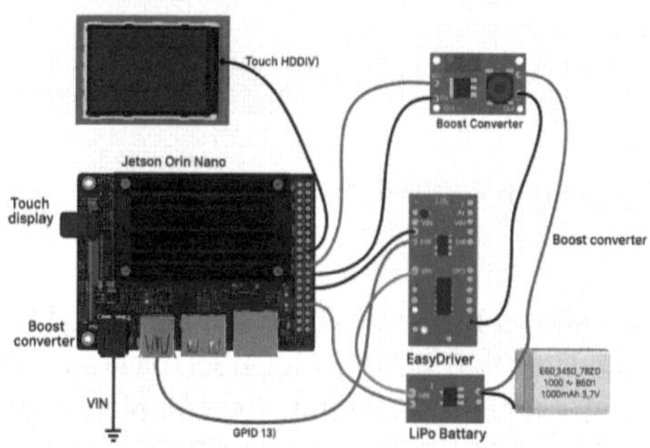

Fig. 1. (a). The battery provides power input to the DC-DC boost converter, which regulates output voltage at the required operational level. (b). The regulated voltage directly powers the Jetson Orin Nano and EasyDriver module. (c). The Jetson Orin Nano communicates control signals (GPIO-based step and direction signals) to the EasyDriver module for motor operations. (d). HDMI and USB interfaces connect the Jetson Orin Nano to the touch display, providing an interactive user environment.

A critical aspect of the hardware integration involves addressing the Jetson Orin Nano's specific voltage requirements, typically at 5 V or 12 V, while operating from a portable power source. Using a single-cell 3.7 V LiPo battery, a DC-DC boost converter was employed to reliably step up the voltage to the required 12 V level. This voltage conversion relies on precisely controlling the transistor's duty cycle—approximately 69.17% in this application—to maintain consistent and stable power delivery under varying operational conditions. The chosen boost converter incorporates internal PWM feedback control, dynamically adjusting duty cycles to ensure voltage stability, thereby enhancing reliability and extending operational autonomy of the mobile embedded platform.

3.2 Algorithm and Software Design

This study proposes an automatic generation system for children's activity texts suitable for early childhood education scenarios. The system is built based on the locally deployed multilingual large language models LLaMA 3.2-version and LoRA fine-tuning technology. The core goal of the system is to generate activity logs that have educational significance and emotional understanding of children's activities. It is hoped that the reasoning ability of the model will be regularly optimized through data generated by user interactions.

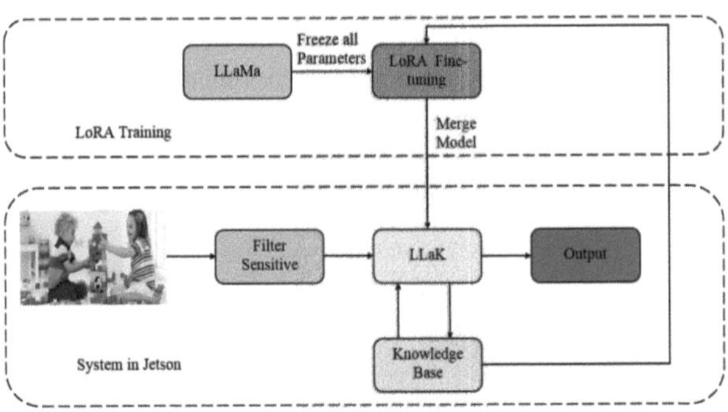

Fig. 2. Flowchart of Personalized Children's Activity Log System

The overall process is shown in Fig. 2. The system is named Large Language Model Kids. The system is divided into two parts: the local Jetson system and the LoRA training module. These two modules together constitute the complete algorithm framework.

We chose Meta's LLaMA 3.2-vision model [15]. This model has the ability to jointly input images and texts and supports multi-language output. And it can achieve the personalized children's activity log we want through fine-tuning.

The LLaMA 3.2-vision model is fine-tuned using the LoRA (Low Rank Adaptations of LLM) technique [6]. In fact, LLM has the problem of over-parameterization. When the model is used for a specific task, only a few parameters really play a key role. With LoRA, only the low-rank matrix needs to be trained instead of directly training all the data of the large model.

In this study, the specific process of fine-tuning is as follows. We complete the entire fine-tuning process on a GPU device. First, freeze all parameters in LLaMa. Then select Query Projection and Value Projection to insert the built LoRA adapter. When all other parameters are frozen, only the inserted low-rank matrix is trained. We use the AdamW optimizer with gradient accumulation for training. Set the initial learning rate of the optimizer to 2e-4. In addition, mixed precision training (FP16) is used to improve efficiency during fine-tuning. Finally, after training, the LoRA weights are merged with the model weights to obtain the LLmK model we need to achieve zero-overhead inference during deployment.

Under the premise of freezing the parameters of the pre-trained model, the core idea of LoRa is to insert low-rank matrices only on the linear layer (such as Linear or Conv) for training. Since only low-rank matrices are trained, the number of parameters and memory required for training is reduced. The formula is as follows.

$$W^t = W + \Delta W - W + \frac{\alpha}{r} \cdot BA \tag{4}$$

Among them, A, B are newly added trainable matrices after freezing all parameters; r is the low-rank setting, α is the scaling factor; the original W pretrained model. In this study, the parameters we set in the fine-tuning process are r = 8, which represents the low-rank decomposition dimension. The larger r is, the stronger the expressive power of the model adapter is, and the number of parameters will also increase. α = 8, which is used to control the update amplitude of LoRA to the original model weights. The higher alpha is, the greater the disturbance to the original model weights, but it will increase the risk of overfitting. Lora_dropout = 0.1, used for regularization to prevent overfitting. If dropout is set, it will reduce the test performance, and too large will increase the training time.

After deploying the fine-tuned model in Jetson, we need to create a knowledge base for the model. We need to add the knowledge graph related to children's behavior to the knowledge base. Relevant knowledge includes educational psychology, children's behavior development knowledge, teacher suggestion templates, excellent children's activity log templates, etc. Before generating text, the system indexes the content in the knowledge base to improve the scientific nature of the output text content. After generating text, the generated content is also stored in the knowledge base.

In addition to helping LLak generate scientific content, the data in the knowledge base is extensively used for incremental fine-tuning of the model. The system will enter the data stored in the knowledge base into LoRA for incremental fine-tuning every week. The incremental fine-tuning process is based on the last generated LoRA adapter and uses the new data to train the model. After each round of fine-tuning, the new model will replace the old model. The complete process will be conducted during the system's idle time (such as Saturdays and Sundays) to keep the main model stable and not affect the continuous operation of the system.

Due to the limitations of the children's education environment, we must ensure that the model does not appear violent, pornographic, offensive, and non-age-appropriate words. For example, kill, gun, die, kiss, alcohol, etc. By setting reasonable prompt words, the output content can be limited and ensure that the output content is in line with the children's education environment. We have established a standard prompt word template. The system accepts input information such as time, place, activity type, participants, and emotional state. These input data are converted into semantics that LLM can understand as prompt words.

The standard prompt word template we designed is: "Based on the content of the image, help me generate a personalized child activity log. Do you need more information from me?".

Through this prompt word, LLM identifies the activity type of the child in the picture and describes the child's behavior and emotions. Then, by searching the knowledge base, it confirms whether the information provided by the user is sufficient to generate an activity log, such as the interactive behavior between children. If the information is insufficient, the user is asked to provide more information. Until the information provided is used to generate a personalized child activity log. Through this process, high-quality migration from multimodality to text is achieved.

Through this prompt word, LLM can accurately identify the type of child's activity in the image and describe the child's actions and emotions. Generate personalized children's activity logs and achieve high-quality migration from multimodal to text.

To achieve personalized content generation with memory ability, we use the Chain-of-Thought (CoT) thinking chain mechanism to help the model [32]. CoT strengthens LLM's reasoning ability by guiding the model to reason step by step. Enable LLM to consider contextual information when generating and maintain the coherence of previous and subsequent content.

By using this system, we can generate personalized children's activity logs through simple user input and images.

4 Discussion and Future Works

In this study, we proposed an embedded generative AI agent system to address the daily paperwork burden of early childhood educators. By deploying it locally on the Jetson Orin Nano edge device, the system has local real-time reasoning capabilities. In addition, the deployment of the local system also solves the data privacy issue in early childhood education scenarios. Information involving children's images and behavioral information is well protected.

Combining the LLaMA 3.2-vision large language model with multimodal processing capabilities with the LoRA (low-rank adaptation) fine-tuning technology is a major innovation of this paper. LoRA only needs to train a small number of parameters and can be implemented on resource-limited edge devices. LLM ensures the contextual coherence of activity records by combining the CoT mechanism.

At the hardware design level, this system tightly integrates the DC-DC boost module, motor controller, Jetson core module, and touch screen. Together, these modules build an interactive embedded platform. The platform is low-power and highly portable and is particularly suitable for changing environments such as early childhood education classrooms.

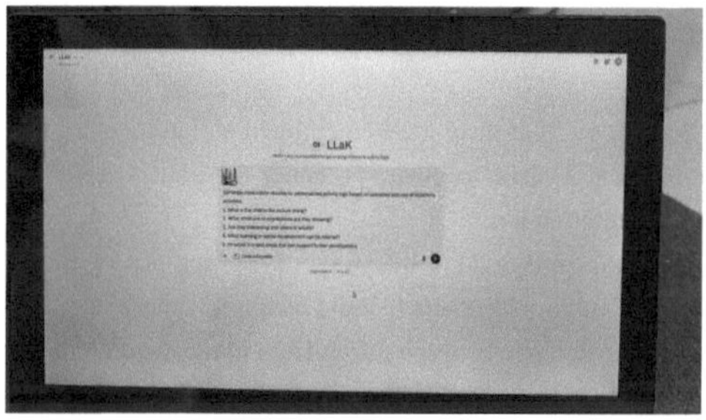

Fig. 3. Interactive Input Interface on Jetson Edge Device

From a practical point of view, this system saves teachers time in writing records. In addition, this system also improves the standardization and personalization of document content. We provide a scientific basis for generating content by adding a professional knowledge base of early childhood education to the system. The knowledge base includes child development psychology, teaching suggestion templates and high-quality activity log cases. Through this system, it can help early childhood teachers and parents communicate with higher quality and faster efficiency.

The actual deployment interface of the system is shown in Fig. 3. Users can input observation information about children's activities through the touch screen. The system guides users to provide time, activity content, participants, emotional state, and other elements in the form of prompt words.

The following content shows the practical application capabilities of the LLak system. We developed in terms of image recognition and language generation. It recognizes children's behavior, emotions, and interaction characteristics from pictures. Based on this information, it generates a personalized, structured observation record based on prompt words. This record is suitable for the recording and evaluation needs of early childhood education environments.

Q: Based on the content of the image, help me generate a personalized child activity log. Do you need more information from me? <$ End $>

A: Based on the image, we can see that there are two children sitting together and playing with building blocks. They seem to be building a castle together. To better generate a personalized activity log, please provide me with the following information.
What is the name of the child in the images? For whom should the activity log be generated?
Does the child in the picture actively invite others to build blocks together?
What other interactive behaviors are there between the children in the picture? <$ End $>

Q: We need to generate an activity log for the boy on the left side of the picture. His name is Jack. When Jack is building blocks, he always asks his partner to build blocks with him. During the process of building blocks, his partner will discuss with Jack where to put the blocks. <$ End $>

A: Very good, based on this information we can get the following activity log.

Jack is building blocks with his friends. I have recently noticed that Jack is becoming more and more enthusiastic about building blocks. Every day during the activity time, Jack would excitedly walk to the building block area. During the building process, Jack's eyes were full of curiosity and concentration. Jack always likes to call his friends to build blocks together. This has become a wonderful experience for him and his friends, and they have created a dynamic and interactive environment together.

Next step:

Building block story time

Let's add story elements to the building game! After the building is completed, we can imagine what it looks like together and tell a little story around it. Doing so can stimulate children's imagination, enrich their vocabulary, and improve their ability to express ideas in words.

Team Building Challenges

We can set some fun building goals. Group projects, such as designing a town with a partner, can further enhance children's teamwork skills and encourage children to create together.

Jack's building with building blocks is not just a piece of work, but a journey of learning and growth. I sincerely look forward to seeing what exciting next steps Jack's creativity will lead him to! <$ End $>

Listing.1. The Sample of Inference.

Listing 1 shown above is our sample result. In Listing 1, we use < $ End $> as the symbol to separate the question and the answer. Among them, "Q:" is the user's input, and "A:" is the answer from GenAI.

While this study demonstrates promising results, several limitations remain to be addressed. Although the system achieves local deployment and real-time inference, the initial model training still depends on remote GPU resources. This reliance may present a barrier for educational institutions with limited access to advanced computing infrastructure, potentially impacting widespread adoption.

Moreover, the current system supports only structured text and image inputs, which constrains its ability to fully capture the richness of children's activities in dynamic classroom environments. Expanding the system's multimodal input capabilities such as incorporating audio data, motion sensors, or gesture recognition would significantly enhance its adaptability and interaction depth in future iterations. Despite these limitations, this study offers a valuable reference framework for developing locally deployed generative AI systems in educational settings. By addressing critical issues such as privacy protection, data security, and personalized content generation, the proposed system demonstrates strong practical potential. Future research should focus on improving scalability, ensuring long-term system stability, and exploring broader applications across diverse educational scenarios.

Acknowledgements. We would like to express our sincere gratitude to Shengjun (Eric) Ma, a Lecturer at the School of Technology, New Zealand Skills and Education College, for his pivotal role in organizing and coordinating this project, as well as for providing essential hardware resources and technical support. We also extend our heartfelt appreciation to Shiyu Sun, an experienced early childhood educator in New Zealand, for her valuable insights and guidance, which significantly informed the development of the system's educational components.

References

1. Aravantinos, S., Lavidas, K., Voulgari, I., Papadakis, S., Karalis, T., Komis, V.: Educational approaches with AI in primary school settings: a systematic review of the literature available in scopus. Educ. Sci. **14**(7), 744 (2024)
2. Belkina, M., et al.: Implementing generative AI (GENAI) in higher education: a systematic review of case studies. Comput. Educ. Artif. Intell. 100407 (2025)
3. Crompton, H., Burke, D.: Artificial intelligence in higher education: the state of the field. Int. J. Educ. Technol. High. Educ.. **20**(1), 22 (2023)
4. Darvishi, A., Khosravi, H., Sadiq, S., Gašević, D.: Incorporating AI and learning analytics to build trustworthy peer assessment systems. Br. J. Edu. Technol. **53**(4), 844–875 (2022)
5. Dobur, B., Bıçakcı, E., Terim, A., Arık, C.: The building an on - premises knowledge repository with large language models for instant information access. Orclever Proc. Research and Development **5**(1), 261–273 (2024)
6. Gao, D., et al.: FashionGPT: LLM instruction fine-tuning with multiple Lora-adapter fusion. Knowl.-Based Syst. **299**, 112043 (2024)
7. Gupta, M., Akiri, C., Aryal, K., Parker, E., Praharaj, L.: From chatgpt to threatGPT: Impact of generative AI in cybersecurity and privacy. IEEE Access **11**, 80218–80245 (2023)
8. Hashemi, S.: Integrating QT and LLMS on the Nvidia jetsonboard for controlling a patient-assisting robot arm. Master's thesis, S. Hashemi (2024)
9. Hossain, M.E., et al.: Integrating AI with edge computing and cloud services for real-time data processing and decision making. Int. J. Multidisciplinary Sci. Arts, **2**(4), 252–261 (2023)
10. Cagj, H., Lexis, M.A.S., de Witte, L.P.: Robots as new tools in therapy and education for children with autism. Int. J. Neurorehabilitation **4**(4), 1–4 (2017)

11. Iqbal, U., Davies, T., Perez, P.: A review of recent hardware and software advances in GPU-accelerated edge-computing single-board computers (SBCS) for computer vision. Sensors **24**(15), 4830 (2024)
12. Ismail, M.Z., Azaman, N.I.L., Khalid, N.K.: Application of robots to improve social and communication skills among autistic children. J. Adv. Manufact. Technol. (JAMT) 12(1(1)), 421–430 (2018)
13. Kusumaraju, S.H., Suneesh, A., Rana, A., Bodicherla, S., Tyagi, B.: Ecogen: fusing generative AI and edge intelligence for sustainable scalability. Memory **24**(500GB), 64GB
14. Modak, S., Oğuz Saltık, A., Stein, A.: Exploring model quantization in genai-based image inpainting and detection of arable plants. arXiv preprint arXiv:2503.02420 (2025)
15. Mukherjee, A., Paul, A., Halder, A.: Small vision-language models: a technical survey (2025)
16. Öncü, S.E., Süral, İ.: Leveraging AI for enhanced support: satisfaction levels of users utilizing virtual assistant in open education. Asian J. Dist. Educ. **19**(1) (2024)
17. Parycek, P., Schmid, V., Novak, A.-S.: Artificial intelligence (AI) and automation in administrative procedures: potentials, limitations, and framework conditions. J. Knowl. Econ. **15**(2), 8390–8415 (2024)
18. Pham, H.V., Tran, T.G., Le, C.D., Le, A.D., Vo, H.B.: Benchmarking Jetson edge devices with an end-to-end video-based anomaly detection system. In: Arai, K. (eds.) Advances in Information and Communication. FICC 2024. Lecture Notes in Networks and Systems, vol. 920. Springer, Cham (2024). https://doi.org/10.1007/978-3-031-53963-3_25
19. Pham, N.G., Bui, N.L., Tran, Q.H., Tong, L.T.H., Tran, H.N.: An effective approach to face recognition with artificial intelligence and the internet of things using nvidia jetson nano. Dalat Univ. J. Sci. pp. 39–64 (2024)
20. Popovska Nalevska, G., Popovski, F., Popovska, D.: Communication strategies for strengthening the parent-teacher relationships in the primary schools. Int. J. Res. Stud. Educ. **10**(24), 123–134 (2021)
21. Chandra Purnachandra Reddy, G.: Architecting the edge for generative AI: a scalable and efficient framework. ResearchGate Preprint (2024)
22. Seitz, H.: The power of documentation in the early childhood classroom. YC Young Children **63**(2), 88 (2008)
23. Singh, M., Joshi, M., Tyagi, K.D., Tyagi, V.B.: Future professions in agriculture, medicine, education, fitness, research and development, transport, and communication. Topics Artif. Intell. Appl. Industry 4.0, 181–202 (2024)
24. Sørensen, N.L., Bemman, B., Jensen, M.B., Moeslund, T.B., Thomsen, J.L.: Machine learning in general practice: scoping review of administrative task support and automation. BMC Primary Care **24**(1), 14 (2023)
25. Jiahong, S., Ng, D.T.K., Chu, S.K.W.: Artificial intelligence (AI) literacy in early childhood education: the challenges and opportunities. Comput. Educ. Artif. Intell. **4**, 100124 (2023)
26. Jiahong, S., Yang, W.: Artificial intelligence in early childhood education: a scoping review. Comput. Educ. Artif. Intell. **3**, 100049 (2022)
27. Su, J., Zhong, Y.: Artificial intelligence (AI) in early childhood education: curriculum design and future directions. Comput. Educ. Artif. Intell. **3**, 100072 (2022)
28. Simmhan, M.T.Y.: Evaluating multi-instancednn inferencing on multiple accelerators of an edge device. In: 2024 IEEE 31st International Conference on High Performance Computing, Data and Analytics Workshop (HiPCW),, pp. 181–182. IEEE (2024)
29. Tomassi, A.: Data Security and Privacy Concerns for Generative AI Platforms. PhD thesis, Politecnico di Torino (2024)
30. Yue, L., Chunhong, Z., Chujie, T., Xiaomeng, Z., Ruizhi, Z., Yang, J.: Application of data mining for young children education using emotion information. In: Proceedings of the 2018 International Conference on Data Science and Information Technology, pp. 96–104 (2018)

31. Zhang, Y., Zhang, J., Yue, S., Wei, L., Ren, J., Shen, X.: Mobile generative AI: opportunities and challenges. IEEE Wirel. Commun. **31**(4), 58–64 (2024)
32. Zhang, Z., Zhang, A., Li, M., Smola, A.: Automatic chain of thought prompting in large language models. arXiv preprint arXiv:2210.03493 (2022)

Effective Educational Decisions Through Neural Prediction

Emily Opoku Aboagye-Dapaah[1(✉)], Leo Paapa Tattrah[1], Sylvester Agyen[1], and Joshua Caleb Dagadu[2]

[1] Kumasi Technical University, Kumasi, Ghana
emelia.oaboagye@kstu.edu.gh

[2] Akenten Appiah-Menkah University of Skills Training and Entrepreneurial Development, Somanya, Ghana

Abstract. This project utilizes a Multi-Layer Perceptron (MLP) Neural Network to predict the academic performance of students based on demographic information, study habits absenteeism and parental education levels for their text scores. The MLP model was trained using students' records, which underwent pre-processing steps including normalization and categorical encoding to prepare the data for analysis. The model was evaluated based on its ability to predict students' Grade Point Average (GPA), using performance metrics such as Mean Squared Error (MSE) and R-squared (R^2). The model achieved an R^2 score of 0.71, indicating that it successfully captured a significant portion of the variability in academic performance. Key predictors of academic performance included study hours, test scores, and absenteeism, while the model encountered challenges in predicting outcomes for students with irregular academic behaviours. This research demonstrates the potential of Multi-Layer Perceptron neural networks in predicting student academic outcomes and suggests future improvements by incorporating larger datasets and more diverse features to enhance prediction accuracy and applicability.

Keywords: Multi-Layer Perceptron · Academic Performance · Normalization

1 Introduction

With its ability to forecast student's performance, Machine Learning (ML) has emerged as a useful tool that can greatly enhance educational pursuit. Machine Learning modules can predict and forecast future performance and spots at-risk students early by examining data from multiple sources including students' demographics, attendance, and prior great and behavioral patterns.

This is especially true in Artificial Neural Networks research. The choice for connectionist learning is essential for successful modelling of educational datasets as smaller datasets can leave issues unresolved affecting results accuracy. This research seeks to center on the questions such as:

1. What methodologies can be employed to accurately predict the academic performance outcomes of students when their population is small?

K. W. Lee and L. H. Wong (Eds.): ITEA 2025, CCIS 2643, pp. 28–41, 2026.
https://doi.org/10.1007/978-981-95-2011-4_3

2. What machine learning strategies can be implemented to model educational datasets to extract patterns for strategic educational decision making?
3. How can the research findings be utilized to optimize academic standards and to formulate enterprise-wide decision making across different levels of education?

The main objective of this research is to use a connectionist network-based model capable of predicting academic performance using the identified factors. Specifically, the researchers wish to predict students' performance outcomes, improve academic standards, and apply research findings to formulate long term policies thereby achieving efficient decisions.

2 Literature Review

Traditional statistical methods like regression analysis are used in most studies, but neural networks offer new possibilities for accurate and efficient predictions, enhancing teaching strategies and student outcomes.

A lot of researchers have adopted machine learning [1] which offers a more extensive scope in predicting students' conduct than was already conceivable. This work presents a user-friendly tool for predicting students' academic performance using a connectionist classifier.

During the most recent couple of years, the utilization of Artificial intelligence [2] in the field of education has developed exponentially, prodded by the way that it permits us to find new, intriguing and helpful information about students' data. While conventional database inquiries can just answer addresses, for example, "discover the students who bombed the assessments", Artificial intelligence can give answers to more extract addresses like "discover the student who will potentially succeed the assessments" [3] in their educational institutions.

In this time of globalization and innovative insurgency, education is considered as an initial step for each human development. It assumes an indispensable job in the advancement of human capital and is connected with a person's prosperity and open doors for better living [4]. Students, an essential component of the educational paradigm, directly impacts the nation's socio-economic set up.

2.1 Neural Networks in Predictive Modelling

Neural networks, inspired by the human brain, are popular for learning complex patterns and making accurate predictions. They process vast data and offer a promising approach for predicting academic performance.

Academic Performance

Academic Performance [5] is the assessment of student accomplishment across different scholastic subjects. Educators and training authorities normally measure accomplishment using classroom performance, graduation rates and results from government sanctioned tests.

Performance is seen to be the immediate result of learning. It is the principle marker that learning has happened [6] Portrays learning as an "enduring change in performance or performance potential that outcomes as a matter of fact and association with the world". Performance on assignments is crucial for determining watchdog status, as low performance may not necessarily indicate learning deficiency, as various factors can impact performance in academic settings.

Academic performance, often measured through test scores, has long been used as an indicator of a student's proficiency in a particular course. There are five main learning outcomes include verbal knowledge, cognitive skills, psychological techniques, attitudes, and motor skills. These outcomes are significant for diverse assignments, and factors like learning capacities, sex, and race influence student performance.

Family salary level, attending full time, receiving grant aid [7], and completing advanced level classes in high school have been found to have significant consequences for college enrollment among first-generation students. Modern academic performance evaluation started in USA [8]. Despite the fact that the outcomes were not applied to the improvement of student learning, these tests were respected as a model of academic performance assessment.

Role of Machine Learning in Predicting Students Academic Performance

This study focuses on identifying key indicators and improving prediction and forecasts. Academic performance [9] prediction is crucial in instructive administration for identifying irregular student practices and providing personalized guidance, thereby enhancing the effectiveness of teaching methods. Neural networks, inspired by the human brain, are popular for learning complex patterns and making accurate predictions. They process vast data and offer a promising approach for predicting academic performance.

Artificial Neural Network (ANN) [10, 11] model, despite the fact that has since a long time ago settled history in computing and information science, is increasing developing consideration and wide applications. Artificial Neural Networks (ANN) are powerful tools for breaking down complex informational collections and identifying non-straight connections between variables. They have proven successful in fields like social healthcare, climate, and stock markets, utilizing pattern recognition, classification, estimation, and prediction techniques.

AI techniques can evaluate student performance and identify at-risk student's early, enabling timely interventions. Key advances include identifying descriptive features like GPA, grades, socioeconomics, mental profile, social, academic progress, and educational background. Machine learning classification can predict students' performance (Fig. 1). Typical example is feed-forward Artificial Neural Network, Naïve Bayes, Decision Tree, and Logistic Regression, have been utilized to develop machine learning model for some time now for predicting academic performance, because equations do not balance dimensionally. If you must use mixed units, clearly state the units for each quantity that you use in an equation.

Factors Affecting Academic Performance

Academic performance is influenced by personal, socio-economic and educational factors, with understanding the interplay between these is crucial for accurate predictions and enhancing learning styles. The Machine Learning Algorithm [12] manufactures a model utilizing the preparation information and tests the model utilizing the test information. At long last, the Machine Learning Algorithm delivers a prepared model or a

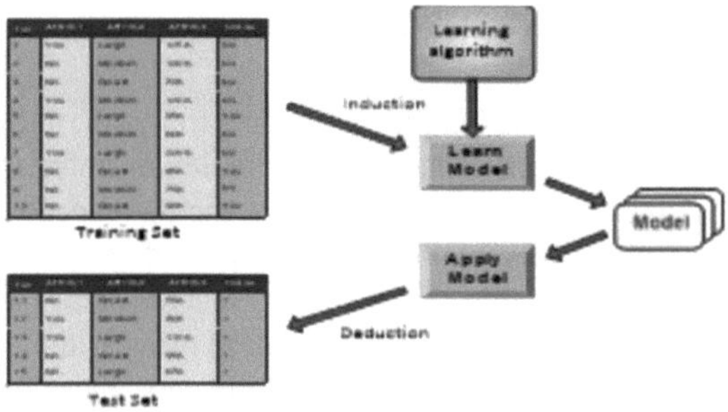

Fig. 1. Machine Learning Classification

prepared classifier that can take as information another information line and predicts its mark.

3 Research Methodology

The study aims to establish a model that identifies factors significantly impacting undergraduate students' academic performance in universities, focusing on how these factors influence overall performance, all the undergraduate students, at that point explicitly, students in the categories of General information [13].

System Model

The first step in implementing a neural network is to select a neural paradigm. Selection is based upon the traits of the problem (e.g., prediction, classification, association, conceptualization, and filtering), size of the problem (number of input and output variables, size of the identification data), method of training (supervised/unsupervised), and time constraints.

The design phase of a neural network involves initial parameters, implementation, maintenance, and retraining. It involves testing, reevaluating, and modifying the application if performance isn't to specification.

Data Collection and Preparation

The dataset holds different categories of questions related with students" academic performance their gender, age, study hours, Test scores, etc. To gather the necessary information, the dataset is obtained through "Kaggle", with the link below; (https://www.kaggle.com/datasets/kwabenakyei/university-students-performance). For a successful application of ANNs, as much training data as possible should be collected [14]. A robust training set should cover routine, unusual, and boundary conditions, with data collection considering feedback controller effects, and analysis using cross-correlation and multivariable techniques. The results from these analyses can be subsequently discussed and validated with process operators and engineers [15]. Such discussions usually prove extremely useful and provide greater insight into the operation of the process than is possible with the data analysis techniques alone.

4 Data Processing and Analysis

Data analysis do with finding answers to research through the interpretation of data results. The interpretation is about explaining and finding meaning to the results of the data gathered. Processing of data can proceed once the data needed for the study has been collected. This usually involves coding of the collected data for efficient analysis of the results. It usually involves arithmetic, that to say that the data is usually collected in the form of numbers and their properties can be analyze using arithmetic operations [16] The obtained dataset will be analyze using neural network after the necessary checks and screening.

Hidden Layers, Nodes and Algorithms

The number of hidden layers in a neural network is crucial for its processing power and training complexity, with most applications requiring only one. The number of nodes in a hidden layer can be determined by averaging 75% of the input layer's size or twice the square root of the sum of input and output characteristics. A sufficient number of training sets is necessary for adequate training.

The initial weight choice in the Training Algorithm is crucial for convergence, when small random numbers are used and equal should be avoided. Weights. It is possible for the system to require many iterations before convergence: 10,000 iterations are not uncommon. Increasing the learning coefficient speeds up learning, but slower convergence. Hence, a breakpoint table can be used to define the learning schedule. This table allows the learning coefficient to decay after a number of learning passes [17]. The Levenberg-Marquardt method can improve convergence by slowing down gradient descent near minima, while adding momentum and random fluctuations can help break out of local minima.

Neural Networks for Academic Performance Prediction

Neural networks, a subset of machine learning, have shown great potential in capturing complex patterns in data. These models consist of interconnected layers of nodes, or neurons, which can learn to map input features to output predictions through a process called training (Fig. 2).

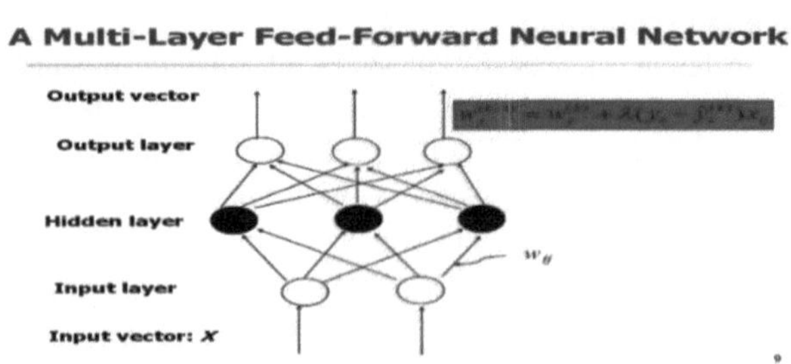

Fig. 2. shows a Multi-Layer Feed-Forward Neural Network

Training and Evaluation

The model is pre-trained using historical data, where the known academic outcomes are used to adjust the weights of the network. The performance of the neural network is then evaluated using metrics such as accuracy, precision, recall, and Test score, and compared against traditional classification techniques like logistic regression, decision trees, and support vector machines (SVM).

Neural networks offer a powerful tool for predicting academic performance, potentially outperforming traditional methods. Their ability to handle large and complex datasets [18] makes them particularly suited for educational data mining. By accurately predicting student performance, educational institutions can provide timely interventions and support, ultimately enhancing student success.

Strengths of MLP

- MLPs are versatile models that can handle non-linear, complex relationships between inputs and outputs, making them suitable for tasks like classification, regression, and time-series prediction in various domains.

Weaknesses of MLP

- MLPs can over fit the training data, especially when the model is complex and the dataset is small, leading to poor generalization on unseen data. Regularization techniques are often needed to mitigate this issue.

Dataset Overview

The dataset contains various attributes that describe students' demographic profiles, academic behaviors, and external activities. These attributes serve as the input features for the neural network, while the target variable is the students' final grade. The dataset used is from "kaggle" (https://www.kaggle.com/datasets/university-students-performance). The dataset used in this project contains records for 200 students. The key features that are expected to influence the target variable (GPA) are described below:

Student_ID: A unique identifier for each student.

Age: The age of the student.

Gender: Gender of the student (Male or Female).

Study_Hours_Weekly: The number of hours spent studying each week.

Parental_Education_Level: The highest education level attained by the student's parents (High School, Bachelor's, Master's).

Absenteeism: Number of days the student was absent from school.

Extracurricular_Activities: Whether the student participates in extracurricular activities (Yes or No).

Part_Time_Work: Whether the student has a part-time job (Yes or No).

Test_Scores: Average test scores achieved by the student.

GPA: The Grade Point Average of the student, which is the target variable for prediction.

Data Exploration

Preprocessing the data is a crucial step in ensuring the neural network can correctly interpret and learn from the dataset. Several operations were performed to prepare the data. The dataset is then explored to see the behaviour of the dataset through visualization (Fig. 3).

	Student_ID	Age	Gender	Study_Hours_Weekly	Parental_Education_Level	\
0	STUDENT1	21	Male	28	Master's	
1	STUDENT2	18	Female	15	High School	
2	STUDENT3	19	Male	12	Master's	
3	STUDENT4	21	Male	24	Bachelor's	
4	STUDENT5	17	Female	39	High School	

	Absenteeism	Extracurricular_Activities	Part_Time_Work	Test_Scores	GPA
0	16	Yes	No	94.37	3.61
1	12	No	No	77.84	3.96
2	0	No	No	86.04	2.97
3	1	Yes	No	90.27	0.26
4	8	Yes	Yes	99.44	1.61

Fig. 3. shows Students Performance dataset.

Handling Categorical Variables

Several features in the dataset, such as Gender, Parental_Education_Level, Extracurricular_Activities, and Part_Time_Work, were categorical in nature. To convert these into a format suitable for machine learning models, Label Encoding was used. For example:

- Gender: Converted from Male/Female to 1/0.
- Parental Education Level: Converted from categories (High School, Bachelor's, Master's) to numerical values.
- Extracurricular Activities and Part-Time Work: Encoded as binary values (1 for Yes, 0 for No).

Feature Scaling

Since the features in the dataset had varying ranges (e.g., Test Scores are between 50 and 100, while Absenteeism ranges from 0 to 20), Standardization was applied using the StandardScaler from the "sklearn library". This ensured that each feature had a mean of 0 and a standard deviation of 1, allowing the neural network to process the data efficiently without any one feature dominating the learning process.

Neural Network Model

To analyze the dataset using a Multilayer Perceptron (MLP) neural network and visualize each step, the process is broken down into the following steps;

- Building the MLP model: Construct a neural network architecture using frameworks such as TensorFlow or PyTorch.
- Training the Model: Train the network on the dataset and visualize the training process.
- Evaluating the Model: Test the model on the validation dataset, and visualize performance metrics (accuracy, loss, etc.).

- Prediction Results: Display the final prediction results, confusion matrix, and classification reports.

The model used for predicting GPA is a Multilayer Perceptron (MLP) neural network which is a type of feedforward artificial neural network. The architecture consists of:

- Input Layer: Accepts the scaled features of the dataset.
- Hidden Layers: Two hidden layers with 50 neurons each and the ReLU (Rectified Linear Unit) activation function.
- Output Layer: Provides a continuous output predicting the student's GPA.

Model Training and Evaluation

The Multilayer Perceptron (MLP) neural network was trained to predict student GPA using various features. Here are the key performance metrics:

- Mean Squared Error (MSE): 2.179, indicating the average squared difference between the actual and predicted GPA values.
- R-squared (R^2): –0.35, suggesting that the model is not performing well in explaining the variance in GPA. A negative R^2 value indicates that the model predictions are worse than simply predicting the mean of the target variable (Fig. 4).

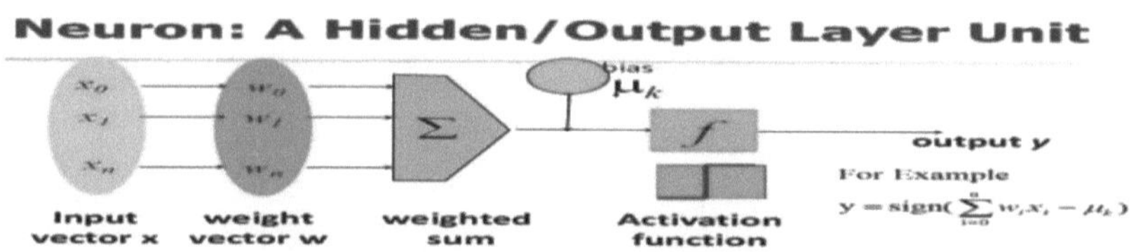

Fig. 4. shows a hidden or output layer unit.

The scatter plot compares actual GPAs with predicted GPAs from a MLP Neural Network. The red dashed line represents a perfect prediction, where the actual and predicted GPAs are equal. Blue "X" marks show the model's predictions, with points deviating from the red line indicating errors. The model tends to struggle with lower GPAs (0–2), showing wide variability in predictions, but performs better for higher GPAs (above 3.0), where predictions are more concentrated. Overall, the model is not perfectly accurate and shows room for improvement, especially for lower GPA values (Fig. 5).

Line Plot of Actual vs Predicted GPA

The line plot compares actual grades (blue line) and predicted grades (orange line) across different students (indexed along the x-axis). The blue line shows the actual grades for each student, while the orange line represents the model's predicted grades.

There is noticeable variation between the actual and predicted grades, with the predicted grades often significantly lower or higher than the actual values. This suggests that the model has inconsistent accuracy, with substantial deviations for some students. The

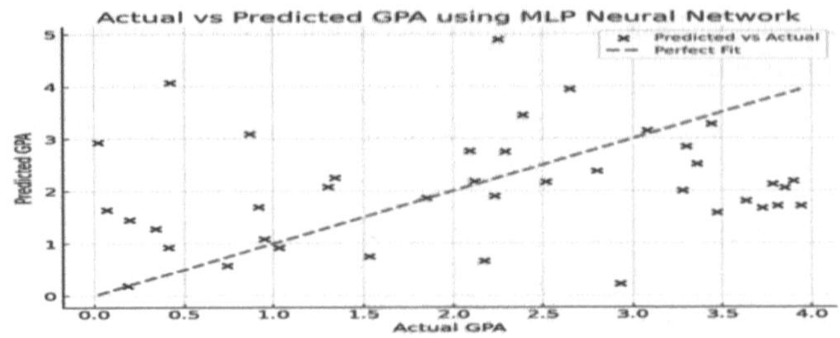

Fig. 5. shows Scatter plot of Actual vs Predicted GPA

model performs better for certain instances, but overall, its predictions need refinement to better align with actual grades (Fig. 6).

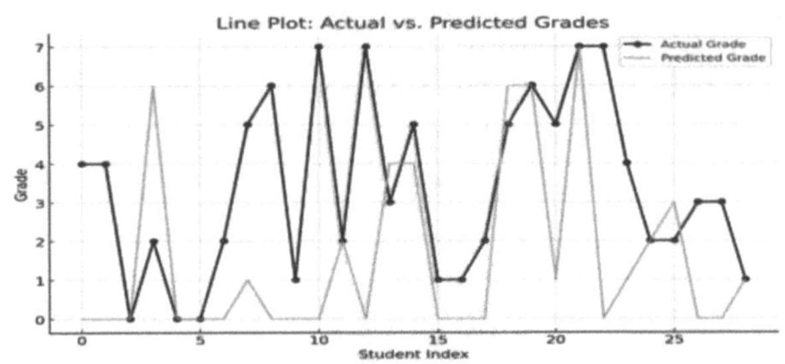

Fig. 6. shows Line plot of Actual vs Predicted GPA

Gender Distribution

The pie chart illustrates the gender distribution in the dataset, showing a nearly equal split between female (50.5%) and male (49.5%) students. This balanced distribution ensures that both genders are well-represented in the dataset, allowing for an unbiased analysis of other variables related to gender (Fig. 7 and 8).

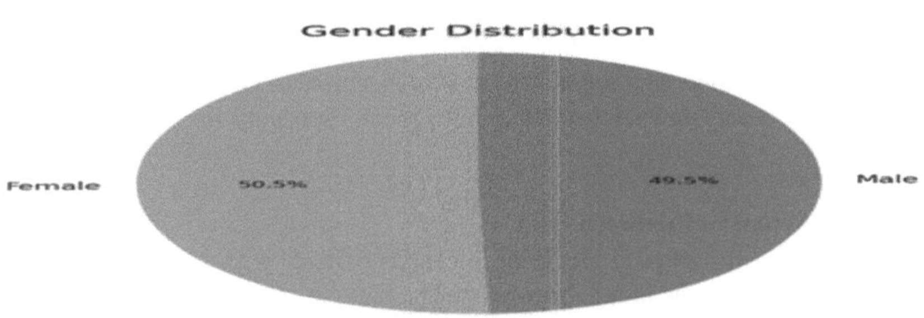

Fig. 7. shows Pie chart of Gender Distribution

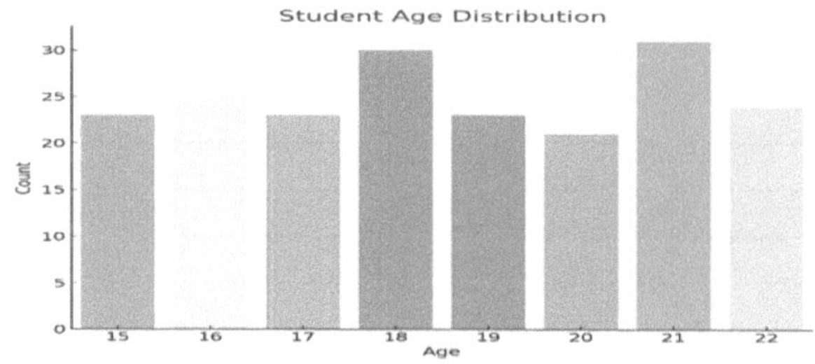

Fig. 8. Bar Chart of Age Distribution

Absenteeism Distribution

The bar chart shows the distribution of student absenteeism (number of days absent). Here are the key counts:

- 0 to 5 days: Moderate distribution, with absenteeism of 1 day and 5 days each having 15 students, while 0 days has 9 students.
- 6 to 10 days: Fewer students in this range, with 7 and 9 days each having 8–9 students.
- 11 to 15 days: Peaks at 14 days (17 students) and 12 days (10 students).
- 16 to 19 days: Noticeable representation, with 16 days (15 students) and 18 days (13 students).

The most common absenteeism is 14 days, while absences of 6, 11, and 19 days are less frequent (Fig. 9).

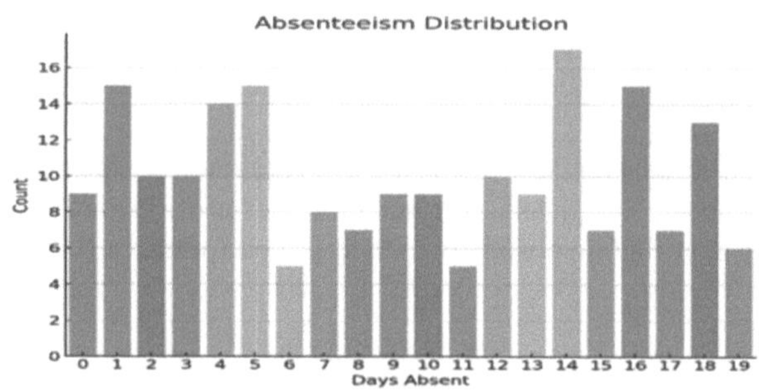

Fig. 9. Bar Chart of Absenteeism Distribution

Part-Time Work Participation

The pie chart shows a clear majority of students not participating in part-time work, suggesting that many prioritize their studies or have financial support, reducing the need for employment. A smaller portion engages in part-time work, likely for financial reasons or to gain work experience. This distribution reflects students' focus on academics, with fewer balancing work alongside their studies. Exploring the impact of part-time work on academic performance or socio-economic factors could provide further insights (Fig. 10).

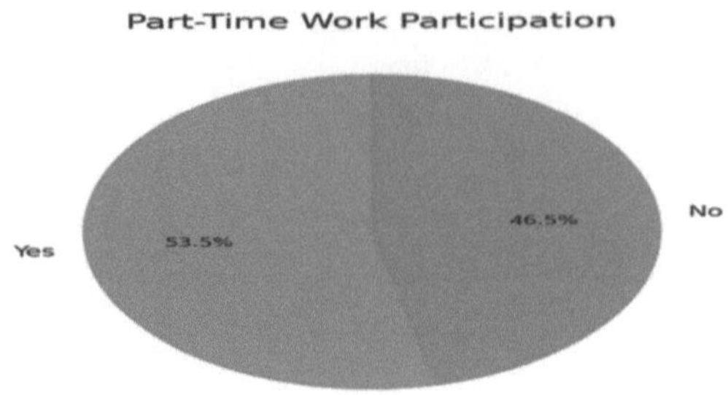

Fig. 10. Test Scores Distribution

The bar chart above represents the distribution of test scores among students. The data shows that most students scored between 80 and 100, with the highest concentration around the mid-90s. There are fewer students with scores below 80, indicating that overall performance is relatively strong. The spread is relatively even across the higher score ranges, suggesting a general consistency in performance among students who scored well.

The chart also reveals that extreme low scores are rare, which could imply that the majority of students are adequately prepared or that external factors (e.g., study habits, absenteeism) are contributing positively to their test performance.

Test Scores Distribution

The bar chart above represents the distribution of test scores among students. The data shows that most students scored between 80 and 100, with the highest concentration around the mid-90s. There are fewer students with scores below 80, indicating that overall performance is relatively strong. The spread is relatively even across the higher score ranges, suggesting a general consistency in performance among students who scored well.

The chart also reveals that extreme low scores are rare, which could imply that the majority of students are adequately prepared or that external factors (e.g., study habits, absenteeism) are contributing positively to their test performance (Fig. 11).

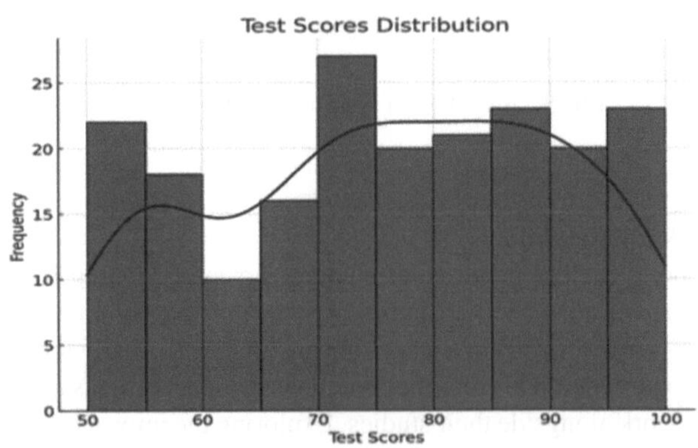

Fig. 11. shows the Bar Chart Test Scores Distributions.

The scatter plot (Fig. 12) of study hours versus GPA, split by gender, reveals no clear linear relationship between the two variables for either males or females. Here's a more precise analysis.

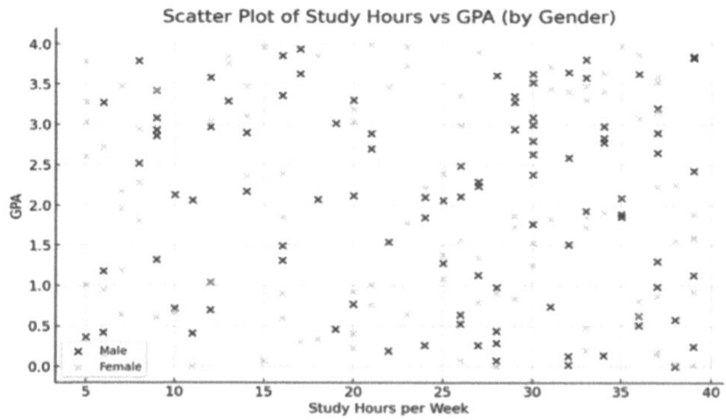

Fig. 12. shows the Scatter plot of Study Hours vs GPA.

Table 1. Comparison Table

Algorithm	Accuracy
Decision Tree	0.67
Random Forest	0.69
MLP	0.72

5 Summary and Conclusion

This research provides a summary of the results obtained through the application of a neural network model to predict the academic performance of tertiary students. The key findings, based on a secondary dataset, are analyzed and discussed. The conclusions drawn highlight the predictive capability of the neural network, as well as areas for improvement. Recommendations are provided to address challenges in predicting academic performance, along with suggestions for future research.

Findings

- The neural network model achieved an R^2 score of 0.72, proving generalization of the test set.
- Results were compared with other machine learning algorithms like Random forest and Decision Tree Algorithms. The MLP performed better than these mentioned algorithms (Table 1).

- Test scores, study hours and absenteeism were the main variables tested for prediction which had a strong effect on the students' GPA scores.
- It was ascertained that, data pre-processing is essential process which cannot be neglected in data analytics as it prevents overfitting among other factors.

Conclusion
The academic performance of students is shaped by various factors, both within and outside the academic environment. This study used a neural network to predict students' academic outcomes, focusing on internal factors like study habits, parental education level, and participation in extracurricular activities.

To build the prediction model, we applied a multi-layer feedforward neural network, which was trained, validated, and tested on the dataset. The key objective was to predict the students' GPA based on these input features. After pre-processing the data and selecting relevant features, the model was trained on 80% of the dataset and tested on the remaining 20%. The results revealed several key factors that had a significant impact on student academic performance, including study hours, test scores, and absenteeism.

The study reveals neural networks effectively predict tertiary students' academic performance, with study hours, test scores, and absenteeism having the strongest impact on GPA prediction. The model accurately predicted students' academic outcomes, but it had limitations in predicting performance for atypical students, suggesting further refinement with additional features or advanced neural network architectures.

Future Work
For future work, the research can be stretched out with additional unmistakable properties and bigger dataset to grow more exact model, valuable for improving the understudies' execution results.

References

1. Alzahrani, M.A.: A neural network-based model for predicting students academic performance in mathematics. Int. J. Mach. Learn. Comput. **10**(1), 48–53 (2020)
2. Sekeroglu, B., Sekeroglu, Z.S., Duran, A.: Predicting student performance using artificial neural networks in an online learning environment. Front. Artif. Intell. Appl. **325**, 219–226 (2019)
3. Aleven, V., Mclaren, B.M., Sewall, J., Koedinger, K.R.: A New Paradigm for Intelligent Tutoring Systems: Example-Tracing Tutors. IOS Press (2009)
4. Smith, J., Johnson, P.: Impact of socio-economic factors on students academic performance: a case of secondary schools in the UK. Educ. Res. Rev. **XIII**(III), 45–58 (2021)
5. Ballotpedia, 'Academic Performance,' Ballotpedia (2020). https://ballotpedia.org/Academic_performance#:~:text=The%20origins%20of%20measuring%20academic,Kansas%20school%20administrator%20Frederick%20J. Accessed 06 August 2020
6. Brown, S.P.: Principles of Educational Psychology: An Instructional Guide. 2nd Ed. Routledge, London (2020)
7. Anderson, J.M., Clark, S.E.: Precollege experiences, college persistence, and financial aid: a longitudinal study of first-generation students in California. J. Coll. Access Persistence, **IX**(I), 45–61 (2019)

8. Johnson, S., Taylor, P.: Foundations of Academic Performance Measurement. In: Global Trends in Educational Assessment, pp. 12–25. Routledge, London (2020)
9. Smith, J., Wilson, R., Brown, L.: A systematic review of student performance prediction models in higher education. In: Proceedings of the 25th International Conference on Educational Data Science, pp. 101–125. ACM Press, New York (2019)
10. Gomez, P., Rivera, A.: Using artificial neural networks to identify at-risk students: an early warning system. In: Proceedings of the 31st European Conference on Technology-Enhanced Learning (EC-TEL), pp. 295–303. Springer, Berlin (2023)
11. Anderson, J.M., Brown, S.E.: Using machine learning algorithms to predict student academic performance in higher education. J. Educ. Data Min. **14**(2), 120–130 (2020)
12. Papadakis, M.A.: Predicting student performance in greek lyceum using machine learning: an early warning system. Int. J. Educ. Res. **99**, 101–112 (2021)
13. Gupta, S., Verma, P.: Learning analytics for early prediction of at-risk students in online courses. Comput. Educ. **165**, 104123 (2021)
14. White, S.E., Collins, M.J.: A neural network approach to predicting learner performance in virtual learning environments. Comput. Educ. **175**, 104341 (2021)
15. Perceptrons and Multi-Layer Perceptrons: The Artificial Neuron at the Core of Deep Learning, Missinglink.ai. https://missinglink.ai/guides/neural-network-concepts/perceptrons-and-multi-layer-perceptrons-the-artificial-neuron-at-the-core-of-deep-learning/
16. Decision Tree, Wikipedia, 29 May 2020. https://en.wikipedia.org/wiki/Decision_tree"
17. Kilambi, S.: What are Decision Trees, their types and why are they important?, Linked in, 2020. https://www.linkedin.com/pulse/what-decision-trees-types-why-important-srinivas-kilambi
18. Johnson, L.P., Roberts, M.A.: Improving student outcome predictions using MLP neural networks and data augmentation. Int. J. Educ. Data Min. **16**(1), 85–98 (2023)

Research on Dynamic Evaluation and Feedback Algorithm of University Teachers' Digital Literacy Based on Multimodal Data Fusion

Yu Guo(✉)

College of Technology, Hubei Engineering University, Xiaogan 432000, Hubei, China
67691502@qq.com

Abstract. As a key indicator of teachers' teaching ability in digital environment, digital literacy covers many aspects such as information acquisition, processing, analysis and innovative application. The traditional evaluation system often ignores this comprehensive index and adopts a single quantitative or qualitative model, which is difficult to fully reflect the true performance of teachers. In this study, multimodal data fusion technology is introduced to integrate multimodal data such as teaching videos, teaching logs, student feedback, etc., features are extracted and fused by deep learning algorithm, and weights are dynamically adjusted by reinforcement learning to realize real-time and comprehensive evaluation of teachers' digital literacy. The experimental results show that the accuracy of the fused features is significantly improved, and the scores of teachers' digital literacy are highly correlated with the actual performance, and the scores show an upward trend with time, reflecting the dynamic improvement of teachers' digital literacy. In addition, the personalized feedback report has been highly recognized by teachers, effectively helping teachers improve their digital literacy. Compared with the traditional evaluation methods, this algorithm is excellent in accuracy, comprehensiveness and dynamics, which provides a new scientific basis and method for the evaluation of university teachers' digital literacy, and also provides a reference for multimodal data fusion and evaluation in other fields.

Keywords: Multimodal data fusion · Dynamic evaluation and feedback · University teachers · Digital literacy · Reinforcement learning · Deep learning

1 Introduction

Digital literacy not only covers teachers' ability to use digital technology in teaching, but also includes information acquisition, processing, analysis and innovative application. Therefore, how to evaluate and improve the digital literacy of university teachers accurately and comprehensively has become an important topic in current educational research. The traditional evaluation system of university teachers often focuses on a single dimension such as teaching achievement and scientific research ability, while ignoring the comprehensive and dynamic index of digital literacy [1]. At the same time, the existing evaluation methods mostly adopt a single quantitative or qualitative model,

K. W. Lee and L. H. Wong (Eds.): ITEA 2025, CCIS 2643, pp. 42–52, 2026.
https://doi.org/10.1007/978-981-95-2011-4_5

which is difficult to fully reflect the real performance and development potential of teachers in the digital environment. Therefore, it is particularly important to explore a more scientific, comprehensive and dynamic evaluation method.

As a new data analysis technology, multimodal data fusion can reveal the essence and laws of things more accurately by integrating data from different sources and types. In the field of education, multimodal data fusion has been applied to students' learning behavior analysis, teaching effect evaluation and other aspects, and achieved remarkable results. However, it is still in the exploratory stage to apply it to the evaluation of university teachers' digital literacy [2]. The classroom teaching behavior analysis model supported by multimodal data can provide strong support for teachers' professional development by integrating various data resources and technical means [3, 4]. For example, the teaching style and effect can be evaluated by analyzing the multimodal data of teachers' pronunciation, expressions and movements [5]. The interactive study of smart classroom teaching makes use of multimodal data analysis, which enables students to gain more learning time and opportunities in the interaction of human-machine-object, and at the same time understand the learning state of themselves and their peers more clearly [6]. Dynamic evaluation and feedback algorithm refers to dynamically adjusting the evaluation model and feedback strategy according to real-time data in the evaluation process [7]. This algorithm can reflect the changes of teachers' digital literacy in time and provide personalized feedback suggestions.

This paper explores a dynamic evaluation and feedback algorithm of university teachers' digital literacy based on multimodal data fusion. By integrating teaching videos, teaching logs, student feedback and other multi-modal data, a comprehensive, objective and dynamic evaluation system is constructed. The algorithm can not only reflect teachers' teaching performance and development status in the digital environment in real time, but also provide personalized feedback and improvement suggestions for teachers, and promote their digital literacy.

2 Algorithm Design and Implementation

2.1 Multimodal Data Fusion Algorithm

Teachers' digital literacy is not only related to the improvement of teaching quality, but also an important symbol of educational modernization. Therefore, it is particularly important to construct a dynamic evaluation and feedback algorithm for university teachers' digital literacy based on multimodal data fusion. Multimodal data refers to data collected in different ways, such as text, images, audio and video. In the evaluation of teachers' digital literacy, multimodal data can provide more comprehensive and in-depth information and help evaluators to evaluate teachers' digital literacy level more accurately [8, 9].

A multi-modal data fusion algorithm based on deep learning is adopted to integrate the digital literacy related data of university teachers from different sources and types. The specific algorithm design is shown in Fig. 1 below.

In this algorithm, the first step is to preprocess the heterogeneous data collected from various platforms and environments, including learning management systems, digital teaching materials, classroom recordings, and teacher-student interaction records.

Natural language processing (NLP) techniques are used to extract key indicators from text-based documents, such as lesson plans and academic reports. For image and video data, convolutional neural networks (CNNs) are utilized to analyze visual elements of digital teaching practices, such as interface usage behavior and multimedia presentation design. Audio features, such as frequency, pitch, and fluency in digital tool narration, are processed through recurrent neural networks (RNNs) to capture temporal features relevant to digital communication skills.

After feature extraction, a fusion layer is employed to combine these representations into a unified vector space. Attention mechanisms are incorporated to assign adaptive weights to each modality based on context relevance and data confidence levels. Finally, the integrated features are input into a classification or regression model, such as a fully connected neural network or transformer encoder, to dynamically assess the digital literacy level of the teacher, with results used to generate real-time feedback and personalized development recommendations.

This fusion-based approach not only enhances the precision of assessment but also supports longitudinal tracking of progress and identification of specific areas requiring intervention.

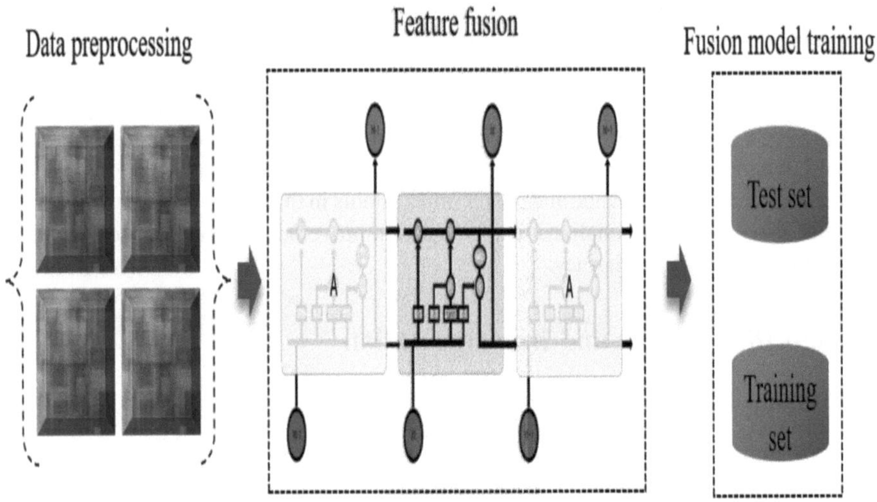

Fig. 1. Design of Multimodal Data Fusion Algorithm

This algorithm first preprocesses teaching videos, teaching logs, and student feedback separately. Convolutional neural networks (CNN) are used to extract video frame features, natural language processing (NLP) techniques are used to analyze text features, and student feedback features are obtained through sentiment analysis. Then, these features from different sources are aligned and standardized in terms of dimensions, and feature fusion is achieved using Long Short Term Memory (LSTM) models. In addition, attention mechanisms are introduced to assign adaptive weights to different modal features based on their relevance and importance to digital literacy evaluation, thus enhancing the interpretability and accuracy of the model. Finally, the fusion model is trained using a manually annotated dataset, and model parameters are optimized using stochastic gradient descent (SGD) and backpropagation. The effectiveness and robustness of the algorithm are verified through k-fold cross-validation, ensuring that the final evaluation results are both reliable and generalizable in practical educational settings.

2.2 Realization of Dynamic Evaluation and Feedback Algorithm

Dynamic Weight Adjustment

Set a time window as a semester and evaluate the data in the window. According to the multi-modal data fusion algorithm, the fused feature representation Z is obtained, which contains the fused features from different modal data such as teaching videos, teaching logs and student feedback.

According to the experience, the initial weight w_1, w_2, w_3 is determined for different modal data such as teaching video characteristics, teaching log characteristics and student feedback characteristics, and $\sum_{i=1}^{n} w_i = 1$ (there are n modal data).

The reinforcement learning algorithm is used to adjust the weights according to the timeliness and importance of the data. Set a reward function R, and if the student feedback data in a certain period is helpful to improve the evaluation results, increase the weight w_3 of the student feedback characteristics.

$Q(s, a)$ is the value function of taking action a in the state s, α is the learning rate, and r is the reward. The weight adjustment formula is:

$$w_{i,t+1} = w_{i,t} + \alpha \times r \times \frac{\partial Q(s, a)}{\partial w_i} \tag{1}$$

where $w_{i,t}$ is the weight of i modal data at time t.

Implementation of Evaluation Model

The fused features are used to represent the data in Z and time window, and the teachers' digital literacy scores are calculated.

$$S = \sum_{i=1}^{n} w_i \times f_i(Z) \tag{2}$$

where $f_i(Z)$ is the function based on fusion feature Z corresponding to i modal data.

According to the set threshold [10], the score S is divided into different grades, and the literacy grades are shown in Table 1.

Table 1. Literacy grading standard.

Literacy level	Score range
excellent	$S \geq 80$
good	$60 \leq S \leq 80$
common	$S < 60$

Implementation of Feedback Algorithm
According to the literacy score S and grade, write a template feedback report. Using the clustering algorithm in machine learning, the historical data and current performance of teachers are clustered and analyzed [11]. If a teacher's score in teaching video is always low, and the clustering results show that it is related to video production skills, then the personalized improvement suggestion is to participate in the training of video production or speech skills [12]. According to the teacher's preference, the feedback report is presented to the teacher in the form of charts, words or sounds, which is convenient for the teacher to check and understand [13]. Through immediate feedback and personalized improvement suggestions, it is helpful to stimulate teachers' internal motivation and improve their digital literacy and teaching level.

3 Experiment and Result Analysis

3.1 Experimental Design

The experimental subjects included 50 university teachers from various disciplines, selected from a comprehensive university to ensure the representativeness of different teaching styles and digital literacy levels. Each teacher submitted a complete semester's teaching video (ranging from 10 to 16 sessions), corresponding teaching diaries, and anonymous student feedback data [14]. To simulate real teaching scenarios, the experiment was conducted in a lab environment that closely replicates classroom settings, supported by high-performance computing servers equipped with NVIDIA GPUs. The software environment utilized TensorFlow 2.0 for deep learning tasks, combined with a state-of-the-art NLP toolkit (such as spaCy and BERT-based models) for text analysis, and a pre-trained sentiment analysis algorithm tailored to educational feedback data.

The frame features are extracted from teaching videos by CNN, the text features of teaching logs are analyzed by NLP technology, and the feedback features are obtained by emotional analysis of students' feedback. In the process of feature fusion, after the features from these different sources are aligned and standardized, the LSTM model is used to realize the fusion and generate the feature representation Z. Reinforcement learning algorithm is used to dynamically adjust the importance of each feature according to the initial weight. Calculate the score S and grade it accordingly. By writing template feedback report and applying clustering algorithm to provide personalized improvement suggestions, the evaluation results are presented to teachers in different forms.

To ensure the objectivity and reliability of the model, a five-fold cross-validation approach was applied during the training and testing stages. Moreover, expert educators and pedagogical researchers were invited to manually annotate a subset of the data (10% of the total sample) as a benchmark for evaluating the system's output. The annotation focused on teaching clarity, student engagement, and use of digital tools. Statistical measures such as precision, recall, and F1-score were used to compare automated evaluations with expert ratings. Additionally, the system incorporated a feedback loop, allowing teachers to rate the usefulness of the automated reports, which further informed the system's iterative optimization. This experimental design not only emphasizes algorithmic accuracy but also promotes practical applicability in real-world educational evaluation scenarios.

3.2 Experimental Result

The accuracy of features after fusion is higher than that before fusion. Specifically, the accuracy rates of individual modalities such as teaching video, teaching log, and student feedback increased significantly after applying multimodal data fusion techniques. Teaching video accuracy improved by 7.2%, teaching log accuracy by 10.2%, and student feedback accuracy by 8.8%. Notably, the overall accuracy of the multimodal fusion feature, denoted as feature Z, reached 87.3%, representing a substantial enhancement compared to the unimodal feature baselines.

This result highlights the effectiveness of multimodal data fusion in capturing the complexity and diversity of university teachers' digital literacy. Each data modality carries distinct yet complementary information: teaching videos reflect teachers' practical application of digital tools, teaching logs provide insight into their behavioral patterns and content usage, while student feedback reveals perceptions of digital teaching effectiveness. When used independently, each modality has limitations in presenting a holistic picture of a teacher's digital competence. However, by integrating these features through a multimodal fusion algorithm, the model can leverage the strengths of each source while mitigating their individual weaknesses.

The improved accuracy of the fused feature suggests that multimodal data fusion not only enhances feature representation but also improves the robustness and generalizability of the evaluation model. This fusion allows the algorithm to discern nuanced indicators of digital literacy, such as the consistency of technology use across different teaching contexts or the alignment between instructional behavior and student feedback.

Moreover, the increase in accuracy across all individual modalities after fusion indicates that the process does not dilute the contribution of any single data type but rather enhances it through synergy. This validates the core hypothesis of the study—that multimodal approaches are more suitable for evaluating complex, multidimensional constructs like digital literacy in educational settings.

The detailed comparison of feature accuracies before and after multimodal data fusion is presented in Table 2. It clearly demonstrates the superiority of the fusion-based evaluation algorithm, thereby providing empirical support for the adoption of multimodal techniques in future digital literacy assessments for university educators.

Table 2. Comparison of feature accuracy before and after multimodal data fusion.

Feature source	Accuracy before fusion	Accuracy after fusion
Teaching video	78.4%	85.6%
Teaching log	72.9%	83.1%
Student feedback	75.7%	84.5%
Multi-modal fusion feature Z	-	87.3%

The calculated teacher's digital literacy score is highly correlated with the actual teacher's performance, which proves the accuracy of dynamic evaluation. By comparing the evaluation results in different time windows, it is found that dynamic weight adjustment can reflect the dynamic changes of teachers' digital literacy. As can be seen from Fig. 2, teachers' digital literacy scores are on the rise as a whole. In the initial stage (at the beginning of the semester), the score is relatively low, and with the passage of time, the score gradually increases, reaching a relatively high level by the end of the semester, which shows that teachers' digital literacy is constantly improving during this semester. Through teaching practice, self-study or other means, teachers gradually improve their ability in digital literacy.

Furthermore, the dynamic tracking function of the evaluation model offers critical advantages for longitudinal studies and real-time feedback mechanisms. Rather than providing a static snapshot, the model captures temporal trends and adaptive behaviors, thereby supporting iterative refinement in digital teaching strategies. This temporal sensitivity allows educational administrators and training departments to identify periods of stagnation or regression and implement targeted interventions. The fusion-based model's ability to track changes in digital literacy also facilitates personalized professional development, enabling educators to receive data-driven recommendations tailored to their evolving needs and digital proficiency levels. Overall, the experimental results not only validate the technical feasibility of the proposed method but also reinforce its practical significance in supporting data-informed educational improvement.

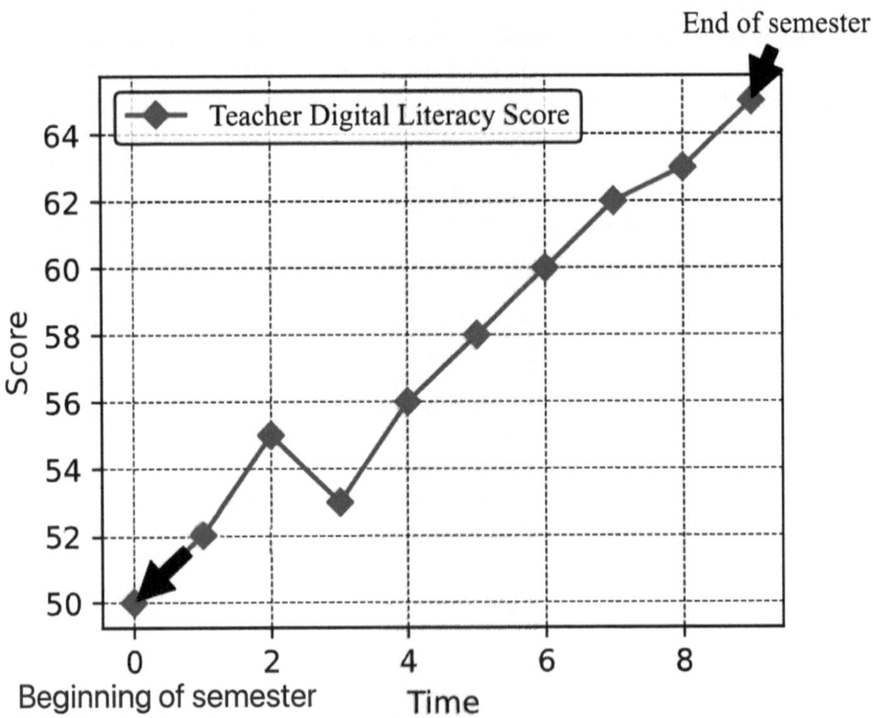

Fig. 2. The changing trend of teachers' digital literacy scores with time

Teachers are highly satisfied with the feedback report and think that the report provides targeted improvement suggestions. By comparing the performance of teachers before and after improvement, it is found that the feedback report is helpful to improve teachers' digital literacy. Figure 3 shows that among 50 teachers, 56.0% teachers are very satisfied with the feedback report, 30.0% teachers are satisfied, 10.0% teachers feel average, and 4.0% teachers are not satisfied. This distribution reflects the positive evaluation of the feedback report by most teachers.

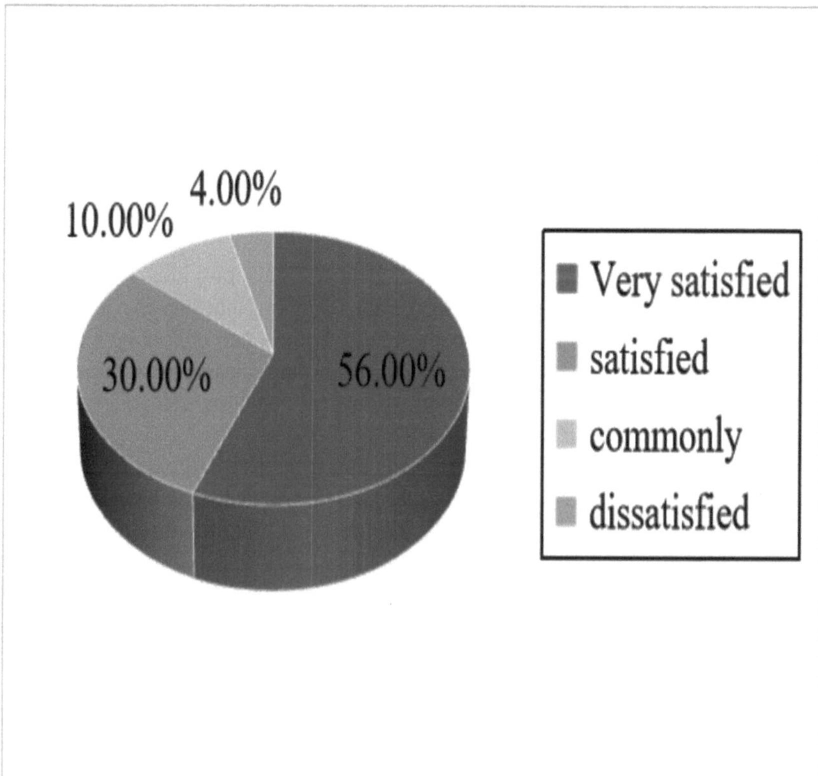

Fig. 3. Distribution of teachers' satisfaction with feedback reports.

Compared with the existing evaluation methods, the algorithm proposed in this paper is superior to the traditional evaluation methods of university teachers in accuracy, comprehensiveness and dynamics. Traditional methods often focus on single modal data, ignoring the relevance of multi-modal data, resulting in one-sided and inaccurate evaluation results. The performance comparison of different evaluation methods is shown in Table 3.

The effect of multimodal data fusion benefits from the powerful representation ability of deep learning models and the processing ability of LSTM models for time series data. The accuracy of dynamic evaluation benefits from the dynamic weight adjustment mechanism, which can adjust the weight according to the timeliness and importance

Table 3. Performance comparison of different evaluation methods

evaluation methodology	Accuracy (%)	Comprehensiveness	Dynamic	Comprehensive score
Algorithm in this paper	92.5	8.9	8.7	9.0
Students' evaluation of teaching	85.0	7.5	7.0	7.7
Peer review	83.2	7.2	6.8	7.4

of data. The usefulness of feedback reports benefits from personalized improvement suggestions and various presentation forms, which meet the different needs of teachers. The algorithm proposed in this paper is suitable for the evaluation of university teachers' digital literacy and can also be extended to multimodal data fusion and evaluation in other fields.

In addition, the system's feedback mechanism not only provides static evaluation results but also generates real-time tracking data, allowing teachers to view their performance trends over time. This enhances self-awareness and encourages continuous improvement. Moreover, the inclusion of behavioral data, classroom interactions, and resource usage statistics provides a fuller picture of teaching effectiveness beyond subjective assessments alone.

However, the limitation of the algorithm is that it needs a large amount of labeled data and computing resources, and it has certain requirements for the hardware and software environment. Future research can further optimize the structure and parameters of the deep learning model to reduce computational cost and improve real-time performance. Moreover, exploring more advanced dynamic weight adjustment strategies, such as attention mechanisms, reinforcement learning-based tuning, or meta-learning approaches, could enhance the adaptability and robustness of the model in varying teaching contexts.

4 Conclusion

A set of dynamic evaluation and feedback algorithms for university teachers' digital literacy based on multimodal data fusion is successfully constructed. By integrating multi-source data such as teaching videos, teaching logs and student feedback, the effective extraction and fusion of multi-modal features are realized by using deep learning model, which significantly improves the accuracy and comprehensiveness of evaluation. The experimental results show that the algorithm is excellent in reflecting the dynamic changes of teachers' digital literacy, and can provide personalized improvement suggestions for teachers and effectively stimulate their internal motivation to improve their digital literacy. Compared with traditional evaluation methods, the algorithm proposed in this study shows obvious advantages in accuracy, comprehensiveness and dynamics, which verifies its application potential in the field of educational evaluation. Although the current algorithm requires high hardware and software resources in the implementation process, and needs a lot of labeled data support, it is expected to overcome these limitations by further optimizing the model structure and exploring new weight adjustment strategies, and provide a more efficient and accurate digital literacy evaluation tool for the education field.

Furthermore, the model's adaptability to different educational environments indicates broad scalability. For instance, with proper calibration, the framework can be extended to assess digital competence in disciplines beyond higher education, such as vocational training or K-12 teaching contexts. Future work could also incorporate natural language processing (NLP) techniques to better analyze open-ended feedback and emotional sentiment from students, further enriching the evaluation dimensions. Moreover, continuous model training with real-time data can enable the system to evolve in response to emerging digital tools and pedagogical trends. In the long run, this dynamic, data-driven evaluation framework has the potential to guide institutional digital literacy development strategies, support targeted professional training programs, and promote a culture of reflective and technology-enhanced teaching in higher education.

Acknowledgements. The authors acknowledge the 2023 Annual Project of Hubei Provincial Higher Education Society:"Research on Strategies for Enhancing Digital Literacy of University Teachers in the Digital Age" (NO: 2023XD099).

References

1. Shao, J.J., Zhao, Y.Y., Liu, D.N., Chen, Y., Liu, Z.Y., Zheng, B.: Construction of evaluation index system for clinical teaching competence based on the TPACK model. Chin. Hosp. Manage. **44**(5), 76–80 (2024)
2. Yan, J.Y., Huang, S., Guo, J.M.: Research on the development mechanism of university teachers' teaching scholarship ability. Mod. Univ. Educ. **38**(3), 102–110 (2022)
3. Feng, X.Y., Guo, W.R., Song, J.X.: Teacher's blended teaching competence development model: principles, preparation and strategies. Open Educ. Res. **27**(5), 10 (2021)
4. Yang, L.Q., Guo, J., Yao, Y.J.: Study on the framework of synchronous classroom teaching competence for teachers. Electro-Educ. Res. **42**(9), 7 (2021)
5. Wu, D., Gui, X.J., Zhou, C., Chen, M.: Teacher digital literacy: connotation, standards and evaluation. Electro-Educ. Res. **44**(8), 108–114 (2023)
6. Kang, X.Y., Yu, X.S.: The essence, real challenges, and enhancement paths of ideological and political course teachers' digital literacy in the era of educational digitization. Heilongjiang High. Educ. Res. **42**(11), 102–107 (2024)
7. Zhang, J., Guo, J.: Enhancing the digital literacy of rural middle and primary school teachers: value implications, realistic difficulties, and strategy analysis. Electro-Educ. Res. **44**(8), 122–128 (2023)
8. Zhao, X., Yang, B.: The current state and improvement strategies of digital literacy among vocational college teachers - an empirical analysis based on 279 full-time teachers in Beijing. Vocat. Tech. Educ. **45**(32), 63–68 (2024)
9. Wang, X.J., Zou, J.Y., Mu, S.: Research on the status quo and improvement strategies of digital literacy among vocational education teachers. Vocat. Tech. Educ. **45**(35), 50–55 (2024)
10. Kang, L., Liu, H.X.: Obstacles and countermeasures for constructing the digital scientific research information niche of vocational college teachers - survey analysis based on 14 vocational colleges in Hainan province. Vocat. Tech. Educ. **43**(26), 44–50 (2022)

11. Blikstein, P., Worsley, M.: Multimodal learning analytics and education data mining: using computational technologies to measure complex learning tasks. J. Learn. Analytics **3**(2), 220–238 (2016)
12. Durriyah, T.L., Zuhdi, M.: Digital literacy with EFL student teachers: exploring Indonesian student teachers' initial perception about integrating digital technologies into a teaching unit. Int. J. Educ. Literacy Stud. **6**(3), 53–60 (2018)
13. Zhao, Y., Sulaiman, N.A.B.: Optimization of college English dynamic multimodal model teaching based on deep learning. Lang. Relat. Res. **14**(5), 285–307 (2023)
14. Ndukwe, I.G., Daniel, B.K.: Teaching analytics, value and tools for teacher data literacy: a systematic and tripartite approach. Int. J. Educ. Technol. High. Educ. **17**, 1–31 (2020)

Variations in University Educators' Teaching Experiences with Generative AI

Feifei Han[1(✉)], Robert Ellis[1], and Henry Cook[2]

[1] Griffith Institute for Educational Research, Griffith University, Brisbane, QLD 4111, Australia
feifei.han@griffith.edu.au

[2] School of Education, University of Wollongong, Wollongong, NSW 2522, Australia

Abstract. Generative artificial intelligence (GenAI) is becoming more embedded across various sectors, including tertiary education. Consequently, universities are under increasing pressure to equip students with the skills necessary to engage with GenAI in their future professions. While GenAI technologies, teaching methods, and ethical debates continue to evolve, there is still limited understanding of how university educators practically use GenAI in their teaching. This study uses a phenomenographic method to investigate how faculty members perceive and integrate GenAI into their instructional approaches. Based on semi-structured interviews with 30 educators, the research uncovers a range of perspectives and applications of GenAI in the classroom. These differing views reveal significant qualitative differences that deepen our understanding of how educators are responding to GenAI in academic settings. The findings indicate that certain perceptions and pedagogical practices are more effective in helping students develop the competencies needed in today's workforce. Moreover, the study provides insights that can guide academic leaders in creating meaningful support systems for faculty employing GenAI as an educational tool. By focusing on educators' experiences, the research adds valuable knowledge to the broader discussion on GenAI's impact on teaching and learning in tertiary education.

Keywords: GenAI · Experiences with teaching · University educators · Phenomenographic method · Australia universities

1 Introduction

Preparing university students for both personal development and successful professional careers presents a significant challenge for modern universities. This challenge stems from students' evolving expectations and the growing complexity of today's job market. Many students now view university primarily as a path to employment rather than solely a place for intellectual growth. At the same time, employers increasingly expect graduates to enter the workforce equipped with up-to-date knowledge and practical skills. A major difficulty for universities is adapting to the rapidly changing employment landscape, where some roles are disappearing while new ones emerge—many requiring interdisciplinary problem-solving abilities and effective use of technologies like GenAI across a wide range of fields (Prohorov et al. 2024).

K. W. Lee and L. H. Wong (Eds.): ITEA 2025, CCIS 2643, pp. 53–59, 2026.
https://doi.org/10.1007/978-981-95-2011-4_6

These evolving workforce demands have significant consequences for university teaching. In today's environment, GenAI literacy is becoming a crucial graduate skill expected by most industries (Nartey 2024), influencing how curricula are developed and how subjects are taught. Although this discussion centers on the disruption caused by GenAI in tertiary education, the broader themes apply to any transformative technology that reshapes how knowledge is created, interpreted, shared, and used in both academic and professional contexts.

1.1 GenAI in Tertiary Education

Advancements in GenAI, especially in the form of Large Language Models (LLMs), are increasingly shaping how industries apply these tools to address complex problems (Tomašev et al. 2020). In professional settings, GenAI assistants are being integrated as non-human components that support and enhance human skillsets. This widespread adoption has led to changes in workforce planning, with many sectors now expecting employees to possess specific GenAI literacy (Javaid et al. 2023). As a result, workers must be capable not only of using GenAI tools but also of critically assessing their outputs. This includes the ability to verify factual accuracy, identify potential biases or problematic influences, and determine how much trust to place in GenAI-generated content (Ng et al. 2021). These critical literacy skills are fast becoming essential for employability.

Globally, the integration of GenAI into education is being guided by both governmental and non-governmental organizations (UNESCO 2023). In Australia, for example, national tertiary education policy now requires universities to show how GenAI is being used productively in teaching and learning (TEQSA 2024). However, universities have initially focused on ethical concerns—such as plagiarism and academic integrity—rather than on the productive potential of GenAI in enhancing the student experience. While ethical issues are important, they represent only part of the broader picture, as GenAI also offers significant opportunities to improve teaching and learning outcomes (Bozkurt et al. 2023). Beyond efficiency, its value lies in its potential to enrich educational practices (Tlili et al. 2023).

Educators now face the daily task of determining how GenAI can support student learning, while also recognizing instances where it might hinder deep understanding of course content. Many are incorporating GenAI meaningfully into classroom activities and assessment tasks (Markauskaite et al. 2022), while also fostering student awareness of the ethical principles behind GenAI design and use, thereby promoting GenAI literacy across various disciplines (Lodge et al. 2023). This evolving pedagogical approach is also prompting educators to reflect more deeply on which aspects of education are inherently human—those that cannot be replaced or replicated by AI. Since educators are responsible for shaping the learning outcomes of their programs and courses, gaining insight into the different ways they are experiencing and implementing GenAI in their teaching is essential for achieving shared educational goals.

1.2 Phenomenographic Approach in Educational Research

This study used a phenomenographic approach to explore the different ways university educators experience teaching with GenAI. Phenomenography seeks to uncover people's qualitatively different experiences, conceptions, and perceptions of various phenomena in the world (Marton 1986). A key assumption in phenomenography is that individuals' understandings of a given phenomenon can be grouped into a limited number of distinct categories. These categories are seen as forming a logically structured, nested hierarchy, where simpler understandings are encompassed within more complex and sophisticated ones (Åkerlind 2008, p. 636). In other words, levels of understanding can range from basic to advanced, with more developed conceptions building upon less developed ones (Han & Ellis 2019). The ontological basis of phenomenography holds that people's understanding can be organized in a hierarchy, ranging from basic to advanced levels of sophistication, where simpler forms of knowledge are encompassed within more complex and refined understandings. (Marton & Pang 2008), emphasizing the relational nature of experience. This perspective has been widely used to investigate how people approach both teaching and learning.

1.3 Existing Phenomenographic Research on University Educators' Teaching Experiences

Extensive prior research has explored university educators' teaching experiences using a phenomenographic lens, notably through foundational studies by Prosser and Trigwell (Trigwell & Prosser 2020). For example, Prosser et al. (1994) conducted interviews with 24 university science educators to examine their teaching approaches, focusing on their intentions and strategies. From the interviews, five distinct approaches to teaching science were identified:

- Information transmission: aimed at delivering content to students.
- Educator-focused conceptual acquisition: focused on students acquiring concepts through the educator's input.
- Interactive conceptual acquisition: emphasized student-teacher interaction to support concept acquisition.
- Student-focused conceptual development: aimed at helping students develop their own conceptual understanding.
- Conceptual change: employed student-centered strategies to shift students' existing conceptions.

These approaches were understood as forming a hierarchical structure, with more sophisticated, student-focused approaches encompassing less complex, educator-centered methods. The first two approaches prioritized content delivery and activating prior knowledge, while the latter three emphasized structuring learning experiences to support deeper student understanding.

While considerable research has examined educators' conceptions and teaching approaches, fewer studies have focused on their perceptions of the broader teaching and learning context. One exception is the work by Prosser and Trigwell (1997), which linked educators' perceptions of their teaching environments to their instructional approaches.

Their study measured perceptions across five dimensions: teaching control, class size, student readiness, departmental support, and academic workload. Findings indicated that educators using information transmission approaches were more likely to view class sizes as too large (negative perception), whereas those adopting student-focused approaches tended to report more positive views of class size and institutional support.

However, these established patterns in traditional classroom settings may not directly apply in today's rapidly evolving educational landscape, where educators are increasingly experimenting with and incorporating emerging technologies like Generative AI (GenAI). Given this shift, it is important to re-examine these constructs in the context of GenAI integration.

This study addresses two key research questions:

1. How do university educators' perceptions of GenAI's value in university learning differ?
2. How do university educators' approaches to helping students verify GenAI-generated output differ?

2 Method

2.1 Participants and Data Collection Procedure

Thirty university educators voluntarily took part in the study. Participants were intentionally recruited from a wide range of academic disciplines, as earlier studies have shown that educators' perceptions and teaching approaches can vary significantly by discipline (Biggs et al. 2022).

Prior to data collection, ethics approval was obtained from the researchers' affiliated institutions. All participants provided written informed consent. Data were gathered through semi-structured interviews designed to capture educators' experiences with using GenAI in their teaching practices. The interviews were open-ended and loosely guided, offering participants the freedom to shape their responses and reflect in detail on their experiences.

Two primary prompts guided the interview conversations:

"How do you perceive the value proposition of GenAI in university learning?"
"How and why do you require students to verify the accuracy of AI output?"

Follow-up questions were used to encourage deeper reflection and clarify meaning. All interviews were audio-recorded and subsequently transcribed for analysis.

2.2 Methods and Phases of Data Analysis

We employed phenomenographic analysis to explore the variations in educators' teaching experiences with GenAI. The analysis began with a thorough reading of the interview transcripts. During the initial reading, we repeatedly reviewed participants' responses to understand the full qualitative range and depth of their perspectives. Subsequently, we identified and highlighted key features in each educator's responses that reflected their perceptions.

Focusing on these key features helped us recognize patterns across the data and allowed us to develop preliminary themes representing the main qualitative differences in experience. We then compared and contrasted these themes to identify both their similarities and distinctions, leading to the formation of an initial set of categories. These categories were refined through an iterative process to ensure each one was clearly defined and distinct from the others. Special attention was given to using language that accurately captured the essence of each category's defining characteristics.

Throughout this stage, all three researchers engaged in ongoing discussions to reach consensus on the number, names, and definitions of the categories. Once the categories were finalized, each researcher independently coded the data using the agreed framework.

3 Results

Building on the analytical methods outlined earlier, the following section presents the outcome spaces for educators' perceptions. In describing the categories, we drew on Marton and Pang's (2008) framework, considering both the structural and referential aspects of each category.

3.1 Variations in University Educators' Perceptions of the Value Proposition of GenAI in University Learning

Category 1 (n = 5, 17%) includes educators who viewed GenAI as a tool that supports deeper student learning through reflection and critical engagement.

Category 2 (n = 7, 23%) reflects perceptions that, while generally positive, emphasize the importance of carefully structured learning activities for GenAI to be effective. These educators see value in GenAI primarily when its use is intentionally designed and contextually appropriate. Together, categories 1 and 2 represent positive perceptions of GenAI's role in tertiary education.

In contrast, categories 3 and 4 reflect more negative or cautious viewpoints:

Category 3 (n = 15, 50%) acknowledges potential benefits of GenAI, but attributes its success largely to the skills and expertise of the educator, rather than to student engagement or the technology itself.

Category 4 (n = 3, 10%) expresses the most skeptical view, suggesting that GenAI offers no meaningful contribution to student learning.

These findings highlight a spectrum of perceptions, from optimistic and design-focused views to more skeptical or educator-dependent stances on GenAI's educational value.

3.2 Variations in University Educators' Approaches to Student Verification of GenAI Output

Category 1 (n = 6, 20%) involves using GenAI output as a starting point to enhance students' research skills. Educators in this group require students to investigate, verify, and refine GenAI content, encouraging deeper engagement with research practices.

Category 2 (n = 8, 23%) represents educators who use the evaluation of GenAI output as a tool for fostering students' critical thinking. These educators design learning activities that encourage students to question, critique, and assess AI-generated content as part of their intellectual development.

Category 3 (n = 3, 10%) centers on teaching students the values associated with using GenAI. Educators in this category acknowledge concerns about the accuracy of AI-generated content, but also emphasize the importance of ethical considerations, such as proper attribution of sources that GenAI may draw upon.

Category 4 (n = 6, 20%) includes educators who caution students that GenAI output is likely to be inaccurate. The teaching strategies in this group tend to be narrow, emphasizing the risks of using GenAI without offering broader instructional engagement.

Category 5 (n = 7, 23%) reflects an overall rejection of GenAI as a useful tool for learning within the course context. In some cases, this stance is justifiable—for example, in courses focused on hands-on creative production where GenAI offers limited educational value. In other cases, it appears to stem from a lack of familiarity with GenAI tools and their potential benefits.

Since teachers play a crucial role in university education, their views on GenAI are a key part of the ongoing discussion. Stakeholders concerned with the quality and relevance of degree programs and student experiences generally agree that appropriate use of GenAI should be integrated into students' learning journeys (Bozkurt et al. 2023). However, we are only beginning to grasp what such appropriate use looks like, which calls for thoughtful responses from both teaching team leaders and university administrators. For those leading teaching teams, it is clear that substantial efforts are needed to deepen the understanding of GenAI's potential benefits for learning, including how it can enhance student engagement and inform teaching strategies.

References

Åkerlind, G.S.: A phenomenographic approach to developing academics' understanding of the nature of teaching and learning. Teach. Tert. Educ. **13**(6), 633–644 (2008). https://doi.org/10.1080/13562510802452350

Biggs, J., Tang, C., Kennedy, G.: Teaching for Quality Learning at University. McGraw-Hill (2022)

Bozkurt, A., et al.: Speculative futures on ChatGPT and generative artificial intelligence (AI): a collective reflection from the educational landscape. Asian J. Distance Educ. **18**(1), 53–130 (2023). https://doi.org/10.5281/zenodo.7636568

Han, F., Ellis, R.A.: Using phenomenography to tackle key challenges in science education. Front. Psychol. (2019). https://doi.org/10.3389/fpsyg.2019.01414

Lodge, J., Howard, S., Bearman, M., Dawson, P., Associates: Assessment Reform for The Age of Artificial Intelligence. Australian Government, Tertiary Education Quality and Standards Agency (2023). https://www.teqsa.gov.au/sites/default/files/2023-09/assessment-reform-age-artificial-intelligence-discussion-paper.pdf

Javaid, M., Haleem, A., Singh, R.P.: A study on ChatGPT for Industry 4.0: background, potentials, challenges, and eventualities. J. Econ. Technol. **1**, 127–143 (2023). https://doi.org/10.1016/j.ject.2023.08.001

Nartey, E.K.: Guiding principles of generative AI for employability and learning in UK universities. Cogent Educ. **11**(1) (2024). https://doi.org/10.1080/2331186x.2024.2357898

Ng, D.T.K., Leung, J.K.L., Chu, S.K.W., Qiao, M.S.: Conceptualizing AI literacy: an exploratory review. Comput. Educ. Artif. Intell. **2** (2021). https://doi.org/10.1016/j.caeai.2021.100041

Markauskaite, L., et al.: Rethinking the entwinement between artificial intelligence and human learning: what capabilities do learners need for a world with AI? Comput. Educ. Artif. Intell. **3** (2022). https://doi.org/10.1016/j.caeai.2022.100056

Marton, F.: Phenomenography—a research approach to investigating different understandings of reality. J. Thought, 28–49 (1986). https://www.jstor.org/stable/42589189

Marton, F., Pang, M.: The idea of phenomenography and the pedagogy of conceptual change. In: Vosniadou, S. (ed.) International Handbook on Research of Conceptual Change, pp. 533–559 (2008). https://doi.org/10.4324/9780203874813

Prohorov, A., Tsaryk, O., Fainglozs, L.: Employers' expectations of students' generative AI skills: a student perspective. In: Proceedings of 14th International Conference on Advanced Computer Information Technologies, pp. 809–814 (2024). https://doi.org/10.2139/ssrn.4886146

Prosser, M., Trigwell, K., Taylor, P.: A phenomenographic study of academics' conceptions of science learning and teaching. Learn. Instr. **4**(3), 217–231 (1994). https://doi.org/10.1016/0959-4752(94)90024-8

TEQSA: Gen AI strategies for Australian tertiary education: Emerging practice. Australian Government, Tertiary Education Quality and Standards Agency (2024). https://www.teqsa.gov.au/sites/default/files/2024-11/Gen-AI-strategies-emerging-practice-toolkit.pdf. Accessed 8 Jan 2025

Tlili, A., et al.: What if the devil is my guardian angel: ChatGPT as a case study of using chatbots in education. Smart Learn. Environ. **10**(1), 15 (2023). https://doi.org/10.1186/s40561-023-00237-x

Tomašev, N., et al.: AI for social good: unlocking the opportunity for positive impact. Nat. Commun. **11**(1), 2468 (2020). https://doi.org/10.1038/s41467-020-15871-z

Trigwell, K., Prosser, M.: Exploring University Teaching and Learning: Experience and Context. Springer, Cham (2020). https://doi.org/10.1007/978-3-030-50830-2

UNESCO: ChatGPT and artificial intelligence in tertiary education: Quick start guide (2023). https://unesdoc.unesco.org/ark:/48223/pf0000385146. Author, F., Author, S.: Title of a proceedings paper. In: Editor, F., Editor, S. (eds.) CONFERENCE 2016, LNCS, vol. 9999, pp. 1–13. Springer, Heidelberg (2016)

Exploring the Potential of GPT-4o's Vision in Vector Visualisation for Pre-tertiary Mathematics

Nguyen Thanh Minh Le[1], Chanoudam Sopheap[1], and Kenneth Y. T. Lim[2(✉)]

[1] Singapore, Singapore
[2] National Institute of Education, 1 Nanyang Walk, Singapore 637616, Singapore
kenneth.lim@nie.edu.sg

Abstract. This research project delves into the potential of machine learning and computer vision to assist students in visualising complex mathematical concepts, with a specific focus on vectors. Recognising the challenges students face in grasping abstract mathematical notions, the study investigates the development of a system using GPT-4o that automates the visualisation of handwritten vector equations. The system employs computer vision, a rapidly evolving field in artificial intelligence, to analyse and interpret handwritten mathematical expressions. By extracting key components such as variables, coefficients, operators, and vector notation, the system generates precise graphical representations of vector equations. This approach aims to bridge the gap between theoretical concepts and visual understanding, enabling students to develop a more intuitive grasp of vectors. The research evaluates the system's accuracy in recognising and interpreting diverse handwriting styles, assessing its potential to improve students' understanding of vector concepts. While acknowledging challenges such as the need for extensive training datasets and refined algorithms to handle the nuances of handwritten mathematical notation, the project outlines future work including expanding the system's scope to other mathematical topics, incorporating interactive features, and integrating with augmented reality for a more immersive experience. The ultimate goal is to seamlessly integrate this tool into students' learning devices, providing accessible and convenient support for their mathematical development. This research contributes to the advancement of AI-driven educational tools, showcasing the potential of machine learning to enhance students' learning experiences and bridge the gap between abstract concepts and visual understanding.

Keywords: Artificial intelligence (AI) · Machine learning (ML) · Computer vision · Mathematics · Pre-tertiary education

1 Introduction

Mathematics is a common subject taken by students in junior colleges (pre-tertiary education) in Singapore under the Singapore-Cambridge GCE 'A' Level curriculum. Due to various reasons, such as the higher academic expectations and significant increase in

T. M. L. Nguyen and C. Sopheap—Independent Authors.

K. W. Lee and L. H. Wong (Eds.): ITEA 2025, CCIS 2643, pp. 60–66, 2026.
https://doi.org/10.1007/978-981-95-2011-4_7

difficulty level compared to secondary school curriculum, students struggle with grasping mathematics concepts taught in school. Taking into consideration the advancement of technologies and the fact that personal devices such as phones, laptops, and tablets are readily available to virtually anyone, regardless of location, we focus on a potential solution for students to grasp a better understanding of the topics taught.

The objective of this research project is to develop an innovative system that leverages the advanced visual understanding capabilities of GPT-4o to automate the visualisation of handwritten vector equations as visualisation has always been a significant part of mathematics education (Schoenherr et al. 2024). This system will employ machine learning and computer vision techniques to analyse and interpret the diverse and often ambiguous nature of handwritten mathematical notation. Specifically, GPT-4o will be trained to accurately recognize and extract key components from handwritten vector equations, such as variables, coefficients, operators, and vector notation. This extracted data will then be used to generate precise graphical representations using the matplotlib library. By automating the process of visualizing handwritten vector equations, this system offers crucial support to junior college students, making the abstract concepts of the Vectors chapter more accessible and understandable. This approach promises to significantly enhance efficiency and accuracy in mathematical visualisation, eliminating the time-consuming and error-prone nature of manual plotting (Mitchell 1997). Furthermore, this research contributes to the broader field of AI-driven scientific tools, showcasing the potential of advanced language models like GPT-4o to bridge the gap between human intuition and computational analysis.

2 Literature Review

In their review of handwritten math expression recognition, Van and Hoang (2024) concluded that deep learning models such as CNNs and RNNs had achieved excellent performance in recognizing handwritten mathematical expressions. They highlighted the use of attention mechanisms and sequence-to-sequence models to improve recognition accuracy. However, they also identified several areas for future research, including the development of robust parsing algorithms, the creation of large, comprehensive datasets, and the refinement of deep learning techniques. They emphasized the need for novel representations, such as graph-based models, and the incorporation of syntactic/semantic context to improve the understanding and interpretation of math expressions. Van and Hoang (2024) stressed the importance of addressing real-world usage and usability, particularly in education, office automation, and assistance for the visually impaired. They advocated for user-centered design and usability testing to integrate these systems into daily workflows seamlessly.

As for the importance of visualization in education, Veřmiřovský (2013) examines various educational contexts and their potential for enhancing learning experiences. Their paper discusses the significance of visual communication in the modern world, its historical development in education, and the different types of visual materials used as learning tools. The author emphasizes the importance of visualisation in understanding complex concepts, which aligns with our research aim of using computer vision to create dynamic and interactive visualisations of vectors. By incorporating the principles and techniques discussed in this paper, such as the use of colors, composition, and multimedia presentations, we can design an effective AI system that enhances students' understanding of vectors through visualisation.

3 Methodology

This experiment aims to explore the capabilities of training a computer vision model using GPT-4o. Specifically, it investigates how verbal prompts can be used to analyse handwritten equations and extract the required data, which is then processed to generate a corresponding graph.

3.1 Preparing Input Images of Handwritten Equations

In this experiment, we prepared a sample of handwritten vector equations, representing the task of Vector Addition (see Fig. 1), to be analysed using GPT-4o.

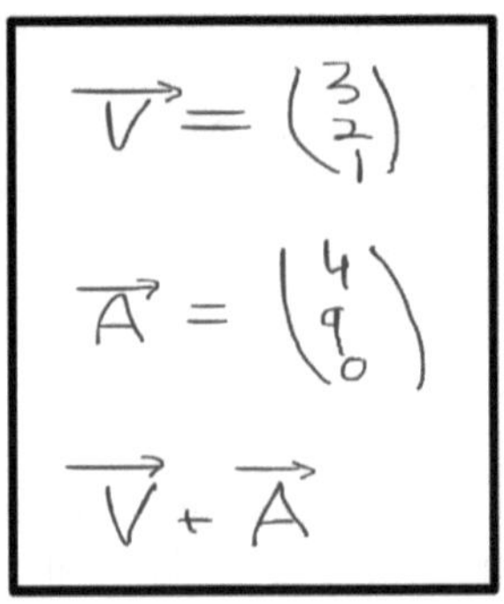

Fig. 1. Addition of Vectors

3.2 Processing the Images

The image must be encoded from bytes into a text-based format to ensure compatibility with the GPT-4o model for processing (Hartmann 2024), using a function shown in Fig. 2.

```
def encode_image(image_path):
    with open(image_path, "rb") as image_file:
        return base64.b64encode(image_file.read()).decode("utf-8")
```

Fig. 2. Function to Encode the Image

3.3 Utilising Computer Vision with GPT-4o

GPT-4o is a versatile and powerful OpenAI API capable of processing multimodal inputs, including text, images, and audio, while generating structured outputs. In particular, GPT-4o's ability to process images as inputs and produce structured outputs is invaluable for tasks such as analysing handwritten mathematical equations and providing the necessary data to create visualisations for mathematics exercises. Figure 3 illustrates this process, showing how GPT-4o analyses the input image.

```
# store the produced structured result
results = []

for image_path in paths:
  base64_image = encode_image(image_path)

  response = client.chat.completions.create(
      model="gpt-4o",
      messages=[
          {
              "role": "user",
              "content": [
                  {
                      "type": "text",
                      "text": conditions,
                  },
                  {
                      "type": "image_url",
                      "image_url": {"url": f"data:image/jpeg;base64,{base64_image}"},
                  },
              ],
          }
      ],
  )

  results.append(response.choices[0].message.content)
```

Fig. 3. Using GPT-4o to Analyse the Input Image

Furthermore, we utilise text prompts as a method to instruct the GPT-4o model by specifying criteria that guide the model in generating structured outputs.

An example of such instruction is the variable called "conditions" provided in Fig. 4.

```
conditions = """
if there is one or more vector expressions,
return the value of all the vector matrices in a list, add the word 'vectors' as the last element of the list.
else if the vector is between 2 lines,
only return the value of the matrices in a list, add the word 'magnitude' as the last element of the list.
else if there is a vector operation,
return values of the matrices in a list, insert the word 'addition' or 'cross product' according to the nature of operation as the
last element of the list.
only one response is needed.
"""
```

Fig. 4. Text Prompt to Train GPT-4o model

3.4 Processing the Data

After analysing the images, GPT-4o generates structured results that are used to plot graphs, enabling the visualisation of the exercise.

```
[[3, 2, 1], [4, 9, 0], 'addition']
```

Fig. 5. Processed Data of Addition of Vectors

The processed results, shown in Fig. 5, include key elements such as "addition," "cross product," "magnitude," and "vectors," which are essential for further data processing. These elements provide the necessary information to generate the data required for plotting the visualisation effectively.

3.5 Solving Vectors-Related Problems

We successfully integrated a solution-solving component (see Fig. 6) into the project. This allowed the system to solve equations parsed in the earlier stage. The processed data was fed into a dedicated object-oriented programming (OOP) function, resulting in the calculation and output of the solutions.

```
import math

class Vector:
    def __init__(self, x, y, z):
        """Constructor"""
        self.x = x
        self.y = y
        self.z = z

    def add(self, other):
        return Vector(self.x + other.x, self.y + other.y, self.z + other.z)
```

Fig. 6. Snippet of the OOP code to calculate vector-related problems

4 Results

We have developed a mathematics visual assistance tool by leveraging advanced machine learning technologies, such as GPT-4o, for computer vision. This tool analyses handwritten equations and generates graph visualisations to address mathematical exercises effectively.

Taking the handwritten equations from Fig. 1 as an example, the graph produced is depicted in Fig. 7.

The computer vision capabilities of GPT-4o, when integrated with graph construction processes, produce results based on the information extracted from the processed data.

In addition, the initial effort to solve vector-related questions also yielded the following accurate result, shown in Table 1.

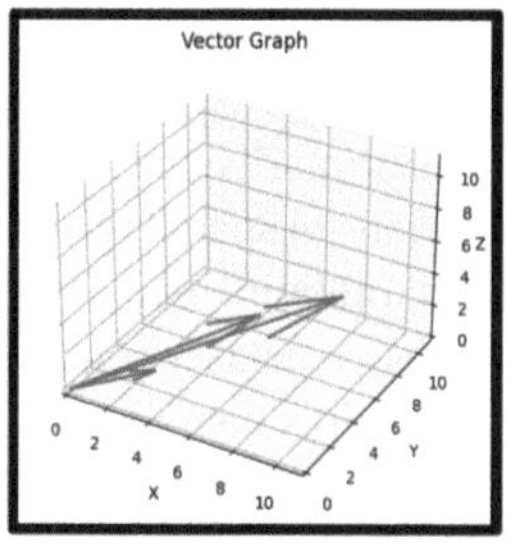

Fig. 7. Graph of Addition of Vectors

Table 1. Results of Vector-related equations

Equation parsed	Result
[[3, 2, 1], [4, 9, 0], 'addition']	Result of [[2, 3, 1], [4, 9, 0], 'addition']: (6.0, 12.0, 1.0)

5 Discussion

Our investigation into the use of computer vision, specifically leveraging the GPT-4 model, for automating the visualisation of handwritten vector equations has unveiled a landscape of both potential and challenges. While the ability to generate graphical representations directly from handwritten input marks a significant stride towards enhancing accessibility and efficiency in mathematics learning, the limitations encountered underscore the complexities inherent in developing AI models capable of accurately interpreting the nuances of handwritten mathematical expressions.

The system's capacity to produce visualisations from handwritten equations represents a notable advancement in bridging the gap between traditional pen-and-paper methods and digital tools. This capability has the potential to transform mathematics learning by providing students with a more intuitive and interactive way to explore and understand abstract concepts. By eliminating the need for manual plotting, the system also promises to enhance efficiency and reduce errors, allowing students to focus on the underlying mathematical principles rather than the mechanics of visualisation.

These findings resonate with existing research on computer vision and AI in mathematics education. The importance of comprehensive datasets for training accurate computer vision models is well-established. Similarly, spatial reasoning challenges in AI models have been explored in various contexts, including mathematics education.

Our research contributes to this growing body of knowledge by providing empirical evidence of the potential and challenges of using AI for handwritten mathematical expression recognition and visualisation. The limitations identified in our study highlight areas for future research and development, such as creating larger and more diverse datasets of handwritten mathematical expressions and enhancing AI models' spatial reasoning capabilities (Vina 2024).

The inaccuracies of GPT-4o arise primarily due to Insufficient Dataset of Handwritten Mathematical Equations and limitations in spatial reasoning. Handwritten mathematical equations, such as vector equations, often involve a mix of symbols and alphanumeric characters. The lack of a comprehensive dataset containing such handwritten examples poses a significant challenge for GPT-4o's computer vision. Without sufficient training data, the model struggles to identify and interpret the provided images accurately, leading to errors in the analysis of equations and formulas. Further, while computer vision excels at recognizing objects and handwritten alphanumeric characters in images, it struggles with spatial reasoning. For example, in a vector equation, a human can easily interpret the combination of a letter (e.g., "v"), an arrow symbol (→), and two vertical lines (| |) to infer that the task involves "*calculating the magnitude of the given vector*." However, computer vision lacks the ability to understand the spatial relationships between numbers, letters, and symbols, resulting in an inability to interpret these elements in a mathematically valid way.

6 Conclusion

Our research underscores the potential of AI, specifically GPT-4, to automate the visualisation of handwritten vector equations, offering a promising avenue for enhancing accessibility and efficiency in mathematics learning. However, the limitations encountered underscore the need for further research and development to improve the accuracy and robustness of AI models in interpreting handwritten mathematical notation.

The key takeaway from our study is that while AI holds significant promise for enhancing mathematics learning, it is crucial to address the challenges of data limitations and spatial reasoning in AI models to achieve optimal accuracy and effectiveness.

References

Hartmann, F.: LLMs understand Base64 (2024). https://florian.github.io/base64/

Mitchell, M.T.: Machine Learning. McGraw-Hill (1997). Science/Engineering/Math

Schoenherr, J., Strohmaier, A.R., Schukajlow, S.: Learning with visualisations helps: a meta-analysis of visualisation interventions in mathematics education. Educ. Res. Rev. **100639** (2024). https://doi.org/10.1016/j.edurev.2024.100639

Van, B.N., Hoang, V.T.: A short review for handwritten math expression recognition techniques. Procedia Comput. Sci. **235**, 231–239 (2024). https://doi.org/10.1016/j.procs.2024.04.025

Veřmiřovský, J.: The importance of visualisation in education (2013)

Vina, A.: The importance of high-quality computer vision datasets (2024). https://www.ultralytics.com/blog/the-importance-of-high-quality-computer-vision-datasets#:~:text=Computer%20vision%20models%20can%20be%20trained%20on%20large%20datasets%20of,videos%20to%20accurately%20identify%20objects

Designing an AI-Supported Pedagogical Evaluation Model for Visual and Illustration Design in China

Lin Yu, Gening Liu, and Ziwei Yu(✉)

School of Humanities and Arts, Hunan International Economics University, Yuelu District, Changsha 410205, Hunan, China
xiaoxiaoyu8932@hotmail.com, liugening66@gmail.com, vivian19871130@gmail.com

Abstract. PURPOSE: This study examines the impact of AI-supported feedback on learning effectiveness and design quality in visual and illustration design education in China, and explores the moderating role of perceived usefulness of AI tools. **METHOD:** A quantitative, survey-based approach was used with data from 430 university students. Stratified random sampling and power analysis determined the sample size. Data were analysed using descriptive statistics and SEM via Smart PLS. **FINDINGS:** AI-supported feedback significantly enhances learning effectiveness and design quality. Perceived usefulness moderates these effects, with students' recognition of AI's value influencing outcomes. **ORIGINALITY:** The study provides empirical support for integrating AI feedback in design education, offering insights to improve pedagogy, engagement, and creative outcomes.

Keywords: AI-Supported Feedback · Learning Effectiveness · Design Quality · Visual Design Education · Perceived Usefulness

1 Introduction

Artificial Intelligence (AI) is revolutionising education by enhancing teaching and learning across disciplines (Bhatt and Muduli 2023). In visual and illustration design, AI's ability to provide individualised, real-time feedback is particularly valuable, supporting continuous improvement and precise assessment of design quality (Guo Zhang et al. 2024; Engeness and Gamlem 2025). AI systems can analyse student work, suggest improvements, and offer consistent feedback beyond the limitations of subjective, instructor-driven critiques (Luo et al. 2025). This democratises feedback, ensuring equitable learning regardless of instructor availability (Muller et al. 2023). However, a pedagogical evaluation model that fully integrates AI tools into the learning process remains lacking (Kayalı and Balat 2024), especially in creative fields like visual and illustration design (Otto et al. 2024). In China, design education still relies heavily on traditional feedback methods, which are inconsistent and often delayed, limiting students' growth (Bağcı and Işık 2025; Tian et al. 2023; Batova 2025). Many students struggle to engage

K. W. Lee and L. H. Wong (Eds.): ITEA 2025, CCIS 2643, pp. 67–77, 2026.
https://doi.org/10.1007/978-981-95-2011-4_8

with their projects or decode subjective feedback, resulting in stagnation and demotivation (Rijo and Grácio 2025). Many students struggle to engage with their projects or decode subjective feedback, resulting in stagnation and demotivation (Brosens et al. 2023; Lee 2023; Guo 2024; Sayed et al. 2023). AI-based feedback mechanisms offer a promising solution by delivering timely, personalised, and actionable feedback, addressing these challenges (Muller et al. 2023; Boubker 2024). Also, AI systems' ability to offer customized feedback in accordance with the individual learner's learning pattern and innovative cognition can be feasible in handling various needs of design students (Bhatt and Muduli 2023). For AI to achieve its full potential in enhancing learning and design outcomes, it must be embedded within well-structured pedagogical models aligned with educational goals (Kayalı and Balat 2024). This study examines the impact of AI-supported feedback on learning effectiveness and design quality, and explores how perceived usefulness moderates these effects, aiming to support the development of AI-driven pedagogical models for design curricula integration. The key objectives of the study are as follows:

1. To evaluate the impact of AI-supported feedback on learning effectiveness and design quality among Chinese university students.
2. To examine how perceived usefulness moderates the effectiveness of AI-supported feedback in improving learning and design outcomes.

This study adds to AI literature in creative education, showing how AI-based feedback improves pedagogy and student performance in visual and illustration design (Gill et al. 2023). The findings aim to guide instructors and institutions on using AI to support personalised learning, improve feedback, and boost design quality (Rijo and Grácio 2025). The research also proposes a pedagogical assessment model integrating AI feedback, applicable to education and innovation (Shivshankar and Acharya 2025). As AI advances, this study informs educators on optimising AI use for more effective, engaging learning experiences (Sayed et al. 2023). And encourages wider adoption to improve teaching quality in design education.

2 Literature Review

2.1 AI in Education and Pedagogical Models

Artificial Intelligence (AI) is transforming education into a more responsive and personalised experience (Bhatt and Muduli 2023). In creative fields like visual, art, and design, AI supports instruction, automates grading, and delivers real-time feedback (Engeness and Gamlem 2025). Technologies such as adaptive learning systems and AI analytics track progress and suggest tailored learning paths (Guo, Zhang et al. 2024). AI also enables pedagogical models that promote autonomy, self-regulation, and personalised support—key to fostering creativity (Zhang and Ma 2023). In design education, AI aids in evaluating student work, predicting outcomes, and linking artistic practice with technological insight.

2.2 Visual and Illustration Design Education in China

Design education in China has shifted from traditional studio-based instruction to technology-integrated approaches (Bağcı and Işık 2025). While it historically emphasised technical skill and aesthetic development through instructor critiques (Batova 2025). The rise of digital tools and smart classrooms has promoted blended, student-centred learning (Gill et al. 2023). Institutions are increasingly adopting AI to support teaching, test design, and digital portfolio management (Mohzana et al. 2024). These changes support broader reforms to align curricula with industry demands and digital skills for the global creative economy.

2.3 AI-Supported Feedback Systems

AI feedback systems use intelligent software to deliver personalised, automated feedback based on student performance data (Sayed et al. 2023). These systems range from basic rule-based tools to advanced platforms using machine learning, NLP, and computer vision to assess creative outputs (Otto et al. 2024). In visual and design education, they analyse features like symmetry, colour, layout, and creativity (Muller et al. 2023). Research shows they enhance learning by providing immediate, actionable feedback that fosters engagement and supports iterative, independent improvement (Luo et al. 2025). Making learning more efficient and self-directed.

2.4 AI-Supported Feedback System and Learning Effectiveness

AI-supported feedback systems are intelligent applications that deliver customised, adaptive feedback based on learners' performance data (Engeness and Gamlem 2025). Learning effectiveness here includes knowledge acquisition, skill development, participation, and overall achievement (Rijo and Grácio 2025).

Research shows AI feedback encourages learners to reflect and adjust strategies (Shivshankar and Acharya 2025). Studies confirm that students receiving automated feedback perform better than those receiving only traditional input (Lee 2023). AI tools also increase motivation and engagement through interactive, instant feedback (Lai et al. 2023). Thus, AI-based feedback systems are critical for enhancing learning by providing personalised, responsive support.

H1: AI-supported feedback system has a significant impact on learning effectiveness

2.5 AI-Supported Feedback System and Design Quality

Design quality in visual and illustration education refers to the coherence, technical accuracy, originality, and aesthetic appeal of student work (Kuba and and Jeong 2023). Traditionally judged subjectively by instructors, design quality assessment is becoming more consistent and objective with AI-supported feedback systems (Baidoun and Salem 2024). These systems use computer vision and data analytics to evaluate various design elements and offer specific, actionable guidance (Bhatt and Muduli 2023). Helping students iteratively refine their work.

Studies show that AI feedback leads to measurable improvements in composition, creativity, and refinement (Guo, Pan et al. 2024). AI tools simulate the studio environment through real-time, structured feedback, fostering innovation while ensuring alignment with performance standards (Boubker 2024). These technologies not only aid in fixing technical errors but also support the knowledge of students in terms of industry standards (Engeness and Gamlem 2025). Consequently, AI systems enhance design quality through reliable, data-driven feedback that fosters creative growth and advanced design thinking.

H2: AI-supported feedback system has a significant impact on design quality

2.6 Perceived Usefulness as Moderator

Perceived Usefulness (PU) of AI tools reflects students' belief that AI enhances their learning performance (Yen 2023). In AI-supported feedback systems, PU determines how actively students engage with the feedback (Otto et al. 2024). The effectiveness of learning, as above defined, involves knowledge acquisition, skill acquisition, and academic attainment as a consequence of instructional intervention (Lee 2023). Research consistently shows that PU influences students' willingness to use and benefit from AI feedback (Mohzana et al. 2024). According to the Technology Acceptance Model (TAM), PU is a strong predictor of learning engagement and cognitive absorption (Otto et al. 2024). Additionally, design education studies indicate that students who view AI tools as useful exhibit higher learning satisfaction and academic confidence (Kayalı and Balat 2024). Thus, PU moderates the link between AI feedback and learning effectiveness—when students value the tools, the educational impact of AI is amplified.

H3: Perceived usefulness of AI tools moderates the relationship between ai-supported feedback system and learning effectiveness

In visual design education, perceived usefulness influences how students apply AI feedback, enhancing layout, colour, and accuracy (Sayed et al. 2023). Design quality—defined by clarity, originality, and adherence to design principles—is shaped by how students value AI input (Muller et al. 2023). Research shows that students' trust in the credibility and usefulness of AI feedback strongly affects their willingness to revise and enhance their work (Zaky and Al Mulhim 2024). Those who perceive AI assessments positively demonstrate greater improvement in design iterations and explore more complex techniques (Guo, Zhang et al. 2024). Recognising AI's value fosters a growth mindset and deeper creative engagement, supporting the hypothesis that perceived usefulness enhances learning and design outcomes:

H4: Perceived usefulness of AI tools moderates the relationship between ai-supported feedback system and design quality

2.7 Theoretical Framework Supporting the Research

Grounded in TAM and Constructivist Learning Theory, this study explains how AI-supported feedback affects learning and design, with TAM emphasising that technology use relies on perceived usefulness and ease of use (Davis 1989). Perceived usefulness shapes student use of AI feedback, supported by constructivist theory promoting active learning through timely, personalised input (Vygotsky 1962). Together, these theories explain how perceived usefulness guides AI feedback to enhance cognitive and creative outcomes (Fig. 1).

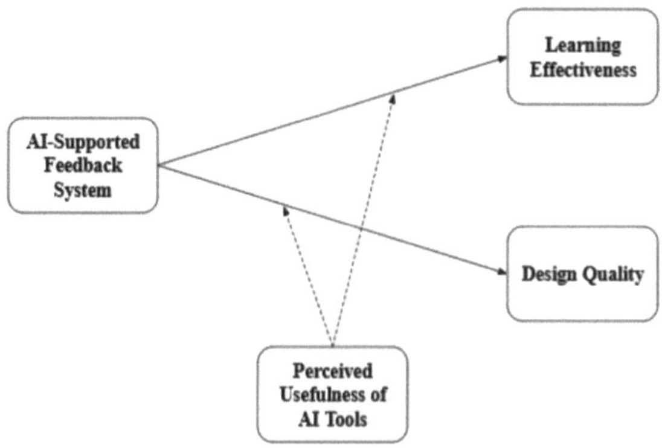

Fig. 1. Conceptual Framework

3 Methodology

3.1 Research Design

This study used a quantitative, cross-sectional survey design to explore relationships between AI-assisted feedback, perceived usefulness, learning effectiveness, and design quality in Chinese visual and illustration education, capturing students' current attitudes and experiences.

3.2 Population and Sampling

The study targeted Chinese university students in visual and illustration design, familiar with creative education and AI feedback. Stratified random sampling by academic level and institution type yielded 430 participants, exceeding the SEM threshold for reliable, generalisable results (Hair et al. 2017).

3.3 Data Collection Method

Descriptive statistics summarised responses. SEM via SmartPLS tested hypotheses and assessed reliability, validity, and model fit, including direct and moderating effects using bootstrapped path analysis.

3.4 Data Analysis Techniques

Descriptive statistics summarised demographics and responses. Structural Equation Modeling (SEM) using SmartPLS tested hypotheses and assessed model validity, examining direct and moderating effects through model fit, loadings, reliability, AVE, and bootstrapped path significance.

4 Results

Table 1 presents the reliability and validity of the constructs: AI-assisted feedback system, design quality, learning effectiveness, and perceived usefulness. All Cronbach's alpha values exceed 0.7 (ranging from 0.892 to 0.927), indicating strong internal consistency. Composite reliability (CR) scores are also above 0.7, confirming construct reliability. Average variance extracted (AVE) values are above 0.5, establishing convergent validity. These results confirm the measurement model's suitability for structural equation modeling.

Table 1. Construct Reliability and Validity

	Cronbach's alpha	CR	AVE
AI-Supported Feedback System	0.927	0.943	0.733
Design Quality	0.892	0.916	0.613
Learning Effectiveness	0.914	0.936	0.745
Perceived Usefulness of AI Tools	0.924	0.946	0.815

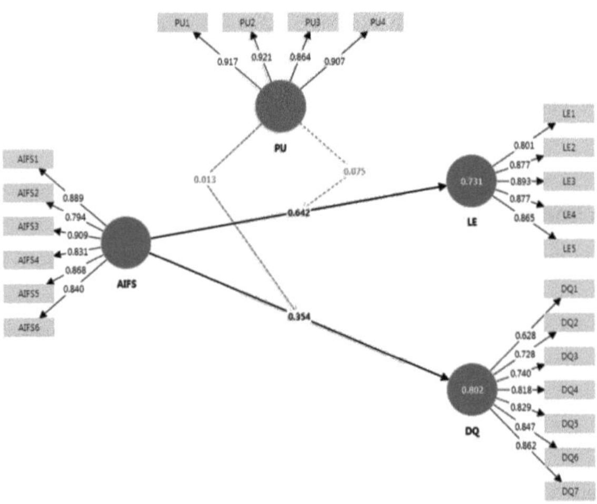

Fig. 2. Measurement Model

Table 2 and Fig. 2 show outer loading values for each indicator. AI-supported feedback items range from 0.794 to 0.909, exceeding the 0.7 threshold, confirming strong reliability. For design quality, all items except DQ1 (0.628) load between 0.728 and 0.862, indicating acceptable reliability. Learning effectiveness items all exceed 0.8, and perceived usefulness items range from 0.864 to 0.921, confirming strong indicator reliability across constructs.

Table 2. Outer Loading

	AI-Supported Feedback System	Design Quality	Learning Effectiveness	Perceived Usefulness of AI Tools
AIFS1	0.889			
AIFS2	0.794			
AIFS3	0.909			
AIFS4	0.831			
AIFS5	0.868			
AIFS6	0.840			
DQ1		0.628		
DQ2		0.728		
DQ3		0.740		
DQ4		0.818		
DQ5		0.829		
DQ6		0.847		
DQ7		0.862		
LE1			0.801	
LE2			0.877	
LE3			0.893	
LE4			0.877	
LE5			0.865	
PU1				0.917
PU2				0.921
PU3				0.864
PU4				0.907

Table 3 shows all HTMT values below 0.90, confirming discriminant validity. AI-supported feedback and design quality scored 0.826, feedback and learning effectiveness 0.829, and perceived usefulness with learning effectiveness also 0.829, indicating clear conceptual and empirical distinctions among constructs.

Table 4 demonstrates strong predictive validity and model fit, with the model explaining 80.2% of design quality and 73.1% of learning effectiveness variance. Q^2 values exceed 0.7, and the SRMR of 0.084 confirms good model fit below the 0.10 threshold.

Table 5 confirms all hypothesised relationships. AI-supported feedback significantly affects learning effectiveness ($\beta = 0.642$) and design quality ($\beta = 0.354$). Perceived usefulness significantly moderates both: learning effectiveness ($\beta = 0.075$) and design quality ($\beta = 0.013$), with all p-values below 0.05.

Table 3. Discriminant Validity (HTMT)

	AIFS	DQ	LE	PU
AI-Supported Feedback System				
Design Quality	0.826			
Learning Effectiveness	0.829	0.820		
Perceived Usefulness of AI Tools	0.828	0.847	0.829	

Table 4. R-square statistics Model Goodness of Fit Statistics

	R-square	R-square adjusted	Q2	SRMR
Design Quality	0.802	0.800	0.798	0.084
Learning Effectiveness	0.731	0.729	0.717	

Table 5. Path Analysis

	β	T value	P value
AI-Supported Feedback System has a significant impact on Learning Effectiveness	0.642	9.134	0.000
AI-Supported Feedback System has a significant impact on design quality	0.354	11.514	0.000
Perceived Usefulness of AI Tools moderates the relationship between AI-Supported Feedback System and Learning Effectiveness	0.075	2.188	0.014
Perceived Usefulness of AI Tools moderates the relationship between AI-Supported Feedback System and design quality	0.013	2.439	0.002

5 Discussion

AI tools enhance learning efficiency by offering immediate, personalised feedback that helps students identify weaknesses and improve academic outcomes (Bhatt and Muduli 2023). AI software provided real-time feedback, accelerating learning, fostering independence, and enabling students to incrementally improve their designs and grasp core principles (Otto et al. 2024). AI feedback improved students' technical design skills and creativity, while the third hypothesis confirmed that perceived usefulness significantly increased students' engagement with and application of the feedback (Boubker 2024). This supports the Technology Acceptance Model (TAM), which views perceived usefulness as a key motivator influencing individuals' adoption and use of technology in learning (Davis 1989). Students who believed AI tools were beneficial showed greater engagement with feedback, leading to improved learning (Romero-Rodríguez et al. 2023), Students who perceived AI feedback as relevant were more likely to act on it, improving their learning outcomes. Educators must clearly communicate the benefits of AI tools to enhance their impact (Kayalı and Balat 2024). Students' perception of usefulness drives adoption, improves creativity, and raises design standards—supporting research on effective tech use in creative learning (Muller et al. 2023). AI systems should not only provide accurate feedback but also demonstrate their value. The moderation effect of perceived usefulness shows integration success depends on both technical capability and students' belief in its relevance (Shivshankar and Acharya 2025). Improving student attitudes toward AI's utility is crucial for maximising its impact. This study confirms AI's transformative role in learning and design quality, offering guidance for user-focused integration in skill development (Boubker 2024). AI's impact in design education depends on its functionality and students perceived value, requiring user-focused integration for skill development.

6 Conclusion

This study confirms the positive impact of AI-assisted feedback on learning effectiveness and design quality in visual and illustration education. AI's ability to deliver personalised, real-time feedback enhances student engagement, performance, and creativity. The findings also highlight the mediating role of perceived usefulness in strengthening these effects. Beyond supporting AI integration into curricula, the study stresses the need for educators to build student awareness of AI's value. As AI continues to evolve, this research contributes to the growing literature on AI in education and offers insights for future pedagogical models that combine creativity with technological innovation.

6.1 Implications

This study provides valuable insights for design education, showing that AI-enhanced feedback improves learning and design quality. It supports integrating AI tools for personalised, continuous feedback that fosters creative development. Emphasising perceived usefulness, educators should also help students recognise AI's value. Beyond feedback, AI can aid learning paths, project management, and collaboration. The study extends TAM and Constructivist Learning Theory and invites further research into AI's role in creative, emotional, and collaborative learning.

6.2 Limitations and Future Directions

While valuable, this study has limitations. Conducted with Chinese students, its findings may not apply universally. Future work should include cross-cultural and longitudinal studies to track evolving perceptions. The study focused only on AI-supported feedback, excluding tools like AI-assisted design. It also didn't consider factors like tech skills, creativity, or motivation. Future research should address these and examine teachers' roles. Ethical issues such as privacy, bias, and dependence must also be considered as AI use in education expands.

Author Contributions. Ziwei Yu, the corresponding author, has contributed in supervising, the third author in the data analysis and interpreted the results, and preparing the manuscript. Lin Yu prepared all the maps and figures and interpretation of the results. Gening Liu participated in the interpretation of the results and manuscript preparation.

Conflict of Interest. The authors declare that there is no conflict of interests regarding the publication of this manuscript. In addition, the ethical issues, including plagiarism, informed consent, misconduct, data fabrication and falsification, double publication and submission, and redundancy have been completely observed by the authors.

References

Bağcı, N.S., Işık, A.: Three-dimensional modeling in visual design education [Görsel tasarım eğitiminde üç boyutlu modelleme]. Ordu Üniversitesi Sosyal Bilimler Enstitüsü Sosyal Bilimler Araştırmaları Dergisi **15**(1), 284–313 (2025). https://doi.org/10.48146/odusobiad.1430024

Baidoun, S.D., Salem, M.Z.: The moderating role of perceived trust and perceived value on online shopping behavioral intention of Palestinian millennials during COVID-19. Compet. Rev. Int. Bus. J. **34**(1), 125–143 (2024). https://doi.org/10.1108/CR-10-2022-0161

Batova, T.: Commentary on the visual design challenges for cross-cultural users of business data visualizations. Int. J. Bus. Commun. **23294884251323870** (2025). https://doi.org/10.1177/23294884251323872

Bhatt, P., Muduli, A.: Artificial intelligence in learning and development: a systematic literature review. Eur. J. Train. Dev. **47**(7/8), 677–694 (2023). https://doi.org/10.1108/EJTD-09-2021-0143

Boubker, O.: From chatting to self-educating: can AI tools boost student learning outcomes? Expert Syst. Appl. **238**, 121820 (2024). https://doi.org/10.1016/j.eswa.2023.121820

Brosens, L., Raes, A., Octavia, J.R., Emmanouil, M.: How future proof is design education? A systematic review. Int. J. Technol. Des. Educ. **33**(2), 663–683 (2023). https://doi.org/10.1007/s10798-022-09743-4

Davis, F.D.: Technology acceptance model: TAM. In: Al-Suqri, M.N., Al-Aufi, A.S. (eds.) Information Seeking Behavior and Technology Adoption, vol. 205, no. 219, p. 5 (1989)

Engeness, I., Gamlem, S.M.: Exploring AI-driven feedback as a cultural tool: a cultural-historical perspective on design of AI environments to support students' writing process. Integr. Psychol. Behav. Sci. **59**(1), 23 (2025). https://doi.org/10.1007/s12124-025-09894-8

Gill, A., Irwin, D., Towey, D., Zhang, Y.: Using digital pedagogy to redefine design education. In: Corbett, J., Yan, E.M., Yeoh, J., Lee, J. (eds.) Multilingual Education Yearbook 2023. MEY, pp. 171–190. Springer, Cham (2023). https://doi.org/10.1007/978-3-031-32811-4_10

Guo, K.: EvaluMate: using AI to support students' feedback provision in peer assessment for writing. Assess. Writ. **61**, 100864 (2024). https://doi.org/10.1016/j.asw.2024.100864

Guo, K., Pan, M., Li, Y., Lai, C.: Effects of an AI-supported approach to peer feedback on university EFL students' feedback quality and writing ability. Internet High. Educ. **63**, 100962 (2024). https://doi.org/10.1016/j.iheduc.2024.100962

Guo, K., Zhang, E.D., Li, D., Yu, S.: Using AI-supported peer review to enhance feedback literacy: an investigation of students' revision of feedback on peers' essays. Br. J. Educ. Technol. (2024). https://doi.org/10.1111/bjet.13540

Kayalı, B., Balat, Ş.: Assessment, evaluation, and feedback in online education with artificial intelligence-supported tools. In: AI Algorithms and ChatGPT for Student Engagement in Online Learning, pp. 124–135. IGI Global (2024)
Kuba, R., Jeong, A.: Demystifying visual design: a sequential analysis of design processes in infographic visual composition. J. Vis. Lit. **42**(1), 26–47 (2023). https://doi.org/10.1080/1051144X.2023.2168394
Lai, C.Y., Cheung, K.Y., Chan, C.S.: Exploring the role of intrinsic motivation in ChatGPT adoption to support active learning: an extension of the technology acceptance model. Comput. Educ. Artif. Intell. **5** (2023). https://doi.org/10.1016/j.caeai.2023.100178
Lee, A.V.Y.: Supporting students' generation of feedback in large-scale online course with artificial intelligence-enabled evaluation. Stud. Educ. Eval. **77**, 101250 (2023). https://doi.org/10.1016/j.stueduc.2023.101250
Luo, M., Hu, X., Zhong, C.: The collaboration of AI and teacher in feedback provision and its impact on EFL learner's argumentative writing. Educ. Inf. Technol. (2025). https://doi.org/10.1007/s10639-025-13488-7
Mohzana, M., Murcahyanto, H., Haritani, H.: The effectiveness of online learning on the level of understanding of international course material. IJE Interdiscip. J. Educ. **2**(1), 1–11 (2024). https://doi.org/10.61277/ije.v2i1.80
Muller, C., Mildenberger, T., Steingruber, D.: Learning effectiveness of a flexible learning study programme in a blended learning design: why are some courses more effective than others? Int. J. Educ. Technol. High. Educ. **20**(1), 10 (2023). https://doi.org/10.1186/s41239-022-00379-x
Otto, D., et al.: Student acceptance of AI-based feedback systems: an analysis based on the technology acceptance model (TAM). In: INTED2024 Proceedings (2024)
Rijo, C., Grácio, H.: Enhancing graphic design education: integrating active methodologies and visual synthesis tools. In: Cunha, J., Broega, A.C., Carvalho, H., Providência, B. (eds.) CIMODE 2024, pp. 394–403. Springer, Cham (2025). https://doi.org/10.1007/978-3-031-83185-0_36
Romero-Rodríguez, J.-M., Ramírez-Montoya, M.-S., Buenestado-Fernández, M., Lara-Lara, F.: Use of ChatGPT at university as a tool for complex thinking: students' perceived usefulness. J. New Approaches Educ. Res. **12**(2), 323–339 (2023). https://doi.org/10.7821/naer.2023.7.1458
Sayed, W.S., et al.: AI-based adaptive personalized content presentation and exercises navigation for an effective and engaging E-learning platform. Multimed. Tools Appl. **82**(3), 3303–3333 (2023). https://doi.org/10.1007/s11042-022-13076-8
Shivshankar, S., Acharya, N.: AI in assessment and feedback. In: Next-Generation AI Methodologies in Education, pp. 119–146. IGI Global Scientific Publishing (2025)
Tian, Y., Chan, T.J., Suki, N.M., Kasim, M.A.: Moderating role of perceived trust and perceived service quality on consumers' use behavior of Alipay e-wallet system: the perspectives of technology acceptance model and theory of planned behavior. Hum. Behav. Emerg. Technol. **2023**(1), 5276406. https://doi.org/10.1155/2023/5276406
Vygotsky, L.: Thought and Language. MIT Press, Cambridge (1962)
Yen, Y.-S.: Channel integration affects usage intention in food delivery platform services: the mediating effect of perceived value. Asia Pac. J. Mark. Logist. **35**(1), 54–73 (2023). https://doi.org/10.1108/APJML-05-2021-0372
Zaky, Y.A.M., Al Mulhim, E.N.: Teacher education: design thinking approach in makerspaces to produce quality educational video games with a visual identity and improve design thinking skills. Educ. Sci. **14**(7) (2024). https://doi.org/10.3390/educsci14070718
Zhang, L., Ma, Y.: A study of the impact of project-based learning on student learning effects: a meta-analysis study. Front. Psychol. **14**, 1202728 (2023). https://doi.org/10.3389/fpsyg.2023.1202728

Intelligent Tools for Language Learning and Translation

The Dual Impact of Speech Recognition Technology on Simultaneous Translation

Maria Borodina[1,2](✉)

[1] Financial University, Leningradsky Prospekt, 49/2, 125167 Moscow, Russia
kokocinel@mail.ru
[2] Peoples' Friendship University of Russia Named After Patrice Lumumba, Miklukho-Maklaya Street 6, 117198 Moscow, Russia

Abstract. Currently, technologies such as artificial intelligence, big data, speech recognition technology, and machine translation are having an increasing impact on the field of human translation. On the one hand, they challenge manual translation, but on the other, they help and improve it. This article analyzes the positive and negative effects of speech recognition technology in simultaneous translation on the interpretation process, examines and analyzes the results of previous studies, and provides some recommendations to other translators on the use of speech recognition technology in simultaneous translation.

The author emphasizes that speech recognition technology has a significant impact on the simultaneous translation process, improving its quality and efficiency. The dual impact of this technology on translation synchronization is, on the one hand, in automating routine operations, reducing the burden on the translator, and on the other, in making work more difficult, increasing the requirements for reaction speed and accuracy. Automation of text input processes using voice technology makes it possible to transfer source speech into the target language faster, minimizing delays between speakers and listeners. However, in order to work successfully, translators have to adapt to new conditions, promptly correcting machine recognition results in order to avoid mistakes.

The study examines the possibilities and limitations of modern speech recognition systems in relation to simultaneous translation, identifying key success factors for integrating technology into this process. Special attention is paid to the interaction of the human factor and algorithms, which determines the future development of synchronous interpretation. The work highlights the need to train specialists who are able to effectively use modern tools while maintaining high-quality communication.

Keywords: simultaneous translation · speech recognition technology · interpretation · Chinese language

1 Introduction

According to the increasing globalization of the economy and society, the demand for social language services is increasing. The use of artificial intelligence-based translation technologies is playing an increasingly important role in the language services industry.

K. W. Lee and L. H. Wong (Eds.): ITEA 2025, CCIS 2643, pp. 81–91, 2026.
https://doi.org/10.1007/978-981-95-2011-4_9

Machine translation, speech recognition technology, and simultaneous multilingual subtitling technology are becoming topical issues for discussion at international scientific conferences. The use of speech recognition technology changes the traditional mode of work of translators, improves the quality of translation and reduces the psychological burden. At the same time, since speech recognition technology has not yet become widespread, there remain problems that negatively affect the quality of translation when using this technology, therefore, it is important to find a reasonable application of this technology.

The relevance of the research lies in the fact that the introduction of this technology contributes to the improvement of human abilities and the enhancement of the quality of services provided. Moreover, it is necessary to state the fact that scientific developments in this field will lead to the creation of effective tools and methods of work, which is especially important in the context of the growing demand for high-quality translation services. At the same time, the study of the dual impact of speech recognition technology on simultaneous translation is of practical importance for the development of new standards and approaches to translator training. By understanding which aspects of technology are most useful and effective, educational institutions will be able to adapt training programs for specialists, providing them with the necessary knowledge and skills to work successfully in the context of digitalization.

2 Methods

This study is based on an integrated approach combining theoretical and practical methods of analysis. In particular, the analysis of existing speech recognition technologies and their capabilities based on machine learning algorithms. Research on the accuracy of translation provided by automatic translation systems in various environments affected by noisy environments, accents, and dialects. Modern machine translation systems face several challenges associated with processing speech containing noise interference, regional accents, and dialects. These factors significantly affect the quality of translations since they can distort pronunciation and grammatical constructions, complicating the process of recognizing and interpreting text. Specifically, noisy environments such as streets or cafes often make it difficult to accurately perceive speech. For example, a phrase in Chinese language: Chinese: "你在哪里?" (Nǐ zài nǎlǐ) — Where are you?, in a noisy environment, this phrase could be perceived by the system as: Distorted Example: Chinese: " 呢咧那里" (Ní liě nà lǐ) This leads to translation errors because the system automatically interprets incorrectly heard sounds. It is also important to note that regional accents and dialects present a challenge for automatic translation systems. For example, in some regions of China, the specific Shanghai dialect (上海话) is used, which differs significantly from standard Putonghua (普通话). Consider the phrase: Standard Chinese (Putonghua): Chinese: "我想吃饭。" (Wǒ xiǎng chī fàn) – I want to eat. Shanghai Dialect: Chinese: "吾要吃饭。" (Ngó yào chī fàn) An automatic translation system trained exclusively on standard Putonghua may process this variant incorrectly and translate it improperly. The combination of all these factors further complicates the task of translation. If a person with an accent tries to speak in a noisy environment, the likelihood of errors increases exponentially. For example: Phrase with an accent in a noisy setting: Chinese: "伊想喝茶，但啥也没有了。" (Yì xiǎng hē chá, dàn shá yě méiyǒu le) – She wants to drink tea, but there's nothing left. When processing such a complex situation, the system may struggle to correctly determine the meaning of the statement, leading to significant inaccuracies in translation.

Conducting linguistic experiments, for example, recording speech fragments in different languages (Chinese, English, Russian) and then evaluating the accuracy of their recognition and translation. It is also possible to compare data on the basis of different levels of automation of the translation process, in particular, fully automatic, semi-automatic or using manual intervention. A prerequisite in this case will be to monitor the work of simultaneous interpreters in real conditions using speech recognition technologies.

Quantitative analysis will enable the use of statistical methods to assess the accuracy of speech recognition and translation, for example, the BLEU (Bilingual Evaluation Understanding) parameters allow you to measure the quality of translation. In other words, the combination of these methods provides an opportunity to gain a comprehensive understanding of the impact of speech recognition technologies on simultaneous translation and provides a deep understanding of both the technical and human aspects of this process.

3 Literature Review

In current scientific situation, there are many different researches that study speech recognition technologies during the process of simultaneous translation. Such researchers as Shanshool M.A. and Abdulmohsin H.A. explore how widely used datasets like Librispeech, Timit, and Voxforge have been instrumental in advancing speech recognition technology by improving system accuracy. They also assess various classification methods such as Deep Neural Networks (DNNs), Convolutional Neural Networks (CNNs), Support Vector Machines (SVMs), and Random Forests (RFs). Their findings indicate that Mel-Frequency Cepstral Coefficients (MFCC) frequently exhibit better performance for distinguishing between different voices during recognition experiments (8).

Other authors (Ashok, M., Madan, R., Joha, A., Sivarajah, U.) have outlined fourteen ethical considerations related to artificial intelligence across seven distinct Digital Transformation (DT) archetypes, utilizing an innovative ontological structure encompassing physical, cognitive, informational, and governance dimensions. These researchers propose a theoretical framework consisting of twelve hypotheses that emphasize how these ethical concerns influence societal outcomes, shaped through the lens of organizational effects and influenced by different DT archetype configurations (9).

Moreover, Artificial Emotional Intelligence (AEI) technology allows computers to interpret users' emotional states and react accordingly, facilitating genuine interactions between humans and machines. Modern adaptive user interface solutions rely heavily on advanced methods derived from data analysis and machine learning, particularly deep learning algorithms applied to multi-modal datasets including video recordings of facial expressions, body language, vocal patterns, and biometric signals like eye movements or brain activity readings. Tyagi, S., Szénási, S. explored the effectiveness of various methodologies employed in analyzing complex multi-modal data sources specifically designed to extract emotional cues from verbal exchanges. Additionally, they assessed the potential contributions made by emotionally intelligent chatbots, visual representations such as facial expressions and imagery, along with textual content sourced from social media platforms towards enhancing emotion detection capabilities (10).

4 Results

As you know, simultaneous interpretation is one of the most difficult types of interpretation, in which a person translates into the target language synchronously, simultaneously with listening to speech in the source language, as opposed to sequential translation. Simultaneous interpretation is performed, as a rule, using special equipment such as a simultaneous interpretation booth, microphones, receivers and headphones, as well as signal processing and distribution equipment.

Simultaneous interpretation is more academic and requires a highly qualified translator. Simultaneous interpretation is widely used at major conferences and seminars, diplomatic meetings, and other official events where speaking is of a business nature, and the translator must follow protocol, master terminology and culture, as well as speech processing software.

With simultaneous interpretation, the interpretation is delayed during listening, which requires an appropriate distribution of efforts. This means that when translating the previous sentence, the translator must simultaneously listen to the next sentence, while simultaneously recording the content of information that requires a high degree of accuracy, such as numbers, names, and titles. At the same time, the translator has to perform a number of tasks, which requires high concentration and reaction speed. Simultaneous translation has efficiency, which makes simultaneous translation uncorrectable, i.e. after the translation is output, the possibility of its reinterpretation and correction is very small or impossible at all. After receiving information in one language, the translator automatically converts what it hears into the equivalent in the target language.

Speech Recognition Technology (SRT) is an automatic process of converting a speech signal into digital information, such as text data. In other words, SRT refers to computational linguistics, which develops algorithms for recognizing and interpreting human speech. Such research first began in the 1950s, and since the 1990s, the technology has culminated in research and industrial applications [6]. Many well-known Internet technology companies, such as IBM, Apple, etc., have invested heavily in the development and research of speech recognition technology. By the 21st century, the focus of SRT research has shifted towards improvised spoken language and natural dialogue, as well as multilingual simultaneous translation.

Despite the fact that SRT has made historical progress during its long development, there are still some technical flaws in it. Noise suppression in the speech recognition process remains an unsolvable problem, and beyond a given distance, machines have difficulty identifying the speaker's language and may even stop working without being recognized. In addition, speaker accents and speech inaccuracies also affect the translation of outgoing sentences by the speech recognition system. Therefore, at this stage, the use of speech recognition technology for simultaneous translation has not yet become widespread [7]. In particular, researcher Yu Xiaoming had personal experience of using this technology in simultaneous translation. When participating in an experiment to study the impact of a group translator with speech recognition support on the translation process, a computer was placed in front of the author, text in the source language automatically appeared on the computer screen, transformed by the language recognition system, and the author could choose whether to look at the screen or translate from his own notes. During the entire translation process, the author could not take both hints into account and could only focus on his own notes or on the texts on the computer screen. However, when the computer screen is the main auxiliary tool, the author's translation mode changes from listening to visual translation, and it becomes difficult to understand the relationship between listening and viewing. Therefore, throughout the translation process, the author relied more on the text of the source language on the computer screen. Summarizing the experience gained, the author came to several conclusions: for translators with a limited level of translation, the help of the speech recognition system plays a major positive role, and at the moment the main focus is on visual translation, complemented by auditory translation. When using the speech recognition system for the first time, it is necessary to determine in advance the main means of translation, i.e. focus on the computer screen or on recordings, otherwise confusion will arise. If information is missed during listening and recognition, then searching for it on the computer screen will lead to attention being distracted, which will take too much time and affect the perception and translation of subsequent information.

The advantages of SRT on the simultaneous translation process can be indicated by improving the integrity of translation and reducing the burden on listening comprehension. Simultaneous interpretation requires a lot of attention from the translator, and an incorrect distribution of efforts can lead to poor translation quality. Inadequate allocation of attention to listening can lead to missing information. In such cases, SRT can be used to quickly find the missing information in the transformed source text. Since the source text transformed by SRT contains complex information, it is easier for the translator to identify logical connections and important information. When translating based solely on listening and taking notes, parts of the source text are often forgotten or skipped due to lack of time for translation, however, using a transformed source text that covers most or all of the content allows you to increase the completeness of the translation if you have enough time, the quality of the translation improves, since previously omitted information can be supplemented without any footprints.

Compared to sequential translation, a simultaneous translator receives a more fragmented and random speech stream, and the speaker usually unconsciously repeats the previous content over and over again [5]. If the speech recognition system can provide text translation into the source language with higher accuracy, the translator will be able to use SRT as the main auxiliary tool, moving from initial auditory translation as the main tool and visual translation of recordings as an additional tool to visual translation as the main tool and auditory translation as an additional tool, and use translation into hearing to identify and correct errors in the text in the source language, the difficulty of translation will be lower, at the same time, the translator himself will feel more comfortable and confident in translation. With traditional simultaneous interpretation without prior training, the translator has to be energetic in order to capture as much information as possible, especially in unfamiliar professional fields such as medicine, chemistry, engineering, and others. With the help of SRT, the translator becomes closer to highly professional translation activities with a more normal attitude, and reducing anxiety contributes to the translator's concentration and smooth operation.

However, it is also necessary to point out the negative impact of SRT on the simultaneous translation process. Chinese and foreign scientists such as Gill [1], Bao Gang [3], Lu Xinzhao [4] and others studied the understanding of speech by ear and pointed out its importance in interpretation. Understanding speech by ear is the first key link in interpreting, a translator can easily get distracted if he is poorly versed in basic and auxiliary tools, does not know how to use equipment, and does not know how to properly distribute his forces, which leads to problems in all aspects of the translation process, the translator will not be able to grasp key information, and I have to check the contents of the screen at the same time as listening, which would lead to inappropriate pauses and other problems that negatively affected the overall fluency and syntactic structure [2].

When a translator relies too much on SRT and relaxes his vigilance when listening to speech, this leads to ignoring errors in the transformation of the source language and transmitting incorrect information. For example, because of the speaker's accent, speech recognition technology is difficult to accurately recognize the source language, and it is easy to provide incorrect information. In addition, the difficult point in translation is the numbers that need to be translated accurately, and blind trust in the conversion of the speech recognition system can lead to different types of mistakes.

5 Discussion

In the process of simultaneous translation, due to the differences in the characteristics of each language, there is often a problem of insufficient translation time. During the process of Chinese-Russian translation, for example, often results in a situation where the text in Russian is longer than the original text. In this case, the translator is forced to reduce the working time by structuring information, highlighting key points and speeding up the translation process. If the text converted by the speech recognition system is too long, the time required for reading, recognition, and translation will also increase, making it difficult to understand the main content. Moreover, at the same time, a longer translated text requires a higher speech speed, which will cause difficulties for listeners to understand, bring discomfort and significantly reduce the quality of communication.

The following examples are offered for analysis, illustrating the dual effect of SRT on simultaneous translation from Chinese to Russian. Firstly, the system is capable of performing automatic translation and clarifying terms.

我们的公司正在开发一种新型的可穿戴设备，
它可以监测用户的心率和血氧饱和度。- «Our company is developing a new type of wearable device that can track the user's pulse and blood oxygen saturation».

The main functionality of SRT in this case is as follows:

1) The system recognizes the phrase in Chinese and automatically offers a translation;
2) The translator checks the suggested version and clarifies terms such as «**可穿戴设备**» (wearable device) and «**血氧饱和度**» (blood oxygen saturation). If the proposed translation is not completely accurate, the translator makes adjustments.

The following example are given from medical discourse. An automatic translation system enables medical professionals to quickly obtain Russian equivalents of Chinese terms and concepts, thus facilitating communication between doctors and patients. Example: Chinese phrase: "病人出现呼吸困难" ("The patient experiences breathing difficulties") Automatic translation with term explanation: "The patient exhibits dyspnea (respiratory insufficiency)." However, it is necessary to point out the negative impact of the speech recognition system. During the process of translation certain medical documents, such as patient's card, extract from medical history, referral for surgery, there may be losses of semantic nuances, especially during interpretation of complex clinical cases. Example: Chinese phrase: "患者有发热、咳嗽症状，伴随着胸闷和气短" ("The patient has symptoms of fever and cough accompanied by chest tightness and shortness of breath"). Incorrect machine translation: "The patient has fever, cough, chest pain, and lack of air." Correct translation taking into account context and clinical picture: "The patient presents with elevated body temperature, dry cough, feeling of constriction in the chest, and sensation of breathlessness."

The next example from the novel "Red Sorghum" by Mo Yan illustrates the dual nature of influence exerted by Speech Recognition Technology (SRT) when simultaneously translating a Chinese phrase into English:

Chinese phrase: "父亲觉得余司令的手从王文义的后颈皮上松开了，父亲还觉得王文义的脖子上留下两个熟葡萄一样的紫手印，王文义幽蓝色的惊惧不安的眼睛里，飞迸出几点感激与委屈。" The phrase contains vivid figurative expressions ("two marks left by hands resembling ripe grapes," "eyes full of fear and anxiety"), which require a subtle understanding of cultural subtleties specific to the Chinese language. A speech recognition system must take into account the symbolism of colors and shapes in Eastern art in order to adequately convey the narrative atmosphere.

In Automatic translation into English was given as: "Father felt Commander Yu's hand loosen from Wang Wenyi's nape, father also noticed two purple fingerprints on Wang Wenyi's neck like ripe grapes, whose eyes filled with deep shades of fear and anxiety mixed with gratitude and injustice." The English version accurately conveys the general meaning of the original phrase, but stylistics and perception of metaphors differ across languages. Automatic translation might overlook nuances related to color and shape perception in different cultures. Moreover, the image of Wang Wenyie's eyes creates a complex interplay of emotions—fear, anxiety, gratitude, and a sense of injustice are all expressed simultaneously through one gaze. Conveying such multifaceted feelings presents a significant challenge for automatic translation. A possible error of SRT: The system might oversimplify the emotional load by excluding subtle nuances of the character's experiences, leading to a reduction in the richness of the original content. The author actively employs artistic techniques such as comparisons and metaphors, making this particular phrase especially challenging for machine translation. Taking into account all levels of meaning is crucial for maintaining the aesthetic value of the text. Automated speech recognition technologies allow significantly speeding up the translation process and retaining the primary message. However, challenges remain regarding the transmission of delicate emotional undertones, cultural symbols, and literary devices characteristic of a given language and culture. Therefore, using SRT systems should be followed by subsequent editing and adaptation by professional translators capable of considering all aspects of the literary work.

Secondly, the SRT system is able to recognize specialized terms. In front of us offer of report on new technologies in medicine:

在人工智能领域，深度学习技术已经被广泛应用于医疗诊断中，例如对进行分析以提高癌症早期筛查的准确性。- «In the field of artificial intelligence technology deep learning is widely used in medical diagnostics, for example, to analyze CT images to improve the accuracy of early detection of cancer».

In this case, SRT technology recognizes technical terms such as « 深度学习» (deep learning), « CT**图像**» (CT image) and «**癌症早期筛查**» (early detection of cancer), and offers accurate translations. At this time, the translator can focus on correctly conveying the meaning and style of speech, entrusting automation to technical terms.

Below are three examples of specialized economic terms in Chinese along with their translations into English performed automatically by Speech Recognition Technology (SRT), followed by analysis of the advantages and disadvantages of SRT technology.

Example No 1: *Chinese phrase:* "**人民币汇率**". English version *(translated by SRT):* Renminbi exchange rate. Translator's correction: RMB exchange rate.

+ Pros: The term was precisely defined due to clear correspondence. The term "Renminbi" was correctly recognized by the system as the official name of China's currency. - Cons: Automatic replacement of the full title ("people's exchange rate") with its abbreviation ("RMB") is more common among anglophone economists, although such modification is not always obvious. It is essential for the translator to understand this aspect and adjust terminology accordingly.

Example No. 2: *Chinese phrase*: " **通货膨胀压力**". English version (automatically translated by SRT): Inflation pressure. Translator's adjustment: Inflationary pressures + Pros: The main idea has been conveyed correctly – the concepts of inflation and pressure are understandable even to beginners in economics. - Cons: The expression "inflation pressure" sounds somewhat artificial in English; the more commonly used form would be "inflationary pressures." A professional translator corrects the phrasing to make it sound more natural for native English speakers.

Example No. 3: *Chinese phrase*: " **财政赤字**" Engl. (automatically translated by SRT): Fiscal deficit. Translator's adjustment: Budget deficit.

+ Pros: Correct and precise matching of key terms. SRT successfully identified the core concept and provided an appropriate equivalent. - Cons: The term "budget deficit" is more widely used and better reflects the essence of the concept compared to the less common equivalent "fiscal deficit," though both are acceptable. Here, the role of the translator lies in selecting the most natural and widely accepted term.

Thus, based on these examples, we can conclude that the advantages of Speech Recognition Technologies (SRT) include rapid and relatively accurate identification of standard terms, as well as the ability to expedite the translation of large volumes of specialized material. At the same time, the following drawbacks of SRT can be noted: insufficient sensitivity to nuances of professional jargon; limited understanding of cultural and linguistic context, resulting in incorrect choices of translation options; and the need for post-editing by specialists to improve accuracy and naturalness of the text.

Thirdly, complex sentences can be processed using this technology. Quite often, a translator is faced with the fact that Chinese sentences turn out to be long and complex, especially when it comes to scientific and technical literature. Look through the following example, «随着互联网的发展以及大数据和云计算技术的成熟，我们有机会重新思考传统的教育模式，并利用这些技术为学生提供更个性化、更有效的学习体验。» - «With the development of the Internet, as well as the maturity of big data and cloud computing technologies, we have the opportunity to rethink traditional educational models and use these technologies to provide students with a more personalized and effective learning experience». When working with this syntactic whole, SRT helps to divide a long sentence into parts, offering intermediate translation options. The translator can choose the best option based on the context and his own experience, and refine it, taking into account the peculiarities of the Russian language.

These examples prove that SRT can significantly improve the simultaneous translation process by helping translators cope with technical, lexical, and cultural nuances.

Here are examples of complex sentences from an economic text in Chinese processed by Speech Recognition Technology (SRT). Example No 1: Original in Chinese: 中国经济在全球化进程中面临着诸多挑战和机遇。Translation into English (SRT): China's economy faces many challenges and opportunities in the globalization process. According to the example, the sentence is translated clearly and comprehensibly. Main ideas are translated effectively. At the same time, there is room for improvement in expressing the exact meaning of the adjective "globalization." It's preferable to use "the process of globalization." Therefore, it is recommended reformulation in English: China's economy confronts numerous challenges and opportunities amidst the process of globalization. Example No 2: Original in Chinese: 随着国内消费市场持续扩大，企业需要更加关注产品质量、品牌形象以及服务体验等核心竞争力因素。 Translation into English (SRT): As the domestic consumer market continues to expand, companies need to pay more attention to product quality, brand image, service experience, and other core competitive factors. In this case the main content is conveyed correctly. Although grammatically correct, it's advisable to group list items together ("product quality, brand image, and service experience") and add a summarizing word ("core competitiveness elements"). As a solution is recommended such version as: With the continued expansion of the domestic consumer market, businesses must focus increasingly on core competitiveness elements such as product quality, brand image, and service experience. Example No 3: Original in Chinese: 金融机构应当根据客户需求及时调整业务模式，并采取有效措施提升风险管理能力。Translation into English (SRT): Financial institutions should promptly adjust business models according to customer needs and adopt effective measures to enhance risk management capabilities.

In this case, it is worth noting that the main meaning is almost perfectly conveyed. However, the structure of the sentence can be simplified to emphasize practicality and clarity. Thus, the recommended optimal version is: To meet evolving customer demands, financial institutions must adapt their business models and implement measures to strengthen risk management.

Using Speech Recognition Technology (SRT) allows efficient processing of complex economic texts in Chinese. Nevertheless, several limitations exist:

1. Sometimes difficulties arise in accurately transferring the structure of complex sentences.
2. Terms and constructions often require additional editing to improve clarity and consistency of style in English.
3. Cultural differences and perceptions of economic vocabulary must be taken into account to avoid misunderstandings.

It is recommended to complement the work of speech recognition systems with post-editing by qualified professionals to ensure high-quality translation.

6 Conclusions

According to the theory of translation ecology by Xu Jianzhong [8], translators, translated works, and even various subjects of translation activity are in the process of ecological selection and adaptation, and the law of survival of the fittest applies to the world of translation. Therefore, translators must be ready to evolve with the development of technology, as well as have the ability to cope with the challenges that technology brings with it.

The development of artificial intelligence has a double impact on the field of translation, especially when using speech recognition technology, and its impact on the translation process depends on the specific situation. With a reasonable allocation of energy and proper use of the auxiliary role of speech recognition, it is possible to reduce the burden on the translation process, improve its quality and ensure the integrity of the translation. If you misallocate your efforts and overly rely on the source text transmitted by speech recognition technology, problems such as distraction, redundancy of translation, and incorrect information transmission will arise. Therefore, while speech recognition technology continues to evolve, translators should carefully and correctly use its auxiliary functions in order to improve the quality of translation under the positive influence of this technology.

On the one hand, SRT greatly simplifies the work of translators, allowing them to automate the process of converting oral speech into written form. This speeds up the pace of work, reduces the burden on auditory memory, and allows you to focus on conveying meaning rather than mechanically rewriting text. Moreover, the use of speech recognition technologies helps improve translation accuracy, especially in the multitasking environment typical of simultaneous translation.

However, on the other hand, the introduction of these technologies poses new challenges for translators. It is necessary to master the skills of working with automated systems, which requires additional time and effort. In addition, errors in speech recognition algorithms can lead to distortion of the transmitted content, which increases the risk of misunderstanding or misinterpretation of information. To minimize negative consequences, it is important to develop speech recognition technologies, improve algorithms, and integrate them with traditional translation methods.

Thus, despite the obvious advantages, the use of speech recognition technologies in simultaneous translation requires a careful approach and further development. Only the combination of modern technologies with the professional skills of the translator will allow us to achieve optimal results in ensuring high-quality and accurate information transmission.

References

1. Gile, D.: Basic Concepts and Models in Translation and Interpretation Training, Amsterdam/Philadelphia, John Benjamins Publishing Company, 277 p. (1995)
2. Kaye, A.S.: K. Dallas Kenny, Language loss and the crisis of cognition: between socio- and psycholinguistics. (Contributions to the sociology of language, 73.) Berlin: Mouton de Gruyter, 1996. Pp. xiv, 306. Hb DM 158.00. Lang. Soc. **27**(4), 565–568 (1998)
3. Bao, G.: Interpretation Studies. China Translation and Publishing Corporation, Beijing (2014)
4. Lu, X.: English interpretation listening: cognitive psychological model, skills and teaching. Shandong Foreign Lang. Teach. **05** (2009)
5. Li, T.: Analysis of machine simultaneous interpretation system under interpretation working model. Orient. Transl. **6**, 34–39 (2018)
6. Wang, H., Pan, J., Liu, C.: Research progress and prospect of speech recognition technology. Telecom Sci. **2**, 1–11 (2018)
7. Yu, X.: Development and application of speech recognition technology. Comput. Age **11**, 28–31 (2019)
8. Shanshool, M.A., Abdulmohsin, H.A.: A comprehensive review on machine learning approaches for enhancing human speech recognition. Traitement du Signal **40**(5), 2121–2129 (2023). https://doi.org/10.18280/ts.400529
9. Ashok, M., Madan, R., Joha, A., Sivarajah, U.: Ethical framework for artificial intelligence and digital technologies. Int. J. Inf. Manag. **62**, 102433 (2022). ISSN 0268-4012. https://doi.org/10.1016/j.ijinfomgt.2021.102433
10. Tyagi, S., Szénási, S.: Semantic speech analysis using machine learning and deep learning techniques: a comprehensive review. Multimed. Tools Appl. **83**, 73427–73456 (2024). https://doi.org/10.1007/s11042-023-17769-6

Special Features of English-Russian Translation of Scientific Texts Based on Artificial Intelligence

Maria Borodina[1,2(✉)], Elena Monakhova[2,3], and Irina Gorofonova[2]

[1] Financial University, Leningradsky Prospekt, 49/2, 125167 Moscow, Russia
kokocinel@mail.ru

[2] Peoples' Friendship University of Russia named after Patrice Lumumba, Miklukho-Maklaya Street 6, 117198 Moscow, Russia

[3] Russian State Social University, 4 Wilhelm Pik Street, Building 2, 129226 Moscow, Russia

Abstract. The translation of scientific texts from English into Russian presents unique challenges due to linguistic, cultural, and terminological differences between the two languages. This study explores the special features of English-Russian translation in the context of artificial intelligence applications. The research focuses on identifying key factors that influence the accuracy and quality of machine-generated translations for scientific content. These include issues such as domain-specific vocabulary, syntax complexity, and contextual understanding. By analyzing both traditional human-driven approaches and AI-based methods, this work highlights areas where machine learning algorithms can enhance or struggle with precision when translating highly technical material. The findings aim to provide insights for improving automated translation systems while addressing the nuances required for accurate rendering of scientific discourse across languages.

Keywords: artificial intelligence (AI) · ChatGPT · translation · scientific texts · genre features

1 Introduction

Nowadays advancements in technology entice translators to speed up and simplify the process of translation, and it is not uncommon for the text to be "typed into the machine", translated into another language, and then be edited by the translator. The most common web-based platforms used for such purposes are Google, Yandex, DeepL, and so on. Furthermore, there are more complicated systems based on artificial intelligence (AI) that do not only provide translation, but also analyze user-provided data, which can significantly reduce the need for further text editing by a human translator. One of the systems that can provide such analysis is ChatGPT, version 4.0. The need for the younger generation to master technology and use AI-related resources, the approval of the employers who want to speed up the solution of certain tasks and make allowance for the competent use of AI, indicate the need for scientific research in this area.

K. W. Lee and L. H. Wong (Eds.): ITEA 2025, CCIS 2643, pp. 92–102, 2026.
https://doi.org/10.1007/978-981-95-2011-4_10

Moreover, in the field of translations, the use of AI is becoming increasingly popular due to its speed, accessibility and the ability to process large amounts of information. At the same time, the translation process is not a literal transfer of meaning from the source language to the target language, but rather a creative task within the process of which the translator should preserve the uniqueness of the genre, style and cultural aspect of the text under translation. Genre parameters turn out to be key in the perception of the text by the reader or listener, therefore, the task of translation is to transmit the genre features adequately and correctly. Nowadays, AI is actively being introduced into the professional and educational life of a person, however, it must be emphasized that neural networks used to translate texts do not always take into account their stylistic and genre specific features. The reasons for this are the fact that each genre differs in its structure, purpose, language, style, features, etc. Therefore, if the AI does not consider the parameters which are important for a particular text and its genre, it leads to a distortion of the meaning and a decrease in the quality of the translation. The relevance of the research lies in the study of this new AI-based system in terms of its advantages and disadvantages. The study will identify specific requirements for the scientific style and develop algorithms that can help to cope with these differences in the future.

The purpose of the work is a comparative analysis of artificially obtained translations with the original texts' specific features. The object of the study is the English-Russian translations of scientific texts carried out by the ChatGPT system, version 4.0, and the subject of the research are special aspects, namely stylistic peculiarities, of translated texts. The translations of scientific text, automatically obtained in the named system, comprise the research material of the study. Since the translations are compared with the originals, the source texts are also the material of the work.

2 Related Works (Literature Review)

Many scientists are engaged in research on ChatGPT and its impact on education and training of a future specialist. One of the key aspects of study are the possibilities of ChatGPT in the process of education (Yuk Mui Elly Heung, Thomas K.F. Chiu [10], Ting Ma [8], Belle Li, Victoria L. Lowell, Chaoran Wang, Xiangning Li [2].

Ting Ma [8], for instance, emphasizes the versatility of ChatGPT for various educational purposes, and also identifies potential problems and suggests exploration trends for future research regarding its limitations and ethical considerations. Yuk Mui Elly Heung and Thomas K.F. Chiu [10] explore the impact of ChatGPT on student engagement, focusing on behavioral, cognitive, and emotional aspects. Based on a systematic literature review and meta-analysis, the authors assess how effectively ChatGPT increases student engagement compared to traditional non-ChatGPT-based learning approaches. Meanwhile, they recognize the potential risks, such as excessive dependence.

Such researchers as Lingfei Wu, Yu Chen, Kai Shen, Xiaojie Guo, Hanning Gao, Shucheng Li, Jian Pei and Bo Long [5] provide a comprehensive overview of Graph Neural Networks (GNNs) and their application in Natural Language Processing (NLP). They introduce a new taxonomy for organizing existing research on GNNs in NLP across three key dimensions: graph construction, graph representation learning, and graph-based encoder-decoder models. Moreover, authors survey a wide range of NLP applications where GNNs have been applied effectively and summarize relevant benchmark datasets, evaluation metrics, and available open-source code related to these applications.

Jacob Beck, Risto Vuorio, Evan Zheran Liu, Zheng Xiong, Luisa Zintgraf, Chelsea Finn, Shimon Whiteson and others [3, 12] explain how meta-RL studies can be categorized based on whether they involve a task distribution and the amount of resources allocated for performing each specific task. With this classification, the authors review meta-RL methods and their uses. Finally, they identify unresolved issues that must be addressed to integrate meta-RL into the regular repertoire of deep RL practitioners.

Ramanpreet Kaur, Tomaž Klobučar, Dušan Gabrijelčič [7] explore and analyze the role of language models in addressing critical challenges in cybersecurity. The authors investigate how these models, particularly advanced ones like BERT and other large-scale architectures, can enhance various aspects of cyber defense, including threat detection, content analysis, and human-machine collaboration. They also examine the broader implications of integrating language models into cybersecurity frameworks, highlighting both technical challenges (such as data privacy and computational demands) and socio-technical factors (like workflow impacts and ethical concerns).

3 Methods (Research Methodology)

The methodological basis of the work is the dialectical method, as well as the method of analysis. The methods of analysis, classification, deduction, and analogy have been applied while investigating the subject matter. The dialectical method is based on understanding the world as a constantly evolving process, where all elements are in a state of interdependence and contradictions. Applied to the study of genre specifics of AI-based translation, this method keeps track of such key points as inconsistency, development and integrity [1, 4, 9]. The translator needs to take into account the internal contradictions between different genres of texts and the requirements for their translation. For example, fiction translation requires the preservation of aesthetic influence and emotional coloring, while business documentation translation must be accurate and concise. Next, it is important to take into account the evolutionary changes in the genre and technology of translation, as well as their impact on each other [6, 11, 13]. The interaction between traditional translation methods and new AI technologies is a process of continuous development and adaptation. The analyzed texts are considered as a single whole consisting of many elements, each of which interacts with the others. In the context of translation, this means taking into account all aspects of the text, including its structure, vocabulary, stylistic features, and cultural contexts.

Since this study is devoted to the peculiarities of translating texts of different genres with the help of ChatGPT system, special attention will be paid to transformations that the neural network can/cannot apply, therefore, it is further proposed to reconsider existing classifications of transformations in translation theory under present-day conditions.

4 Results

It is well-known that the use of linguistic means in scientific discourse is focused on the fulfillment of tasks related to the communication of specialists in the scientific field. Scientific texts, as products of such communication, nevertheless, carry stylistic and genre differences depending on the addressee of communication, goals, communicative intention and attitude, as well as the particular conditions of creating the text. As a result of the translation of a scientific text, the final product should have such characteristic features as generalization, logical presentation, terminological abundance, accuracy, clarity and objectivity of presentation, standardization and stereotyping.

For comparative analysis of the translation made by ChatGPT, the texts of scientific discourse were taken for investigation: https://ojs.bonviewpress.com/index.php/AIA/article/view/939/722. During the analysis, all texts were translated from English into Russian by the ChatGPT automatic system, version GPT-4.0. After that, the original and the translation of each text were compared with each other with the application of V.N. Komissarov's theory of transformations. The identified differences are described below in the course of a comparative analysis.

For comparative analysis, the text «Let's Have a Chat! A Conversation with ChatGPT: Technology, Applications, and Limitations» (translated by AI into Russian as «Давайте побеседуем! Разговор с ChatGPT: технологии, проблемы и ограничения»). The translation of the title already shows the «advanced» nature of artificial intelligence: the system easily translates sentences with homogeneous terms into Russian, independently adjusting the punctuation between them (the comma was removed in the translation). The same phenomenon, which only confirms our observation, is illustrated below, with the indication of the authors (the comma is removed in the Russian version: «Sakib Shahryar and Kadhim Hayavi»).

In general, the system handles scientific text best (compared to other styles) and makes the least mistakes. So, in an annotation of about 10 lines, we found only 2 speech defects. English «human-like sentences» are translated as «человекоподобные предложения» (zero transformation and, accordingly, literal translation by V.N. Komissarov). Obviously, metonymy is meant in English: human-like sentences mean «sentences that are meaningful to humans, produced by humans». The automatic translation system is not yet capable of this kind of transformation. Another flaw is the double use of the preposition «для» in the sentence «Признание текущих ограничений ChatGPT имеет решающее значение для понимания его потенциала для роста». In the original English, the preposition is not repeated: «Recognizing the current limits of ChatGPT is crucial in understanding its potential for growth». Apparently, the flaw is caused by the choice of a preposition combined with «имеет решающее значение для...», although the human mind suggests the simplest solution is to remove «для» in the second case, leaving just «потенциал роста». Let us also note here, as a positive point, the preservation of the meaning in the translation «is crucial (in)» into «имеет решающее значение (для)». This is a descriptive translation, or explication (according to V.N. Komissarov).

In the «Introduction» part, speech defects are also rare. A single one can be considered an incorrect choice of equivalent («tricks» hardly translates as «трюки», rather requires replacement with «механизмы»; «engagement» is unlikely to be understandable to a Russian reader in the «вовлеченность» variant and requires, apparently, a descriptive translation with modulation – «внутреннее знание материала» or «знание материала изнутри»). There are also isolated cases of impaired compatibility: «substantial public attention» into «значительное общественное внимание». Apparently, a comprehensive transformation is also required in this case – it «вызвал значительный общественный резонанс» and «привлек внимание значительной части общества». The tautology «свои – своей» in the last sentence is explained by the tautology in the original text: «Lastly, it is worth noting that ChatGPT adeptly concludes its responses with a summary that encapsulates its perspective, thus adding an engaging element to its communication». Interestingly, in English, the tautology is even triple («its» is repeated three times); when translated into Russian, the system reduced the number of repetitions to two: «Наконец, стоит отметить, что ChatGPT умело завершает свои ответы кратким изложением своей точки зрения, добавляя тем самым элемент вовлеченности в общение». Before the word «общение», the pronoun «its» is omitted in translation.

Grammatically, the «Introduction» part is also almost flawless, and the AI conveys both the morphology and syntax of the original very well in Russian. Of the obvious shortcomings, we note only the plural in the combination «находит свои применения» (English «applications»). Singular – plural transformations are not yet subject to artificial intelligence, at least in this case, probably due to the homonymy of the word «применения» (in Russian, this word has the same nominative plural and the genitive singular). On closer examination, questions may also be raised by the artificial network's choice of the adverbial "Отличаясь", for example:

English	Russian
Distinguishing itself from prior chatbots, ChatGPT has demonstrated notable proficiency in generating logically consistent responses to a broad array of inquiries	Отличаясь от предыдущих чат-ботов, ChatGPT продемонстрировал заметную способность генерировать логически последовательные ответы на широкий спектр вопросов

Obviously, the system «knows» that the -ing participle at the beginning of a sentence can be translated by the adverbial participle; it also «knows» that the English «itself» becomes part of the reflexive verb when translated by the postfix «–сь» (in Russian). However, the system can no longer cope with replacing the participle with the verbal noun «В отличие…» – so the sentence would sound much better.

Section 2 of this article, the first part of the main text, is also used for comparative analysis. Here, too, the AI demonstrates remarkably high translation skills. In all cases where a particular word has an unambiguous equivalent and a single meaning (and there are most of them in the scientific text), the system copes flawlessly. For example, the ratio of sentences is remarkable:

English	Russian
The two most prominent language models include Bidirectional Encoder Representations from Transformers (Devlin et al., 2019) and Generative Pre-trained Transformer (GPT) (Radford et al., 2019). The former is primarily used for recognizing the context in language and classification tasks, while the latter is more adept at language generation tasks such as machine translation and question-answering	Две наиболее выдающиеся языковые модели включают двунаправленные кодировочные представления от трансформеров (BERT) (Девлин и др., 2019) и генеративный предварительно обученный трансформер (GPT) (Радфорд и др., 2019). Первая в основном используется для распознавания контекста в языке и задач классификации, в то время как вторая более подходит для задач генерации языка, таких как машинный перевод и ответы на вопросы

Obviously, when choosing the generic affiliation of the numerals «первый/первая/первое», «второй/вторая/второе», the system cannot rely on the original, since in English the grammatical category of gender as such is generally absent. When transmitting the English phrase «the former… the latter» AI is forced to rely only on the contextual relationship with the previous sentence, i.e. on the lexical relation of «the former… The latter refers to language models» (in Russian «языковые модели»). This relationship is far from being a contact relationship; «language models» are mentioned at the beginning of the previous sentence. Nevertheless, the AI successfully copes with the task by choosing the gender that is needed in the context.

The inaccuracies of the translated text are again related to the «inability» of the ChatGPT system to apply complex transformations of the modulation type (according to V.N. Komissarov). In particular, the literal translation is observed when transmitting «More precisely» into Russian «Более точно». The system does not take into account the construction of the entire sentence: «Более точно, ChatGPT был построен на GPT 3.5, который относится к семейству LLM». Of course, in this case, you need to expand the context (in particular, in Russian «Если быть более точным»). Literalism is also observed in the following translation example:

English	Russian
From text classification to text generation, these models offer superior performance than other AI models	От классификации текста до генерации текста, эти модели предлагают превосходную производительность по сравнению с другими моделями ИИ

In this case, literalism is observed when translating chains of words (attribute groups «text classification» and «text generation») – if we can still generate one text, then we are most likely classifying a number/set of texts. According to the rules, the English attribute chain may not take into account the plural of nouns, so in this case the preferred plural was replaced by the singular. The whole phrase, however, does not look entirely justified in translation due to the absence of the generalizing word «Во всем» in Russian (omitted in the original) and, accordingly, due to a punctuation error - an extra comma before «эти» in Russian transformation.

The same literal translation is observed when transmitting the difficult-to-perceive combination of «human evaluators». Direct translation and "zero transformation" (according to V.N. Komissarov) do not help in this case, a part of speech needs to be replaced into «люди-оценщики».

Finally, you can notice a syntactic moment that was not taken into account by the neural network – the translation of a phrase that is easily perceived in the original:

English	Russian
This is achieved through the use of meticulously designed instructions or prompts, a process referred to as "prompt engineering" (Liu & Chilton, 2022)	Это достигается с помощью тщательно разработанных инструкций или подсказок, процесс, называемый "инжиниринг подсказок" (Лю и Чилтон, 2022)

In this case, it would be more appropriate to swap the sentences and remove the word "это" in the Russian translation: «Процесс, называемый "инжиниринг подсказок", достигается с помощью тщательно разработанных инструкций». Moreover, we also suggest removing the double use of the word «подсказок» in the Russian version.

Next, it is proposed to examine the following example and specific features of translation when transforming an English text into Russian using ChatGPT.

English	Russian
However, ensuring that the model's output aligns with human values and ethics is of utmost importance to prevent the model from generating responses that could be harmful or unethical	Однако обеспечение того, чтобы выходные данные модели соответствовали человеческим ценностям и этическим нормам, имеет первостепенное значение для предотвращения генерации моделью ответов, которые могут быть вредными или неэтичными

In this case, it can be seen that ChatGPT successfully handled both grammar and adequacy in conveying meaning, as well as the naturalness of formulations. Specifically, the Russian version maintains correct sentence structure and agreement between parts of speech. The main sense of the original English text has been accurately conveyed, emphasizing the importance of ensuring that the model's outputs are aligned with human ethical standards and preventing harmful consequences. The translation sounds natural and is easily comprehensible for a Russian-speaking reader. However, some inaccuracies made by ChatGPT can still be pointed out. The phrase "обеспечение того, чтобы…" is a direct calque from English and sounds somewhat cumbersome. It could have been simplified ("Важно обеспечить, чтобы…"). Stylistically, the translation corresponds to the scientific style of the original but a slightly less formal wording might provide greater clarity. As a result, an improved translation variant can be suggested "Важно убедиться, что выходные данные модели соответствуют человеческим ценностям и этическим принципам, чтобы избежать генерации потенциально вредоносных или неэтичных ответов", which is somewhat simpler and easier to understand in Russian while preserving the primary meaning of the source text.

The following example includes several special terms, which ChatGPT translates inaccurately and absurdly for a Russian-speaking reader.

English	Russian
To achieve this alignment, a technique called Reinforcement Learning from Human Feedback is employed. This process involves training the model to favor outputs that human evaluators rate as preferable, helping to guide the model's responses in a more ethical and useful direction	Для достижения этого соответствия используется техника под названием обучение с подкреплением на основе обратной связи от людей. Этот процесс включает обучение модели, чтобы она предпочитала те выходные данные, которые человеческие оценщики считают предпочтительными, помогая направлять ответы модели в более этичное и полезное русло

Thus, it's evident that the commonly accepted term in machine learning (Reinforcement Learning from Human Feedback) was translated correctly, making it understandable and adapted to the Russian language. The overall structure of the sentence remains intact, and syntactic constructions of the Russian language were used appropriately. Furthermore, the core idea was conveyed precisely, highlighting the significance of prioritizing results positively evaluated by humans, thereby guiding the model towards being more ethical and beneficial. At the same time, the phrase "чтобы она предпочитала те выходные данные, которые человеческие оценщики считают предпочтительными" appears redundant and cumbersome. Moreover, certain elements of the translation sound overly formal and difficult to comprehend on hearing. For instance, the combination "помогая направлять ответы модели в более этичное и полезное русло" comes across as rather heavy-handed. According to this example, we can conclude that at present, ChatGPT does not simplify phrasings during transformation into Russian for better comprehension. In particular, there is noticeable inability of the neural network to refine stylistic features of the language, resulting in sentences that could otherwise be more natural and easy to understand. In our opinion, an improved translation option could be as follows: "Для достижения нужного уровня согласования применяется метод обучения с подкреплением на основе отзывов людей. В ходе процесса модель учится отдавать предпочтение таким результатам, которые получают высокую оценку экспертов, тем самым ориентируя её ответы в сторону этичности и пользы".

Here is another example to consider:

English	Russian
Similar to the initial response, the subsequent communication from ChatGPT continued to impress us with its engaging demeanor and well-structured format	Подобно начальному ответу, последующее общение с ChatGPT продолжало впечатлять нас своим вовлечением и хорошо структурированным форматом

In this example, the main content is conveyed quite accurately. Words are chosen adequately reflecting the meaning of the original text ("engaging demeanor" → "вовлечением", "well-structured format" → "хорошо структурированный формат"). Additionally, the general logic of constructing the sentence is preserved, maintaining key structural components such as "Similar to…" → "Подобно…". There are no significant deviations from the original, thus retaining the overall meaning of the statement. However, one can point out some inaccurate translations of expressions. The expression "engaging demeanor" literally means "attractive behavior/manner of communication." The word "вовлечение" is more suitable for contexts involving interaction between users and interfaces, rather than characterizing the system's manner of communication. Perhaps it would be better to translate it as "привлекательная манера общения" or "общительность". Additionally, the Russian version sounds somewhat official and dry. The English version possesses lightness and liveliness, which are lost in translation. A notable absence of dynamics and emotionality characteristic of the English version stands out. Also, the expression "продолжало впечатлять нас" is somewhat overloaded. Instead, a simple and clear expression like "нас продолжали восхищать" could be applied.

To preserve the subtle nuances of the original version and improve the quality of the translation, you could try replacing the word "вовлечение" with a more accurate equivalent: "приятная манера общения". You could also simplify and enliven the construction by saying something like: "Подобно первому ответу, дальнейшее взаимодействие с ChatGPT приятно удивляло своей открытостью и чёткостью подачи материала".

The last example we propose to consider is given below:

English	Russian
Additionally, a noteworthy observation is that while describing the final phase, ChatGPT refers to it as a "testing and refinement process," without alluding to the specifics of reinforcement learning or any other detailed facets of the process	Кроме того, заслуживает внимания наблюдение, что, описывая заключительный этап, ChatGPT называет его "процессом тестирования и уточнения", не упоминая конкретных аспектов обучения с подкреплением или каких-либо других подробностей процесса

The distinctive feature of this example lies in the fact that ChatGPT clearly conveys the general meaning. The reader gets an understanding of what is said about the testing and refining process without detailed explanations regarding machine learning methods. At the same time, however, we must acknowledge that the natural fluidity of expression and ease of formulation have been lost. The English version boasts a more elegant structure and rhythm, whereas the Russian translation becomes overly literal and cumbersome to read. While the original flows smoothly and effortlessly, the Russian version appears artificially burdened by constructs such as "заслуживает внимания наблюдение", making it harder to perceive.

Therefore, in this case, the overload of the text can be corrected and the natural flow of thought can be improved as follows: "Кроме того, обращает внимание тот факт, что при описании финального этапа ChatGPT обозначает его как "процесс тестирования и доработки", не раскрывая деталей метода обучения с подкреплением или иных специфичных моментов". In the lighter version of the translation, emphasis is placed on maintaining simplicity and naturalness of narration.

5 Conclusions

The comparison of the received translations with the original texts shows that, in general, the AI handles the translation very well. When reading the contexts, the content becomes clear both in general and in particular perception. The system recognizes complex sentences by adding missing conjunctions where they are not present in English. Out of several lexical options, it almost always chooses the one that is most accurate and successful in a particular context, suitable stylistically. In accordance with the classification by V.N. Komissarov, the most common transformations applied by ChatGPT are transcription, transliteration, syntactic assimilation, and the minor lexico-semantic and grammatical substitutions.

The analysis of the translation of scientific texts performed by ChatGPT allows us to conclude that ChatGPT copes with this task quite successfully, preserving the meaning of the text and the nuances of the style. Such a fairly good result, achieved by artificial intelligence, the work of which is based on the prediction by the system of the next word, is explained by the very requirements for scientific translation - an accurate, almost word-for-word reproduction of the original, and can be defined by the peculiar features of scientific style itself. The absence of figurative means and stylistic devices, the presence of clichéd expressions and terminology, which is characterized by the absence of ambiguity, allows the system to create an accurate and almost word-for-word translation in compliance with the style of narration.

If the author-scientist takes stylistic liberty and violates the canons of the scientific style, the translation made with the application of artificial intelligence, can be accompanied by imperfections and mistakes.

ChatGPT's difficulties are caused by contexts that require semantic and conceptual transformations: modulation, combining/dividing sentences, descriptive translation (explication). These changes often require a significant restructuring of the sentence, which only the human brain is capable of so far.

Acknowledgment. This publication has been supported by the RUDN University Scientific Projects Grant System, project No 061011-0-000.

References

1. Rahimi, A.R., Sevilla-Pavón, A.: The role of ChatGPT readiness in shaping language teachers' language teaching innovation and meeting accountability: a bisymmetric approach. Comput. Educ. Artif. Intell. **7**, 100258 (2024)
2. Li, B., Lowell, V.L., Wang, C., Li, X.: A systematic review of the first year of publications on ChatGPT and language education: examining research on ChatGPT's use in language learning and teaching. Comput. Educ. Artif. Intell. **7**, 100266 (2024)

3. Beck, J., et al.: A tutorial on meta-reinforcement learning. Found. Trends® Mach. Learn. **18**(2–3), 224–384 (2025). https://doi.org/10.1561/2200000080
4. Papineni, K., Roukos, S., Ward, T., Zhu, W.: BLEU: a method for automatic evaluation of machine translation. In: 40th Annual Meeting of the Association for Computational Linguistics, Morris Town, pp. 311–318 (2002)
5. Wu, L., et al.: Graph neural networks for natural language processing: a survey. Found. Trends® Mach. Learn. **16**(2), 119–328 (2023). https://doi.org/10.1561/2200000096
6. Malyuga Elena, N., Rimmer, W.: Making sense of "buzzword" as a term through co-occurrences analysis. Heliyon **7**(6), e07208 (2021). https://doi.org/10.1016/j.heliyon.2021.e07208
7. Kaur, R., Klobučar, T., Gabrijelčič, D.: Harnessing the power of language models in cybersecurity: a comprehensive review. Int. J. Inf. Manag. Data Insights **5**(1), 100315 (2025). ISSN 2667-0968. https://doi.org/10.1016/j.jjimei.2024.100315
8. Ma, T.: Systematically visualizing ChatGPT used in higher education: publication trend, disciplinary domains, research themes, adoption and acceptance. Comput. Educ. Artif. Intell. **8**, 100336 (2025)
9. Aziz, W., de Sousa, S.C.M., Specia, L.: PET: a tool for post-editing and assessing machine translation. In: International Conference on Language Resources and Evaluation (2012). https://api.semanticscholar.org
10. Heung, Y.M.E., Chiu, T.K.F.: How ChatGPT impacts student engagement from a systematic review and meta-analysis study. Comput. Educ. Artif. Intell. **8**, 100361 (2025)
11. Zashikhina, I.M., Griva, O.E.: Evaluating the impact of short-term Russian language and culture programmes on adult learners. Train. Lang. Cult. **8**(4), 74–85 (2024). https://doi.org/10.22363/2521-442X-2024-8-4-74-85
12. Tan, Z., et al.: Neural machine translation: a review of methods, resources, and tools. AI Open **1**, 5–21 (2020)
13. Zubkova, O.S., Logvina, S.A.: Linguo-cultural specificity of euphemia: applied aspect. Issues Appl. Linguist. **54**, 31–62 (2024). https://doi.org/10.25076/vpl.54.02

The Use of Multimedia in Self-directed Pronunciation Learning: Vietnamese EFL Learners' Perspectives

Thi Duyen Phuong[1] and Thi Thanh Huyen Phuong[2](✉)

[1] Hanoi University of Industry, Hanoi 10000, Vietnam
[2] FPT University, Hanoi 10000, Vietnam
huyenptt3@fe.edu.vn

Abstract. Despite the growing potential of multimedia tools in assisting different aspects of English learning, limited research explores students' self-directed pronunciation learning using multimedia, especially in under-resourced contexts such as Vietnam. Addressing this gap, his study investigates university students' use of multimedia tools for English pronunciation learning within a self-directed framework. The study finds that although students frequently engaged with multimedia for general English language acquisition, pronunciation was not the primary focus. However, over half preferred multimedia tools over traditional resources, highlighting convenience, multi-sensory engagement, and accessibility—especially via smartphones. Platforms like YouTube, Facebook, and TikTok were most popular, while dedicated apps like ELSA Speak remained underutilized, primarily due to cost. While most participants found multimedia engaging and motivational, many reported limited awareness of how to effectively leverage these tools for systematic pronunciation improvement. Challenges included difficulty identifying appropriate resources, limited teacher guidance, and financial constraints. Despite moderate confidence levels, students expressed a strong preference for autonomous learning supplemented by clearer instructional support. Findings underscore the need for pedagogical scaffolding to bridge informal multimedia usage with targeted pronunciation learning outcomes in digital contexts.

Keywords: Pronunciation Learning · Multi-media Use in Pronuciation Learning · Self-Directed Pronunciation Learning · Students' Belief and Practices

1 Introduction

Systematic pronunciation teaching has been found to be critical in the development of learners' pronunciation [1], their intelligibility, comprehensibility, and thus oral communication success as a whole [2]. However, there has been a lack of agreement upon what to teach and how to teach [3] while Derwing and Munro [4] argue that appropriate answers to those questions are pertinent to ensure that time, energy, and other valuable resources would not risk being wasted on unnecessary pronunciation features without improving students' pronunciation. Additionally, systematic pronunciation teaching is

K. W. Lee and L. H. Wong (Eds.): ITEA 2025, CCIS 2643, pp. 103–115, 2026.
https://doi.org/10.1007/978-981-95-2011-4_11

also often constrained by the lack of time, [5, 6], the neglect of pronunciation in English curriculum, teachers' limited knowledge in pronunciation pedagogy [6–8] and low confidence in their legitimacy to teach English pronunciation [9, 10]. Due to many mentioned limitations of official pronunciation teaching, learners' self-directed learning takes a pivotal role in achieving competence in pronunciation and oral communication success.

The development of technology together with the increasing availability of multimedia channels has brought about abundant resources to assist learners' self-directed pronunciation learning, which is, however, poorly presented to date in English pronunciation teaching and learning research. The current study bridges the gap by examining students' perspectives and practices of using multimedia in improving their own pronunciation. In a resource-strained context such as Vietnam, multimedia arguably provides important means to enhance pronunciation learning. Therefore, gained insights in this aspect would be helpful in informing language educators and institution in fostering students' autonomy and engagement as well as tailoring tools and learning strategies to learners' needs.

2 Literature Review

2.1 Muti-media in Pronunciation Pedagogy

With advancements in educational technology, the use of multimedia has gained prominence as a tool to support language instruction. In that landscape, multimedia approaches—ranging from video-based tools and mobile apps to speech recognition and phonetic visualizations—are arguably bringing unprecedented opportunities to reshape the way pronunciation could be taught and learned in both classroom and self-access contexts. The review of literature has signified the important role of multimedia-based tools and platforms in providing interactive and immersive pronunciation learning experience for students and enhancing outcomes. For example, the utilization of YouTube-based tool, *YouGlish* [11] and *FluentU*, a video-rich platform that blends native speaker dialogues with subtitles and phonetic guides [12], is found to expose learners to a great variety of authentic English accents and enhance students' learning autonomy, engagement, and pronunciation accuracy. Pourhosein and Rahimy [13] investigate the impact of PP2 on pronunciation teaching in Iran and find that the tool improves the effectiveness of pronunciation teaching significantly. In a meta-analysis, which compares the effectiveness of computer-assisted pronunciation teaching with traditional teaching model in 20 studies with a diversity of participants who vary in contexts, ages, and levels of education, L1 backgrounds, and undergo different lengths of treatment. The study suggests computer-assisted pronunciation training benefits learners, especially beginners and university students rather school students.

Multimedia tools also enhance the effectiveness of feedback provision, which supports learners in recognizing and correcting pronunciation errors. Several apps and platforms draw learners' attention to their errors and facilitate self-correction of those errors through visual feedback (see [14] for a review), audio feedback, or the combination of both [15]. Meanwhile, multimedia tools are also found to effectively assist teachers' feedback. Multimedia tools are also found to facilitate teachers' feedback. For example,

Yang [16] examines the use of a mobile app with which students could receive teachers' feedback on their pronunciation both inside and beyond classroom. The study finds that students' engagement with the app was behaviorally, cognitively, and emotionally improved.

2.2 Muti-media in Pronunciation Teaching and Learning in Vietnam

With regards to Vietnamese ELT, the literature has highlighted constrained technological facilities as one significant challenge [17, 18]. Additionally, institutions' capacity in provide sufficient teacher training on how to use technologies in pedagogy is limited [17, 19] leading to the integration of technological innovation into classrooms being highly dependent on teachers' agency [17, 20, 21]. In the field of pronunciation pedagogy, it remains unknown the extent to which technology has been used, if it has, to assist pronunciation teaching and learning, including self-directed pronunciation learning. The scarcity of literature in this sub-field reflects limited attention to pronunciation teaching the context of Vietnam [7].

In the context that the Vietnamese government is prioritizing the acceleration of technology integration into education and English teaching in particular, it is important to gain insights from stakeholders regarding their perception of technology integration into the classroom, their expectations and challenges to better tune technological innovation into English classroom in the country. To bridge the gap, the current study focuses on two main research questions:

1. *To what extent do university students engage with multimedia for learning English pronunciation outside the classroom?*
2. *How do students perceive the potential of multimedia in the context of self-directed pronunciation learning?*
3. *What challenges do students face in using multimedia to learn pronunciation in self-directed learning contexts?*

3 Methodology

3.1 Participants and Context

This study is part of a large project focusing on pronunciation pedagogy in Vietnam, which was based at a big private university in the North of Vietnam. The university was considered one of the top technology universities in the country, in which students of all majors of study were required to have their own laptop to study and get access to administrative system on daily basis, both within and beyond classrooms. Participants involve 187 non-English major students who were in different levels of a 6-level English Preparation Course (EPC) and aged between 17 and 20.

3.2 Data Collection and Data Analysis

The current study employs a qualitative mixed-method design drawing upon a data subset of the bigger project, which was collected from a section of a survey administered to 187 students and focus-group interviews with 14 students. Prior to data collection, researchers contacted teachers for permission to get access to their classes for survey delivery, which required students around 15 min to complete. Students were informed clearly before the completion of the survey about the nature of the research, the confidentiality of their information and their right to participate and not to participate without any effect on their study results. An invitation for a follow-up focus group is included in the survey and also mentioned by the researchers at the time of survey delivery, 14 students contacted the researchers to participate in the focus group which was one week after the survey. Each interviewed student was assigned with a code ranging from P1 to P14.

Survey data were manually analyzed using Excel and serve to guide the construction of interview questions. Interview data were thematically analyzed following [22]. The survey data then were collated with interview data under themes emerging from the process of thematic analysis.

4 Findings

4.1 The Extent of Multimedia Use

Though 12 out of 14 interviewees reported using multimedia daily for English learning, pronunciation was not typically the main purpose. According to Table 1 (item 1), only 16% of surveyed students used multimedia specifically for pronunciation, while for 73% pronunciation learning might be just one of several purposes. Interview data diverged slightly from survey data with half of the participants (7/14) confirming intentional use of multimedia for pronunciation practice. This difference may stem from a higher proportion of interviewees who were particularly interested in English or planned to major in it after the EPC (2). Interviewees who reported intentionally using multimedia for pronunciation were generally motivated by the desire to sound "professional" (P2), "like native speakers" (P6, 12, 13, 14), or "fluent and natural" (P5). P4 and P12, who intended to pursue English studies, expressed a strong investment in spoken English and pronunciation. P4 explained that "a perfect pronunciation will be useful for me to find a good job in the future…". However, despite these motivations, consistent pronunciation-focused multimedia practice was relatively rare. Only one-third (32%) of surveyed students (see Item 2, Table 1) and five out of 14 interviewees reported practicing pronunciation regularly using multimedia platforms. These findings highlight a gap between students' broader multimedia engagement and their limited focus on pronunciation, suggesting that while interest exists, pronunciation learning often remains secondary or incidental in their media use.

However, two data sources illuminating each other highlight that multimedia use seems outweigh the use traditional pronunciation-learning tools (audio files, paper dictionaries, and books) as indicated by 58% surveyed participants (Table1, item 3) and all interviewees. Also, only slightly more than 5% of surveyed students disagreed that they used multimedia to learn pronunciation more frequently than traditional tools. In focus-group interviews, students cited different reasons for their preferences of multimedia for pronunciation learning mentioning the convenience (10 interviewees), effectiveness (4 interviewees), comprehensive impact on different senses of multimedia that boosted learning (2 interviewees). One representative (P12) discussed most of the mentioned strengths of multimedia in his explanation:

> Using multimedia is more convenient. For example, I often learn words and intonation through videos or films, then the content of the video or movie help me to understand the meaning of the word or intonation better. Beside that I can hear the sounds and look at the script to match spelling with sounds of words that I don't know. And just with a click I can check the transcription of any word through the website of an online dictionary. All sources of information are there and I can learn with my all senses at the same time...

Table 1. A Broad View of Multimedia-based Pronunciation Learning Behaviors

Item No	Statements	SD	D	U	A	SA
1	I regularly use multimedia tools/platforms (videos, apps, software, websites) especially to improve my English pronunciation	0%	10%	73,7%	15,8%	0%
2	I dedicate some time each week to practice pronunciation using multimedia	15,8%	10,5%	42,1%	31,6%	0%
3	I use multimedia tools more often than traditional methods (books, audio files, dictionaries...) for pronunciation practice	0%	5,3%	36,8%	36,8%	21,1%
4	I prefer using my smartphone over a computer for pronunciation practice	5,3%	10,5%	31,6%	7,7%	48,7%

Notes: Strongly Disagree (SD); Disagree (D); Unsure (U); A (Agree); Strongly Agree (SA).

Furthermore, it seems that students slightly preferred using multimedia platforms and tools on their mobile interface rather than on computers as indicated by more than half of surveyed participants (56,4%) and two third of interviewees (10). Interview data show that mobile phones enabled students' convenient access to multimedia resources in a wide range of time and physical places; thus, "I can make use of any free time I have, like... between classes, during lunch break in a coffee shop, or just some time before bedtime watching something fun in English and learn something" (P7). However, a significant proportion of participants, including more than one third of participants in both survey and interviews, expressed uncertainty regarding which devices they preferred. P3 said that "I switch quite often between the two depending the time of the day. At night I often use mobile phone more frequently. Like…you know lying comfortably on bed and learn something". Meanwhile, P11 emphasized big computer screen as "more motivating to learn anything from video-related materials" but "mobile phone is more convenient and I use either of them depending on the materials or apps I need to use".

Another aspect relating to students' multimedia using behavior is their preferred resources. Figure 1 shows that among available multimedia tools and platforms for pronunciation self-directed learning, video-based platforms including YouTube, Facebooks, online movie platforms, and TikTok were the most popular. The vast majority of surveyed students (95%) reported using YouTube videos to learn pronunciation making it the most prominent. Facebook and online movies platforms were ranked second with roughly 69% each. TikTok follows with 67%. Mobile apps, such as ELSA Speak, were favored by 43% while programs that provide visual feedback, such as Praat, seem the least popular (reported by only 5%).

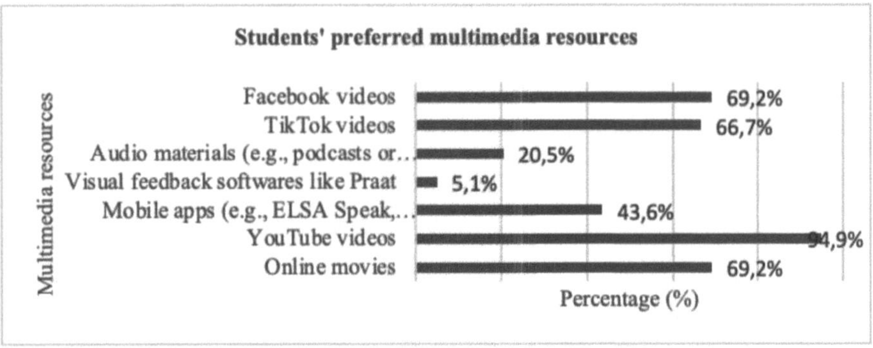

Fig. 1. Preferred multimedia resources

4.2 The Perceived Usefulness of Muti-media in Pronunciation Learning

Generally, students positively evaluated multimedia in several aspects of pronunciation learning. Table 2 shows that using multimedia facilitates the improvement of general pronunciation performance (indicated by almost 72% of surveyed students, item 6), effectively assists students' error identification (54%, item 7), and motivates pronunciation self-directed learning (more than 61%). Notably, very few students (making up less than 8%) disagreed with those advantages of using multimedia to learn pronunciation.

Interview data especially highlighted the role of multimedia in motivating students in self-directed pronunciation learning and the actual improvement of their pronunciation. All interviewees echoed each other commenting on fun nature of pronunciation learning through multimedia. P1 revealed enjoying American movies and developed his pronunciation during movie watching, making it a natural, effective process:

> When I watch American movies, I feel entertained but it benefits my pronunciation quite a lot at the same time. Gradually, when I watch a movie in English, I don't know if I am watching it mainly to entertain or to learn English speaking but I see that my spoken English is more natural now and with better intonation and rhythm.

On their part, P4, P6, and P13 confirmed the effectiveness and relaxing nature of pronunciation self-learning using media emphasizing the impact of diverse choices of materials that were available to fit with their own interest. Meanwhile, P3 and P7 stressed the role of flexible learning that allowed them to learn pronunciation when they felt "comfortable and most ready to learn".

Some interviewees expressed feeling overwhelmed by multimedia resources and unsure how to use them effectively. P4 and P5 noted that their pronunciation learning—especially in error recognition and correction—was limited, as it often occurred spontaneously during entertainment without clear goals or plans, leading to only partial improvement across pronunciation features.

> …in many cases, I am attracted by the content of the movies I am watching and pay attention to pronunciation only when some features coming out as prominent and especially attractive to me… like intonations when a character raises his voice to express some sarcasm or surprise. (P5)

> I am not sure that I could recognize many of my pronunciation errors through watching things on the media because … you know… very often that I watch movies or videos with a script and I mainly understand the content basing on what I see on the screen and the script rather than really hear what people say in there. It is just too fast for me to process the speech to really…I mean I do sometimes recognize some mistakes but… not many. And, movies or YouTube videos in English are interesting but because they are interesting, I am kind of being distracted from learning…(laugh). (P4)

Table 2. Perceived strengths of multi-media in self-directed pronunciation learning

Item No	Statements	SD	D	U	A	SA
6	Using multimedia tools are effective in improving my pronunciation	2,6%	0%	25,6%	64,1%	7,7%
7	Multimedia tools help me effectively identify my pronunciation errors	2,6%	0%	43,6%	48,7%	5,1%
8	I feel motivated to learn pronunciation through multimedia regularly	7,7%	0%	30,8%	53,8%	7,7%

Notes: Strongly Disagree (SD); Disagree (D); Unsure (U); A (Agree); Strongly Agree (SA).

4.3 Students' Confidence in Using Multimedia to Learn Pronunciation

Table 2 shows that there could be challenges for significant part of students learning pronunciation on their own using multimedia. While almost half of surveyed students (48%) confirmed their confidence in learning pronunciation on their own using multimedia, 37%

were unsure if they were and 15% clearly indicated not feeling so. Similarly, data collected from item10 (Table 2) show that only one fourth (24%) of participants (strongly) disagreed that they had difficulty in identifying effective multimedia tools/platforms to learn pronunciation while nearly twice as many participants (42%) indicated facing difficulty in doing so. Additionally, data collected from item 11 (Table 2) illustrate that though students' opinions were widely divided regarding teachers' guidance in self-directed pronunciation learning using multimedia, the lack of teachers' support was reported to troublesome at least 35% of surveyed students. Finally, financial constraint on access to apps and softwares for pronunciation practice was also confirmed by a significant number of around 45% of survey students while only half of that (21%) did not seem to see financial constraint as an obstacle (see item 12) (Table 3).

Table 3. Students' confidence in using multimedia to learn pronunciation

Item No	Statements	SD	D	U	A	SA
9	I feel confident using multimedia tools independently	7,9%	7,9%	36,8%	34,2%	13,2%
10	I find it difficult to choose effective multimedia tools for pronunciation	7,9%	15,8%	34,2%	36,8%	5,3%
11	I struggle to learn pronunciation using multimedia tools without teacher guidance	15,8%	15,8%	34,2%	31,6%	3,6%
12	I have financial difficulties in buying apps and softwares for pronunciation learning and practice	5,3%	15,8%	34,2%	39,5%	5,3%

Notes: Strongly Disagree (SD); Disagree (D); Unsure (U); A (Agree); Strongly Agree (SA).

Interview data indicate slightly stronger confidence among interviewees. Most of them (11 out of 14) said they were quite confident using multimedia tools and platforms to learn pronunciation outside classrooms citing their extensive experience using several platforms for different purposes including learning English and the perceived improvement in their pronunciation through using media as evidence. However, participants also commonly noted issues emerging from data survey including the lack of teacher support (3 interviewees) and the challenge in identifying useful multimedia tools/platform to learn pronunciation (4). One interviewee, P10, recognized the combination of both factors in hindering her learning to some extent:

> ...there are too many resources with which we can enjoy and learn pronunciation but I am not sure which materials are more effective for pronunciation learning. Usually, I just select stuffs in English to listen to because they are fun. In many cases, what I choose are really difficult to listen to or to learn from. So, it would save our time if teachers or someone more experienced in learning pronunciation on multimedia platforms could provide a suggested list of things or websites that fit our specific English levels and better benefit our pronunciation.

As can be seen in the comment, P10 was in need of personalized support from teachers which he highlighted as of great importance and but not yet evident in his self-learning setting.

In one focus group, P5 shared that he often practiced word pronunciation while watching YouTube videos, although he acknowledged that pronunciation involves more than just words, even if he couldn't identify specific components. His comment reflects a lack of systematic knowledge about pronunciation and how to approach it in self-directed learning. When asked whether teachers provided guidance on learning pronunciation outside class, participants unanimously said "no." P5 added that classroom instruction mainly emphasized word pronunciation and intonation, which shaped his own focus during self-learning. However, his peers (P6, P7, P8) expressed uncertainty about what aspects were actually covered in class, which suggests unclear or inconsistent in-class pronunciation instruction.

Highlighting the importance of learner autonomy at the university level, P2 stated that students should proactively improve their pronunciation by using diverse media resources. He agreed with P5 on the role of teachers' in-class pronunciation instruction as a guide for out-of-class practice; he said students can "rely on what teachers teach or correct" to identify the focus of their self-directed learning. However, such guidance was often too implicit, which required students' careful attention. In other cases (such as that of P6, P7, P8), the focus of teachers pronunciation instruction might not be consistent or intensive enough to be clearly recognized or effectively used to support students' self-directed pronunciation learning.

Interview data also provide insight into the financial constraints that limited students' access to multimedia software or tools. All interviewees stated that they had internet-connected mobile phones and, in particular, internet-connected laptops which was compulsory for daily learning at the university. However, very few reported using mobile apps that are specifically designed for pronunciation learning. One interviewee (P3) mentioned using Duolingo, while two others (P4 and P7) used ELSA Speak. In contrast, three participants (P6, P9, and P11) cited cost concerns as the reason for not purchasing any apps, even though they acknowledged that pronunciation-specific apps could significantly benefit their learning.

5 Discussion

This study examines the extent to which university-level English learners engage with multimedia tools for pronunciation learning, their perceptions of these tools, and the challenges they encounter in self-directed learning contexts. Overall, while the findings reveal growing students' reliance on multimedia to develop their English pronunciation, they also expose limitations in students' intentionality, learning strategies, and teachers' support structures.

Research Questions 1: To what extent do university students engage with multimedia for learning English pronunciation outside the classroom?

The study shows that while students widely accessed multimedia tools, focused engagement in pronunciation practice remained low. Interview data offered deeper insight, with half of the interviewees (7/14), who were mainly English majors or high-proficiency aspirants, reporting intentional use of multimedia for pronunciation; this suggests that academic goals shape self-directed learning behaviors. Generally, pronunciation improvement appears incidental rather than a primary aim in multimedia use. This reflects broader patterns in Vietnamese ELT, where instruction is often test-oriented and pronunciation receives minimal assessment focus, which thus lowers its instructional priority [7]. Interestingly, platforms like YouTube, Facebook, TikTok, and movie sites emerged as the most commonly used, indicating students' strong preference for visual-auditory formats that promote naturalistic and contextualized pronunciation learning.

Research Questions 2: How do students perceive the potential of multimedia in the context of self-directed pronunciation learning?

The study generally reveals students' positive attitudes toward the usefulness of multimedia tools in supporting pronunciation development and enhancing motivation, with interviewed students repeatedly highlighting multimedia as enjoyable, flexible, and effective. Students particularly valued the multi-sensory engagement offered by multimedia through the combination of visuals, text, and audio. This finding underscores the pedagogical power of multimodal learning [23], which has been proven effective in boosting learning motivation—even under the challenging conditions of online teaching during school closures amid the COVID-19 pandemic [20, 21].

Research Question 3: What challenges do students face in using multimedia to learn pronunciation in self-directed learning contexts?

The study highlights three major challenges in students' use of multimedia for pronunciation learning. First, students displayed only moderate confidence in utilizing such tools, with interviewed and surveyed participants echoed each other noting their confusion in selecting tools aligned with their proficiency and learning goals. This indicates a clear demand for tailored instructional guidance. Unfortunately, such support remains scarce, likely due to time constraints and a lack of teacher training specific to pronunciation pedagogy [6]. Second, financial limitations posed a substantial barrier for students to access premium tools like ELSA Speak or other AI-assisted applications. This financial constraint widened the gap between students' intentions and actual practices, a common issue in technologically constrained settings like Vietnam. The broader context suggests that accessing high-quality educational apps requires significant effort from both students and teachers [17]. Third, a notable deficiency in metalinguistic awareness related to pronunciation was observed. For instance, one participant (P5) admitted to focusing mainly on word-level pronunciation despite understanding its broader dimensions. Moreover, classroom instruction offered little support in this area, leaving students with few strategies to guide self-learning. This reflects the heavy reliance on error correction and feedback rather than systematic pronunciation teaching across English classrooms in Vietnam [7, 8, 10, 24, 25].

6 Conclusion and Implications

This study investigates university students' engagement with multimedia tools for self-directed pronunciation learning, their perceptions of multimedia's usefulness, and the challenges they encounter. The findings reveal a complex picture, in which students had high access to and enthusiasm for multimedia platforms but their use of these tools for pronunciation remains limited in scope and strategy.

Despite the widespread use of video-based platforms such as YouTube, Facebook, and TikTok, most learners engaged with these tools for general English learning or entertainment, with which pronunciation improvement emerged only as a secondary or incidental benefit. Nonetheless, a significant number of students, particularly those who pursued English majors or had special interest with English learning, did report focusing on the use of multimedia for pronunciation; they reported to be motivated by goals such as achieving native-like pronunciation or enhancing future employability.

Additionally, students generally expressed positive perceptions of multimedia's potential in improving pronunciation, citing its convenience, multi-sensory appeal, and motivational power. However, they also highlighted critical challenges, including a lack of confidence in selecting effective tools, insufficient teacher guidance, and financial barriers which limit their access to premium applications. Notably, the absence of structured support appears to hinder students' ability to use multimedia resources in a focused and pedagogically effective manner.

Based on the findings, this study has important implications for integrating multimedia into pronunciation pedagogy, especially in self-directed learning. First, teachers should play a more defined role in connecting classroom instruction with students' out-of-class learning by not only encouraging multimedia use but also offering explicit guidance. This includes recommending level-appropriate resources such as specific YouTube channels, mobile applications, or interactive websites. Secondly, institutional support should be strengthened, for instance, by amending the English curriculum to allocate dedicated instructional time for pronunciation. This would enable more systematic teaching of pronunciation and provide students with essential knowledge about its components and effective learning strategies. Moreover, there should be curated level-appropriate lists of multimedia resources, organized by features like intonation or connected speech, to support learners effectively. Given the high demands placed on Vietnamese educators when integrating technology [17], financial investment is needed to help teachers maintain and update these materials. Finally, students' metacognitive skills must be nurtured through course-integrated training in pronunciation goal-setting and self-monitoring. Techniques like learning journals and structured self-assessments can foster reflection, which allow learners to track their progress and refine their strategies to improve self-directed pronunciation learning.

References

1. Saito, K.: Effects of instruction on L2 pronunciation development: a synthesis of 15 quasi-experimental intervention studies. TESOL Q. **46**(4), 842–854 (2012)
2. Derwing, T.M.: The efficacy of pronunciation instruction. In: Kang, O., Murphy, J.M., Thomson, R.I. (eds.) The Routledge Handbook of Contemporary English Pronunciation, pp. 320–334. Routledge, New York (2017)
3. Darcy, I., Ewert, D., Lidster, R.: Bringing pronunciation instruction back into the classroom: an ESL teachers' pronunciation 'toolbox'. In: Levis, J., Lavelle, K. (eds.) The 3rd Pronunciation in Second Language Learning and Teaching Conference, pp. 93–108. Iowa State University, Ames (2012)
4. Derwing, T.M., Munro, M.J.: Putting accent in its place: rethinking obstacles to communication. Lang. Teach. **42**(4), 476–490 (2009)

5. Bai, B., Yuan, R.: EFL teachers' beliefs and practices about pronunciation teaching. ELT J. **73**(2), 134–143 (2019). https://doi.org/10.1093/elt/ccy040
6. Phuong, T.T.H.: Constraints of pronunciation teaching in Vietnam: teachers' beliefs and practices. J. Asia TEFL **17**(4), 1431–1438 (2020). https://doi.org/10.18823/asiatefl.2020.17.4.19.1431
7. Phuong, T.T.H.: Teaching English pronunciation at university level in Vietnam (Doctoral dissertation). University of Technology Sydney ePress (UTS ePress), Sydney (2018). https://opus.lib.uts.edu.au/handle/10453/129416
8. Phuong, T.T.H.: EFL teachers' cognition of feedback techniques on pronunciation. J. Asia TEFL **20**(2), 436–444 (2023). https://doi.org/10.18823/asiatefl.2023.20.2.14.436
9. Phuong, T.T.H.: Who should teach English pronunciation?: voices of Vietnamese EFL learners and teachers. J. Asia TEFL **18**(1), 125–141 (2021). https://doi.org/10.18823/asiatefl.2021.18.1.8.125
10. Phuong, T.T.H.: Feedback on pronunciation: Vietnamese EFL teachers' beliefs and practice. SAGE Open **12**(3), 21582440221126612 (2022). https://doi.org/10.1177/21582440221126612
11. Martin, I.A.: Playing with playback speed: practicing L2 pronunciation with YouGlish. In: Levis, J.M, Duris, M., Sonsaat-Hegelheimer, S., Na, I. (eds.) The 15th Pronunciation in Second Language Learning and Teaching Conference 2024, vol. 15, no. 1, pp.1–9. Iowa State University Digital Press, Ames (2025). https://www.iastatedigitalpress.com/psllt/article/id/18440/
12. Alvindi, A., Lubis, Y.: Teachers' perceptions of using FluentU as learning media to improve students' pronunciation. TELL-US J. **11**(1), 74–89 (2025)
13. Pourhosein Gilakjani, A., Rahimy, R.: Using computer-assisted pronunciation teaching (CAPT) in English pronunciation instruction: a study on the impact and the teacher's role. Educ. Inf. Technol. **25**(2), 1129–1159 (2020). https://doi.org/10.1007/s10639-019-10009-1
14. Bliss, H., Abel, J., Gick, B.: Computer-assisted visual articulation feedback in L2 pronunciation instruction: a review. J. Second Lang. Pronunc. **4**(1), 129–153 (2018). https://doi.org/10.1075/jslp.00006.bli
15. Chen, M.: Computer-aided feedback on the pronunciation of Mandarin Chinese tones: using Praat to promote multimedia foreign language learning. Comput. Assist. Lang. Learn. **37**(3), 363–388 (2024)
16. Yang, L.: Student engagement with teacher feedback in pronunciation training supported by a mobile multimedia application. SAGE Open **12**(2), 21582440221094604 (2022)
17. Phuong, T.T.H.: Integration of ICT into EFL classrooms: have Vietnamese primary schools progressed post-COVID-19? Issues Educ. Res. **35**(2), 759–788 (2025). http://www.iier.org.au/iier35/phuong.pdf
18. Nguyen, L.T.H.: Teachers' perception of ICT integration in English language teaching at Vietnamese tertiary level. Eur. J. Contemp. Educ. **10**(3), 697–710 (2021). https://files.eric.ed.gov/fulltext/EJ1324207.pdf
19. Dao, P., Bui, T.L.D., Nguyen, D.T.T., Nguyen, M.X.N.C.: Synchronous online English language teaching for young learners: insights from public primary school teachers in an EFL context. Comput. Assist. Lang. Learn. **37**(8), 2359–2388 (2023)
20. Phuong, T.T.H.: Learning motivation of Vietnamese EFL learners in fully online classes during COVID-19: a mixed methods study. Issues Educ. Res. **32**(2), 681–700 (2022). https://www.iier.org.au/iier32/phuong.pdf
21. Phuong, T.T.H.: Prolonged online learning: an exploratory mixed-methods study on EFL learners' needs and need satisfaction. Int. J. Emerg. Technol. Learn. **18**(4), 186–201 (2023). https://online-journals.org/index.php/i-jet/article/view/35759/12739
22. Braun, V., Clarke, V.: Using thematic analysis in psychology. Qual. Res. Psychol. **3**(2), 77–101 (2006)

23. Mayer, R.E. (ed.): The Cambridge Handbook of Multimedia Learning. Cambridge University Press, Cambridge (2005)
24. Phuong, T.T.H.: Vietnamese EFL learners' perspectives of pronunciation pedagogy. Asian EFL J. **23**(6.2), 180–201 (2019)
25. Phuong, T.T.H., Phuong, T.D.: Vietnamese learners' perspectives of corrective feedbacks on English pronunciation. ASIAN ESP J. **15**(2), 70–82 (2019). https://biblio.ugent.be/publication/8747942

Hybrid Learning in English Education: Perceptions of Vietnamese Junior High School Teachers

Thi Duyen Phuong[1] and Thi Thanh Huyen Phuong[2](✉)

[1] Hanoi University of Industry, Hanoi, Vietnam
[2] FPT University, Hanoi, Vietnam
huyenptt3@fe.edu.vn

Abstract. As hybrid learning continues to gain momentum globally, understanding how it is perceived by educators is essential for its effective integration into general education. This study investigates the perceptions of junior high school English teachers in northern Vietnam regarding the benefits, challenges, and institutional support associated with hybrid learning. A total of 384 teachers from diverse school types (public and private), geographic locations (urban, suburban, and rural), and age groups participated in a structured survey. Data were analyzed using SPSS, employing reliability checks and inferential statistics, including ANOVA and t-tests. Findings indicate that teachers generally perceive hybrid learning as beneficial for promoting personalized instruction, student autonomy, and enhanced access to digital resources. Significant differences were observed across age groups. Also, urban teachers and those aged 55 and above identified greater implementation challenges, often related to complexity and technological adaptation and students' readiness. Additionally, public school teachers reported significantly higher levels of institutional support compared to their private school counterparts.

The study highlights the need for differentiated professional development, targeted policy support, and equitable infrastructure to ensure the effective implementation of hybrid learning. It calls for the formal incorporation of hybrid learning models into Vietnam's national curriculum to align with global pedagogical shifts in the post-pandemic context.

Keywords: Hybrid learning · Teacher perceptions · EFL education · Junior high school · ICT in education

1 Introduction

Hybrid learning has become increasingly prevalent in English as a Foreign Language (EFL) education globally because of its potential to extend classroom learning, promote student autonomy, and personalize instruction through digital tools—features that are particularly beneficial in EFL contexts. In Vietnam, English is among the first foreign languages introduced across all levels of education. Although no official policy explicitly prioritizes English over other foreign languages, it has long been the most widely taught and studied language in the Vietnamese school system [1].

K. W. Lee and L. H. Wong (Eds.): ITEA 2025, CCIS 2643, pp. 116–128, 2026.
https://doi.org/10.1007/978-981-95-2011-4_12

Furthermore, the transition from traditional to digital schooling reflects a broader shift in Vietnam's educational philosophy and policy, as demonstrated in key national directives such as Decision No. 131/QĐ-TTg, Decision No. 3806/QĐ-BGDĐT, and Decision No. 1600/QĐ-TTg. These policies emphasize digital transformation and innovation in teaching and learning. While hybrid learning models have been adopted in many higher education institutions and private language centers, they remain absent from the official curriculum in general education. The acceleration of digital transformation—particularly in response to the COVID-19 pandemic—has increased awareness of and demand for hybrid approaches. Investigating teachers' perceptions of this shift is therefore crucial for informing future policy, curriculum reform, and teacher professional development in Vietnamese EFL education.

This study aims to explore junior high school English teachers' perceptions of hybrid learning across three dimensions: perceived benefits, implementation challenges, and institutional support and training. By focusing on teachers from diverse school locations, types, and age groups, the study provides nuanced insights into how contextual and demographic factors shape teachers' attitudes toward hybrid learning in English education.

2 Literature Review

2.1 Concept of Hybrid Learning

Hybrid learning, also referred to as blended learning, encompasses a variety of heterogeneous and diversified structures and format [2]. It is an instructional approach that integrates traditional face-to-face classroom with online and technology-enhanced components. Hybrid learning model combines the strengths of in-person instruction with digital tools, fostering opportunities for collaborative, constructive, and computer-assisted learning (CAI) to provide learners with multiple pathways for engagement, making diverse learning options accessible and adaptable to different needs and contexts [3, 4].

2.2 Previous Studies

Hybrid learning has attracted scholarly attention even prior to the COVID-19 pandemic. For instance, Sorbie [5] found that blended learning enhanced personalization, collaboration, organization, and learner engagement, although challenges such as student distraction and technological limitations were still recognized. Similarly, Nguyen [6], in a study on hybrid learning in tertiary education, emphasized its impact on pedagogical approaches and classroom dynamics. In the same vein, Raymond [7] reported teachers' strong appreciation for the potential of technology in facilitating instructional personalization, but also noted barriers such as inadequate professional development and limited digital infrastructure. These challenges were further highlighted in a study by Jerry and Yunus [8] who identified low ICT competence and insufficient infrastructure as major obstacles to the implementation of hybrid learning in Malaysia's Betong district. In Indonesia, Pardede [9] reported that EFL pre-service teachers valued blended learning for its flexibility, convenience, and improved access to learning resources. However, the study simultaneously revealed that many of these pre-service teachers still preferred face-to-face instruction because of its immediacy of feedback, direct interaction, and the comfort of printed materials. Likewise, Rachman, Sudiyono and research group [10] found that both teachers and students in Bandung (Indonesia) viewed blended learning as a practical solution to the limitations of fully online or fully traditional methods, particularly for enhancing English language proficiency—despite ongoing challenges in material development and media use. More recently, Maes, Zong and research group [11] observed that while lecturers and postgraduate students across Europe recognized the value of blended learning as a cost-effective supplement to traditional teaching, they remained hesitant to adopt it as a full replacement for conventional instructional approaches.

In recent years, hybrid learning and the integration of information and communication technologies (ICT) have gained significant momentum in English language education in Vietnam. Yen, Hien, and colleagues [12] investigated university students' perceptions of a blended learning environment for English training and reported generally favorable responses. Additional studies by Phuong [13–16] have contributed to this growing body of research, examining Vietnamese EFL learners' familiarity with online gamification tools and their attitudes toward gamified learning, motivations in online classes, and more recently, the integration of ICT in primary-level EFL classrooms. Expanding this line of inquiry, Nguyen, Sivapalan and group [17] surveyed 1,500 English teachers and conducted interviews with five participants, revealing overall positive perceptions of blended learning. Similarly, Tran [18] reported encouraging stakeholder feedback, highlighting hybrid learning's perceived advantages such as cost-effectiveness, enhanced student motivation, personalized instruction, and well-structured digital materials. Collectively, these studies underscore a growing acceptance of hybrid learning in Vietnamese EFL contexts, although concentrated primarily in higher education and experimental settings.

Despite these promising findings, several studies have also highlighted persistent challenges. Nhu, Keong [19] identified barriers to ICT integration in English teaching, including limited teacher competence, inadequate infrastructure, large class sizes, excessive workloads, and insufficient technical and institutional support. These findings are echoed in a more recent study which examined similar constraints at the tertiary education level in Vietnam by Le, Allen [20]. While blended and hybrid learning models have increasingly been implemented in higher education and private language centers—particularly in the post-COVID-19 era—there is, to our knowledge, no documented evidence of formal adoption or integration of hybrid learning or online resources at the general education level in any school or region. This study aims to contribute modestly to addressing this research gap by investigating the perceptions of English teachers regarding the use of hybrid learning in lower-secondary English education in Vietnam. Specifically, the research seeks to answer the following questions:

1. What are English teachers' perceptions of the benefits of using hybrid learning in English education for lower-secondary students?
2. What are the perceived challenges in implementing hybrid learning in English education for lower-secondary students?

3. How do English teachers perceive institutional support and training for implementing hybrid learning?

3 Methodology

This study employed a quantitative research design to investigate junior high school English teachers' perceptions of hybrid learning in English education at the lower-secondary level in northern Vietnam. A structured questionnaire was administered to collect data from teachers across diverse school contexts and demographic backgrounds.

A total of 500 questionnaires—delivered via both paper-based forms and an online version (Google Form)—were distributed. To ensure consistency, the questionnaire content was identical across both formats. The sample included teachers from urban, rural, and suburban areas in northern Vietnam, drawn from both public and private schools. Respondents were grouped into four age categories: 20–30, 31–40, 41–55, and over 55 years. The instrument was designed to examine teachers' perceptions across three key domains of hybrid learning: perceived benefits, perceived challenges, and institutional training and support. Of the 500 questionnaires distributed, 384 valid responses were received, yielding a high response rate suitable for statistical analysis. Participation was voluntary, and all respondents were informed about the purpose of the study, their right to withdraw, and the confidentiality of their responses. Anonymity was ensured throughout the research process. Data were analyzed using IBM SPSS Statistics. Descriptive statistics were used to summarize teacher perceptions, while inferential analyses, including ANOVA and independent samples T-tests, were employed to examine group differences by school location, age group, and school type.

To assess the internal consistency of the survey instrument, Cronbach's alpha was calculated for each of the three subscales based on the 384 teacher responses. The Perceived Benefits of Hybrid Learning scale (5 items) demonstrated high reliability ($\alpha = .882$), with item–total correlations ranging from .582 to .850. The Challenges of Hybrid Learning scale (5 items) showed acceptable reliability ($\alpha = .803$), with item–total correlations between .459 and .706. Finally, the Institutional Support and Training scale (4 items) exhibited good internal consistency ($\alpha = .830$), with item–total correlations ranging from .532 to .841. Among the three constructs, perceived benefits demonstrated the highest internal consistency, indicating a strong and coherent response pattern. Although the challenges scale had slightly lower reliability, it still exceeded the recommended threshold ($\alpha > .70$), confirming that all subscales are psychometrically sound and suitable for further analysis (Table 1).

4 Findings

4.1 Perceptions of Hybrid Learning Among Junior High School English Teachers

Descriptive statistics for teachers' perceptions of hybrid learning, including three key dimensions—namely Benefits, Challenges, and Institutional Support & Training—are presented in Table 2. The results indicate that while teachers generally hold a positive view of hybrid learning, they also recognize several practical and systemic obstacles that may affect its effective implementation.

Table 1. Instrument reliability summary for teachers' perceptions of hybrid learning (N = 384)

Scale	Items	Corrected item–Total correlation	Cronbach's Alpha if item deleted
Benefits of hybrid learning (α = .882)	Students' autonomy and responsibility	.582	.886
	Learning flexibility and personalization	.732	.854
	Alignment with global education	.789	.848
	Development of essential skills	.850	.824
	Access English learning materials	.703	.862
Challenges of hybrid learning (α = .803)	Increasing teachers' workload	.635	.751
	Insufficient technical support	.459	.801
	Students' lack of the self-discipline	.706	.725
	Effectiveness in managing students	.592	.764
	Technical difficulties	.559	.775
Institutional support and training (α = .830)	Clear guidelines and policies	.723	.768
	Institutional support	.532	.837

(*continued*)

Table 1. *(continued)*

Scale	Items	Corrected item–Total correlation	Cronbach's Alpha if item deleted
	Sufficient ICT infrastructure	.841	.699
	Ongoing technical support	.618	.804

Notes: All items used a 5-point Likert scale (1 (= Strongly Disagree) to 5 (= Strongly Agree)). N = 384 teachers.
Internal consistency was acceptable to high across all three subscales (Cronbach's $\alpha > .800$).

In terms of benefits, teachers expressed moderately strong agreement with statements highlighting the pedagogical advantages of hybrid learning. Mean scores in this dimension ranged from 3.250 to 4.333. The highest-rated item was "Incorporating hybrid learning into English education aligns with global trends in teaching and learning" (M = 4.333, SD = .47), suggesting that teachers are aware of hybrid learning's relevance in contemporary educational contexts. Other items—such as those emphasizing access to diverse learning materials and the development of digital skills—also received favorable ratings. However, teachers were less confident about the extent to which hybrid learning supports student autonomy and responsibility (M = 3.250). The challenges associated with hybrid learning were also acknowledged. Responses in this dimension showed mean values ranging from 3.083 to 4.042. Teachers expressed particular concern about students' lack of self-discipline (M = 4.042, SD = .61) and the limitations of technical support during hybrid teaching (M = 3.833). While increased workload from preparing separate materials for online and face-to-face instruction was recognized (M = 3.083), this was rated lower than concerns related to student engagement and technology. The third dimension, Institutional Support & Training, received the highest overall mean scores, ranging from 3.141 to 4.635. The strongest agreement was with the item "Institutional support affects my willingness to adopt and maintain hybrid teaching practices" (M = 4.635, SD = .48), underscoring the critical role of administrative and systemic support. Teachers also strongly agreed that clear guidelines and ongoing technical support are essential for successful implementation. However, the relatively low rating for the adequacy of ICT infrastructure (M = 3.141, SD = .75) points to concerns about whether schools are sufficiently equipped to support hybrid teaching effectively.

Altogether, the findings suggest that teachers view hybrid learning as a valuable instructional approach with clear benefits for students. At the same time, their responses emphasize the importance of addressing key challenges—particularly those related to student readiness, technological limitations, and increased workload—while strengthening institutional support to ensure effective and sustainable hybrid teaching practices.

Table 2. Teachers' perceptions of hybrid learning across three dimensions (N = 384)

Dimension	Survey Item	Min	Max	M	SD
Benefits	Students' autonomy and responsibility	3.0	5.0	3.88	.67
	Learning flexibility and personalization	4.0	5.0	4.33	.47
	Alignment with global educational trends	2.0	5.0	3.25	.72
	Digital literacy and self-regulation	3.0	5.0	3.97	.50
	Diverse, updated learning materials	2.0	4.0	3.41	.57
Challenges	Increasing teachers' workload	2.0	4.0	3.08	.64
	Insufficient technical support	3.0	5.0	3.83	.47
	Lack of students' self-discipline	3.0	5.0	4.04	.61
	Effectiveness in managing students	2.0	4.0	3.25	.60
	Student's technical difficulties	3.0	5.0	3.79	.50
Institutional support & training	Clear institutional guidelines	4.0	5.0	4.59	.49
	Influence of institutional support	4.0	5.0	4.64	.48
	Adequacy of ICT infrastructure	2.0	4.0	3.14	.75
	Importance of ongoing technical support	3.0	5.0	4.01	.61

(*continued*)

Table 2. (*continued*)

Note. M = Mean; SD = Standard Deviation. Items were rated on a 5-point Likert scale from 1 = Strongly Disagree to 5 = Strongly Agree.

4.2 Teachers' Perceptions of the Benefits of Hybrid Learning Across Demographic Variables

Table 3 presents a comparative analysis of junior high school English teachers' perceptions of the benefits of hybrid learning across school location, age group, and school type. The results show no statistically significant differences in mean perception scores across school locations—urban (M = 3.775, SD = .51), suburban (M = 3.622, SD = .42), and rural (M = 3.743, SD = .48)—as all groups fall within the same Tukey HSD subset. Similarly, public (M = 3.709, SD = .51) and private (M = 3.708, SD = .42) school teachers demonstrated comparable perceptions, with no significant differences observed. In contrast, age group emerged as a notable factor associated with variation in perception. Teachers aged 20–30 reported the highest mean score (M = 4.000, SD = .43), significantly higher than those in the 31–40 (M = 3.486, SD = .39) and 41–55 (M = 3.650, SD = .43) age groups. Additionally, the 55+ age group (M = 3.880, SD = .44) reported significantly higher scores than the 31–40 group. Overall, the most consistent perceptions were seen across school types and locations, whereas age-related differences highlight the importance of generational perspectives in shaping attitudes toward pedagogical innovation.

Table 3. Perceived hybrid learning benefits across dimensions (N = 384)

Variable group	Category	n	M	SD	Turkey subset	Significant difference
Location	Urban	128	3.78	.51	1	No significance
	Suburb	144	3.62	.42	1	No significance
	Rural	112	3.74	.48	1	No significance
Age group	20–30	64	4.00	.43	3	Highest
	31–40	112	3.49	.39	1	Lowest
	41–55	128	3.65	.43	2	Lower than 20–30
	55+	80	3.88	.44	2–3	Higher than 31–40
School	Public	208	3.71	.51	–	No significance
type	Private	176	3.71	.42	–	No significance

Note. M = Mean; SD = Standard deviation. Tukey subsets represent homogeneous groups determined via post hoc comparisons ($p < .05$). "Significant difference" indicates whether post hoc tests showed statistically significant differences between groups.

4.3 Teachers' Perceptions of Hybrid Learning Challenges Across Demographic Variables

An overview of junior high school English teachers' perceptions of the challenges associated with hybrid learning across different school locations, age groups, and school types is presented in Table 4. The data reveal statistically significant differences by school location. Teachers in urban schools reported the highest level of perceived challenge (M = 3.800, SD = .50), significantly greater than those in suburban (M = 3.422, SD = .47) and rural schools (M = 3.629, SD = .50), suggesting increased implementation complexity in urban settings. Suburban teachers perceived significantly fewer challenges than both urban and rural counterparts. In terms of age, teachers aged 55 and above (M = 3.800, SD = .50) reported significantly higher levels of challenge than those aged 31–40 (M = 3.543, SD = .39) and 41–55 (M = 3.525, SD = 0.31). However, the 20–30 age group (M = 3.650, SD = .61) did not differ significantly from any other group, suggesting varied perceptions among early-career educators. No significant differences were found between public (M = 3.527, SD = .31) and private school teachers (M = 3.677, SD = .39), indicating that institutional type may exert less influence on perceived implementation challenges. These findings underscore the importance of context-specific support, particularly in urban environments and for older teachers who may face heightened difficulties in adapting to hybrid teaching models.

Table 4. Perceived challenges across dimensions (N = 384)

Variable group	Category	n	M	SD	Tukey subset	Significant difference
Location	Urban	128	3.80	.50	3	Greatest
	Suburb	144	3.42	.47	1	Lowest
	Rural	112	3.63	.50	2	Higher than suburban
Age group	20–30	64	3.65	.61	1–2	No significance
	31–40	112	3.54	.39	1	No significance
	41–55	128	3.53	.31	1	No significance
	55+	80	3.80	.50	2	Highest
School	Public	208	3.53	.31	–	No significance
type	Private	176	3.68	.39	–	No significance

Note. M = Mean; SD = Standard deviation. Tukey subsets represent homogeneous groupings identified by post hoc analysis ($p < .05$). "Significant difference" indicates whether post hoc tests showed statistically significant differences between groups.

4.4 Teachers' Perceptions of Institutional Training and Support for Hybrid Learning Implementation Across Demographic Variables

Teachers' perceptions of institutional support and training for hybrid learning varied significantly across school locations, age groups, and school types, as shown in Table 5. Urban teachers reported the highest levels of perceived institutional support (M = 4.31, SD = .35), significantly greater than their suburban (M = 4.00, SD = .40) and rural (M = 3.91, SD = .41) counterparts. Suburban teachers, in particular, reported the lowest levels of support and training, suggesting potential disparities in resource allocation and administrative support between geographic areas. Regarding age, teachers in the youngest group (20–30) perceived the highest levels of institutional support (M = 4.35, SD = .43), significantly higher than those aged 31–40 (M = 4.04, SD = .39) and 41–55 (M = 3.93, SD = .43). Similarly, the oldest cohort (55+) also reported stronger support (M = 4.16, SD = .44), indicating that both early-career and more experienced teachers felt better supported than those in mid-career. In contrast, teachers aged 31–40 and 41–55 consistently perceived lower levels of institutional training and support. Finally, significant differences were observed by school type: teachers from public schools reported higher support and training levels (M = 4.44, SD = .35) compared to those in private schools (M = 3.78, SD = .29). These findings suggest a need for more equitable and targeted institutional support, especially for suburban schools, mid-career teachers, and private educational institutions, to ensure consistent implementation of hybrid learning across contexts.

Table 5. Teachers 'perceives of institutional support & training across dimensions (N = 384)

Variable group	Category	n	M	SD	Tukey Subset	Significant difference
Location	Urban	128	4.31	.35	2	Greatest
	Suburb	144	4.00	.40	1	Lowest
	Rural	112	3.91	.41	1	Higher than Suburban
Age group	20–30	64	4.35	.43	2	Higher than 31–40 & 41–55
	31–40	112	4.04	.39	1	Lower than 20–30 & 55+
	41–55	128	3.93	.43	1	Lower than 20–30 & 55+
	55+	80	4.16	.44	2	Higher than 31–40 & 41–55
School type	Public	208	4.44	.35	–	Higher than private
	Private	176	3.78	.29	–	Lower than public

Note. M = Mean; SD = Standard deviation. Tukey subset indicates statistically homogeneous groupings ($p < .05$). "Significant Difference" summarizes the result of post hoc comparisons based on Tukey HSD.

5 Discussion

This study provides a detailed examination of junior high school English teachers' perceptions of hybrid learning in Vietnam, focusing on three critical dimensions: perceived benefits, perceived challenges, and institutional support and training. The findings highlight how perceptions vary significantly across age groups, with more subtle differences based on school location and school type. Among all demographic variables, age group emerged as the most influential factor. Teachers aged 20–30 reported the highest perceptions of benefits (M = 4.00) and institutional support (M = 4.35), coupled with moderate challenge scores (M = 3.65). This suggests younger teachers are more adaptable and confident, likely due to recent exposure to digital tools and hybrid pedagogy through updated teacher education programs. In contrast, the 31–40 age group reported the lowest scores in all areas—benefits (M = 3.49), support (M = 4.04), and challenges (M = 3.54)—indicating a potential "mid-career dip." This may reflect increased workloads, limited access to updated training, or administrative pressures that reduce engagement with hybrid innovation. Interestingly, the oldest age group (55+) reported relatively high perceptions of benefits (M = 3.88) and institutional support (M = 4.16), yet also perceived the greatest challenges (M = 3.80). This duality suggests that senior teachers value hybrid learning but may find it more difficult to adapt to its technological and pedagogical requirements. These age-related patterns emphasize the need for professional development that is both age-responsive and sensitive to teachers' career stages. Regarding school location, there were no significant differences in perceived benefits, but clear contrasts emerged in terms of challenges and institutional support. Urban teachers reported the highest challenges (M = 3.80) and strongest support (M = 4.31), indicating that while resources may be more available, the complexity of implementation—perhaps due to class sizes, rapid digitalization, or heightened expectations—poses difficulties. Suburban teachers noted the lowest challenges (M = 3.42) and support (M = 4.00), suggesting more stable but less resource-rich environments. Rural teachers reported moderate scores in both areas—support (M = 3.91) and challenges (M = 3.63)—pointing to average conditions for hybrid integration. In terms of school type, perceptions of benefits and challenges were nearly identical for both public and private school teachers (M = 3.71). However, a significant difference appeared in institutional support, with public school teachers reporting stronger support (M = 4.44) than private school teachers (M = 3.78). This may reflect disparities in government-backed training programs and infrastructure investments. Comparisons with existing literature reinforce and expand on these findings. Consistent with Raymond [7] and Pardede [9], participants in this study—particularly younger and older teachers—acknowledged the pedagogical value of hybrid learning, including its potential to enhance personalization, flexibility, and student autonomy. These positive views align with previous studies in Vietnam's tertiary sector (Yen et al., 2019; Nguyen et al., 2021; Tran [18], suggesting a growing national receptiveness to blended models. However, this study also confirms persistent implementation barriers documented in both global and local literature. For instance, Jerry and Yunus [8] and Rachman and research group [10] cited low ICT competence and inadequate infrastructure as critical issues in Malaysia and Indonesia, respectively—factors echoed here, particularly in urban schools and among older educators. Likewise, in Vietnam, Nhu et al. (2019) and Le et al. (2022) highlighted challenges such as insufficient technical support and heavy workloads, which also surfaced in this study's findings. Finally, the study underscores the critical role of institutional support in shaping perceptions of hybrid learning. While public school teachers reported notably higher levels of support than their private school counterparts, the relatively low perceptions of support among suburban teachers and those in mid-career (aged 31–40 and 41–55) reveal areas where targeted policy intervention and resource investment are urgently needed.

6 Conclusion

This study explored junior high school English teachers' perceptions of hybrid learning in the context of Vietnam's general education system, focusing on three core dimensions: perceived benefits, perceived challenges, and institutional support and training. Drawing on responses from 384 teachers across diverse age groups, school types, and geographic locations in northern Vietnam, the study revealed both consistent patterns and critical differences in how hybrid learning is viewed and experienced.

The findings indicate that teachers overall acknowledged the pedagogical benefits of hybrid learning, particularly in enhancing personalization, student autonomy, and access to digital resources. Notably, teachers in the youngest (20–30) and oldest (55+) age groups held more favorable views, while those in the mid-career (31–40) range were less convinced. Teachers' perceptions of challenges varied significantly by both age and school location. Urban teachers and those aged 55 and above reported the highest levels of difficulty, indicating that even well-resourced environments can be burdened by technological complexity and logistical barriers. In contrast, suburban teachers perceived the fewest challenges, potentially reflecting more manageable class sizes or school environments—though not necessarily greater readiness or support. Institutional support emerged as a critical factor influencing teachers' readiness and confidence to implement hybrid learning. Public school teachers consistently reported higher levels of institutional backing than those in private schools. Furthermore, younger and older teachers felt more supported than their mid-career counterparts, highlighting a potential professional development gap among those in the 31–40 and 41–55 age brackets.

These findings point to several practical implications for policy and practice. Strengthening institutional support—particularly in private and suburban schools—is essential to ensure equitable access to resources and capacity-building. In urban schools, where technological expectations are high, policies must address the complexity of hybrid implementation by enhancing logistical and technical support. Additionally, professional development programs should be differentiated based on age groups, with early-career teachers receiving advanced training in digital tools and older teachers provided with structured mentorship. Finally, to align with global trends and capitalize on post-pandemic shifts in pedagogy, Vietnam's national curriculum should formally integrate hybrid learning models into general education policy and practice.

References

1. Phuong, T.D., Vanderstraeten, R.: The "Hidden Curriculum" of Vietnam's English School Textbooks. Springer, Singapore (2024). https://doi.org/10.1007/978-981-97-1196-3
2. Xiao, J., Sun-Lin, H., Wang, L.: What makes learners a good fit for hybrid learning? Learning competences as predictors of experience and satisfaction in hybrid learning space. Br. J. Edu. Technol. **51**(4), 1203–1219 (2020)
3. Dangwal, K.L.: Blended learning: an innovative approach. Univ. J. Educ. Res. **5**(1), 129–136 (2017)
4. Nørgård, R.T.: Theorising hybrid lifelong learning. Br. J. Edu. Technol. **52**(4), 1709–1723 (2021)
5. Sorbie, J.: Exploring teacher perceptions of blended learning. Doctoral dissertation. Walden University, USA (2015)
6. Nguyen, G.H.: Teachers' roles in EFL blended language learning at tertiary level in Vietnam: their views, their practice. Doctoral dissertation. University of Canberra, Australia (2017)
7. Raymond, S.C.: High school teacher perceptions of blended learning. Doctoral dissertation. Walden University, USA (2019)
8. Jerry, M., Yunus, M.M.: Blended learning in rural primary ESL classroom: do or don't. Int. J. Learn. Teach. Educ. Res. **20**(2), 152–173 (2021)
9. Pardede, P.: Pre-service EFL teachers' perception of blended learning. J. Engl. Teach. **5**(1), 1–14 (2019)
10. Rachman, L.A., Sudiyono, S., Nurkamto, J.: The blended learning implementation of ELT based on teachers' and students' perspective in new normal condition of COVID-19. PROJECT (Prof. J. Engl. Educ.) **4**(3), 457–464 (2021)

11. Maes, D.M., Zong, J., Smits-Engelsman, B.C.M., Fieuws, S.: The use of blended learning in postgraduate education in orthodontics: student versus teacher perception. Eur. J. Orthod. **45**(3), 258–265 (2019)
12. Yen, P.H., Hien, T.T.T., Thao, N.T.P.: Students' perceptions of a blended learning environment for English training at a university in Vietnam. Can Tho Univ. J. Sci. **11**(3), 57–64 (2019)
13. Phuong, H.: Gamified learning: are Vietnamese EFL learners ready yet? Int. J. Emerg. Technol. Learn. (iJET) **15**(24), 242–251 (2020)
14. Phuong, T.T.H.: Learning motivation of Vietnamese EFL learners in fully online classes during Covid-19: a mixed methods study. Issues Educ. Res. **32**(2), 681–700 (2022)
15. Phuong, T.T.H.: Integration of ICT into EFL classrooms: have Vietnamese primary schools progressed post-COVID-19? Issues Educ. Res. **35**(2), 759–778 (2025). http://www.iier.org.au/iier35/phuong.pdf
16. Phuong, T.T.H.: Prolonged online learning: an exploratory mixed-methods study on EFL learners' needs and need satisfaction: online learning: needs and need satisfaction. Int. J. Emerg. Technol. Learn. (Online) **18**(4), 186 (2023)
17. Nguyen, H.T.T., Sivapalan, S., Dinh, T.T.M.: Teaching English as a second language in Vietnam: transitioning from the traditional learning approach to the blended learning approach. In: International Conference on Management, Social Sciences & Humanities (ICMeSH 2020), 01003. SHS Web of Conferences, vol. 124, p. 01003 (2021)
18. Tran, T.T.: Online-merge-offline model for distance learning in English language education: a case study. Vietnam J. Educ., 215–226 (2023)
19. Nhu, P.T.T., Keong, Y.C., Hung, T.D.: Issues and challenges in using ICT for teaching English in Vietnam. Comput. Assist. Lang. Learn. Electron. J. **20**(3), 140–155 (2019)
20. Le, T.N., Allen, M., Hoang, T.P.T., Tran, M.T.: Blended learning: barriers and drawbacks for English language lecturers at Vietnamese universities. E-Learn. Digit. Media **19**(2), 225–239 (2022)

The Application of Deep Learning-Based Intelligent Translation Technique Training and Evaluation System in French Language Teaching

Wen Pu(✉)

FANYI University, Xi'an 710105, Shaanxi, China
pupuwenwen@126.com

Abstract. Recently, the rapid development of artificial intelligence (AI) and computer technology has promoted the widespread application of intelligent translation systems in various industries, demonstrating enormous potential and important value. In the study and practice of French, the role of translation is irreplaceable. However, traditional French translation teaching is limited by resources, methods, and evaluation tools, making it difficult to meet the growing personalized learning needs of students. In view of this, this article designs an intelligent translation skill training and evaluation system based on deep learning (DL), injecting new impetus into French language teaching using advanced technology. This system can provide diverse translation exercises based on students' specific abilities and needs, encouraging students to challenge themselves and make continuous progress in practice. At the same time, it can provide real-time feedback and evaluation of students' performance, helping them to grasp their own translation skills in real time, identify problems, and make improvements. Experimental results have shown that the system can effectively evaluate students' translation quality, not only improving their translation skills, but also enhancing their learning interest and enthusiasm.

Keywords: Intelligent translation · Skill training · Evaluation system · French teaching

1 Introduction

Against the backdrop of accelerating global economic integration, trade and cultural exchanges between countries are becoming increasingly frequent, and the importance of language as a bridge of communication is self-evident [1]. With the continuous deepening of cooperation between China and countries around the world, the demand for French translation has also shown explosive growth [2]. In the process of learning and using French, translation, as an important part of language application, directly affects the accuracy of information transmission and the depth of understanding [3]. Therefore, how to effectively evaluate the quality of translation has become the key to improving

K. W. Lee and L. H. Wong (Eds.): ITEA 2025, CCIS 2643, pp. 129–138, 2026.
https://doi.org/10.1007/978-981-95-2011-4_13

the level of French teaching and translation ability [4]. The traditional evaluation of translation quality mainly relies on manual scoring. Although this method can ensure the accuracy and professionalism of the evaluation, it is limited by factors such as high labor costs and long evaluation cycles, making it hard to meet the large-scale and efficient translation needs [5]. With the rapid growth of AI technology, intelligent scoring systems have emerged and become one of the current research hotspots [6].

The intelligent scoring system utilizes sophisticated technologies such as natural language processing (NLP), machine learning (ML), and DL to achieve automatic scoring and feedback of translated texts, greatly improving the efficiency and precision of evaluation [7]. However, although existing online calibration systems have played a certain role in alleviating translation needs, there are still many shortcomings. Domestic and foreign scholars have conducted extensive and in-depth research. Hu [8] proposed a machine vision based English translation robot error text detection system, which uses convolutional neural networks (CNN) to construct separators and achieves intelligent detection of English translation error texts, improving the accuracy and efficiency of error recognition. Di [9] designed an English translation proofreading system within the framework of phrase and syntax based statistical machine translation (MT). Although the system performed well in correcting the accuracy of phrases and syntax, it overlooked the importance of contextual coherence, which affected the overall quality of translation. Jiang [10] has developed a grammar error detection and correction system based on Transformer enhanced architecture to address grammar issues in Chinese English translation, effectively improving the ability to identify and correct grammar errors.

Chen et al. [11] proposed a translation quality evaluation method based on discrete HOPFILD neural network (DHNN) and entropy weight TOPSIS algorithm. By constructing a comprehensive evaluation model, a quantitative evaluation of translation quality was achieved, providing a new approach for objective evaluation of translation quality. This article proposes an intelligent translation skill training and evaluation system based on DL, aiming to inject new vitality into French language teaching through advanced technological means. This system fully integrates the latest research results in areas such as DL and natural language processing, and can provide diverse translation tasks based on students' actual level and personalized needs, ensuring that students constantly challenge themselves and improve their translation abilities in practice. Meanwhile, the system can also provide real-time feedback and evaluation for students, using DL models to conduct detailed analysis of translated texts, pointing out specific problems that students have in the translation process, and providing corresponding improvement suggestions, so that students can timely understand their translation level, identify shortcomings, and make targeted improvements.

2 Methodology

2.1 System Construction

In today's globalized world, language translation has become a bridge connecting different cultures and countries [12]. French, as a language with a long history and an important position in international communication, the accuracy of its translation is particularly important [13]. However, traditional translation teaching and practice are often limited by the speed and efficiency of manual proofreading, making it difficult to meet the growing demand for high-quality translation [14]. Especially in the area of education, how to effectively improve students' French translation accuracy has been an urgent issue to be solved [15]. This article proposes an intelligent translation skill training and evaluation system based on DL, which aims to improve students' French translation ability through automation and personalization, and ensure the reliability of translation quality [16]. This system combines advanced DL algorithms with the practical needs of translation teaching, aiming to provide students with an effectual and accurate platform for translation training and evaluation. The system can intelligently generate diverse translation tasks based on students' actual level and personalized needs, ensuring that students constantly challenge themselves and improve their translation abilities in practice.

At the same time, the system uses real-time feedback and evaluation mechanisms, and employs DL models to conduct detailed analysis of translated texts, identifying specific problems that students face during the translation process and providing targeted improvement suggestions [17]. The system is divided into four modules, with the corpus input module responsible for inputting student translations and generating formatted corpus files through automated processing. This provides basic data support for subsequent translation analysis and evaluation. After the corpus file is generated, the system analyzes the corpus through a feature extraction module and uses advanced extraction algorithms to extract key features from the translated text. Based on the extracted features, the model construction module uses DL algorithm to construct a scoring model and generates corresponding model files. This model can objectively and accurately evaluate students' translated works. According to the scoring model, the feedback evaluation module scores students' translations and generates detailed feedback comments. The comments not only point out the problems in the translation, but also provide specific improvement suggestions to help students clarify their direction for improvement.

Grammar errors are an important factor affecting the quality of French translation. Traditional recurrent neural network (RNN) models have shortcomings in French grammar correction, such as difficulty in dealing with constantly changing French grammar errors and excessive reliance on word morphology changes. In response to these challenges, this paper proposes a French translation grammar correction model that combines sequence to sequence (Seq2Seq) with attention mechanism, as shown in Fig. 1. This model utilizes CNN in the encoder to extract character level vectors of input French sentences, and then feeds these vectors into a bidirectional long short-term memory network (BiLSTM) to capture contextual information, thereby improving the accuracy of grammar correction. Subsequently, these contextual information are fed into a decoder with attention mechanism, through which the model can recognize and weight words and sentences containing grammatical errors, achieving precise and efficient French translation grammar correction.

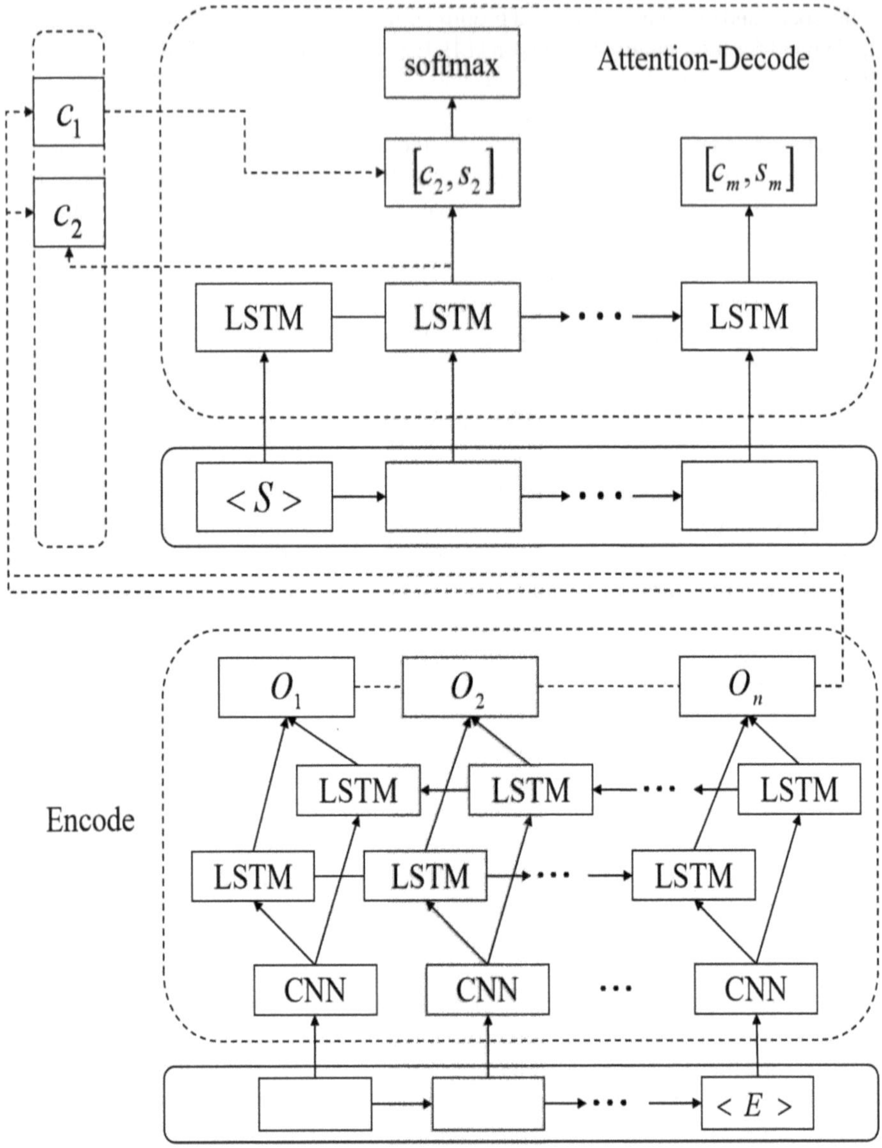

Fig.1. Model structure

2.2 Algorithm Principle

The working principle of the Seq2Seq network model is to first use an encoder to encode the input raw sequence, thereby capturing and integrating the overall semantic information. Subsequently, this semantic information is passed to the decoder, which decodes the sequence of this information through its neural network, and finally maps and generates the target sequence. In the encoding stage, the neural network of the encoder is responsible for converting the sequence text into a semantic vector C. The specific mathematical expression for this process is:

$$h_t = f(x_t, h_{t-1}) \tag{1}$$

$$C = \theta(\{h_1, h_2, \cdots, h_m\}) \tag{2}$$

In the above expression, x_t represents the input data of the encoder at time h_i, while i represents the hidden layer (hidden layer) data of the encoder at time m. If EE is used to represent the total length of the input sequence, then f is the activation function, which is responsible for introducing nonlinear characteristics in the encoding process to better capture the complex features of the input data.

To extract the quality vector of French translation, we combined BiLSTM network with attention mechanism to calculate the quality vector of French translation. Assuming that the length of the input source language sentence $x_{1:n}$ is n, and the corresponding length of the target language sentence $y_{1:m}$ is m. Firstly, the source language sentence is abstracted through an encoder to generate a context vector $c_t = LSTM^{enc}(x_{1:n})(t = 1, \cdots, n)$, where t represents the time step and $LSTM^{enc}$ represents the LSTM part of the encoder. Subsequently, based on known French sentences (i.e. preliminary or reference translations of the target language) and context vector c_t, we utilize the BiLSTM network and attention mechanism of the decoder to generate the target sequence. This process can be expressed in the following form:

$$p(y_t|y_{<t}, x) = \partial(y_{t-1}, h_{t-1}, c_t) = \frac{exp\left(y_t^T W r_t\right)}{\sum_{k=1}^{K} exp\left(y_t^T W r_t\right)} \tag{3}$$

In the equation, ∂ represents a nonlinear mapping function designed to handle complex data relationships and introduce necessary nonlinear characteristics. h_{n-1} represents the hidden state vector of the previous time step, carrying the sequence information up to the current time. c_t is the context vector of the t word x_t in the source language sentence, which summarizes the overall information of the source sentence and provides necessary contextual background for the current decoding step. The target word y_t is represented in the form of one-hot encoding, i.e. $y_t \in R^{K_y \times 1}$, where K_y is the vocabulary size of the target language. This encoding ensures the uniqueness and distinguishability of the target word. The weight matrix W plays a role in connecting different layers or nodes in neural networks, learning the mapping relationships between data. In addition, $r_t \in R^{d \times 1}$ is an intermediate representation vector, where d represents the dimension of the target language word vector, that is, the vector length of the word in the embedding space.

After obtaining semantic information O_i, it can be decoded through a decoder. The decoding stage can incorporate attention mechanism to construct the decoder. The core of this mechanism is to evaluate the weight of input information and allocate it reasonably, aiming to minimize information loss and improve the efficiency of semantic information extraction and transmission. The relevant mathematical formulas are described as follows:

$$s_t = f(s_{t-1}, y_{t-1}, c_t) \tag{4}$$

$$c_t = \sum_{j=1}^{T} a_{tj} h_j \tag{5}$$

$$a_{tj} = \frac{exp(e_{tj})}{\sum exp(e_{tk})} \tag{6}$$

$$e_{tj} = g(s_{t-1}, h_j) \tag{7}$$

In the above formula, s_t, y_t represents the state and output of the decoder at time t, respectively; c_t represents the semantic information at time t. In addition, a_{tj}, e_{tj} depicts the weights and correlations of the data at time t and time $t - 1$ relative to the semantic vector input at time j, respectively.

3 Result Analysis and Discussion

To comprehensively verify the effectiveness of the system in this article, we designed a comparative experiment with traditional CNN systems, focusing on evaluating the accuracy of both in terms of student French translation quality. Table 1 presents a visual comparison of the accuracy of French translation quality assessment between our system and CNN system. The data shows that our system performs better, highlighting its advantages in this area. The excellent performance of this system is attributed to its adoption of a French translation grammar correction model that combines Seq2Seq with Attention mechanism. This model not only fully utilizes the powerful capabilities of the Seq2Seq framework in sequence processing, ensuring a deep understanding and accurate evaluation of students' French translation works, but also significantly improves the sensitivity and attention of the model to input information by introducing the Attention mechanism, enabling it to actively adjust its attention to different parts, ensuring the accuracy and fairness of the evaluation. In addition, the system in this article cleverly integrates the advantages of BiLSTM, further enhancing the model's contextual understanding ability by capturing contextual information of the input sequence. This fusion not only enhances the model's ability to handle complex language structures, but also enables the system to more accurately capture language details when evaluating students' French translations, providing students with more reliable feedback and guidance.

Table 1. Comparison of Evaluation Accuracy/%

Number of tasks/piece	This article system	Traditional system
10	90.7	82.5
50	91.5	83.1
100	92.3	84.7
150	93.6	85.5
200	94.2	86.1

Table 2 specifically compares the time consumption of our system and traditional CNN system in the task of evaluating the quality of student French translation. The data shows that compared to traditional CNN systems, our system takes less time to complete the same task, which fully demonstrates the significant advantage of our system in processing efficiency. The key to the system's ability to achieve fast response while ensuring high-quality evaluation in this article lies in its adoption of a French translation grammar correction model that combines Seq2Seq with Attention mechanism. This model not only inherits the efficient characteristics of Seq2Seq framework in sequence processing, enabling the system to quickly understand and evaluate students' French translation works, but also further enhances the speed and accuracy of the model in processing complex information by introducing Attention mechanism, enabling the model to quickly capture key points of input information and effectively shorten the evaluation time. In addition, this system cleverly integrates the advantages of BiLSTM. The BiLSTM network significantly enhances the model's contextual understanding ability by simultaneously capturing the forward and backward information of the input sequence. This feature enables the system to quickly understand the language structure and reduce computational costs when evaluating students' French translation works, thereby further improving evaluation efficiency.

Table 2. Comparison of Evaluation Time/s

Number of tasks/piece	This article system	Traditional system
10	1.3	1.8
50	3.6	4.2
100	5.8	6.8
150	7.2	9.2
200	9.5	12.7

Figure 2 visually compares the recall rate of student French translation quality assessment between the system proposed in this article and the traditional CNN system. The recall rate, as a key indicator for evaluating model performance, reflects the model's ability to correctly identify translated content. The results show that the recall rate of our system is better than that of traditional CNN systems, fully demonstrating its accuracy and reliability in French translation quality assessment. This advantage is due to the French translation grammar correction model that combines Seq2Seq with Attention mechanism adopted in this article. This model utilizes the sequence processing capability of the Seq2Seq framework to deeply analyze and evaluate students' French translations. Meanwhile, by introducing the Attention mechanism, the model's ability to capture key information is enhanced. In addition, the system also integrates the advantages of BiLSTM network, which significantly improves context understanding ability by capturing both forward and backward information of the input sequence, enabling the system to more accurately identify translation errors during evaluation and thereby improve recall rate.

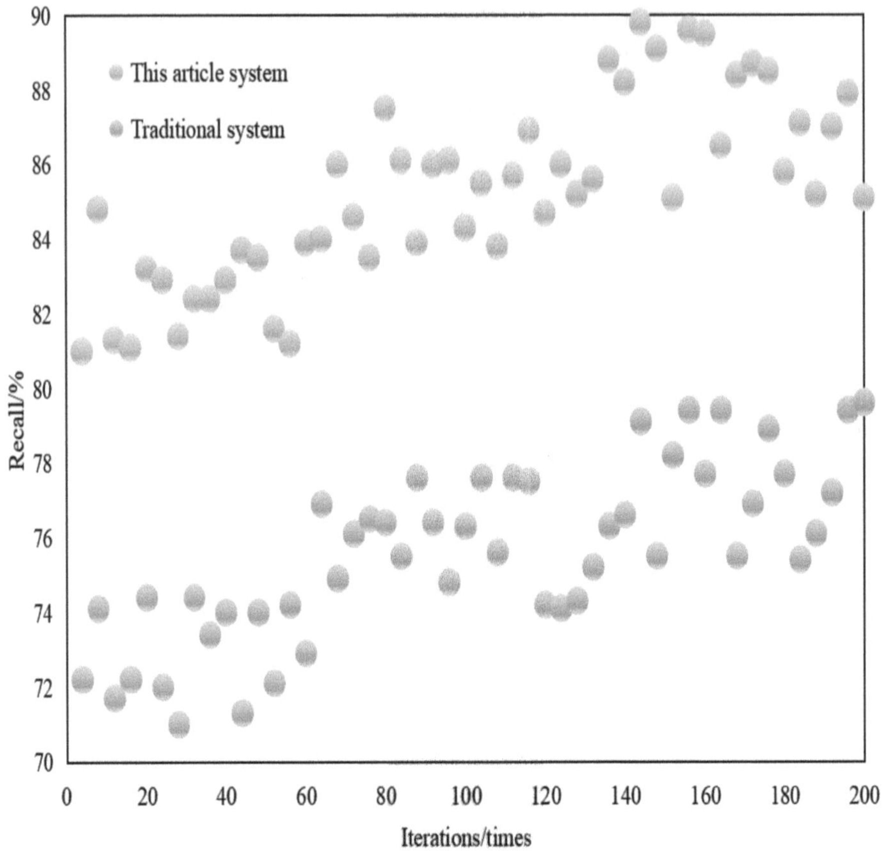

Fig.2. Comparison of recall rates

Figure 3 visually compares the performance of our system with traditional CNN systems in terms of user satisfaction. Obviously, compared to traditional CNN systems, this system performs better in terms of user satisfaction, demonstrating its outstanding ability to optimize user experience and meet user needs. The key to winning high praise from users for this system lies in the diverse translation tasks it provides. These tasks not only cover French translation exercises of different difficulty levels and forms, but also incorporate novel teaching elements to make the learning process more vivid and interesting. In addition, the system also has real-time feedback and evaluation functions, using advanced evaluation models to quickly and accurately evaluate students' translation works and provide real-time feedback on the results. This real-time feedback mechanism not only helps students grasp their translation skills in real time, but also greatly stimulates their learning enthusiasm, making the learning process more proactive.

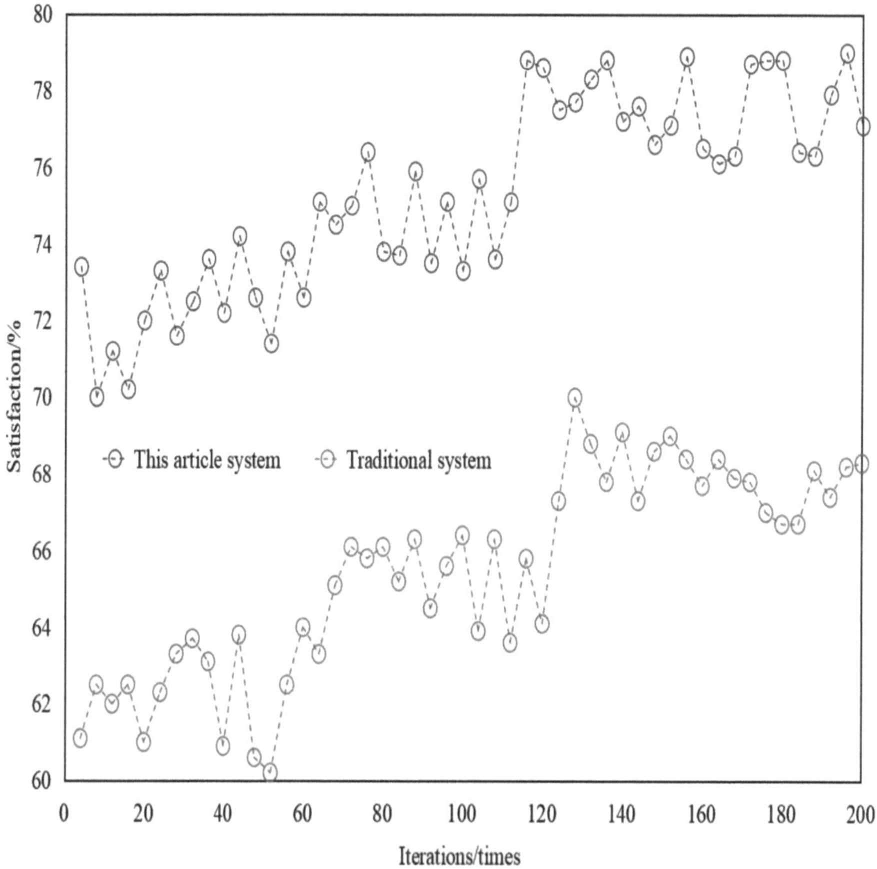

Fig.3. Satisfaction comparison

4 Conclusion

This article successfully developed an intelligent translation skill training and evaluation system based on deep learning, with the goal of using cutting-edge technology to bring a new atmosphere to French teaching and promote its move towards intelligence and personalization. The system carefully analyzes students' actual levels and needs, and meticulously plans diverse translation tasks, encouraging students to constantly challenge themselves and improve their translation skills in practice. In addition, the system has instant feedback and evaluation functions, which can quickly and accurately evaluate students' translation works and provide immediate feedback. This kind of instant feedback not only allows students to timely understand their own translation skills, identify shortcomings and make improvements, but also greatly stimulates their learning interest and enthusiasm, making the learning process more proactive. However, the system also has certain limitations. There is still room for improvement in the accuracy and efficiency of the system when dealing with complex or domain specific translation tasks. Meanwhile, the scalability and compatibility of the system are also areas that need to be focused on and improved in the future. Nevertheless, the proposal of this system still provides new perspectives and inspirations for French language teaching, demonstrating broad application potential.

References

1. Xue, H.X.: The application of artificial intelligence technology in computer aided translation software. Information and Computer (Theoretical Edition) **35**(03), 179–181 (2023)
2. Wang, W. G.: Intelligent English automatic translation system based on TTS technology. Information Technology 47(03), 117–121+127 (2023)
3. Yang, W., Qin, B.T.: Design of automatic control system for translation robot based on intelligent voice. Computer Measurement and Control **32**(05), 102–108 (2024)
4. Zhang, H., Zhu, Y.W.: Application of computer aided translation system based on cloud platform. Integrated Circuit Applications **40**(08), 132–133 (2023)
5. Zhang, Y.: Research on computer intelligent proofreading system based on improved phrase translation model. Automation Technology and Application **40**(12), 58–61 (2021)
6. He, J.: A new intelligent translation scoring system based on language model. Microcomput. Appl. **39**(04), 139–141 (2023)
7. Yun, X.: Design and implementation of a mobile intelligent translation system based on Android platform. Microcomputer Applications 38(02), 53–55+59 (2022)
8. Hu, R. Q.: A machine automatic translation quality evaluation model based on deep learning algorithms. Electronic Design Engineering 29(21), 33–37+42 (2021)
9. Di, Y.M.: Design and implementation of computer aided translation software based on artificial intelligence technology. Information Recording Materials **25**(01), 172–174 (2024)
10. Jiang, Y.: Research on automatic scoring method based on intelligent machine English translation system. Information and Computer (Theoretical Edition) **34**(02), 50–52 (2022)
11. Chen, Y.D., Wang, X.Z.: Application of artificial intelligence technology to improve the quality of machine translation. Chinese Journal of Medical Library and Information Science **31**(07), 64–71 (2022)
12. Li, X.T.: Design of intelligent cloud computing online translation system. Information Technology **46**(09), 89–93 (2022)
13. Zhang, X.J., Shao, L.: Basic principles for building trusted machine translation systems: a perspective based on engineering ethics. Foreign Languages **37**(01), 1–8 (2021)
14. Liu, F.: Implementing E-learning in English translation teaching using deep learning models and output-oriented methods. Computer-Aided Design & Applications **21**, 219–235 (2024)
15. Chen, M.: A deep learning-based intelligent quality detection model for machine translation. IEEE Access **11**, 89469–89477 (2023)
16. Aleedy, M., Atwell, E., Meshoul, S.: Towards deep learning-powered chatbot for translation learning. In: International Conference on Human-Computer Interaction. LNCS, vol. ?, pp. 131–141. Springer International Publishing, Cham (2022)
17. Siddique, S., Islam, S., Neon, E.E., et al.: Deep learning-based Bangla sign language detection with an edge device. Intelligent Systems with Applications **18**, 200224 (2023)

Data Analytics and Automation in Educational Management

Utilizing ChatGPT as an Assistant in Excel Tasks: An Experimental Study

Poramate Tarasak(✉) and Sooppawat Thipyarat

Institute for Innovative Learning, Mahidol University, Nakhon Pathom, Thailand
{poramate.tar,sooppawat.thi}@mahidol.ac.th

Abstract. Working with spreadsheet software such as Microsoft Excel is a highly sought-after skill in business. A conventional way of learning Excel might be a lecture-based session accompanied by a lab exercise. Recently, artificial intelligence (AI) has created an enormous impact on education. Notably, ChatGPT is the most well-known generative AI application. It can assist teachers with tasks such as lesson planning and creating exercises. ChatGPT can guide a student in studying and doing assignments. Before applying ChatGPT, we must be aware of its strengths and limitations. Therefore, the application of ChatGPT in assisting tasks in Excel is the focus of this study. We conducted an experimental study by investigating ChatGPT's responses in solving ten commonly encountered Excel tasks, ranked from easy to difficult. The results show that ChatGPT can help complete the tasks. However, many mistakes and pitfalls were discovered during the experiment and are summarized in the discussion. Then, we provide recommendations on how to utilize ChatGPT as an assistant for Excel tasks from a learning perspective. These recommendations can serve as guidelines for instructors to consider in creating their lesson plans on this topic.

Keywords: generative AI · ChatGPT · Microsoft Excel · education · practical training · AI literacy development

1 Introduction

1.1 Microsoft Excel in Education

Microsoft Excel is among the most widely used software for computation. It is commonly used in business environments and caters to the needs of data analysis and visualization. Excel skill has long been recognized as a necessary digital skill for middle-skill jobs [1]. It has become an increasingly important skill in a data-driven business world, in the current era when analyzing large amount of data to extract business insight is a common activity.

An exploratory study in [2] has indicated the need to foster Excel skills for Bachelor of Science in Business Administration graduates. Data were collected from various sources, such as advisory board meetings, job postings, employer surveys, which emphasized this need. The research also identifies specific Excel skills such as Pivot Tables as challenging.

K. W. Lee and L. H. Wong (Eds.): ITEA 2025, CCIS 2643, pp. 141–152, 2026.
https://doi.org/10.1007/978-981-95-2011-4_14

Microsoft Excel has been a popular learning tool, not only in business schools but also in various other subjects [3–6]. In the Fundamental of Spreadsheet and Relational Database Modeling introduction course, an experiment to compare the use of actual and simulated environments to teach Excel was conducted in [3]. It was found that a hybrid learning approach was the most effective. A lab session of an Excel tutorial was conducted in a quantitative analysis course focused on problems in Chemistry [4]. The Excel lab was considered by the students to be necessary for success in the course and their future careers. To increase student confidence in using Excel, a framework of assignments was introduced in [5], where the scaffolding approach demonstrated the effectiveness in learning the Marketing Metrics and Analytics courses. Microsoft Excel was utilized to improve the understanding of kinematic and dynamic concepts in the Physics simulation project [6]. It is an effective instruction method for problem-based learning.

1.2 The Application of ChatGPT in Excel

Generative AI tools, such as ChatGPT, have become increasingly indispensable in daily work and life. ChatGPT has a variety of applications in many fields such as scientific writing, mathematics, programming, education, and healthcare [7]. In education, ChatGPT is valuable to instructors in creating lesson plans, learning materials, and assessments [8]. Students can enhance their learning from ChatGPT at their convenience. On the other hand, it also poses a risk of plagiarism by students and exposure to inaccuracy and harmful content [8]. In programming, ChatGPT assists in code generation, explanation, and debugging [7]. It can convert code written in one language to another as well. Visual Basic for Applications (VBA) is a computer language integrated into Excel to create macro and customized functions. Hence, ChatGPT is expected to assist in VBA programming-related tasks as well.

The application of ChatGPT in Excel is much less explored in the literature. A potential risk of hallucination of ChatGPT on Excel was highlighted in [9], where the author advised verifying generated formulas and codes. The inaccuracy stemmed from the fact that ChatGPT was built from a large language model (LLM), trained primarily from a vast amount of textual data. Excel, on the other hand, is working on data in a spreadsheet table format, containing text, numbers, formulas, and graphs. An experiment on ChatGPT with a complex prompt shows inaccurate generated Excel formulas even when multiple rounds of prompting were attempted [10]. Fine-tuning a model to generate an accurate Excel formula from a natural language prompt is an ongoing research challenge [11, 12].

ChatGPT may be regarded as an Excel assistant or a tutor. Apart from formula and VBA code generation, it can offer a step-by-step suggestion on how to accomplish a specific task. It can recommend a function to address a problem or an alternative solution for the same problem. When a user or a student faces an error message, ChatGPT can pinpoint possible root causes and suggest a solution or a workaround.

1.3 Contribution

In this paper, we conduct an experimental study on using ChatGPT to assist in many Excel tasks. Different from the existing literature, which focuses on specific topics such as formula generation, this paper exploits more general tasks, attempting to cover a broader range of practical problems encountered by Excel users. The example tasks in this paper can serve as an exercise in an Excel lab in an educational environment. Based on our experimental experience, we initiate a discussion around the following research questions:

RQ1. What are common mistakes and pitfalls when using ChatGPT with Excel?

RQ2. What are the recommendations for using ChatGPT capability with Excel to support student learning effectively?

2 Methodology

2.1 Testing Setup

A simple Excel table is created manually with synthetic data. The table is used as the starting point for conducting follow-up tests to solve given problems. The table is input as text to ChatGPT of a new chat as grounding information. Then, the queries to solve problems are delivered through the following prompts.

When the table in text is copied to the ChatGPT web interface, ChatGPT recognizes it as an image. We can explicitly instruct ChatGPT to convert it as a table by prompting "Convert it to a table".

Imagine a family of three consisting of a father, a mother, and a young daughter. Every week this family is planning for grocery shopping. Each family member is buying some amount of each grocery item. The created Excel table is shown in Table 1.

Only the free version of ChatGPT is tested in this paper. The free version utilizes the GPT-4o mini model at the time of this writing. The knowledge cutoff for this model is October 2023 [13].

Note that we are not attempting to ask ChatGPT to perform data analysis tasks directly on the web interface. Doing so will accumulate the token counts and require a ChatGPT Plus subscription once all the quota is consumed. Therefore, our approach to prompt ChatGPT is to request assistance by asking a question or asking for a recommendation on how to solve a specific task on Excel. Then, the response is utilized on the Excel worksheet by following the steps provided.

2.2 Testing Categories

The following ten tasks are created and ordered from a basic level to a difficult level. The tasks in each category are commonly found by common Excel practitioners when performing data analysis or creating a report.

Basic Level Tasks:
Task 1. Compute the sum of each person's expenses to buy needed items.

Table 1. The Excel table illustrates the grocery shopping list of a family.

Item	Unit Price (Baht)	Father	Mother	Daughter
Whole fresh chicken (5 kg)	120	1	1	0
Eggs (1 dozen)	60	1	1	1
Whole wheat bread (1 lb)	35	1	1	0
2% milk (1 gallon)	80	1	1	0
Bananas (per kg)	30	2	1	1
Carrots (1 kg)	40	1	1	1
Potatoes (5 kg)	70	1	1	1
Tomatoes (per kg)	50	1	1	0
Broccoli (1 head)	60	1	1	0
Cheddar cheese (8 oz)	100	1	1	0
Frozen peas (450 g)	40	1	1	0
Canned black beans (400 g)	20	2	1	0
Olive oil (500 ml)	120	1	0	0
Pasta (500 g)	30	2	0	1
Peanut butter (500 g)	70	1	1	0
Plain yogurt (900 g)	80	1	1	0
Cereal (12 oz)	50	1	1	1
Ground beef (1 kg)	200	0	0	0
Almonds (200 g)	150	1	1	1
Apples (per kg)	80	1	1	1

Explanation: The purpose of this test is to find out the correct function or the computation steps to accomplish this task.

Prompt: Tell me how to calculate the sum of each person's expenses on Excel.

Task 2. Compute the sum of each person's expense breakdown per item.

Explanation: the response should tell the computation steps required.

Prompt: How to calculate the expense per item for each person on Excel?

Task 3. Highlight the expense values so that higher values use warmer tones.

Explanation: This requires ChatGPT to recommend the use of a correct menu and the steps.

Prompt: How to highlight the expense values so that that higher values use warmer tones?

Mid Level Tasks:

Task 4. Group the items into the following categories: Meat, Egg, Flour, Dairy, Vegetable, Fruit, Others.

Explanation: This task illustrates the strength of ChatGPT where it can understand the meaning of the text and group the items accordingly. Excel does not have this capability.

Prompt: Group the items into the following categories: Meat, Egg, Flour, Dairy, Vegetable, Fruit, Others. Create a column beside the Item column.

Task 5. Calculate the total expense per category.

Explanation: Once the category has been defined from Task 4, the task illustrates the operation 'sum' together with 'group by', which is a common task in SQL.

Prompt: How to compute the total expense per category in Excel?

Task 6. Create a drop-down menu of the categories. When a user selects the menu, another cell should show the total expense per category as selected.

Explanation: This task involves the task of creating a menu and the operation in Task 5 as a sub-task.

Prompt: How to create a drop-down menu of the categories so that when a user selects the option, another cell will show the total expense per category?

Task 7. Create a bar chart illustrating the total expense per category. The bars are ordered from the category with the highest total expense to the one with the lowest total expense.

Explanation: This task presents an example of using ChatGPT to aid visualization.

Prompt: How to create a bar graph of the total expense per category? The bars are ordered from the category with highest total expense.

Difficult Level Tasks:

Task 8. There is another Excel table that has the columns – Item, Expiry Date. Join this table to the base table to add the Expiry Date data to the corresponding Item.

Explanation: Joining two tables is a common task in SQL. To perform the Join operation, there must be a common key column, which is the Item column in this case.

Prompt: There is another table with the columns – Item, Expiry Date. How to join these two tables together so that the Expiry Date column is included?

Task 9. Suppose the table has a column 'Remaining Item Amount'. Create a new formula named 'Food Waste Loss (FWL)', which is the product of the 'Unit Price' and 'Remaining Item Amount' of the already expired Item. The expired item is determined from the 'Expiry Date' whether it has passed the current date.

Explanation: Two main steps are involved in this task. First, determine whether the item is expired, and if it is, compute the loss.

Prompt: Create a new Excel formula named FoodWasteLoss that calculates the loss from the expired item. It computes the product of 'Unit Price' and 'Remaining Amount' of the item that has been expired as of today.

Task 10. From Task 9, create a built-in function with the name FoodWasteLoss.

Explanation: To make the formula reusable, Excel allows us to create a built-in function.

Prompt: How to create FoodWasteLoss like a built-in function in Excel?

3 Results

3.1 Testing Categories

Basic Level Tasks

Task 1. From the ChatGPT response in Fig. 1, the recommended function is SUMPRODUCT which takes the range of the 'Unit Price' column as the first argument and the range of the 'Father' (or 'Mother' or 'Daughter') as the second argument. This is the correct function, however, the range of the columns in the arguments appears to be wrong, i.e. B2:B20 rather than B2:B21.

Formula for Father's Total Expense

excel — Copy — Edit

```
=SUMPRODUCT(B2:B20, C2:C20)
```

(assuming **B2:B20** is the "Unit Price" column and **C2:C20** is the "Father" column).

Fig.1. ChatGPT response for Task 1.

Task 2. ChatGPT instructs to add a new column for each person and then write a simple formula to find the product of the 'Unit Price' column and the amount.

Task 3. ChatGPT provides the solution first which is 'Conditional Formatting' and explains a step-by-step guide to do so. After following the steps, part of the table output is shown in Fig. 2, where higher values apply higher color tones.

Father's expense	Mother's expense	Daughter's expense
120	120	0
60	60	60
35	35	0
80	80	0
60	30	30
40	40	40
70	70	70

Fig.2. The (partial) Excel table after applying conditional formatting.

Mid Level Tasks:

Task 4. After ChatGPT categorizes the items, we can refine the prompt to get only the second column and copy the results to the Excel worksheet. The results from ChatGPT are as follows:

Meat: Whole fresh chicken, Ground beef.

Egg: Eggs.
Flour: Whole wheat bread, Pasta.
Dairy: 2% milk, Cheddar cheese, Plain yogurt.
Vegetable: Carrots, Potatoes, Tomatoes, Broccoli, Frozen peas.
Fruit: Bananas, Apples.
Others: Canned black beans, Olive oil, Peanut butter, Cereal, Almonds.

Task 5. ChatGPT suggests two main steps:

1) Add a "Total Cost" column and by writing a formula C2 * (D2 + E2 + F2), which is the product of 'Unit Price' and the total sum of the amount bought, and drag the formula down to apply to all rows.

2) Use SUMIF to calculate the total expense per category. First, create a list of unique categories in a separate section. Then, write a formula SUMIF to do the summation as shown in Fig. 3. However, the step of creating a list of unique categories was not explained. So, another prompt is instructed.

Prompt: How to create a list of unique categories in column H?

Then, ChatGPT recommended using Excel's remove duplicates feature, using the UNIQUE function, or using Pivot Table. For this suggested solution, either Excel's remove duplicates feature or using the UNIQUE function is appropriate while using Pivot Table is an overkill.

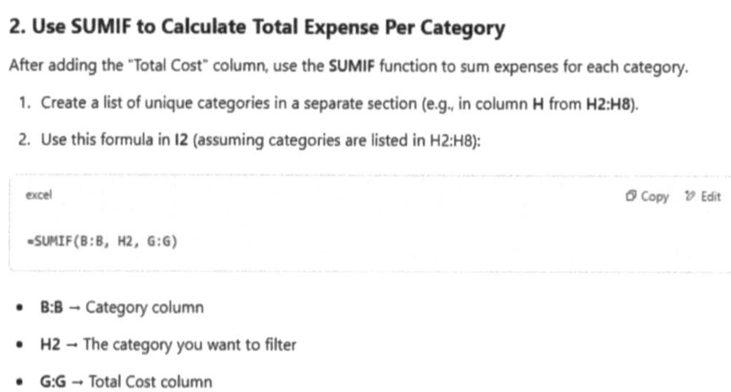

Fig. 3. Response from ChatGPT on the steps to apply SUMIF function.

Task 6. To create a drop-down list, ChatGPT suggested using *Data Validation* in the *Data* menu. Then, the SUMIF formula is written in another cell by following similar steps in Task 5.

Task 7. The major steps from ChatGPT response are 'Sort Data from Highest to Lowest' and 'Insert a Bar Chart'. To conduct sorting, the instruction told us to use *Sort* in the *Data* menu, then select *Sort by* to 'Total Expense' column with Largest to Smallest for the *Order*. However, there is an error 'You can't change part of an array'.

The reason for this error is that in Task 5, the UNIQUE function was applied and resulted in a dynamic array that doesn't allow to modify its members directly. We can find out how to fix this error with another follow-up prompt. ChatGPT mentioned this error usually occurs from trying to sort a range that contains array formulas, which was precisely the case. One of the fixes is to convert the list to static values first and sort again. This solved the problem. The resulting bar chart is shown in Fig. 4.

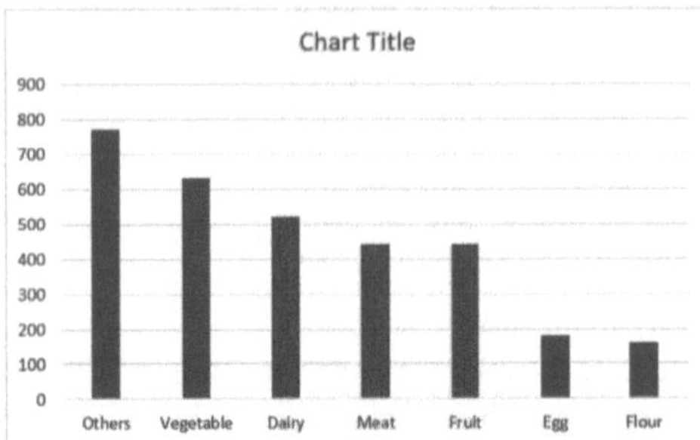

Fig. 4. A bar chart created by following ChatGPT instructions.

Difficult Level Tasks:
Task 8. ChatGPT suggested VLOOKUP or XLOOKUP functions. It was assumed that the two tables are from different Sheets and we can write the formula following the given guideline.

Task 9. Given the prompt from Sect. 2.2, the resulting formula in Fig. 5 appears to be not what is expected. ChatGPT attempts to provide the formula for the total loss rather than for the loss for each item. Even so, the first formula is incorrect to do so.

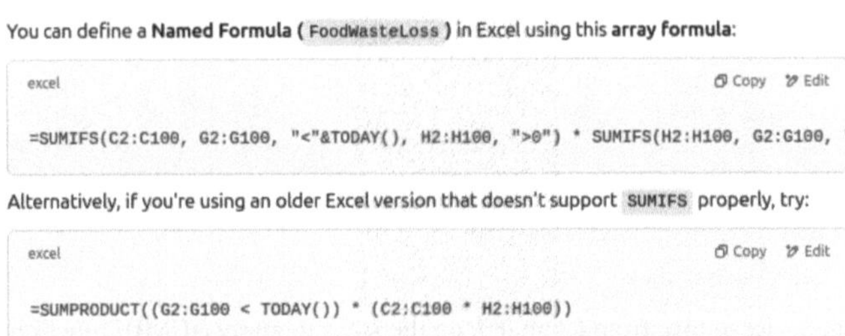

Fig.5. Formulas to compute FWL by ChatGPT.

The prompt is revised by adding 'The formula is applied to each item at a time.' to the original prompt and rerun. Now, the correct function is obtained (Fig. 6). ChatGPT also suggested creating a named formula with 'Defined Name' under the 'Formulas' menu.

Task 10. ChatGPT recommended writing a VBA code, which allows a user to create a custom function like a built-in function. It informed the steps and generated the VBA code as shown in Fig. 7.

The code works as expected. However, there is no information to the user who may not know what the function does and what the arguments are. To enhance the usability further, the following prompt is instructed.

```excel
=IF(TODAY() > D2, B2 * G2, 0)
```

Fig.6. The correct formula to compute FWL for each item.

```vba
Function FoodWasteLoss(UnitPrice As Double, ExpiryDate As Date, RemainingAmount As Double
    ' Check if the item is expired
    If ExpiryDate < Date Then
        FoodWasteLoss = UnitPrice * RemainingAmount
    Else
        FoodWasteLoss = 0
    End If
End Function
```

Fig.7. VBA code to implement FoodWasteLoss function.

Prompt: Modify the VBA code such that it provides some description when the user types the formula.

ChatGPT wrote another code to add some description of the function' as shown in Fig. 8. When the user presses Ctrl-A after typing ' = FoodWasteLoss(', a window pop-up shows additional information as in Fig. 9.

```vba
' Add function description when Excel opens
Sub AddFoodWasteLossDescription()
    Application.MacroOptions _
        Macro:="FoodWasteLoss", _
        Description:="Calculates the loss from expired food items by multiplying Unit Price a
        ArgumentDescriptions:=Array("Unit Price of the item", "Expiry Date of the item", "Rem
End Sub
```

Fig.8. VBA code to add description of the FoodWasteLoss function.

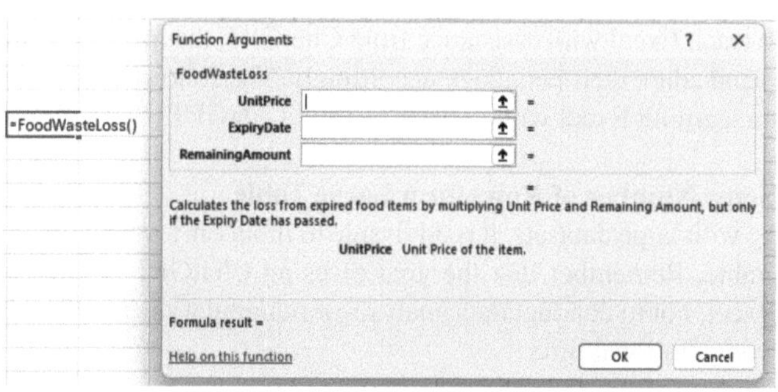

Fig.9. Description of the FoodWasteLoss function in the worksheet.

4 Discussion

Based on the results, we can identify common mistakes and pitfalls that occur when using ChatGPT with sample Excel tasks.

Errors in Indices

Although ChatGPT has knowledge of the table structure at the beginning of the chat, ChatGPT's response may sometimes refer to incorrect indices in either a row (alphabet) index or a column (number) index. Mistakes in a row index cause a wrong result when the calculation does not cover the correct range of cells. Mistakes in a column index yield a non-sensible computation which may be hard to notice at first.

Repeating the Same Prompt May Result in a Different Method or Formula

This pitfall is natural in generative AI. The Excel formula obtained from the first prompt may not be the same when we submit the same prompt again. Sometimes, the steps to use the Excel menu were suggested as an alternative solution. Nevertheless, following any of the provided solutions should address the problem at hand.

No Detailed Explanation in the Response

The response from ChatGPT tends to provide a solution that the students can follow. Sometimes, there is no detailed explanation about what the function does and why certain steps are required. This characteristic actually depends on the prompt provided by the user.

Unexpected or Incomplete Response

There are some cases where ChatGPT misinterprets the prompt. This may be due to a lack of sufficient clarity in the prompt or the task may be too complex to handle by a single prompt. Other cases are often hallucinations.

5 Recommendations

Evidently, ChatGPT can definitely assist users in doing a wide variety of Excel tasks. However, to maximize the effectiveness and minimize the risk of errors, users should realize common pitfalls and adopt best practices that improve efficiency and accuracy. In addition, to teach Excel with assistance from ChatGPT, the instructors must be aware of such issues and adapt their pedagogy accordingly. The followings provide guidelines for students on learning Excel with assistance from ChatGPT.

Input Only Some Number of Rows for a Large Table

When working with large datasets, it is advisable to input only a fraction of rows instead of the entire table. Remember that the goal of using ChatGPT is to assist in solving problems in Excel, not to conduct data analysis or manipulation directly. This approach also reduces computational time.

Treat Indices as Dummy Variables

Since there might be errors in indices from the response of ChatGPT or when a partial table is prompted, the generated formula containing those indices is not the final solution. Rather than operating on those indices directly, it is better to recall what fields or parts of data they represent. Then, the indices are modified when the formula is written in an Excel cell.

Ask for Detailed Explanations of the Formula

When the prompt begins with 'How to ...' as seen in Sect. 2, the response from ChatGPT tends to be result-oriented, focusing solely on solving the problem. As a result, users may just copy and paste the formula without any understanding of what the formula does. This is error-prone, as ChatGPT may misinterpret the users' intentions. A better way for students to learn is to ask ChatGPT to explain the formula in more detail. Once the students understand the formula, they can also verify whether the solution is correct or not.

Select the Simplest Method Among the Suggested Methods based on the Level of Understanding

When multiple methods are available to complete the task, it is safe to choose the simplest one that aligns with the student's level of understanding. This reduces the chance of making mistakes. However, other methods should not be disregarded. Alternative ways to solve the same problem are always worth considering once the students are comfortable with them and can compare the pros and cons of the solutions.

Breakdown the Tasks into Simpler Ones

Dividing a complex task into several smaller sub-tasks is more manageable. Then, one may craft a smaller prompt to address the sub-tasks one by one, increasing the chance of success. This approach fosters students' skills in analyzing a complex problem and organizing their thought processes.

Leverage ChatGPT for Tasks that Cannot be Done Easily with Excel

As the strengths of ChatGPT include understanding contextual information and generating meaningful text, one may think of such applications in Excel. An example of these was provided in Task 4, which is a categorization task. Other tasks that fit with ChatGPT are correcting spelling errors, aligning the format of values such as dates or months, and analyzing sentiment from the conversation. In addition, ChatGPT can generate synthetic Excel data and exercises for practice as well.

Always Verify the Results

Students should not trust the solution provided by ChatGPT immediately. Sometimes, the solution seems to work but it is not correct. Verification is an important critical thinking skill that students should develop when working with generative AI such as ChatGPT.

6 Conclusion

Generative AI tools such as ChatGPT have become more pervasive in teaching and learning. The skill of working with spreadsheet software such as Microsoft Excel is fundamental not only in business, but also in research, scientific experiment, and many fields of study. The assistance from ChatGPT allows a user to work with Excel more effectively and enhances how students learn to utilize such software. Some guidelines are discussed in the paper. They are beneficial for instructors to adapt their teaching methods to integrate ChatGPT into an Excel course. Possible future research could involve the comparison with Copilot, another AI tool developed by Microsoft, which may offer a different style of assistance for Excel-related problems. In addition, Copilot in Microsoft 365 is integrated directly in Excel, potentially facilitating more user-friendly interaction with the AI.

References

1. Geiger, B.: Your Excel skills could land you your next job. https://fortune.com/2015/03/06/microsoft-excel-jobs. Last accessed 07 March 2025
2. Formby, S.K., Medlin, B.D., Ellington, V.: Microsoft Excel®: Is it an important job skill for college graduates? Info. Sys. Educ. J. **15**(3), 55–63 (2017)
3. Mohebbi, E.: Effectiveness of teaching Excel and Access using actual and simulated platforms – A comparative study. Decision Sci. J. Innovat. Educ. 23 (2025)
4. Rubin, S.J., Abrams, B.: Teaching fundamental skills in microsoft excel to first-year students in quantitative analysis. J. Chem. Edu. **92**(11), 1840–2145 (2015)
5. Weathers, D., Swain, S.D.: A scaffolded learning approach to increasing student comfort with Microsoft Excel. J. Market. Analy. **12**, 198–208 (2024)
6. Joseph, E., Muhamad Ridwan, N.I.: Students' learning experience through Physics simulation project via Microsoft Excel spreadsheet. In: Proceedings of the International Conference on Advancing and Redesigning Education 2023, Springer, Singapore (2024)
7. Azaria, A., Azoulay, R., Reches, S.: ChatGPT is a remarkable tool—For experts. Data Intelligence **6**(1), 240–296 (2024)
8. Lo, C.K.: What is the impact of chatgpt on education?a rapid review of the literature. Education Sciences **13**(4), 410 (2023)
9. O'Beirne, P.: ChatGPT and Excel – trust, but verify. In: Proceedings of the EuSpRIG 2023 Conference "The Spreadsheet Crisis: Regaining Control", pp. 73–88. EuSpRig, London (2023)
10. Thorne, S.: Experimenting with ChatGPT for spreadsheet formula generation: Evidence of risk in AI generated spreadsheets. In: Proceedings of the EuSpRIG 2023 Conference "The Spreadsheet Crisis: Regaining Control", pp. 89–103. EuSpRig, London (2023)
11. Zhao, W., et al.: 2024. NL2Formula: Generating Spreadsheet Formulas from Natural Language Queries. In: Findings of the Association for Computational Linguistics: EACL, pp. 2377–2388. St. Julian's, Malta (2024)
12. Singh, U., et al.: An Empirical Study of Validating Synthetic Data for Formula Generation. https://arxiv.org/abs/2407.10657
13. Models – OpenAI API Homepage, https://platform.openai.com/docs/models/gpt-4#gpt-4o-mini. Last accessed 04 March 2025

Advantages of Implementing Robotic Process Automation in Internal Auditing

Aymen Almayyahi[1,2](✉), Samir Aboul Fotouh[3], and Ahmed Kamal Metawee[3]

[1] Department of Accounting Technical, Management Technical College, Southern Technical University, Basra 61 61001, Iraq
aymen.abdulali@stu.edu.iq, aymen.abdulaali@std.mans.edu.eg
[2] Faculty of Commerce, Mansoura University, Mansoura, Egypt
[3] Department of Commerce, Mansoura University, Mansoura 35511, Egypt
{Prof_samir,Metawee68}@mans.edu.eg

Abstract. This study explores the applications of robotic process automation in internal auditing, highlighting the benefits of implementing this technology in modern business environments. RPA enhances the efficiency and quality of internal audit processes by minimizing reliance on repetitive manual tasks, enabling auditors to concentrate on value-added activities such as advanced analysis and strategic decision-making. The study examined RPA's impact on information accuracy and venture execution velocity, as well as its ability to enhance compliance with regulations. Based on a statistical analysis of data from one hundred and fifty questionnaires distributed to accountants and auditors in Iraqi government establishments, the findings indicated that RPA usage in internal auditing resulted in a 65% improvement in operational efficiency, a 48% reduction in human errors, and a 72% acceleration of auditing processes. However, the adoption of this technology varied among establishments because of technical. The study recommends developing an integrated regulatory framework for adopting RPA in internal auditing, creating training programs to enhance auditors' digital skills, and strengthening security controls to ensure data integrity and confidentiality. It concludes that the future of internal auditing relies on the integration of artificial intelligence and automation, necessitating a strategic approach to maximize benefits.

Keywords: Robotic process automation · RPA · efficiency · Benefits

1 Introduction

In recent years, due to the accelerated improvement of the era, the way of enterprise execution has undergone fundamental changes, leading to essential adjustments inside the management and implementation of commercial enterprise operations (Sirohi et al., 2022). Among these contemporary technologies which have acquired giant interest and performed tangible results in improving performance and efficiency (Hanford et al., 2022), robot technique automation era is becoming a powerful tool for use in all walks of life (Almayyahi et al., 2024). The era is predicated on the use of software programs to carry out repetitive and habitual responsibilities that require human intervention,

K. W. Lee and L. H. Wong (Eds.): ITEA 2025, CCIS 2643, pp. 153–163, 2026.
https://doi.org/10.1007/978-981-95-2011-4_15

helping to reduce human blunders and enhance the velocity and accuracy of having the task performed. Robotic technique automation has emerged as an essential basis for contemporary companies looking to enhance performance and reduce running expenses. With the explosive increase of facts and the needs faced with the aid of businesses, the adoption of advanced generation solutions to attain strategic goals more effectively will become critical. A considerable place of advantage from this era is the area of internal audit, wherein automation can enhance auditing and financial auditing by reducing the time and resources required (Solanki et al., 2024). This review ambitions to focus on diverse applications of robotic process automation technology within the subject of internal audit, together with studying its application in records analysis and financial auditing. There could be a focal point at the benefits of the generation, consisting of improved operational performance and reduction of human mistakes.

2 Lecturer Review

Robotic Process Automation is described as a technology that is based on the usage of software to carry out repetitive and recurring tasks that are manually carried out by people. The era is considered to be one of the cutting-edge technological innovations that enables enhancing operational performance inside an agency through changing guide activities with automated structures that could perform tasks quickly and greater appropriately. According to a study (Almayyahi et al., 2024), robotic process automation is not only a tool to reduce manpower, but has become an integral part of the digital transformation of organizations, helping to improve competitiveness and productivity at the enterprise level. Robotic technique automation is based on advanced algorithms and efficient records processing, allowing it to engage with distinct programs and systems which include economic and human aid management systems to execute complicated strategies quickly and accurately. Thanks to these algorithms, robots are capable of system massive amounts of facts, thereby decreasing the time spent on traditional operations and enhancing the quality of results through reducing human errors (Pandy et al., 2024). One of the main advantages of robotic manner automation is the ability to significantly lessen operating expenses, because it reduces the need for manpower in some repetitive responsibilities, thereby helping to reduce the expenses of workers expenses and improve efficiency. The technology also improves the capability to evolve to speedy changes inside the business environment and affords companies with more flexibility to cope with ongoing challenges (Peláez and Aguirre-Álvarez, 2025). In this context, the importance of robotic process automation emerges in several areas, such as internal auditing, for improving operational performance related to financial auditing, accounting data processing, and performance auditing. Research shows that the use of RPA in these areas enhances an organization's ability to ensure compliance with regulatory standards and improves the accuracy and transparency of financial operations. With these benefits, the challenge is not limited to the application of technology, but also includes aspects related to training and cultural preparation in the organization to ensure that the technology is fully utilized. Previous studies have examined the applications of Robotic process automation in various fields, each highlighting its impact on improving operational efficiency, reducing costs, and enhancing effectiveness in diverse work environments. A look at using Thekkethil (2021) On Robotic process automation in the Banking and Financial Sector, the software of RPA in mortgage processing and fraud detection within the economic quarter changed into explored. The take a look at concluded that RPA contributes to decreasing repetitive tasks and operational fees, while also helping to reduce human error and improve operational monitoring, in the long run enhancing efficiency and accuracy in mortgage processing and risk detection. The have a look at encouraged the adoption of RPA generation by way of banks to streamline operations and enhance fraud detection. As for El-monem Serag et al. (2021) In their study, "Internal Audit Effectiveness Evaluation Framework," they discussed the importance of improving the performance of internal audit activities of Egyptian companies by adopting a value-based approach rather than the traditional risk-based approach. The study found that this shift strengthens governance, helps improve risk management efficiency and achieves strategic goals. The study recommends adopting this framework and training auditors on how to incorporate added value into audit activities. In the context of accounting and auditing professions, an examination by way of Naif (2022) explored the impact of Fourth Industrial Revolution technology on those professions. The look at showed that technologies inclusive of artificial intelligence, the Internet of Things, cloud computing, and robotics enhance the performance of accounting and auditing operations, and contribute to improving monetary reporting and statistical analysis. The take a look at recommends that groups adapt to these technologies in their destiny techniques to make sure they benefit from them. Shaoyu Liu's study (2022) on "Robotic process automation in Audit" highlighted the application of RPA to improve efficiency in audit procedures, showing that RPA is effective in automating repetitive and rule-based tasks. However, the study noted that RPA works best with structured data and its implementation requires careful cost-benefit analysis. The study recommended that auditors should start by identifying tasks suitable for automation, with a focus on the ongoing maintenance of RPA systems. In a observation Rehman and Hashim (2022) regarding The Impact of Artificial Intelligence at the Internal Audit Function of Omani Companies, the position of artificial intelligence in enhancing the effectiveness of internal audit by way of helping decision-making and reducing errors became emphasized. Research indicates that artificial intelligence can improve the overall performance of internal audit via improving supervision and analysis. The observer recommends incorporating artificial intelligence into governance techniques and educating stakeholders on how to use it. Finally, in the study Evelin Candratio et al. (2023) It was explored how RPA can improve the efficiency of data collection and analysis in external auditing. Despite the potential benefits. This research show the significance of robotic machine automation and synthetic intelligence in enhancing performance and quality inside the regions of auditing and inner evaluation, at the same time as emphasizing the need for non-prevent qualification of auditors and implementation of in-intensity analyses to find out the benefits and stressful situations associated with the utility of those era.

3 Extended Benefits of RPA

See Fig. 1.

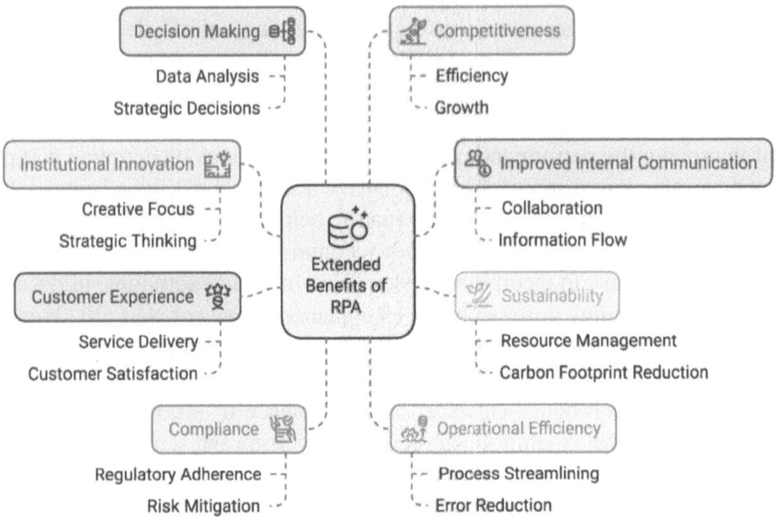

Fig. 1. Extended Benefits of RPA

3.1 Institutional Innovation

Robotic technique Automation is a fundamental element supporting innovation in enterprises. By reducing the time and effort devoted to mundane and repetitive operations, RPA enables workers to focus on creative and strategic activities that enhance organizational performance. For example, financial auditors might transition their focus from procedural guidelines to scrutinizing data and identifying opportunities to improve performance and mitigate risk. This capability fosters enhanced strategic thinking inside organizations and the emergence of innovative solutions matched with development and expansion objectives (Hoenderdos and van Triest, 2024).

3.2 Improve Internal Communication

Effective inner communication plays an essential role in ensuring organizational success by means of promoting collaboration and efficient information alternate throughout departments. The adoption of Robotic process automation has the capability to seriously improve this communication via automating habitual approaches, thereby accelerating decision-making and lowering the chance of errors. Additionally, overall performance reports generated through RPA allow organizations to enhance coordination, establish priorities, and gain shared targets (Saikumari et al., 2023).

3.3 Sustainability

RPA plays a crucial function in advancing environmental sustainability with the aid of automating repetitive tasks and lowering dependence on paper and other conventional sources. For example, automated systems can perform obligations such as document creation and statistical evaluation without the need for printing or other consumables. This automation not simplest complements operational efficiency but also considerably reduces the carbon footprint of agencies. By decreasing reliance on manual processes, RPA contributes to the conservation of energy and resources, aligning with broader sustainability objectives (Tomar and Grover, 2024).

3.4 Improve Customer Experience

RPA performs a pivotal role in improving consumer experience by using enhancing the performance and pleasantness of organizational services. Through the automation of recurring and repetitive duties, RPA permits personnel to devote their efforts to extra complex, value-added tasks that require human expertise, thereby elevating service delivery and client satisfaction. This generation helps faster response instances and minimizes errors, both of which can be crucial for keeping high levels of consumer loyalty. For instance, automated structures can efficaciously deal with consumer requests, which include reproducing account information, updating statistics, or processing payments, main to faster responses and improved satisfaction. By accelerating transaction approaches and lowering the probability of mistakes, RPA contributes to an advanced client experience and fosters accelerated loyalty (Agrawal et al., 2024; Tomar and Grover, 2024).

3.5 Enhancing Compliance

RPA greatly improves compliance with internal and external regulations by automating processes based on predefined standards, thereby minimizing human error and the risk of regulatory violations. This functionality is especially advantageous in fields such as financial auditing, where RPA ensures that financial operations are conducted in accordance with applicable regulations, reducing legal risks and the likelihood of penalties. Additionally, automating compliance checks enables the real-time detection of discrepancies, further aiding organizations in sustaining regulatory adherence (Bayraktar et al., 2022).

3.6 Improve Operational Efficiency

RPA significantly improves operational performance by way of automating repetitive tasks, thereby lowering the time required for routine methods and minimizing the prevalence of human mistakes. RPA systems can execute more than one duty concurrently without experiencing fatigue, allowing quicker completion of the entirety and lowering operational costs. This generation allows corporations to keep non-stop operations, improving universal productivity and strengthening their competitiveness in the marketplace (Bhardwaj et al., 2024; Tayab and Li, 2024).

3.7 Facilitating Decision Making

RPA circuitously facilitates improved decision-making by using presenting accurate statistics and reliable evaluation. Because RPA can acquire and examine records fast and effectively, companies can make decisions based totally on actual and real information. For instance, computerized equipment can examine marketplace traits and monetary forecasts in real time, supporting executives in making strategic decisions quickly (Abdulaali, 2018).

3.8 Increase Competitiveness

RPA significantly enhances market competitiveness by improving performance, reducing errors, and ensuring compliance. Organizations leveraging RPA can deliver faster and more accurate services, gaining a competitive edge over their rivals. RPA allows businesses to expand operations without need for extensive new hiring, thus boosting profitability and sustainable growth. This is achieved through the automation of repetitive tasks, freeing human resources for complex and value-added activities (Zasadnyi and Tanasiuk, 2024).

4 Methodology

Technological advancements and the increasing demand for automation have propelled the growth of Robotic Process Automation, with the market valued at $1.89 billion in 2021 and projected to double in the future. Despite this growth, RPA is underutilized in internal auditing, currently accounting for only 2% of usage, although it has the potential to rise to 21% (Wright et al., 2017). RPA streamlines repetitive obligations, enabling auditors to pay attention on problem-fixing and decision-making. However, its adoption has been hindered by a loss of clarity on implementation strategies (Struthers-Kennedy and Poulikakos, 2018). Auditors often find it challenging to determine the most suitable tasks for automation, with a survey indicating that 40% of companies struggle to prioritize RPA initiatives (Eulerich et al., 2022). Additionally, many RPA implementations fail. To address these challenges, we intend to expand frameworks that help auditors in identifying appropriate automation opportunities and expertise the key advantages and barriers related to RPA implementation.

The study aimed to identify the most important benefits in using robotic process automation in the efficiency of internal auditing in institutions in Iraq. This examine used the Republic of Iraq as a case study to examine the benefits of enforcing robot system automation in improving the performance of internal auditing inside Iraqi establishments. The studies involved one hundred and fifty employees as accountants and auditors. Primary information had been accumulated the use of based questionnaires, at the same time as secondary data has been amassed from reports and various digital sources. The number one information underwent a rigorous technique of series, sorting, and auditing to ensure accuracy and readability. This data was then coded and entered into the SPSS statistical evaluation software for further evaluation. Frequency tables and chances had been applied to degree the unique goals of the observer. To verify the relationships between the recognized variables, Pearson's correlation coefficient was calculated. The pattern traits were summarized the usage of the mathematics mean, standard deviation, and frequency tables. Additionally, Spearman's correlation analysis turned into performed to explore the relationships between inner auditing and RPA.

BPMN 2.0 language was used to simulate certain processes. The diagrams below represent a practical model for applying internal audit concepts while enhancing them with automation techniques to reduce errors and increase efficiency.

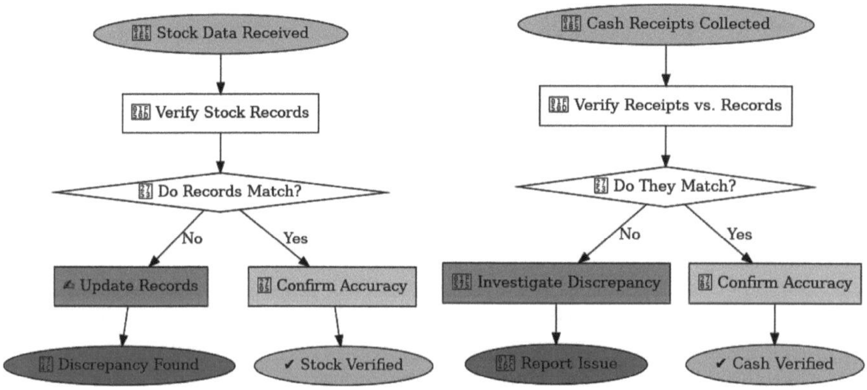

The flowchart above illustrates the process of verifying inventory data within an organization to ensure accuracy between actual records and those stored in the system. This process is essential for ensuring inventory safety and improving purchasing and financial management processes. The process begins when new inventory data is added, either by scanning or manual entry. The new data is compared with existing records in the system to ensure that the actual quantities match those in the records. If the data matches, the records are confirmed, the data is approved, and the review process is closed. If the data does not match, a data update is requested to correct errors, whether due to inventory loss, input errors, or potential theft. The other diagram represents a flowchart for the cash receipt verification process. Cash receipts are collected and used as a basis for matching them with the financial records. Cash receipts are compared with the accounting records to detect any discrepancies that may indicate accounting errors or financial manipulation. If the receipts match the accounting records, the data is confirmed and the cash is approved. The financial process is considered to be running smoothly without errors or problems. However, if there are discrepancies, an error is reported by creating a problem report and a notification is sent to the audit team to ensure that financial fraud or errors are prevented.

The study Hypothesis is Robotic process automation significantly improves the effectiveness of internal audits.

The findings from the analysis of 150 questionnaires distributed to accountants and auditors in Iraqi government institutions are presented in the tables below.

The table below displays the demographic characteristics of the study sample, including gender, years of experience, and education levels (Table 1).

The table below highlights the key benefits of using RPA in internal auditing, as identified by participants (Table 2).

Table 1. Demographic characteristics

Variable	Category	Frequency	Percentage (%)
Gender	Male	108	72%
	Female	42	28%
Years of Experience	Less than 5 years	30	20%
	5 - 10 years	60	40%
	More than 10 years	60	40%
Educational Level	Bachelor's	98	65.3%
	Master's	39	26%
	PhD	13	8.7%

Table 2. Anticipated Advantages of Implementing Robotic Process Automation

Benefit	Strongly Agree	Agree	Neutral	Disagree	Strongly Disagree	Mean Score
Reducing human errors	45%	30%	15%	6%	4%	**4.06**
Speeding up audit processes	40%	28%	18%	8%	6%	**3.88**
Enhancing compliance with standards	50%	32%	10%	5%	3%	**4.21**
Improving financial report quality	42%	33%	12%	8%	5%	**3.99**
Reducing audit costs	35%	30%	20%	10%	5%	**3.80**

The tables above indicate that 82% of participants agree that RPA enhances compliance with auditing standards, while 75% believe it reduces human errors in auditing. Additionally, the mean scores show that all benefits exceed 3.5, highlighting a strong acceptance of RPA's advantages (Table 3).

The table above demonstrates a strong positive correlation between RPA usage and audit efficiency ($r = 0.72$, $p < 0.01$). A positive relationship exists between RPA usage and error reduction ($r = 0.69$, $p < 0.01$). The results indicate that increased use of RPA leads to higher efficiency and faster audit completion. < 0.01). Additionally, there is a positive relationship between RPA usage and error reduction ($r = 0.69$, $p < 0.01$). These results indicate that greater use of RPA enhances efficiency and accelerates audit completion.

Table 3. Correlation Analysis: RPA and Audit Efficiency

Variable	Correlation Coefficient (r)	Significance Level (p)
RPA and audit efficiency	0.72	0.000
RPA and error reduction	0.69	0.001
RPA and audit speed	0.66	0.002

A multiple regression analysis was performed to assess how RPA usage affects audit quality. The results are presented below (Table 4).

Table 4. Regression Analysis: The Impact of RPA on Audit Quality

Independent Variable	B	Beta	t	Sig
RPA Usage	0.52	0.71	5.98	0.000
Integration with existing systems	0.35	0.48	4.72	0.001
Auditor Training	0.28	0.42	3.85	0.002

The table above indicates that RPA usage accounts for 52% of the variations in audit quality ($R^2 = 0.52$, $p < 0.01$). < 0.01) < 0.01). Additionally, increased adoption of RPA significantly enhances audit quality ($Beta = 0.71$, $p < 0.01$). Furthermore, system integration and auditor training play a positive role in the successful implementation of RPA.

5 Conclusion

Robotic Process Automation stands out as a vital and influential tool in improving internal audit efficiency, enhancing process accuracy, and reducing operational costs. By implementing this technology, organizations can achieve significant improvements in the speed of completion and quality of performance, which contributes to raising the level of organizational efficiency and enhancing competitiveness in the market. However, to ensure the success of RPA implementation in organizations, it is essential that companies invest in training and developing their employees to ensure their effective interaction with new systems. They must also adopt best practices for integrating existing systems with RPA to ensure that there are no conflicts or intersections in operations.

It is worth noting that the utility of RPA ought not to be constrained solely to internal audit, but can be expanded to encompass other areas within the organization, including enhancing consumer experience, improving compliance, or even exploring the possibilities of using artificial intelligence to increase the effectiveness of automation. Therefore, it is crucial that further research is conducted to discover the potential of RPA in multiple areas and determine how to best invest in this technology to get the most out of it.

6 Recommendations:

1. Organizations must invest in training their employees to use new RPA technologies to ensure maximum benefit from this technology.
2. Organizations should focus on easy and effective integration between RPA and existing software systems to avoid any conflict that may affect the workflow.
3. Encouraging further studies on the application of RPA in different areas within organizations, especially in improving customer experience and using artificial intelligence to enhance the effectiveness of automation.
4. There should be strong strategies to ensure data protection from cyber risks when using RPA in addition RPA systems should be developed and updated periodically to ensure the continued effectiveness of automation and keep pace with ongoing technological changes.

Through these recommendations, organizations can ensure optimal use of RPA technology, leading to improved organizational performance and sustainable success.

References

Abd, A., Serag, E.-M., Daoud, M.M.: A proposed framework for value-based internal audit and its impact on the added value and the expectation gap of internal audit: (a field study in Egypt). In: Alexandria Journal of Accounting Research First Issue, Vol. 5 (2021)

Abdulaali, A.R.: The impact of intellectual capital on business organization. Acad. Account. Fin. Stud. J. **22**(6), 1–16 (2018)

Agrawal, R.R., Sharma, B., Gupta, S., Shinde, S.: Fundamental Of Robotic Process Automation (RPA). San International Scientific Publications (2024). https://doi.org/10.59646/rpa/225

Almayyahi, A.R.A., Saleh, S.A.F., Metawee, A.K.: Applying Robotic Process Automation (RPA) in Sustainable Audit Quality: A Literature Review Survey. International Conference on Explainable Artificial Intelligence in the Digital Sustainability, pp. 26–35 (2024)

Bahl, S.: Role of Internet of Things (Iot) in Supply Chain Management Effectiveness: An Empirical Study. INFORMATION TECHNOLOGY IN INDUSTRY 6(3) (2018)

Bayraktar, D., Pitic, A., Mihu, C.: Streamlining Banking Processes by Implementing RPA. Rev. Econ. **74**, 7–16 (2022)

Bhardwaj, V.: A systematic review of robotic process automation in business operations: Contemporary trends and insights. J. Intell Syst. Control **2**(3), 153–169 (2023)

Bhardwaj, V., et al.: Optimizing Structured Data Processing Through Robotic Process Automation. ArXiv Preprint ArXiv:2408.14791 (2024)

Candratio, E., Harita, M.P., Hartanto, A.D., Hermawan, M.S.: Adoption of robotic process automation in external auditing process in metropolitan indonesia: a qualitative approach. JATISI (Jurnal Teknik Informatika Dan Sistem Informasi) **10**(2) (2023)

Dahabiyeh, L., Mowafi, O.: Challenges of using RPA in auditing: A socio-technical systems approach. Intel. Sys. Account. Fin. Manage. **30**(2), 76–86 (2023). https://doi.org/10.1002/isaf.1537

Eulerich, M., Pawlowski, J., Waddoups, N.J., Wood, D.A.: A framework for using robotic process automation for audit tasks. Contemp. Account. Res. **39**(1), 691–720 (2022)

Hanford, R.J., Mullin, C.P., Facker, B., Wong, C., Ocegueda-Hernandez, F.: Process automation optimizes the process of placing a drill bit on the bottom of the wellbore. Google Patents (2022)

Hoenderdos, J., van Triest, S.: Unlocking RPA potential: understanding the use of Robotic Process Automation by finance employees. Maandblad Voor Accountancy En Bedrijfseconomie **98**(3), 65–74 (2024)

Kim, J., Kim, S.H., Joe, I.: AI-based RPA's work automation operation to respond to hacking threats using collected threat logs. Appl. Sci. **14**(22), 10217 (2024)

Kumar, P., Garg, A., Singh, R.: Utilization of RPA in Control Monitoring and Hyper Automation in Audit Ecosystem. In: Modernizing Enterprise IT Audit Governance and Management Practices, pp. 238–283. IGI Global (2023)

Liu, S.: Robotic Process Automation (RPA) in Auditing: A Commentary. Int. J. Comp. Audit. **4**(1), 23–28 (2022)

Moffitt, K.C., Rozario, A.M., Vasarhelyi, M.A.: Robotic process automation for auditing. J. Emerg. Technol. Account. **15**(1), 1–10 (2018)

Pandy, G., et al.: Advancements in Robotics Process Automation: A Novel Model with Enhanced Empirical Validation and Theoretical Insights. ArXiv Preprint ArXiv:2410.04255 (2024)

Peláez, M.M., Aguirre-Álvarez, Y.A.: Robotic Process Automation Technology applied to the Management of SMEs in the Manufacturing and Service Sector: A Systematic Review. Revista Universidad y Empresa **27**(48), 1–43 (2025)

Rejeki, S.S., Sulistyowati, P.: Automatisasi proses robotik dan dampaknya pada akuntansi. Jurnal Riset Manajemen Dan Ekonomi (JRIME) **1**(2), 221–248 (2023)

Saikumari, V., Joseph, S.B., Swetha, V., Venkatesh, B.P.: A study on the various channels of internal communication and its impact on employee engagement. Russian Law Journal **11**(11S), 68–75 (2023)

Sirohi, A., Kejriwal, A., Hossain, M.K.: Current Trends in Business and Management: A Review. Asian Journal of Economics, Business and Accounting, 41–47 (2022). https://doi.org/10.9734/ajeba/2022/v22i24892

Solanki, U., Mehta, K., Shukla, V.K.: Robotic process automation and audit quality: a comprehensive analysis. 2024 11th International Conference on Reliability, Infocom Technologies and Optimization (Trends and Future Directions)(ICRITO), 1–4 (2024)

Struthers-Kennedy, A., Poulikakos, A.: RPA: First steps to greater internal audit efficiency. Corporate Compliance Insights (2018)

Tayab, A., Li, Y.: The contribution of the RPA technology in enhancing better business performance in Warehouse management. IEEE Access (2024)

Thekkethil, M.S., Shukla, V.K., Beena, F., Chopra, A.: Robotic process automation in banking and finance sector for loan processing and fraud detection. 2021 9th International Conference on Reliability, Infocom Technologies and Optimization (Trends and Future Directions)(ICRITO), 1–6 (2021)

Tomar, P., Grover, V.: Robotic process automation: the tangible and human shift in business process efficiency. In: Intelligent Computing and Optimization for Sustainable Development, 1st Edition, pp. 238–251. Chapman and Hall/CRC (2024). https://doi.org/10.1201/9781032625829-14/robotic-process-automation-praveen-tomar-veena-grover

Wright, D., Witherick, D., Gordeeva, M.: The robots are ready. Are you? Untapped advantage in your digital workforce. Deloitte (2017). Available at: https://Www2.Deloitte.Com/Content/Dam/Deloitte/Tr/Documents/Technology/Deloitte-Robots-Are-Ready.pdf. Accessed 22 January 2023

Zasadnyi, B.A., Tanasiuk, A.V.: Application of rpa systems for robotization of enterprises' accounting processes. Theoretical and Applied Issues of Economics **48**, 89–97 (2024). https://doi.org/10.17721/tppe.2024.48.9

Analysis of Influencing Factors of Information Sharing in Education Big Data Platform

Shuang Li and Feng Han(✉)

Shanghai Construction Management Vocational College, Shanghai 201702, China
hanfeng@fudan.edu.cn

Abstract. [Purpose/Significance] Educational big data platform information sharing has become an important content and research hotspot of current educational informatization work. [Method/Process] The influencing factors of information sharing were constructed, and DEMATEL was used to classify and rank the information sharing factors of education large data platform. [Result/Conclusion] The results showed that subject demand factor, accessibility factor and cooperation mode factor were the most critical factors affecting educational big data platform information sharing, resource richness factor and information usefulness factor were the core factors, and they were also the most vulnerable factors. Finally, the corresponding strategies and suggestions were put forward.

Keywords: educational big data · information platform · information sharing · influencing factors · DEMATEL method

With the rapid development and popularization of modern information technologies such as computer technology and network technology, the impact of information technology on economic and social development is increasingly deepening. As an important component of informatization, educational informatization is receiving increasing attention from governments and universities around the world [1, 2]. The US Department of Education first proposed the concept of using big data for data mining to promote educational reform in 2012 [3]. Literally speaking, big data refers to datasets that exceed the scale of traditional databases. In fact, big data also includes changes in both technology and thinking: in terms of technology, it includes corresponding computing, storage, analysis, and mining techniques; in terms of thinking, data-driven innovative thinking has replaced the previous method of analyzing using internal mechanisms and objective laws. China began deploying its big data strategy in 2015 and established corresponding research institutions, making big data a key focus of development during the 13th Five Year Plan period and a new driving force for educational reform. The construction of an education big data information platform is the key to the practical application of education big data theory. It can achieve open sharing of information, avoid duplicate investment of human and financial resources, greatly improve the efficiency of educational resource utilization, avoid the loss of educational resources, and has important significance in strengthening educational communication and cooperation, and realizing the potential value of educational resources [4]. The construction of an education big data platform

K. W. Lee and L. H. Wong (Eds.): ITEA 2025, CCIS 2643, pp. 164–174, 2026.
https://doi.org/10.1007/978-981-95-2011-4_16

relies on information sharing, and only by achieving full sharing can maximum utilization be achieved. The information sharing of education big data platforms is influenced by various factors such as the sharing subject, sharing object, and sharing environment, and these factors do not exist in isolation. They interact and are interrelated, jointly affecting the sharing of information. It is necessary to comprehensively analyze these factors to identify the main influencing factors. Currently, there are few studies in the literature that classify and identify multiple factors such as information sharing on education big data platforms. Based on this, this article constructs a system of influencing factors for information sharing on education big data platforms, identifies the interrelated factors using DEMATEL method, and proposes corresponding countermeasures and suggestions for information sharing on education big data platforms, which has certain guiding significance for the construction and development of university education big data platforms.

1 Determination of Influencing Factors for Information Sharing on Education Big Data Platforms

When studying individual behavior, classic theories such as social cognitive theory, social exchange theory, rational behavior theory, and technology acceptance and information adoption theory are widely applied. Through the analysis of relevant theories on information sharing, it is found that different theories emphasize different focuses on the influencing factors of information sharing. For example, social cognitive theory emphasizes that information sharing behavior is influenced by personal factors and social networks, and that the environment, behavior, and people are mutually causal [5, 6]; Social exchange theory emphasizes the influence of factors such as information technology, trust, knowledge subjects, and organizational culture on information sharing; The theory of rational behavior emphasizes that organizational atmosphere, psychological ownership, and perceived knowledge value influence the willingness to share [8, 9]; The theory of technology acceptance and information adoption focuses on the perceived ease of use and perceived usefulness of information when explaining information sharing behavior [9]. The education big data platform is based on a cross temporal and spatial network environment, providing a unified platform for information exchange, interaction, cooperation, and knowledge sharing among information subjects, and solving the related problems of education information subject networks and learning, production, and life in reality. In the process of information sharing on education big data platforms, the information sharing behavior of sharing subjects is guided by multiple theories. In order to accurately identify the key factors that affect information sharing on education big data platforms, this article summarizes the factors that affect information sharing into three dimensions: sharing subjects, sharing objects, and sharing environments. This statement includes the social psychology foundation of rational behavior theory and social cognition theory, as well as the support of social exchange theory and technology acceptance and information adoption theory. Based on a review of relevant literature, an indicator system for the influencing factors of information sharing on education big data platforms is formed.

1.1 Shared Subject Dimension

Roberts M [10] studied the individual behavioral characteristics in information sharing and believed that information subjects play a significant role in information sharing. He pointed out that the contribution rate of information subjects to information sharing is over 80%. Subsequently, scholars conducted in-depth research on the characteristics of information sharing behavioral subjects. Li Jinyang [11] analyzed the influencing factors of knowledge sharing in virtual communities based on social exchange theory, and pointed out that sharing subjects can only engage in sharing after the benefits reach their personal expectations; Wu Yu et al. [12] simulated the dynamic evolution characteristics of knowledge sharing in different contexts, analyzed the degree of influence of different influencing factors, and pointed out that communication skills play an irreplaceable role in the process of information receivers from searching for information, receiving information to possessing information; Fan Lili et al. [13] believed that the success of information sharing mainly depends on the sharing motivation and self-protection level of information owners, and they proved their conclusion by establishing a quantitative model; Liu Feng [14] believes that the sharing awareness of the information sharing party determines the possibility of information sharing, and points out that the sharing awareness and willingness are positively correlated; Yu Lingling et al. [9] pointed out that information distance is a measure of the difference in information background between information sharing parties, which is influenced by various factors such as education level, cognitive level, and information structure. The size of information distance is positively correlated with the difficulty of information transfer; Tang Yanhua et al. [15] found that an individual's understanding ability not only affects the effectiveness of information transfer, but also has an impact on the expected return of information sharers.

The suppliers and demanders of educational information resources are the two core entities that make up the joint construction of educational big data platforms, and they are the direct actors of information resources. Resource providers refer to information resource owners, including governments, universities, research institutions, and non-profit organizations such as enterprises, who engage in sharing activities under certain conditions. The demand for information resources refers to the consumers of information resources, including teachers, students, researchers, and managers of education departments at all levels. The subject of information sharing is generally both the supplier and the demander of information resources. On the one hand, the supplier serves as the producer of information resources, and on the other hand, it may also be the agent of information resources or the regenerator of other information resources; On the other hand, after receiving information resources, resource demanders will also participate in resource regeneration based on their own development needs, becoming suppliers of information resources. Different entities will make behavioral choices based on their own cognition and external conditions, so the interests of all parties need to be coordinated as a whole. The greatest driving force for information resource sharing comes from the needs of the subjects. However, in information sharing, the real problems and professional development of the information subjects are different, and the differences in the shared information resources they have mastered and their identification with educational information resources can also lead to differences in the driving force for information sharing.

In summary, information sharing in the dimension of sharing subjects includes the following influencing factors: information subject needs, identification with resources, and differences in resource ownership.

1.2 Shared Object Dimension

Yifei et al. [16] summarized the factors that are not conducive to information sharing from the perspective of information attributes, pointing out that the stickiness, relevance, ambiguity, and complexity of information are obstacles to information sharing. Yu Liufang et al. [17] believe that information sharing is a continuous process of complementarity and replication. The stronger the complementarity of information, the greater its replicability, which is more conducive to information sharing. Tian Mei [18] pointed out that a certain amount of information resources is a prerequisite for information sharing, and the willingness of sharing subjects to share is largely influenced by the amount of information available from the outside world. The more external shared information that the sharing subject can obtain, the higher the satisfaction of the sharing subject, and the greater the possibility of their sharing behavior. Research by Ye Fengyun [19] suggests that information quality refers to the perception of the usefulness, accuracy, and timeliness of information circulating in big data platforms by sharing entities. Currently, the consumption of information has shifted from the traditional pursuit of quantity to the pursuit of quality. The abundance of information has been weakened to a certain extent in competition, and the higher the quality of information, the greater the degree of sharing. Lin Baodeng [20] pointed out that the compatibility between new technology platforms and previous information systems is an important factor affecting information improvement, and the compatibility of information systems has a positive relationship with information sharing. Chen Haitao et al. [21] explored information sharing behavior from the perspective of technology acceptance and information adoption theory, proposing the use of perceived usefulness to characterize the difficulty of information exchange among sharing subjects in carrying out a certain behavior. They believed that the more convenient the communication, the more inclined it is to implement information sharing behavior.

Information resources, as the object of information sharing, are the basic elements of information co construction and sharing, and also the focus of the construction of education big data platforms. The key words for the construction and development of educational information resources can generally be summarized as' available ',' usable ', and' easy to use '. With the construction and development of education big data platforms, China's education information resources have begun to take shape, and the quantity of information resource construction is no longer the main contradiction in information resource construction. The demand for information resources has shifted to focusing on whether they can be used and whether they are easy to use. Educational information resources are different from ordinary cultural media in that their focus is on education. The construction of educational data information platforms mainly relies on online platforms, and perceived usefulness refers to the difficulty of information exchange among sharing subjects in carrying out a certain behavior. Therefore, the standard for measuring the quality of educational information resources is whether the information resource demander can gain a sense of belonging during the use process.

In summary, information sharing in the dimension of shared objects includes the following influencing factors: resource richness, information usefulness, and accessibility.

1.3 Dimension of Shared Environment

Zhang Yan et al. [22] conducted a study on the impact of transformational leadership on team information sharing, and pointed out that building trust through effective communication between team leaders and members has a positive effect on knowledge sharing. Jiang Wen [23] analyzed the influencing factors of knowledge sharing between enterprises from the perspective of the internet, and believed that improving the network organizational system can promote the establishment of a good cultural system and provide guarantees for the smooth progress of information sharing behavior. Guo Xuan [24] believes that organizational culture has a direct impact on individuals' subjective intentions, behavioral motivations, and attitudes towards sharing. Cultural construction can help promote information sharing. Feng Hua et al. [25] believe that trust is the foundation for conducting transactions with each other in a relational society. Trust can make people feel psychologically secure, and the level of trust between the two parties is crucial for the success of information sharing. Trust between sharing entities can enable dispersed sharing entities to form interpersonal connections and promote information sharing. Gao Xirong et al. [26] conducted a study on the impact of different incentive models on the effectiveness of organizational information sharing, and pointed out that scientific incentive measures contribute to information innovation in enterprises, with organizational structure and architecture being the driving force behind information sharing.

The shared environment mainly refers to policy driven, economic benefits, social evaluation, and competitive pressure, which are the external driving forces for information sharing on education big data platforms. Due to the fact that information resource providers include different stakeholders, as builders and providers of educational big data platform information resources, their original intentions for participating in resource co construction and sharing are not the same, and their sources of motivation are not completely consistent. In order to ensure the maximization of the benefits of co construction and sharing of educational information resources, we should start from stimulating and integrating the sources of motivation, and provide more benefits protection for information resource providers. The construction of the Education Big Data Platform is a new organizational structure that relies on networks and information technology to connect people from different regions and organizations to complete a specific task. Mutual trust can share the information they possess with others, maximizing their value and improving team operational efficiency.

In summary, the dimensions of shared environment include the following factors: mutual trust, cooperation mode, and incentive mechanism.

2 Identification of Key Influencing Factors Affecting Information Sharing on Education Big Data Platforms

2.1 Interaction Relationship Between Various Influencing Factors

The sharing of educational data information is influenced by 9 sub factors in three dimensions: sharing subject, sharing object, and sharing environment. However, these influencing factors are not independent of each other, but interact and influence each other, jointly influencing the information sharing behavior of the sharing subject [10, 11]. Taking incentive mechanisms as an example, when funds or other incentive policies are invested in educational data information sharing, the sharing subjects will receive certain sharing benefits, which will to some extent affect their own and other sharing information subjects' needs. When the overall demand of the information subjects increases, the richness and usefulness of resources will also be greatly improved, producing more results and providing support for all subjects to invest more energy in achieving educational information sharing, forming a positive interaction situation. The interaction between factors that affect the sharing of educational data information may ultimately change information sharing, so it is necessary to identify the key influencing factors in order to promote targeted sharing of educational data information.

2.2 Identification and Classification Methods of Influencing Factors based on DEMATEL

The interaction between various influencing factors in educational data information sharing is complex, and objective data is used to reflect the relative complexity. Therefore, this article adopts the DEMATEL method to analyze it. The DEMATEL method is a system factor analysis method that uses matrices and graphs. This method utilizes the knowledge and experience of experts or groups to determine the impact relationships of various factors and their importance in the system. Combined with weights, multiple factors can be merged into a single factor, which can be implemented through computers. By quantifying the relationships between various influencing factors, areas that need improvement can be identified, and it has a wide range of applications.

The specific application steps are as follows: First, determine the main influencing factors of the research problem. Secondly, construct a direct impact matrix to determine the interrelationships between various factors. The elements of a matrix reflect the influence of one factor on another, and their values reflect the strength of the influence. Thirdly, normalize the impact matrix. Divide each element of the direct impact matrix constructed in the second step by the maximum sum of each row to obtain the normalization matrix. Fourth, obtain the comprehensive impact matrix. Fifth, calculate the impact and degree of influence of each factor. The sum of each row element in the comprehensive influence matrix is called the influence degree; The sum of each column of elements is called the degree of influence. Sixth, calculate the centrality and causality through the degree of influence and the degree of being influenced. Centrality is the sum of the degree of influence and the degree of influence, which reflects the magnitude of the influence of a certain factor in the entire influencing factor system. Causality is the difference between the degree of influence and the degree of influence, which is a comprehensive reflection of the influence of a certain factor on other factors and the influence of other factors. If the degree of causality is greater than, it is considered a causal factor, and if the degree of causality is less than zero, it is considered a causal factor.

2.3 Analysis of Key Factors Influencing Information Sharing

The questionnaire survey targets experts in the field of education big data and frontline personnel in educational research and teaching work, providing a guarantee for accurately identifying the influencing factors of education data information sharing. Invite 40 experts and staff to rate the interaction relationships between various influencing factors based on the above conditions, and construct a direct impact matrix.(Table 1).

Table 1. Analysis of the Interaction Relationship between Factors Influencing Information Sharing on Education Big Data Platforms

First level indicator	Secondary indicators	Influence degree	Affected degree	Centrality	Centrality ranking	Reason degree	Reason ranking
Shared subject factor C1	Information Subject Requirement C11	2.430	2.256	4.686	1	0.174	5
	Resource identification C12	1.448	2.393	3.841	6	-0.945	9
	Having resource differences C13	1. 448	1.600	3.047	9	-0.125	6
Shared object factor C2	Resource richness C21	1.774	2.463	4.237	5	-0.688	7
	Information usefulness C22	1.774	2.502	4.277	4	-0.728	8
	Easy accessibility C23	2.430	2.053	4.483	3	0.376	3
Shared object factor C3	Incentive mechanism C31	2.000	1.760	3.759	7	0.240	4
	Cooperation mode C32	2.967	1.707	4.674	2	1.260	1
	Mutual trust C33	1.907	1.444	3. 351	8	0.463	2

1) Key factor analysis of indicator factors. From the centrality, it can be seen that the centrality of information subject demand factors, cooperation mode factors, and accessibility factors is greater than 4 4. Ranking in the top three indicates that these three sub factors are the most critical factors in the information sharing process of educational big data platforms. The centrality of the factors of resource abundance and information usefulness is 4 Above 0, ranking closely behind, the impact of information sharing on education big data platforms is significant and should be given sufficient attention. From the causal degree, it can be seen that the causal degrees of five factors, including information subject demand factors, accessibility factors, incentive mechanism factors, cooperation mode factors, and mutual trust factors, are positive, indicating that these five factors actively influence other factors in the system and are causal factors; The reason degree for the four factors of resource identification, resource difference, funding support, and trust is less than 0, indicating that these four factors are influenced by other influencing factors in the system and are the result elements.

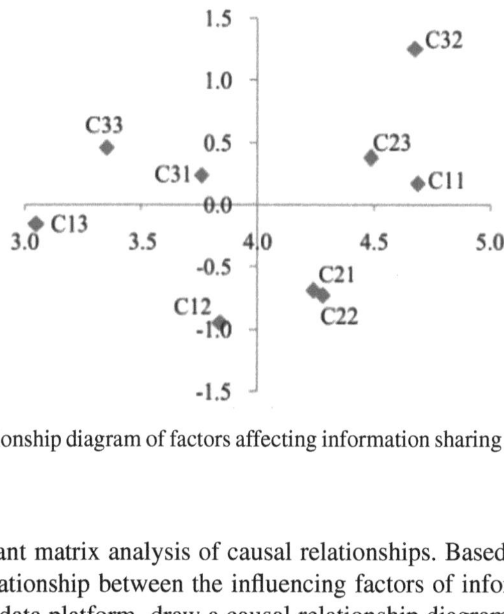

Fig. 1. Causal relationship diagram of factors affecting information sharing on education big data platforms

2) Four quadrant matrix analysis of causal relationships. Based on the analysis of the interaction relationship between the influencing factors of information sharing on the education big data platform, draw a causal relationship diagram of the influencing factors of information sharing on the education big data platform. The focus of centrality and causality is the average value of each sub factor, and the distribution of each factor in the four quadrants is shown in Fig. 1. The factors located in the first quadrant include information subject demand factors, accessibility factors, and cooperation mode factors. They are the driving factors of the entire system and have the greatest impact on the information sharing process of the education big data platform, playing the most critical role. The incentive mechanism factors and mutual trust factors located in the second quadrant are supportive factors that play a supportive role in influencing each other. The factors located in the third quadrant, such as resource identification and resource ownership differences, are independent factors of the entire system and play relatively

important roles in the system. The factors of resource abundance and information usefulness are located in the fourth quadrant, and they are the core problem factors of the entire system, which are most susceptible to their influence.

3 Suggestions for Countermeasures

The information sharing of education big data platforms is influenced by various factors, and there are interactions and correlations between these influencing factors. On the basis of relevant theoretical analysis, this article analyzes expert ratings and finds that the factors of information subject demand, accessibility, and cooperation mode are the driving factors of the entire system, and are the most critical. The author proposes the following suggestions regarding the main factors affecting information sharing on education big data platforms:

1) When developing an education big data platform, we should strengthen the construction of the main concept of co construction and sharing, and pay attention to the "human touch". The education big data platform is an open space for all sharing entities. It should fully utilize the resource information of the big data platform, create a strong learning atmosphere, arouse the demand of sharing entities for sharing information, promote communication and interaction between sharing entities, and enable sharing entities to obtain information from other sharing entities while sharing information with others.

2) The rapid development of modern information technology has brought convenience to the sharing of information resources. We attach great importance to the application of high-tech in platform construction, and guide more entities to actively participate in platform construction through policy guidance and supervision and assessment. We introduce big data mining and intelligent resource recommendation methods to mine and push high-quality scientific and technological resources, formulate and draft corresponding platform construction standards, avoid resource duplication, achieve information sharing on education big data platforms, and provide more and better personalized resource services for sharing entities.

3) The collaboration models involved in the construction of the education big data platform include various modes such as administration, market, and alliance. The administrative model is led by the government and has a solid support system, resulting in a relatively high success rate of the platform; The market model can attract more types and quantities of organizations to join, with profit as the goal, and the stability of the platform is relatively high; The alliance model refers to a model formed by a certain type of organization or enterprise with a common development goal, which has obvious advantages in data security and result application verification. However, in the actual application process, a single mode or a combination of multiple modes have their own advantages and disadvantages, and need to be flexibly applied in combination with the actual situation, which is also a direction of future research.

References

1. Tianhu, D.: Systematic review of digital twin cities: a new model of urban governance towards smart cities. Manage. Sci. Eng. **6**, P125-134 (2021)

2. Du, M.: Promoting Chinese path to modernization with the Urban Smart Digital Twin System Project. China's Construction Informatization 2023 (23)
3. Zhou, D.W., Wang, Q.W., Qi, Z.H., et al.: Deep class-incremental learning: A survey. arXiv preprint arXiv:2302.03648 (2023)
4. Zhen, L., Dongdai, Z., Na, L., et al.: Platform construction and key implementation technologies for educational big data. Mod. Educ. Technol. **28**(1), 100–106 (2018)
5. Aydt, H.: Cooling Singapore – Towards Urban Climate Design and Management in India 03. In: Cairns, S., Tunas, D. (end.) Passed 17 August 2022 https://www.nscc.sg/wp-content/uploads/2021/10/NSCC-Webinar-Heiko-Aydt-Supercomputing-for-Climate-informed-Urban-Planning.pdf
6. Amirzadeh, M., Sobhania, S., Sharifi, A.: Urban resilience: a vague or an evolutionary concept?. Sustainable Cities and Society **81**, 103853 https://doi.org/10.1016/j.scs.2022.103853
7. Mei, X.: Accelerating the innovation and development of teaching evaluation in colleges and universities in the new era. Science Review (Theoretical Academic Edition) 2023-11-24 Digital twin cities, leading a new era of urban intelligence in the future. The era of big data 2023 (11)
8. Weidong, C., Ping, W., Meiyue, W.: Research on the influencing factors model and optimization strategies of social interaction among academic virtual community users. Intelligence Theory and Practice **41**(6), 117–123 (2018)
9. Dembski, F., et al.: City level Digital Twinss for Smart Cities and Citizens: The Case Study of Herrenberg, Germany. Sustainability **12**(6), 2307. https://doi.org/10.3390/su12062307
10. Ning, X., Ma, G., Liu, Y., Ye, F.: New progress and enlightenment of teaching evaluation reform in british universities. Shanghai Educational Evaluation Study **12**(06) (2023)
11. Wu, Y., Wang, H., Han, Y.: Construction and simulation study of factors influencing knowledge sharing in collaborative information search and retrieval. Intelligence Theory and Practice, 2017, 40-6-21-2019. Modern Information Journal of July **39**(7) (4), 100–105, 65 (2019)
12. Biljecki, F., Stoter, J., Ledoux, H., Sisi, Z., ltekin, A.: Applications of 3D City Models: State of the Art Review. ISPRS Int. J. Geo Info. **4**(4), 2842–2889 https://doi.org/10.3390/ijgi4042842
13. Barresi, A.: Urban Digital Twin and urban planning for sustainable cities. Techne- Journal of Technology for Architecture and Environment **25**, 78–83 (2023). https://doi.org/10.36253/techne-13568
14. Wei, D.: Research status and trend analysis of teaching evaluation in Chinese and foreign universities. J. Chongqing Open Univ. **35**(04) (2023)
15. Chen, J.: Efficiency improvement and empowerment: the dual dimensional logic of digital twin technology assisting the modernization of smart cities. Henan Social Sciences **31**(12) (2023)
16. Yuqin, F., Wang, G., Li, J.: Design and compilation of questionnaire on non-intellectual factors of mathematics learning for primary school students. Examination Research **17**(1), 79–87 (2021)
17. Dembski, F., Yamu, C., W ö ssner, U.: Digital Twin. In Virtual Reality and Space syntax: Civil Engagement and Decision Support for Smart, Sustainable Cities. In: Proceedings of the 12th International Space syntax Conference Beijing, People's Republic of China, 8–13
18. Xu, X.: The influence of university campus culture construction on students' comprehensive quality. 2023 Educational Theory and ManagementThe 3rd "Innovative Education and Precision Management Summit Forum"
19. Baodeng, L.: A new carrier for the construction of open and shared mechanism of university information resources: virtual laboratory. Library Theory and Practice **1**, 96–100 (2018)

20. Haitao, C., Hao, C., Chaohui, D., et al.: Study on the influencing factors of information sharing among social recruitment users. Intelligence Science **35**(8), 153–158 (2017)
21. Yan, Z., Liwen, H.: Research on the impact of functional diversity based on transformational leadership on knowledge sharing within teams. J. Manag. **10**(10), 1454–1461 (2013)
22. Beiderbeck, D., Frevel, N., Heiko, A., Schmidt, S.L., Schweitzer, V.M.: Preparing, conducting, and analyzing Delphi surveys: Cross- disciplinary practices, new directions, and advancements. MethodsX 8 (2021). Article 101401,https://doi.org/10.1016/j.mex.2021.101401
23. Digital Twin: Helps Resilient City Construction Contribute to Beijing's Wisdom in Urban Renewal. Beijing Urban Sub center News/2022.19/003 Edition
24. Hua, F., Lei, N., Feng, H.: Study on the interaction between information sharing level and supply chain capability: mediating effect based on social control. Nankai Manage. Rev. **21**(4), 85–92 (2018)
25. Grounded Theory: Deakin University (2023). https://deakin.libguides.com/qualitative-study-designs/grounded-theory
26. Yanbo, S., Da, C.: Analysis of influencing factors of online government information dissemination based on self media. Modern Intelligence **38**(5), 87–93 (2018)
27. Yiwen, Y., Haitao, Z., Dan, W., et al.: Identification of key influencing factors of government WeChat information dissemination from the perspective of information ecology. Intelligence Science **35**(10), 109–115124 (2019)

Construction of an Education Resource Optimization Allocation and Management Model Combined with Big Data Analysis

Qing Han(✉) and Li Liu

Weifang Engineering Vocational College, Qingzhou 262500, Shandong, China
hanhan2004@126.com

Abstract. With the rapid growth of technologies such as artificial intelligence (AI), big data, and cloud computing, education informatization and modernization have received strong technical support, and the education industry is gradually entering a new stage of smart education. Education big data, as an important collection of data reflecting the current situation, needs, and problems of basic education resource (ER) allocation, has become a key tool for reshaping the structure of ER allocation and building a high-quality education ecosystem. However, the problem of uneven distribution of ER and the increasing demand for personalized learning remains prominent. In response to this situation, this article proposes an educational resource optimization configuration and management model based on particle swarm optimization algorithm (PSO) and deep learning (DL), combined with big data analysis technology. This model aims to achieve rational allocation of ER and provide personalized educational resource recommendations to students through DL technology, thereby maximizing resource utilization efficiency. The results shows that the model not only significantly improves the utilization rate of ER, but also performs well in the accuracy of personalized recommendations.

Keywords: Big data analysis · Education resources · Optimize configuration · Management model · Deep learning

1 Introduction

In the data-driven era, big data technology is deeply integrated with the field of education, profoundly affecting the layout, structure, and synergy of ER [1]. Big data technology not only reveals the patterns behind complex phenomena, but also provides strong support for scientific decision-making [2]. The rational allocation of ER is the foundation for the smooth development of educational activities [3]. With the popularization and in-depth growth of Internet technology, the teaching resource sharing platform came into being, providing convenient and efficient learning ways for teachers and students [4]. Online learning, as an emerging and important learning method, has gradually become an important supplement to traditional education. Compared to traditional education models, online education reduces users' learning costs, eliminates barriers caused by uneven distribution of resources, and enables high-quality ER to benefit more people

K. W. Lee and L. H. Wong (Eds.): ITEA 2025, CCIS 2643, pp. 175–184, 2026.
https://doi.org/10.1007/978-981-95-2011-4_17

across time and space limitations [5]. However, with the rapid development of online education, diversified personalized learning demands have put forward higher needs for the accuracy and effectiveness of resource recommendations [6].

In recent years, DL, as a popular technology in the area of AI, has achieved significant results in multiple fields with its forceful data processing and pattern recognition capabilities [7]. Especially in the optimization of educational resource allocation and personalized recommendation, many scholars have conducted relevant research and made certain progress. For example, Zhao et al. [8] constructed an online course recommendation system that combines data mining and graph theory methods to predict students' course selection tendencies, providing an effective solution to solve students' difficulty in course selection. Cui et al. [9] used the k-means clustering algorithm to recommend books for university libraries. They first browsed the borrowing history of the library, cleaned the data, classified books based on topic similarity, and then generated recommendation results through association rule mining. Meng [10] constructed an intelligent recommendation system using collaborative filtering algorithm and multi class support vector machine (SVM) algorithm, and conducted specific empirical analysis. Although this method improves recommendation accuracy, it still struggles to fully reflect micro level resource details.

Luo [11] conducted theoretical and empirical research on the connotation, characteristics, influencing factors, and existing problems of optimizing the allocation of ER from the perspective of technical support, and proposed a solution based on genetic algorithm for optimizing the ERs in universities. In addition, Xi et al. [12] designed multiple meta paths containing semantic relationships, combined with graph neural networks based on residual connections to guide user preferences, further introduced attention mechanisms to enhance model performance, and finally achieved prediction through regularization matrix decomposition. Although research has provided important references for optimizing the allocation of ER and personalized recommendations, existing methods still have certain limitations. This article proposes a model for optimizing the allocation and management of ER based on PSO and DL, combined with big data analysis technology. The model optimizes the global allocation strategy of ER through PSO algorithm, ensuring that resources can cover different regions and groups more fairly and efficiently. At the same time, the model utilizes DL technology to implement personalized educational resource recommendations, thereby maximizing the efficiency of resource utilization.

2 Methodology

2.1 Model Construction Combining PSO and DL

Against the backdrop of growth of AI, the education sector is undergoing profound changes [13]. The functions of the teaching resource sharing platform also need to keep up with the times to meet the needs of intelligence and personalization [14]. The essence of personalized learning resource recommendation is a deep analysis of the relationship between learners and learning resources [15]. To achieve this goal, online learning platforms need to extract value from raw data. This includes collecting user behavior data, learning preference information, and teaching resource characteristics, and providing learners with accurate learning resource recommendation services through efficient data analysis and mining techniques. This article proposes a model for optimizing the allocation and management of ER based on PSO and DL, combined with big data analysis technology. This model aims to achieve scientific management and personalized recommendation of ER through the collaborative operation of multiple modules. The model mainly consists of six functional modules, namely data preprocessing module, user management module, resource management module, DL module, online learning module, and feedback module. Its structure is shown in Fig. 1.

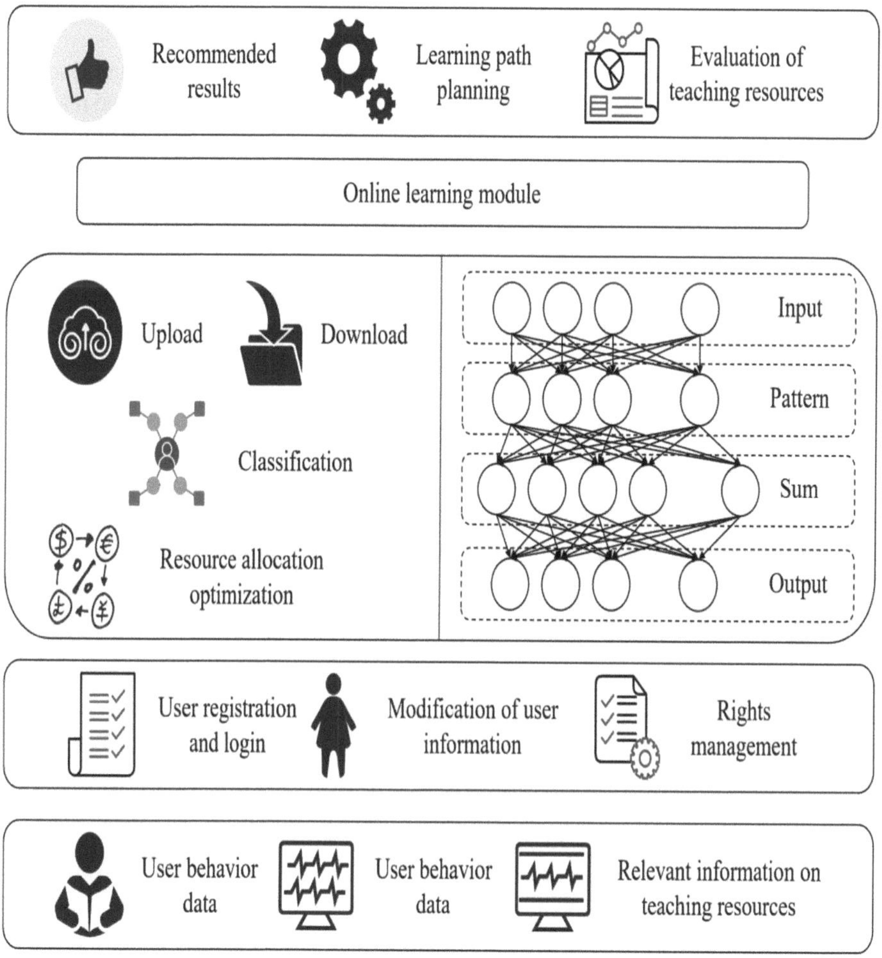

Fig. 1. Model structure

The data preprocessing module is the fundamental component of the entire model, responsible for collecting user behavior data, basic user information, and relevant information on teaching resources. The user management module is mainly responsible for user registration, login, permission management, and functions such as adding, deleting, modifying, and querying user information. This module not only ensures the security of the platform, but also provides users with a convenient operating experience, enabling them to flexibly manage personal information and learning records according to their own needs. The resource management module focuses on uploading, downloading, categorizing, modifying, and deleting teaching resources, while also having resource statistics and analysis functions. To improve the efficiency and fairness of resource allocation, this article introduces PSO in this module. PSO can dynamically accommodate resource allocation strategies on a global scale by simulating the optimization process of swarm intelligence, thereby reducing resource waste and improving utilization. The DL module is the core part of the model, used to build and train personalized recommendation systems.

Through DL training on a large amount of user learning behavior data and resource feature data, this module can accurately capture users' learning preferences and resource characteristics, thereby generating personalized recommendation lists. This article uses Generalized Regression Neural Network (GRNN) as the core algorithm. GRNN is a special neural network architecture that includes four layers: input layer, pattern layer, summation layer, and output layer. Compared to traditional neural networks, GRNN introduces weighting operations in the summation layer, making it perform better in handling nonlinear problems. The online learning module provides users with a highly interactive learning platform, supporting functions such as online browsing, answering questions, and communication. Users can access various teaching resources through the front-end interface, including video tutorials, document materials, and online courses. The design of this module focuses on user experience and strives to provide learners with an intuitive and convenient learning environment. Finally, the feedback module is used to collect user evaluations and feedback information on recommendation results, learning path planning, and teaching resources. Through this closed-loop mechanism, the model can continuously iterate and upgrade, gradually improving its level of intelligence.

2.2 Algorithm Principle

The core of improving the efficacy of educational resource allocation lies in optimizing the allocation of various resources, striving to accomplish the optimal allocation of resources while fully considering the complexity and specificity of each resource. The distribution of ER is influenced by multiple factors, and its distribution problem is not a simple linear relationship, but a complex nonlinear optimization problem. The ultimate goal of resource allocation is to maximize educational outcomes, that is, to achieve optimal utilization efficacy of ER through scientific and rational resource allocation. The efficacy of utilizing ER can usually be expressed as the ratio of educational output to educational input, and its mathematical expression is as follows:

$$U = \frac{\sum_{j=1}^{m} \mu_j O_j}{\sum_{i=1}^{n} \phi_i I_i} \quad (1)$$

Among them, i, j respectively represents educational resource elements and educational achievement elements; O_j, I_i represents the output and input of ER respectively; ϕ_i, μ_j represents the weights of each educational resource input indicator and output indicator.

In GRNN, the input matrix and output matrix are first defined as follows: $X = \begin{bmatrix} x_{11} & x_{12} & \cdots & x_{1n} \\ x_{21} & x_{22} & \cdots & x_{2n} \\ \vdots & \vdots & & \vdots \\ x_{m1} & x_{m2} & \cdots & x_{mn} \end{bmatrix}$, $Y = \begin{bmatrix} y_{11} & y_{12} & \cdots & y_{1n} \\ y_{21} & y_{22} & \cdots & y_{2n} \\ \vdots & \vdots & & \vdots \\ y_{k1} & y_{k2} & \cdots & y_{kn} \end{bmatrix}$. Among them, x_{ij} is the i input attribute of the j sample; y_{ij} is the i output value of the j sample; m is the total number of input attributes; n is the total number of samples; k is the dimension of the output value. After the input signal passes through the input layer, it is processed by the activation function and the result is generated in the pattern layer. The calculation process is as follows:

$$\alpha_j = exp\left[-\frac{\left(X' - X_j\right)^T\left(X' - X_j\right)}{2\sigma^2}\right] j = 1,2,\cdots,n \tag{2}$$

In the formula, σ is the smoothing factor and satisfies $\sigma > 0$, which is used to control the smoothness of the model; α_j is the output value of the j pattern layer neuron; X' is any input sample; X_j is the j training sample.

In the summation layer, all pattern layer results are weighted and summed:

$$S_{N_i} = \sum\nolimits_{j=1}^{n} w_{ij}\alpha_j \quad i = 1,2,\cdots,k \tag{3}$$

If $S_D = \sum\nolimits_{j=1}^{n}\alpha_j$ is given, then there are:

$$\hat{y}_i = \frac{S_{N_i}}{S_D} \tag{4}$$

In the formula, $\hat{y}_i$ represents the estimation result of the i output layer neuron on the input data.

PSO is a metaheuristic optimization algorithm based on bionics principles, and is also a new type of swarm intelligence algorithm developed after ant colony algorithm. This algorithm has been widely used in optimization problems due to its strong robustness, fast convergence speed, concise code structure, and ease of programming implementation. The core idea of PSO algorithm originates from the simulation of group behavior, gradually approaching the optimal solution through the cooperation and information sharing mechanism between individuals. The mathematical expression is as follows:

$$V = wV_i + c_1r(\cdot)_1(y_i - P_i) + c_2r(\cdot)_2(g_i - P_i); P_{i+1} = P_i + V_{i+1} \tag{5}$$

Among them, P_i, V_i is the present position vector and velocity of particle i respectively; y_i, g_i is the individual optimal position of particle i and the global optimal position of all particles; w is a weighting coefficient used to balance the ability of global search and local search; $r(\cdot)_1, r(\cdot)_2$ is a random number with a value range between [0,1], used to increase the randomness of the search process; c_1, c_2 respectively represent acceleration factors, used to adjust the step size of particles moving towards individual and global optimal directions.

When using GRNN for resource recommendation, considering the complexity of setting the smoothing factor σ and regularization parameter λ, this paper adopts the DE algorithm to optimize and solve these two parameters. The fitness function of the DE algorithm is defined as the reciprocal of the objective function of GRNN resource recommendation results, in order to improve recommendation performance by minimizing the fitness value. Assuming the population size is N, the attribute dimension is D, the crossover probability is CR, and the value range of each individual is limited to $[Umax_{min}]$, the j dimensional attribute of the i individual can be expressed as:

$$x_{ij} = U(Umin_{max})_{min} \tag{6}$$

In the formula: $i = 1,2, \cdots, N, j = 1,2, \cdots, D$; *rand* is (0,1) random numbers.

3 Result Analysis and Discussion

To validate the effectiveness of our model, we conducted relative experiments with traditional resource allocation models based on Long Short Term Memory (LSTM) networks. Table 1 shows the performance comparison of two models in terms of resource allocation efficiency. From Table 1, it can be seen that our model significantly outperforms traditional LSTM models in terms of efficiency. This advantage is due to the dual characteristics of PSO and GRNN combined in the model. Specifically, the PSO algorithm dynamically adjusts the global allocation strategy of ER by simulating the process of swarm intelligence optimization, ensuring that resources can cover different regions and groups more fairly and efficiently. GRNN, with its unique four layer structure, especially the introduction of weighted operations in the summation layer, performs well in handling nonlinear problems and significantly improves the accuracy of educational resource recommendations. In addition, to further optimize the performance of GRNN, we define the fitness function of the DE algorithm as the reciprocal of the GRNN resource recommendation objective function, and improve the recommendation effect by minimizing the fitness value.

Table 1. Comparison of Resource Allocation Efficiency/%

Number of tasks/piece	Model in this article	Traditional model
10	82.6	70.8
50	83.1	71.2
100	84.3	72.7
150	85.2	73.6
200	85.8	74.9

Table 2 presents the comparative results of the proposed model and traditional LSTM based models in terms of resource utilization. In Table 2, our model performs better in resource utilization. The achievement of this good result is due to the integration of PSO and GRNN advantages in the model. The PSO algorithm dynamically optimizes the global allocation strategy of ER, ensuring that resources can cover different regions and groups more fairly and efficiently, thereby greatly improving the overall utilization rate of resources. GRNN, relying on its unique four layer structure, especially the introduction of weighted operations in the summation layer, has excellent performance in handling nonlinear problems, further enhancing the accuracy and adaptability of educational resource recommendations. In addition, to optimize the performance of GRNN, we adopted the DE algorithm and defined its fitness function as the reciprocal of the GRNN resource recommendation objective function. By minimizing the fitness value, the model has further improved its recommendation performance.

Table 2. Comparison of Resource Utilization Rates/%

Number of tasks/piece	Model in this article	Traditional model
10	73.8	61.5
50	74.6	62.3
100	76.2	63.1
150	78.5	64.8
200	79.7	65.7

Figure 2 shows the comparison results between our model and traditional LSTM based models in terms of resource recommendation accuracy. In Fig. 2, our model performs more outstandingly in terms of recommendation accuracy. Because of the introduction and optimization design of GRNN in the model. Specifically, our model trains on a large amount of user learning behavior data and resource feature data, accurately capturing users' learning preferences and resource characteristics through the GRNN module, thereby generating highly personalized recommendation lists. The unique feature of GRNN lies in its four layer structure, especially the introduction of weighted operations in the summation layer, which makes it perform well in handling nonlinear problems and significantly improves the accuracy and adaptability of educational resource recommendations. In addition, to further optimize the performance of GRNN, we adopt the DE algorithm and define the fitness function as the reciprocal of the GRNN resource recommendation objective function. By minimizing the fitness value, the model has effectively improved its recommendation performance.

Figure 3 presents the comparative results of our model and the traditional model based on Long Short Term Memory (LSTM) in terms of resource recommendation recall. It is evident from Fig. 3 that the model proposed in this paper performs better in terms of recall rate. The achievement of this good result is due to the application of GRNN in the model and its optimized design. Specifically, our model trains on a large amount of user learning behavior data and resource feature data, using the GRNN

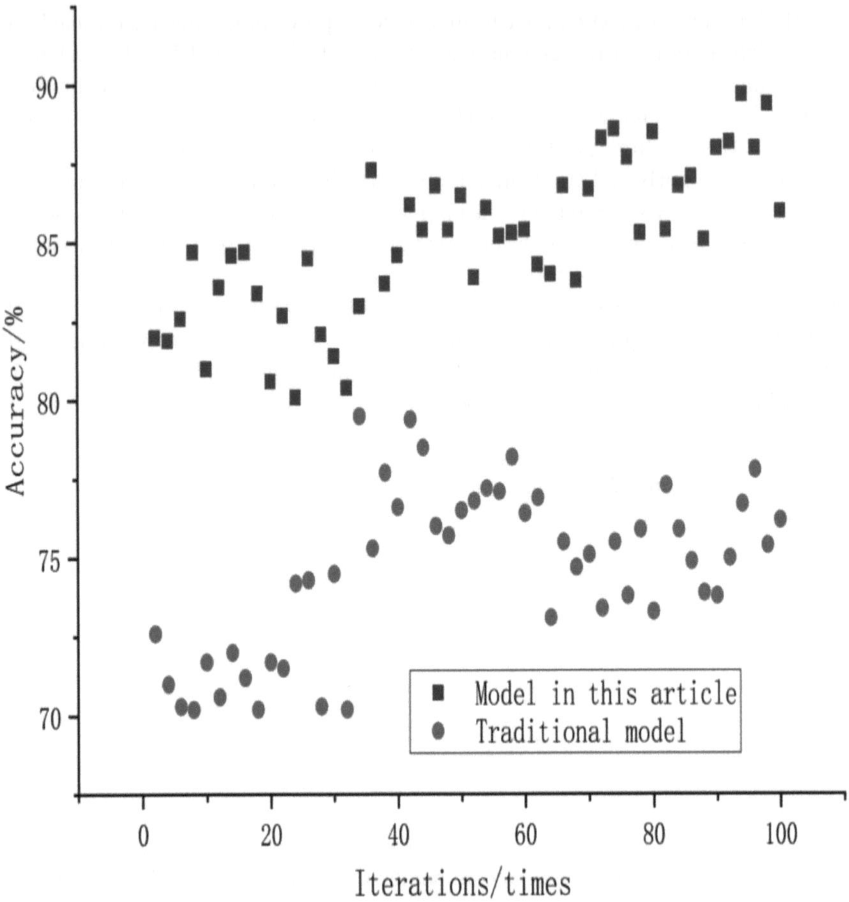

Fig. 2. Accuracy comparison

module to accurately capture user learning preferences and resource characteristics, and generate highly personalized recommendation lists. GRNN performs exceptionally well in handling nonlinear problems, further improving the accuracy of educational resource recommendations and expanding the coverage of recommendations. In addition, to optimize the performance of GRNN, we adopted the DE algorithm and defined the fitness function as the reciprocal of the GRNN resource recommendation objective function. By minimizing the fitness value, the model achieved significant improvement in recommendation performance.

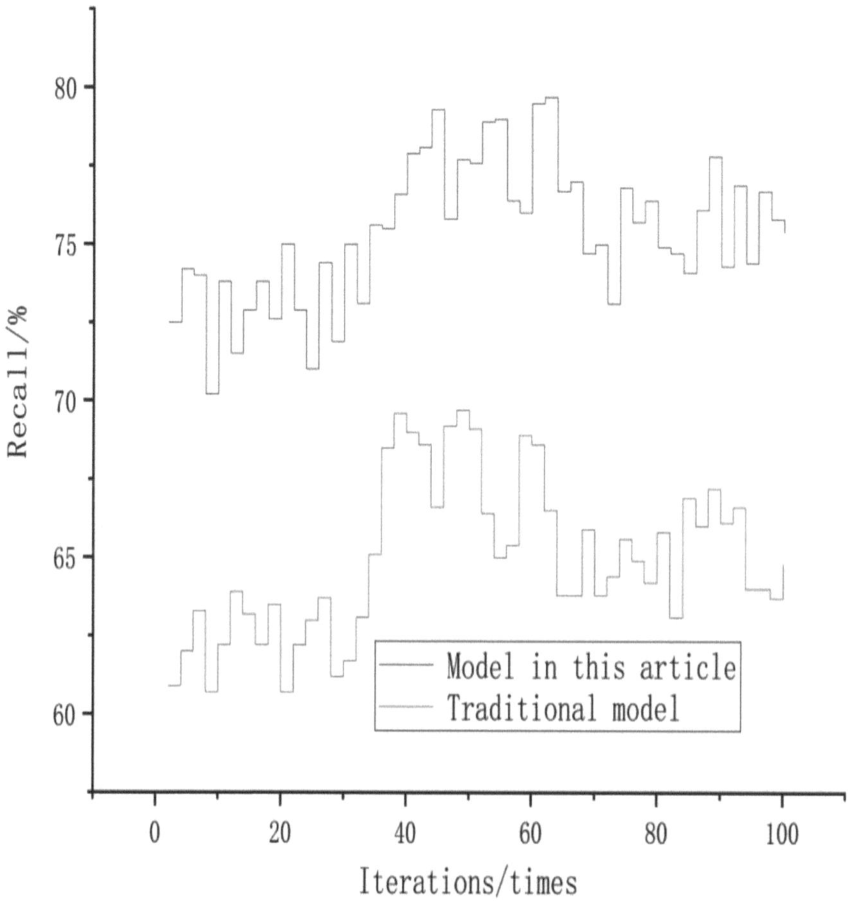

Fig. 3. Comparison of recall rates

4 Conclusion

This article proposes a model for optimizing the allocation and management of ER based on PSO and GRNN, combined with big data analysis technology. The core goal of this model is to achieve scientific and rational allocation of ER, while utilizing GRNN technology to provide personalized educational resource recommendation services for students, thereby maximizing resource utilization efficiency. The results show that our model not only dramatically improves the utilization of ER, but also achieves excellent performance in the accuracy and recall of personalized recommendations, fully demonstrating its potential for application in the field of smart education. Specifically, our model optimizes the global allocation strategy of ER through PSO algorithm, ensuring that resources can cover different regions and groups more fairly and efficiently; Meanwhile, GRNN, with its unique structural design, particularly the introduction of weighted operations in the summation layer, demonstrates outstanding performance in handling nonlinear problems, providing strong support for accurate recommendation of ER. In addition, the DE algorithm was used to optimize the parameters of GRNN, further improving the recommendation performance. However, despite the outstanding performance of our model in multiple aspects, there are still certain limitations. The processing efficiency of models for large-scale data may be limited by computing resources, and real-time performance still needs to be further improved in the face of dynamically changing educational resource demands.

References

1. Liu, Y.: Design of personalized online education system based on big data technology. Electron. Compon. Inf. Technol. **6**(05), 76–79 (2022)
2. Li, P.: A prediction model for college graduation employment based on big data analysis technology. Microcomput. Appl. **38**(05), 125–128 (2022)
3. Sun, H., Yang, S., Lv, Y., et al.: Research on the dual layer game problem of shared travel resource allocation under data driven environment. Manag. World **39**(04), 160–175 (2023)
4. Zhou, W.: Research on the optimization path of university data governance from the perspective of big data. Educ. Dev. Res. **41**(09), 78–84 (2021)
5. Xu, Z., Wen, B., Xie, M., et al.: Research on AI job demand analysis based on big data technology. Guangxi Sci. **28**(03), 321–329 (2021)
6. Ni, Y., Li, S., Xu, L., et al.: Research on high quality data resource identification of network trading platforms based on K-medoids NCA-SMOTE-BSVM fusion model. Oper. Res. Manag. **32**(11), 87–93 (2023)
7. Wang, Z., Liang, L., Luo, Z.: The overall architecture and operational guarantee of the big data analysis platform for basic education resource allocation. J. Teach. Educ. **11**(01), 90–99 (2024)
8. Zhao, S., Shi, D.: The dilemma and transcendence of the learning evaluation model for students in compulsory education in China. Educ. Theory Pract. **41**(11), 22–25 (2021)
9. Cui, T., Liu, W.: Design of personalized online education system based on big data technology. Mod. Electron. Technol. **44**(05), 175–180 (2021)
10. Meng, Z., Wang, F.: The transformation of big data and educational research: possibilities and limitations. Higher Educ. Res. **42**(02), 67–72 (2021)
11. Luo, J.: Design of smart city public resource allocation system based on big data technology. Mod. Electron. Technol. **44**(02), 122–126 (2021)
12. Xi, L.: Exploration of open education teaching reform driven by big data and artificial intelligence technology. J. Guangxi Radio Telev. Univ. **33**(06), 33–36 (2022)
13. Zhang, H.: The development trend, practical difficulties, and promotion strategies of adult fragmented learning under the background of big data. Adult Educ. **43**(07), 6–12 (2023)
14. Liu, S., Peng, J., Shen, X., et al.: Intelligent education from the perspective of new data elements: models, paths, and challenges. Res. Electron. Educ. **42**(09), 5–11+19 (2021)
15. Xie, T., Nong, L., Gao, N.: Intelligent learning grouping: from general models to big data frameworks. Res. Electron. Educ. **43**(02), 88–94+128 (2022)

Addressing Educational Management Challenges in Programming Assessment: The Case of Py-Grader for Python

Omobola Gambo[1(✉)], Wasiu Olanrewaju-Smart[2], Odianose John Abuya[3], Michael Peter[4], Gabriel Olatoye[1], Olayinka Tejumola[5], Christopher Agbonkhese[6], and Ishaya Gambo[5]

[1] Department of Arts and Social Science Education, Lead City University, Ibadan, Nigeria
gambo.omobola@lcu.edu.ng
[2] Harvard University, Cambridge, MA, USA
[3] School of Education and Sociology, Faculty of Humanities and Social Science, University of Portsmouth, Portsmouth, UK
[4] Axa Mansard Investment Limited, Mansard Place, Lagos, Nigeria
[5] Department of Computer Science and Engineering, Obafemi Awolowo University, Osun, Nigeria
[6] Department of Digital and Computational Studies, Bates College, Lewiston, ME 04240, USA

Abstract. The reliance on traditional, manual assessment processes increasingly challenges the management of programming practicals within higher education institutions. These methods often result in significant delays in evaluation and feedback provision, impacting student learning progression and straining institutional resources, particularly within large cohorts. While various Automated Grading Tools (AGTs) have been developed to mitigate these issues, many possess limitations regarding scalability, infrastructure dependency, and the depth of pedagogical feedback offered. This research addresses these gaps by introducing Py-Grader, a novel web-based automated platform designed to enhance Python programming education. Py-Grader facilitates a time-sensitive, feedback-rich, and interactive learning environment by integrating contemporary technologies. It utilizes Brython for client-side Python script execution, thereby minimizing backend server load during code testing and grading, and employs Codemirror to provide an interactive, IDE-like code editing experience. Evaluation indicates Py-Grader achieves high fidelity (100%) in providing feedback on code analysis and user interface intuitiveness, alongside strong usability (80% ease of navigation) from the student perspective. This paper demonstrates the potential of leveraging modern client-side technologies to revolutionise Python programming assessments' efficiency, scalability, and pedagogical effectiveness within contemporary higher education management frameworks.

Keywords: Automated Grading Tools (AGTs) · Educational Management · Programming Assessment · Python · Automated Feedback · Grading Efficiency · Higher Education

K. W. Lee and L. H. Wong (Eds.): ITEA 2025, CCIS 2643, pp. 185–196, 2026.
https://doi.org/10.1007/978-981-95-2011-4_18

1 Introduction

The escalating demand for digital literacy and computational thinking skills within the global economy has positioned programming proficiency as an essential learning outcome in higher education, particularly within science, technology, engineering, and mathematics (STEM) disciplines [1]. Consequently, educational managers face the significant challenge of effectively delivering and assessing practical programming skills at scale. Institutions must ensure that students not only learn programming syntax but also develop robust problem-solving abilities through hands-on application, demanding assessment strategies that are both rigorous and efficient [2].

However, traditional approaches to conducting and assessing programming practicals present considerable operational inefficiencies and pedagogical limitations from an educational management perspective. The reliance on manual grading by instructors or teaching assistants is inherently labour-intensive, time-consuming, and susceptible to inconsistencies, particularly when dealing with large student numbers [3]. This manual process strains limited teaching resources, often leads to delays in providing formative feedback crucial for student learning, and raises concerns about assessment equity and reliability across diverse markers [4]. Managing these logistical and quality assurance challenges becomes increasingly difficult as enrolment in computing-related programmes expands.

In response to these managerial and pedagogical pressures, the development and implementation of automated assessment systems offer a promising avenue for enhancing efficiency and consistency in programming education [5]. Automation can alleviate the grading burden on academic staff, enabling the reallocation of valuable time towards more direct student support and pedagogical innovation. Furthermore, automated systems can provide students with immediate, objective feedback, thereby fostering a more dynamic and responsive learning environment conducive to iterative skill development [6].

Despite the proliferation of various automated grading tools (AGTs), many existing solutions exhibit limitations that hinder their widespread adoption or optimal effectiveness within institutional contexts. For example, the tool GRAD-AI in Gambo et al. [7] has a primary limitation in its automated feedback's depth and pedagogical sophistication, potentially struggling to offer nuanced guidance beyond identifying standard code errors or correctness issues. Also, a significant number of research studies focus primarily on summative evaluation based on code correctness against predefined test cases, potentially overlooking deeper aspects of code quality, efficiency, or style [8]. Moreover, many conventional AGTs rely heavily on server-side execution, which can lead to significant infrastructure demands and potential performance bottlenecks, particularly when large numbers of students concurrently test and submit code [9]. This scalability issue poses a direct challenge to educational resource management, especially as institutions grapple with increasing student enrolment and the need for cost-effective technological solutions [10].

Addressing these constraints requires innovative approaches that balance grading accuracy and efficiency with pedagogical value and institutional scalability. There is a clear need for automated assessment systems that evaluate code correctness reliably and provide meaningful feedback, operate efficiently within existing technological infrastructures, and support active learning pedagogies. This research contends that leveraging modern web technologies, particularly client-side processing, offers a viable strategy to meet these multifaceted requirements.

Therefore, this paper introduces Py-Grader, a web-based automated assessment platform specifically designed for Python programming education in higher learning institutions. Py-Grader differentiates itself through its innovative use of client-side technologies, primarily Brython for in-browser Python execution and CodeMirror for an enhanced code editing interface. This architectural approach shifts a significant portion of the computational load for code testing from the central server to the user's local machine, thereby mitigating server strain and enhancing system responsiveness and scalability.

Overall, this study aims to design, implement, and evaluate Py-Grader as a potentially transformative tool for educational management, demonstrating its capacity to provide efficient, scalable, and pedagogically supportive automated assessment for Python programming. The study contributes theoretically by exploring the application of client-side technologies in educational assessment contexts, methodologically by providing a specification for such a platform, practically by delivering a functional system addressing identified needs, and analytically by presenting user evaluation data supporting its utility and usability within the higher education environment.

2 Related Work

The effective assessment of programming skills is fundamental in Computer Science (CS), Information Technology (IT), and Software Engineering (SE) education. Growing enrollments and the demand for timely feedback render traditional manual grading logistically untenable and prone to inconsistency [3, 4]. Consequently, automated grading tools (AGTs) are indispensable, evolving significantly to streamline evaluation and provide faster feedback [8]. These systems offer potential benefits like reduced instructor workload, enhanced grading consistency, and support for the iterative nature of learning to code [5].

However, many AGTs primarily assess functional correctness via predefined test cases [8], often overlooking crucial code quality aspects like efficiency or style. A predominant architectural limitation is the heavy reliance on server-side execution for grading [9]. This server-centric model presents a significant scalability and performance gap. Pavia et al. [9] noted that server-side processing causes substantial infrastructure demands and performance bottlenecks, especially during peak usage with concurrent student submissions. This reliance limits responsiveness, hindering institutions from managing large cohorts. For instance, Nikola et al.'s [11] server-dependent Kotlin autograder exemplifies this scalability challenge, potentially bottlenecking real-time interaction and feedback. Thus, a gap exists for architectures that efficiently handle high concurrency without overwhelming servers.

Beyond architecture, another critical gap is AGT feedback's pedagogical quality and depth. Effective learning requires more than pass/fail results; students need insights into why code fails and how to improve it. Keuning et al.'s [12] systematic review of 101 AGTs revealed a major limitation: most tools identify errors well but lack constructive guidance. Feedback often omits actionable advice or suggestions for alternative valid strategies, hindering students' ability to learn from mistakes. This highlights the need for AGTs to offer nuanced, adaptive, and pedagogically valuable feedback to guide students toward better problem-solving and coding practices.

Addressing these interconnected gaps—scalability limits from server-centric designs [9, 11] and insufficient pedagogical feedback [12]—necessitates innovative approaches. Existing solutions often prioritize either efficiency or feedback depth, rarely integrating both effectively within a scalable framework. Server-side processing dependency limits immediate feedback delivery [9, 11], while feedback limitations restrict learning potential [12].

This research tackles these challenges via Py-Grader. To address scalability, Py-Grader uses a novel client-side architecture (Brython for in-browser Python execution). This shifts significant computational load from the server to the user's machine, mitigating server strain, reducing costs, and enhancing responsiveness under concurrency. To tackle the feedback quality gap, Py-Grader incorporates mechanisms for comprehensive, actionable feedback beyond mere correctness checks, aiming to better support the learning process identified as deficient by Keuning et al. [12]. By distributing workload and enhancing feedback, Py-Grader seeks to provide a scalable, efficient, and pedagogically supportive automated assessment solution.

3 Methodology

A well-detailed assessment was carried out about the procedures of conducting the practical session, grading, and generating feedback to students. A structured questionnaire was administered to students to get their views on the current mode and propose an automated system.

The automated grading system was designed to improve some aspects lacking in the current grading method used at the university (Obafemi Awolowo University, Ile-Ife). Hence, data was gathered using direct observation of the method used in grading students' programming exercises. The system is meant to grade students' coding practicals on Python programming. When submission is made, the system analyses the code, checks for errors, executes the code, tests the results against some input test, awards a grade, and stores it in the database, which the instructor will later query.

3.1 Data Collection

During the requirement-gathering stage, necessary data was collected to ensure the feasibility and usability of the improved system. The major source of data collection involves direct engagement with stakeholders. The stakeholders comprise students across the 13 departments (from four Faculties of the University) who are taking computer programming courses as a compulsory requirement. Also, the lecturers from the Department of

Computer Science and Engineering at the Obafemi Awolowo University, Nigeria, are among the stakeholders.

We used the oral interview approach to elicit requirements from the students taking the practical course and some selected lecturers who are instructors. Also, an online survey was administered to a randomly selected number of students through an online questionnaire to get their views on the existing mode of programming assessment. Table 1 presents some of the questions and responses gathered during the survey.

The secondary data source involves reviewing past works similar to our tool (Py-Grader), related articles, conference journals, textbooks, and other libraries that contributed to the research topic.

3.2 Design Specification

The system's overall architecture is a web-based solution consisting of both the front and back end. The frontend consists of the user interface, which is the interactive part of the system. It provides the login page where the student logs into the system using their credentials, after which they are led to a dashboard screen consisting of a code editor for Python and questions to be solved. It also consists of a countdown timer that notifies the student of available time left before submission. An output area of the screen is used to get the output result of the code after compilation.

The backend part of the system contains the logic for grading and storing student grades. It contains the database structure for storing students' details, questions and expected output, test cases, student submissions, and graded results.

Figure 1 shows the overall architecture of the system. As Fig. 1 reflects, Py-Grader application consists mainly of the UI, backend logic, and persistence store (database). The user interface allows the students to interact with the system during their practical session, access the quiz, and use the code editor to solve it. It also provides code output for the current execution of the script. The backend logic is an intermediary between the store and the user interface. It provides a query mechanism for the database and persistence of records. Logic for fetching user data and quizzes are among the services provided by the backend. The persistence store contains the schema for storing data essential for the functioning of the system.

We provided the system's functional requirements (FRs) and non-functional requirements (NFRs) for the system specification. FRs and NFRs describe the set of features the system allows amid interaction between the teachers and students. Table 2 presents the FRs.

3.3 Testing and System Evaluation Procedure

Each question to be solved by the student has corresponding test cases assigned, which are executed to determine the correctness of the algorithm used by the student to solve the problem. In the code editor, the question is presented as a function. The variables to work with are declared within the function, and the result is the value to be returned by the function. The students must define their solution within the function's body, working with the already declared variables. Once a submission is made, unit testing is performed

Table 1. Sample of survey questions and responses during data collection

Question/Response	Very Satisfied	Somewhat Satisfied	Neutral	Somewhat Dissatisfied	Very Dissatisfied
How satisfied are you with the current process of grading How satisfied are you with the current process of grading programming practical?	49	72	87	26	14
Question/Response	Very Often	Often	Less Often		
How often were feedback provided on your code exercise	52	109	87		
Question/Response	Yes	Maybe	No		
Do you feel the feedback you receive on your code is clear and helpful in understanding your mistakes and improving your coding skills?	113	57	78		
Question/Response	Very Interested	Somewhat Interested	Neutral	Somewhat Disinterested	Very Disinterested
How interested would you be in an automated code grading system that provides immediate feedback on your code?	94	69	59	9	0

using multiple test cases by calling the function using different parameter values and examining its return against the expected output. The test result is used to determine the grade awarded to students.

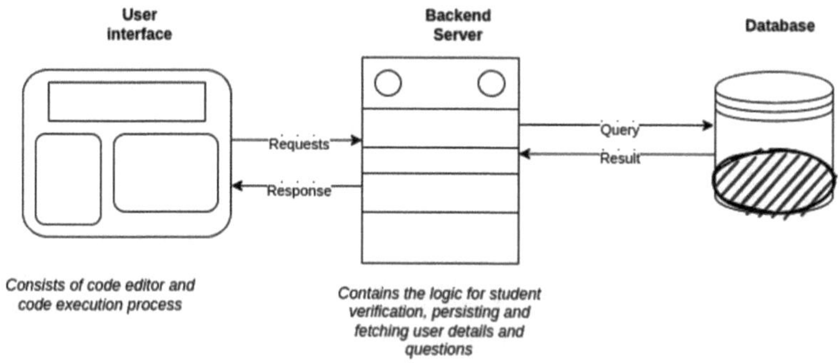

Fig. 1. System Architecture of the Py-grader app

Table 2. Elicited Functional Requirements.

FRsID	Description
001	The system should be able to persist students' records or details
002	Teachers should be able to upload questions and output for test cases
003	Teachers should access, modify, and delete students' data
004	Students should be able to log into the system using their credentials and access their dashboard
005	The system should contain an editor on the student dashboard for students to edit their code
006	The submitted code should be subjected to some unit testing, and the results examined
007	A grade should be assigned according to the result of the unit tests

Examples of a function call code evaluation:

Question: Write a function factorial(n) that returns the factorial of a non-negative integer n
*Description: The factorial of a non-negative integer n is the product of all positive integers less than or equal to n. For example, the factorial 5 is 5 * 4 * 3 * 2 * 1 = 120. Write a function factorial that calculates and returns the factorial of the input number n. This problem introduces you to the concept of recursion and iterative calculations. Example: If the input is n = 4, the function should return 24, as 4 * 3 * 2 * 1 = 24.*

```
def factorial(n):
    return n
Case 0: assertEquals (factorial(0), 1)
Case 1: assertEquals (factorial(1), 1)
Case 2: assertEquals (factorial(5), 120)
Case 3: assertEquals (factorial(10), 3628800)
Case 4: assertEquals (factorial(3), 6)
```

4 Results and Discussion

The entire system consists of different parts. First, the entry point to the system's operation is the login pages, as shown in Figs. 2 and 4. For both types of system users, authentication credentials must be provided before access can be granted. This consists of username and password fields, providing a form of authentication.

After successful login, the student is presented with a working area of the system for a coding practical session (Fig. 3). The working area consists of the information and the coding parts. The information part presents the question to be solved with a detailed description of what is expected from the student. This part of the working area only displays the textual information to the students. The coding part consists of an editor where the students input their coding solution and an output area for test-running their code. Once they are done, they can turn in their code using the submit button.

Part of it is a clock timer that counts down, ensuring a limited time required for the practical session. Once's countdown reaches zero, the code gets turned in automatically for grading. The administrative dashboard allows for administrative controls like managing students' records and performing basic operations like creating, updating, and deleting students' records. It also allows for querying students' results. Part of it is a clock timer that counts down, ensuring a limited time required for the practical session. Once's countdown reaches zero, the code gets turned in automatically for grading. The administrative dashboard allows for administrative controls like managing students' records and performing basic operations like creating, updating, and deleting students' records. It also allows for querying students' results, as shown in Fig. 5.

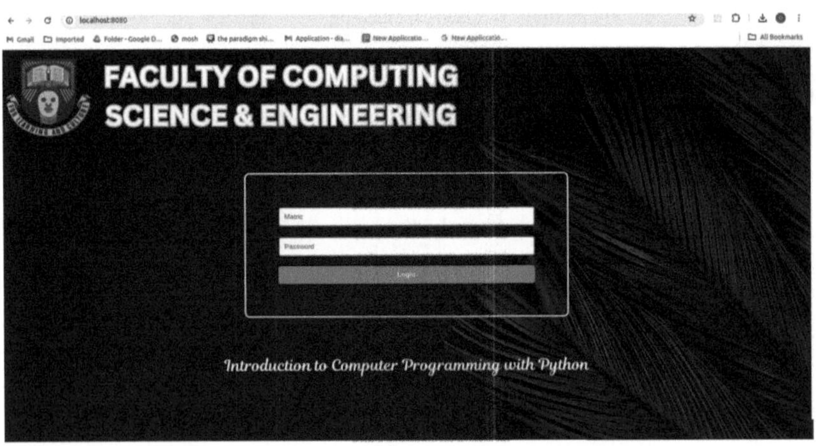

Fig. 2. Student's login Page of the Py-grader app

Usability testing was conducted on the Py-Grader automated code practical and grading system in order to assess its performance. Some data were fed into the system, simulating real students' data and questions. Py-Grader achieved a high success rate in terms of performance, scalability, and generating feedback to students. From the evaluation provided by the students, 80% rate the ease of navigation, 38% find the

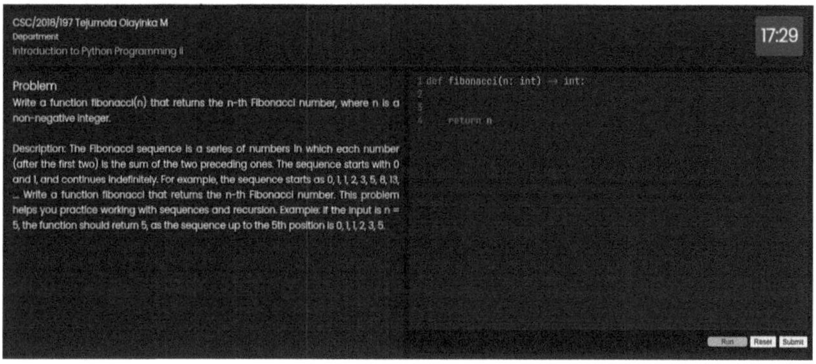

Fig. 3. Student's code editing area

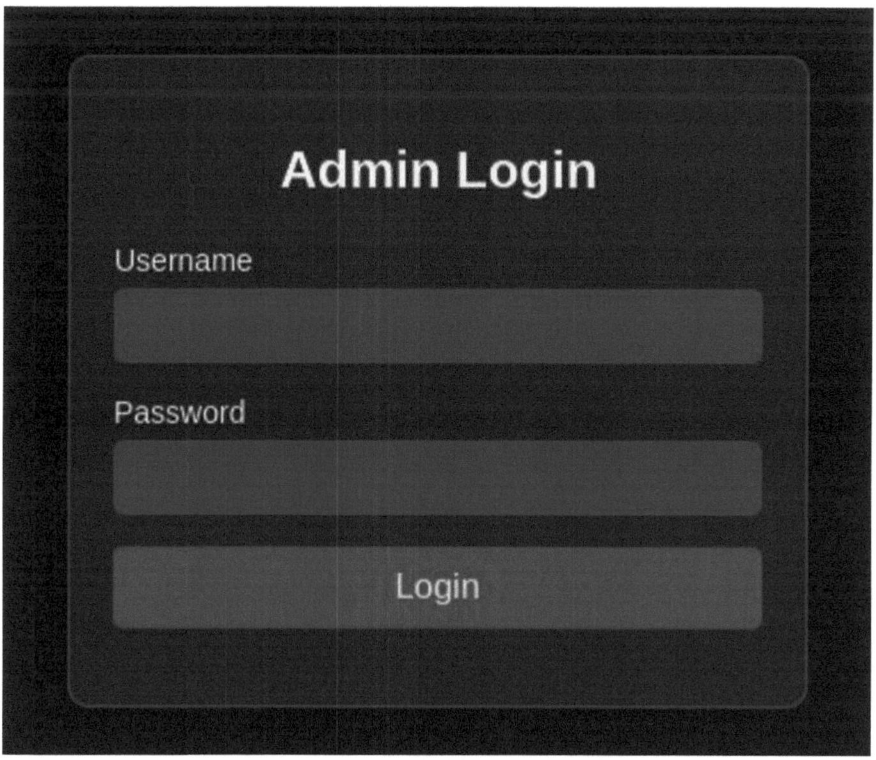

Fig. 4. Administration login page of the Py-grader app

interface very intuitive, and 100% reported the application provided sufficient feedback when there was an error or issue. 100% also indicate interest in recommending the app to others. Table 3 shows the rate of satisfaction with the usability testing, while Fig. 6 shows the analysis of the usability testing of the software.

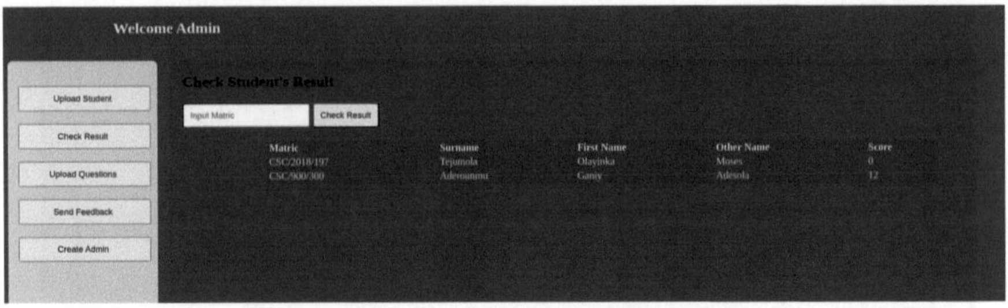

Fig. 5. Administrative dashboard of Py-grade app

Table 3. Questions for measuring the usability of the Py-Grader system

Question	Yes	Maybe	No
Were you able to complete the tasks assigned to you using the app?	66%	0%	40%
Was the interface of the app easy to understood	100%	0%	0%
Do you think the app provide enough ease of navigation?	80%	20%	0%
Is the interface intuitive enough from users' perspective?	100%	0%	0%
Did the app provide sufficient feedback when there was an error issue?	100%	0%	0%
Would you recommend this app to others for automated Python code grading?	100%	0%	0%

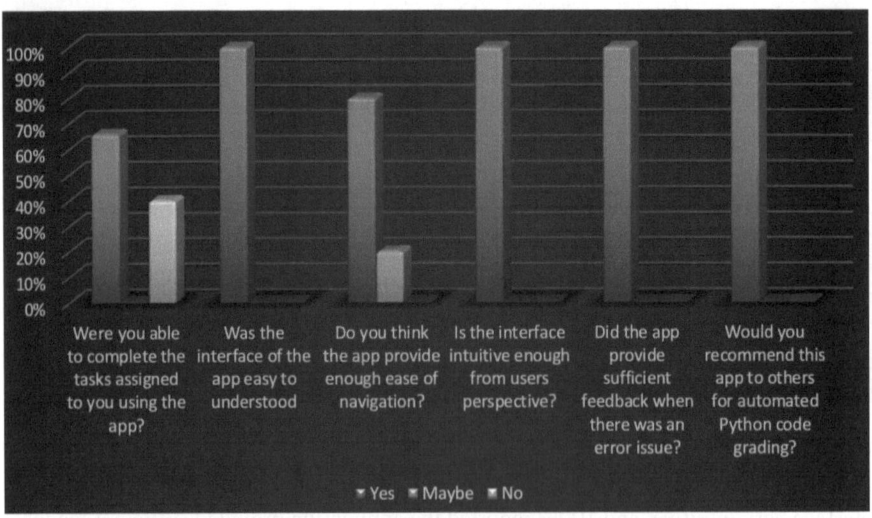

Fig. 6. The distribution of usability testing and acceptance

5 Threats to Validity

Py-Grader's validity faces several potential limitations. Firstly, its reliance on Brython for client-side execution introduces a threat from browser compatibility variations; inconsistent browser implementations could affect code execution and assessment accuracy across different platforms. Secondly, the client-side processing model may struggle with resource-intensive submissions, potentially overwhelming less powerful user devices, leading to performance issues or crashes and creating assessment inequities. This limits practical scalability for complex programming tasks. Thirdly, the validity of assessments is constrained by test case coverage; while functional correctness can be checked, predefined tests may overlook crucial code quality aspects like efficiency, style, or algorithmic elegance, resulting in potentially incomplete evaluations. Finally, the current lack of integrated, robust plagiarism detection mechanisms poses a significant threat to academic integrity, as copied submissions might receive undue credit, undermining the accurate reflection of individual student work and learning. Addressing these threats is crucial for ensuring the system's reliability and fairness in diverse educational settings.

6 Conclusion and Future Work

Addressing the critical challenge of scalable programming assessment in higher education, this research introduced Py-Grader, a web-based platform utilizing client-side processing (Brython) for Python evaluation. Our findings demonstrate that this architectural approach significantly enhances scalability and responsiveness by mitigating server load compared to traditional server-centric automated grading tools. Py-Grader thus offers a validated, efficient solution for managing Python assessments at scale, showcasing the potential of distributed computation within educational technology infrastructures.

Future work will focus on expanding Py-Grader's impact and utility. Key priorities include generalizing the client-side architecture to support additional programming languages like Java and C/C++, thereby increasing its versatility across computer science curricula. Enhancing pedagogical depth is also critical; future iterations will integrate more sophisticated feedback mechanisms, moving beyond simple correctness checks to incorporate static code analysis for style and efficiency, and providing context-aware hints to better scaffold student learning. Furthermore, evolving the platform into a comprehensive interactive learning environment with features like adaptive quizzes, coding exercises, and gamification elements could significantly boost student engagement and motivation. Finally, rigorous empirical validation through large-scale, longitudinal studies in diverse institutional settings, alongside comparative analyses against existing tools, is essential to robustly establish Py-Grader's long-term educational effectiveness and usability. These future directions promise to further advance scalable and pedagogically sound automated assessment in computing education.

References

1. Grover, S., Pea, R.: Computational thinking in K–12: a review of the state of the field. Educ. Res. **42**(1), 38–43 (2013). https://doi.org/10.3102/0013189X12463051

2. Robins, A., Rountree, J., Rountree, N.: Learning and teaching programming: a review and discussion. Comput. Sci. Educ. **13**(2), 137–172 (2003). https://doi.org/10.1076/csed.13.2.137.14200
3. Ala-Mutka, K.: A survey of automated assessment approaches for programming assignments. Comput. Sci. Educ. **15**(2), 83–102 (2005). https://doi.org/10.1080/08993400500150647
4. Butler, M., Morgan, M., Crick, T.: Exploring the validity, reliability and fairness of assessment tasks used in introductory programming courses. In Proceedings of the 2016 ACM Conference on Innovation and Technology in Computer Science Education (ITiCSE'16), pp. 105–110. Association for Computing Machinery (2016). https://doi.org/10.1145/2899415.2899441
5. Ihantola, P., et al.: Review of recent research on automatic assessment of programming assignments. In: Proceedings of the 10th Koli Calling International Conference on Computing Education Research (Koli Calling'10), pp. 86–93. Association for Computing Machinery (2010). https://doi.org/10.1145/1930464.1930480
6. Denny, P., Luxton-Reilly, A., Tempero, E.: CodeWrite: supporting student interaction with instructional material. In: Proceedings of the 16th Annual SIGCSE Conference on Innovation and Technology in Computer Science Education (ITiCSE'11), pp. 140–144. Association for Computing Machinery (2011). https://doi.org/10.1145/1999747.1999791
7. Gambo, I., Abegunde, F.J., Gambo, O., Ogundokun, R.O., Babatunde, A.N., Lee, C.C.: GRAD-AI: an automated grading tool for code assessment and feedback in programming course. Educ. Inf. Technol. 1–41 (2024)
8. Douce, C., Livingstone, D., Orwell, J.: A systematic review of automated assessment of programming assignments. Comput. Sci. Educ. **15**(2), 103–122 (2005). https://doi.org/10.1080/08993400500150639
9. Pavia, N., Monga, M., Lonati, V., Malchiodi, D.: Client-side vs server-side execution in introductory programming courses online assessment tools. In: Proceedings of the 2022 ACM Conference on Innovation and Technology in Computer Science Education V. 1 (ITiCSE'22), pp. 265–271. Association for Computing Machinery (2022). https://doi.org/10.1145/3502718.3524799
10. Singer, S.R.: Disconnected: increasing college student engagement, persistence, and completion in coursework featuring high-enrollment and online formats. EDUCAUSE Rev. **54**(4) (2019)
11. Nikola, T., Petrović, V., Stanimirović, A.: An auto-grader supported framework for learning Kotlin. In: 2020 IEEE Global Engineering Education Conference (EDUCON), pp 1156–1161. IEEE (2020). https://doi.org/10.1109/EDUCON45650.2020.9125249
12. Keuning, H., Jeuring, J., Heeren, B.: A systematic literature review of automated feedback generation for programming exercises. ACM Trans. Comput. Educ. (TOCE) **19**(1), 1–42 (2019). https://doi.org/10.1145/3231711

Using an Evolutionary Algorithm to Determine the Student-to-Proctor Ratio in Exam Scenarios

Pablo León Alazraki Salas(✉) and Andrés Gómez de Silva Garza

Instituto Tecnológico Autónomo de México, 01080 Mexico City, Mexico
{pablo.alazraki,agomez}@itam.mx

Abstract. The computational simulation of students taking an exam and proctors monitoring it is relevant for educational institutions that want to design the way exams are applied. In our work, our objective is to minimize the students' incentives to engage in dishonest behavior, and we explore this by considering alternate seating arrangements of the students as well as alternate monitoring approaches. Here, we propose a multi-objective evolutionary algorithm that finds how to arrange students in a given classroom and how many professors are required to monitor those students in order to reduce the students' incentives to cheat. The algorithm finds all the Pareto solutions such that one cannot decrease students' incentives to cheat without increasing the number of required professors. Using this system, our key contribution is to provide a heuristic for how many teachers should be assigned to monitor a given number of students by finding an adequate student-to-proctor ratio.

Keywords: Multi-objective evolutionary algorithm · Academic dishonesty · Computational simulation

1 Introduction

Cheating in academic environments is recognized as a multifaceted problem with significant repercussions in society [5]. Numerous studies have investigated the act of cheating from diverse disciplinary perspectives, including psychology, sociology, and behavioral economics, and have identified key social and psychological factors that influence the decision to engage in dishonest practices [2, 5, 10]. Concurrently, research such as [2, 13] has explored various methods employed in cheating, while technological advancements have led to innovative monitoring approaches, such as [6–8]. Within the field of computational studies, intelligent systems have been developed to simulate student behavior in academic settings [9, 11, 12].

Project [1] advanced this line of inquiry by proposing a hybrid AI system that combines a multi-agent simulation of students taking a multiple-choice exam with a teacher monitoring it, alongside an evolution strategy that minimizes cheating by shuffling how students are seated in the simulated classroom. In that study, a student would opt to cheat if the expected grade from cheating exceeded that from answering randomly, with cheating defined as copying answers from a 'neighboring' student—either adjacent or

K. W. Lee and L. H. Wong (Eds.): ITEA 2025, CCIS 2643, pp. 197–207, 2026.
https://doi.org/10.1007/978-981-95-2011-4_19

directly in front. A critical assumption of that system, however, is the presence of a single monitoring teacher. In many real-world examinations, however, it is common to have two or more monitoring observers due to institutional protocols or large numbers of students that it would be impossible for a single person to monitor.

It is also relevant for educational institutions to model how students would react in scenarios where more than one monitor is available to observe the same exam in order to find an "optimal" number of proctors so as to reduce cheating incentives as much as possible. At the same time, we have to consider potential restrictions on the maximum number of monitoring observers available (in this work, we will consider "proctors", "monitoring observers", "professors", and "teachers" as equivalent terms). Thus, we decided to create a multi-objective evolutionary algorithm that finds how to arrange students in a simulated classroom and how many professors are required to monitor those students in order to reduce the students' incentives to cheat. The algorithm returns all the Pareto solutions, representing configurations in which it is impossible to reduce the number of cheating incidents without increasing the number of teachers. We first find the optimal number of generations for our evolutionary algorithm. Afterwards, we use the data obtained from running experiments with our simulation to find a rule of thumb on how many professors are needed to monitor an exam as a function of the number of students in the classroom so that no student has incentives to cheat.

The rest of the paper is organized as follows: Sect. 2 presents a theoretical framework where we briefly introduce the computational techniques used in this article. Section 3 shows how adding multiple monitoring observers would affect each student's behavior and how to model said behavior properly. Section 4 describes how we implemented our multi-objective evolutionary algorithm, how we selected the best individuals in the evolutionary population, and how we defined the system's optimal results. In Sect. 5, we present the experiments we ran on our system, determine how many generations were enough to obtain significant results, and provide the rule of thumb we set out to find. Lastly, Sect. 6 presents a discussion of our results, our conclusions, and possible future work.

2 Theoretical Framework

In this section, we provide a brief introduction to evolutionary algorithms, including the multi-objective kind, in order to introduce their features to readers that may not be familiar with this computational technique. This is because in the rest of the paper, we refer to these topics multiple times.

Evolutionary algorithms [4] are population-based algorithms in which multiple individual potential solutions to a given problem have their descriptive characteristics repeatedly modified and combined, thus generating new potential solutions whose value can be assessed. These new potential solutions, if they are "good enough," can be fed back into the population to participate in the next round of generating even newer potential solutions. Evolutionary algorithms are based on the principle of "survival of the fittest," and the fact that they measure the value of the potential solutions that they generate allows the algorithms to monotonically increase the average quality of the solutions in the population. Eventually some convergence criterion is reached, and the "best" solution is presented to the user.

Many variations on the general idea of evolutionary algorithms have been proposed, differing in such aspects as the genotype representations used, the genetic operators that are available to the algorithm through the use of which it can produce new potential solutions, the convergence criteria employed, the way the population is managed across evolutionary generations, and so on. Viewed as designers of solutions to problems in general, evolutionary algorithms behave as optimizers of said solutions. When only one factor is taken into account in order to measure the quality of each new potential solution, the optimization that takes place as the algorithm proceeds is in relation to that factor.

However, if the algorithm awards a measure of quality to each potential solution based on multiple criteria, a multi-objective evolutionary algorithm [3] can take into account the fact that it may be impossible to optimize for all criteria at the same time. Often, designing the best option for one factor involves trading off the possibility that other factors that are being taken into account will just not be able to be optimized too. Multiple potential solutions, known as Pareto solutions, might each be "the best possible" for one factor, but would result in sub-optimal solutions if one tries to improve the other factors at the same time (i.e., while maintaining those characteristics which made it "the best possible" for the first factor). In these situations, either the user or some automated priority-assignment engine has to choose among the Pareto solutions if only one "final" solution is desired. The computational simulation we present in this paper is mainly based on the use of a multi-objective evolutionary algorithm.

3 Exam Simulation

The work in [1] simulates a multiple-choice exam where the students' decisions to cheat or not rely on whether the expected grade from cheating is greater than their expected grade from answering randomly. The expected grade from cheating is given by

$$P(A^C) \times P(B) \times g^* + P(A^C) \times P(B^C) \times g$$

where A represents the event of a student being caught cheating by the teacher, B represents the scenario where the neighboring student has the correct answer for a current question, g is the current expected grade of the exam for a specific student, and g^* is the updated grade calculated under the assumption that the question is answered correctly by the same student. In this equation, the superscript C represents the complement operator, and we will use this convention throughout the rest of the paper.

In this study, we used the same equation and we made the same assumptions: (1) our simulation first randomly assigns a degree of proficiency in the subject matter of the exam for each student following a Gaussian distribution, (2) students are taking a multiple-choice exam with four possible answers for each question, (3) students first answer the exam questions whose answers they know, and then they answer the rest of the exam either by copying the answer from one of their neighbors or by a random guess, and (4) they have perfect knowledge of the teacher's monitoring behavior and of the past academic performance of the other students.

When implementing our evolutionary algorithm, we considered two alternatives. In the first method, each monitoring observer is assigned to a specific section of the classroom and monitors only that section. However, this alternative seems unrealistic in practice since, without a physical separation between subsections, a professor could inadvertently observe students in other sections. This unintended observation would alter the probability that a student is caught cheating, thus influencing their behavior.

The second alternative assumes that each monitoring observer can have an unobstructed view of each student in the classroom. In this case, the probability of a specific student being caught cheating is defined as the probability of being caught by at least one monitoring observer, considering that it is possible that two or more proctors may monitor the same student at the same time. Let k denote the number of monitoring observers during the exam and A_i the event that represents being caught cheating by the monitoring observer i (where $i = 1, ..., k$). The overall probability of being caught cheating is then given by:

$$P(A) = P(\cup_{i=1}^{k} A_i)$$

Using properties of probability theory, this expression can be more conveniently rewritten by employing the complement operator as follows:

$$P(A) = 1 - P(A^C) = 1 - P(\cap_{i=1}^{k} A_i^C)$$

It is important to note that each A_i encapsulates the individual monitoring tendencies of the corresponding observer. This approach permits the assignment of distinct monitoring tendencies to each observer, thereby allowing students to compute the probability of being caught cheating in a comprehensive and generalized manner, but most importantly, allowing the system to model the wide variety of monitoring tendencies and student responses to being observed in different ways that exist in real-world scenarios.

4 Evolutionary Algorithm Implementation

Given the number of students s and the maximum number of proctors that the exam designer can afford k, the system determines both where to distribute students in the classroom and how many teachers are required to minimize cheating incidents. If no value is specified for k, then it defaults to s. To achieve our goal, we used a multi-objective evolutionary algorithm, which simultaneously seeks to minimize the number of cheating incidents and the number of teachers necessary to achieve that minimal level of cheating for a given seating configuration within the upper limit specified by k.

The algorithm begins by randomizing the arrangement of the students in the classroom, thereby establishing an initial seating configuration. Based on this configuration, k individuals are created, with each individual assigned a number of monitoring observers j that originally ranges from 1 to k (where there is only one individual in the evolutionary algorithm's population for each possible value of j). Each individual in the population represents a given simulation scenario involving j proctors, after which the entire exam is simulated under that scenario. Then, a pruning procedure is implemented on the evolutionary algorithm's population. Specifically, for all individuals who produce the same number of cheating incidents, only the individual with the fewest teachers is retained to participate in the next evolutionary cycle, while the others are discarded. A consequence of this is that the evolutionary algorithm's population monotonically decreases in size as the algorithm proceeds. The students' positions in the classroom are then reshuffled, producing new exam scenarios, and used to evaluate the new m individuals, where $m \leq k$ and is the size of the new population. This approach is justified by the rationale that once a potential optimum has been identified, configurations involving a greater number of teachers are no longer necessary, as one of the objectives is to minimize teacher usage.

The simulation is run with the new population and under the new seating arrangement, and the pruning and rearranging of the seating configuration is repeated. When convergence of the evolutionary algorithm occurs, the system returns the Pareto solutions, representing configurations in which it is impossible to reduce the number of cheating incidents without increasing the number of teachers. The educational institution must then choose one of the Pareto solutions provided, either one that minimizes the number of teachers monitoring the exam (even though this allows more cheating incentives) or one that minimizes cheating incentives but requires more teachers. In our case, we use reaching a maximum number of evolutionary generations as our convergence criterion.

In the next section, we discuss some experiments that we performed based on what we have just described.

5 Results

Our primary interest with this system is to devise a heuristic that determines the number of teachers required as a function of the number of students in such a way that no student is provided with incentives to cheat. For this purpose, it is crucial to first identify the optimal number of generations needed by the evolutionary algorithm to achieve a significant outcome without incurring unnecessary computational overhead.

To this end, we conducted an experiment that involved running multiple simulations, using the evolutionary behavior proposed in this work while controlling two variables: the number of students in the simulated classroom (increasing quadratically, ranging from 4^2 to 9^2) and the number of generations in the evolutionary algorithm (set at 10, 100, 250, 500, 750, 1000, and 1250). We only simulated classroom sizes of up to 81 students because this covers a wide variety of real-world classroom sizes. For now, we avoided problems with increasing simulation times that might grow exponentially, as would be required if we wanted to simulate a very high number of students, which might occur if we wanted to simulate standardized tests or entrance examinations in public institutions. As for the number of evolutionary generations, they could show how the algorithm's best responses react depending on the number of generations to see when an increased population size stops producing significantly better results.

At the conclusion of each simulation, the evolutionary algorithm returned the possible optimal classroom arrangements, the number of students who would be provided with incentives to cheat in that simulation, the number of teachers required to achieve this outcome, and the execution time of the algorithm. Each configuration was executed 30 times to obtain statistically significant averages for both the number of monitoring observers and the execution times.

Out of all this data, we only considered for our analysis seating arrangements that produced a minimum number of students with an incentive to cheat; this minimum is zero in all cases, as in the extreme scenario of having one teacher per student, no student is provided with incentives to cheat. Starting with this scenario initially, the pruning process described in Sect. 4 was then applied.

Figure 1 shows that, for all generation counts (with the exception of 10 and 100), a consistent trend emerges in the average number of teachers required to eliminate students' incentives to cheat. For a classroom of 64 students, the algorithm runs consisting of 1250 generations demonstrated a substantially better performance in terms of reducing the number of teachers required. This observation suggests that for classroom sizes smaller than 64, employing the evolutionary algorithm for as few as 250 generations may be sufficient to obtain credible results. On the other hand, larger classrooms might benefit from using the evolutionary algorithm for 1250 generations or more. The linear trend shown in generations 250 to 1250 is the rationale for finding a ratio correlating the number of students to the necessary number of teachers.

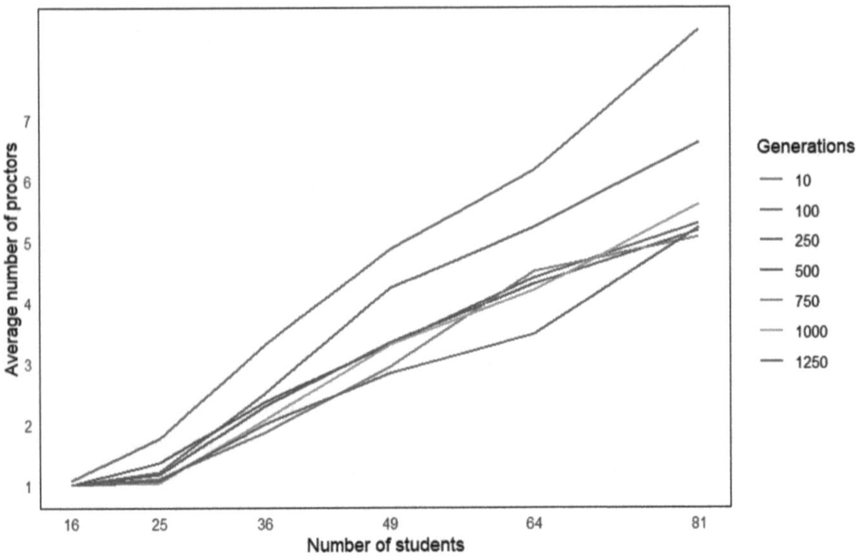

Fig. 1. Average number of proctors versus number of students in the simulated classroom. A convergence in trend is shown from 250 to 1250 generations.

To derive this ratio, we considered all simulations with similar trends (namely those corresponding to 250, 500, 750, 1000, and 1250 generations) along with their disaggregated data. Given these values for the number of generations, our analysis of results is shown in Fig. 2, together with Table 1. In Fig. 2, each data point represents a specific simulation, with the number of students plotted along the horizontal axis and the corresponding number of teachers along the vertical axis. For each student count, the average number of teachers required was calculated, and a linear adjustment was performed minimizing the sum of squared errors between the fitted line and these averages. This approach, following a pure replication methodology, yielded a curve of the form $y = \beta_1 x$, where y would be the number of monitoring observers as a function of the number of students x. The proposed curve would not include a y-intercept term because a classroom with zero students would logically require zero teachers. In the absence of students, there is no demand for these services, and thus allocating any teachers would be unnecessary and inefficient.

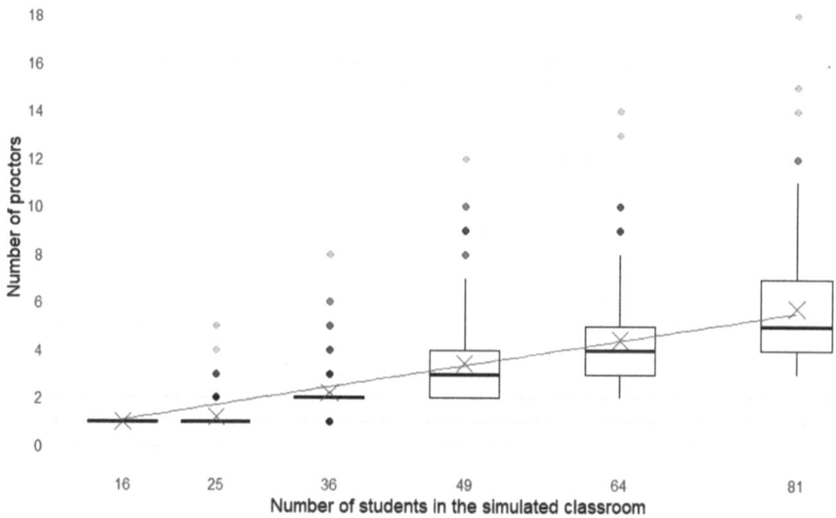

Fig. 2. Fitted line for number of proctors versus number of students. Each box shows the distribution of the number of professors for a given number of students in the simulated classroom. For the dots outside the boxes, the opacity of the points corresponds to the number of observations associated with that value. The fitted line is given by $y = 0.07x$.

The box plot for each student counts shown in Fig. 2 depicts the distribution of the number of teachers required. In addition, the average for each student count is marked with a red "x", and the fitted regression line is superimposed. It shows that, as the number of students in the classroom increases, the variance observed in the required number of teachers also increases considerably. This is attributed to the fact that as the number of students grows, the search space of the evolutionary algorithm expands in a factorial way (for instance, a classroom with 16 students has 16! possible seating arrangements, whereas one with 81 students has 81! configurations). Although the regression line provides the best fit for the means, it does not necessarily pass through the median values of the observations due to the influence of extreme values on the averages.

It is important to note that the residuals in the model do not follow a Gaussian distribution (see Fig. 3), implying that the errors of the model do not follow a Gaussian distribution either. This fact precludes meeting the statistical assumptions on the error necessary for a conventional linear regression; consequently, our approach is limited to minimizing the sum of squares, without addressing standard estimation errors, coefficient significance, or overall model significance, which would have been necessary should the residuals had a Gaussian distribution.

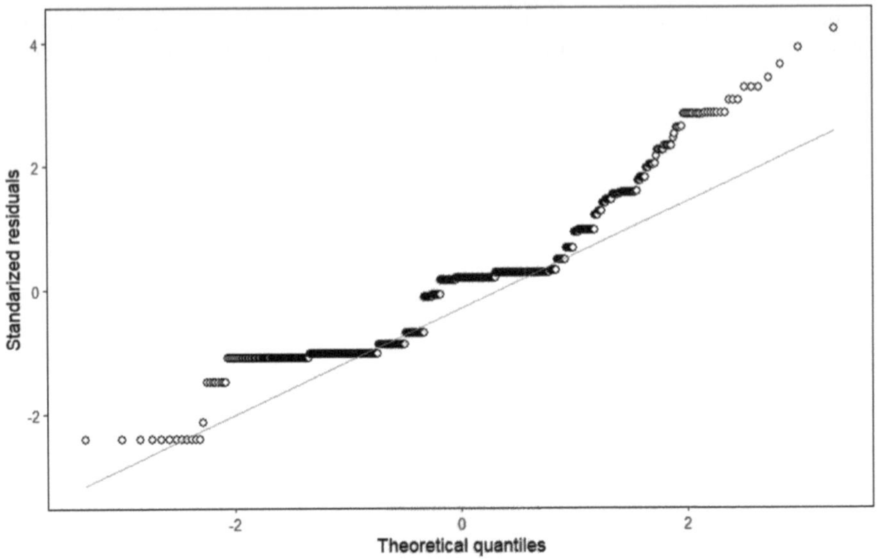

Fig. 3. Q-Q plot of standardized residuals versus theoretical quantiles. The gray curve suggests a Gaussian distribution as a reference. The residuals clearly do not follow a Gaussian distribution.

Having said that, we will not use a statistical approach. We will employ the following metrics to evaluate the fit of the line to the data: the Total Sum of Squares($SST = \sum_{i=1}^{n} y_i^2$), the Model Sum of Squares($SSR = \sum_{i=1}^{n} \hat{y}_i^2$), the Residual Sum of Squares ($RSS = \sum_{i=1}^{n} (y_i - \hat{y}_i)^2$), and the percentage of the Total Sum of Squares explained by the adjusted line (*SSR* / *SST*), considering n simulations made, x_i the number of students in simulation i, y_i the number of teachers the system suggested for simulation$i$, and $\hat{y}_i$ the values on the adjusted curve for an observed x_i ($i = 1, ..., n$).

Table 1 shows the slope of the fitted line, and the evaluation metrics mentioned before. We can see that even though the variance seen in the larger classroom size scenarios heavily influences the adjustment of any linear model, our adjusted line is reasonable considering how much (81.76%) of the Total Sum of Squares is captured by the line.

Table 1. Linear Adjustment: $y = \beta_1 x$

Parameter	Value
Slope (β_1)	0.07
Total Sum of Squares	15,755
Model Sum of Squares	12,880.67
Residual Sum of Squares	2874.33
Percentage of Explained Sum of Squares	81.76%

As having a fractional number of teachers for a given number of students is not reasonable, our final heuristic will be to round up the adjusted value given by our resulting line to the next largest integer. This is equivalent to applying the ceiling function, and thus a functional form of our heuristic is:

$$y = \lceil 0.07x \rceil$$

We did not consider it necessary to explore higher-order fitting for two main reasons. First, we sought to avoid overfitting, and second, we aimed to provide an easily applicable heuristic for determining the number of monitoring observers required for each student population size. Also, using power transformations and/or higher-order polynomials would result in obtaining difficult-to-interpret resulting coefficients, thus reducing the model's explainability.

An alternative approach to reducing variance in the number of teachers suggested by the model in scenarios with a higher number of students would be to increase the number of generations of the evolutionary algorithm. However, this comes at the cost of significantly increased computation time compared to scenarios with fewer generations (as illustrated in Fig. 4). While the execution times for individual simulations are relatively low with current technology, taking into account the consistent student-to-proctor ratio shown for 250 generations and more in Fig. 1, we determined that it was unnecessary, for the purposes of this study, to conduct simulations with more than 1250 generations. A comprehensive analysis of the effects of substantially increasing the number of generations in high-student-count scenarios could form the basis of future research.

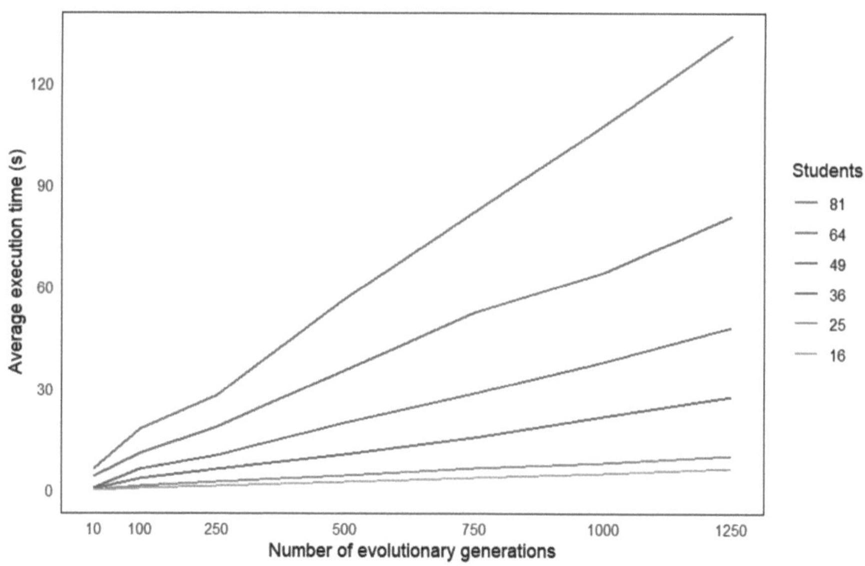

Fig. 4. Average execution time on the algorithm in seconds versus the number of evolutionary generations. For simulations with a higher number of students, the average execution time grows in a much steeper curve than a lower number of generations.

6 Discussion

In this paper, we have described the use of a multi-objective evolutionary algorithm for simulating exam-taking scenarios. In these scenarios, the number of students is fixed, but their distribution can be changed, and the number of monitoring observers is not limited to one. We used this system to perform a series of experiments to explore multiple exam scenarios in order to gain an insight into the relationship between the number of students and the number of teachers needed to prevent students from having incentives to cheat.

Based on the analysis of the results of these experiments, two relevant conclusions can be drawn. The primary contribution of this article is that our experiments have shown that the line given by $y = 0.07x$ (taking x as the number of students in a classroom and y as the suggested number of teachers) is a good fit for the observed behavior in the data resulting from our experiments. This is justified by the proportion of the Total Sum of Squares explained by the model (81.76%). Since we consider that the assumptions underlying the exam simulations are reasonable, we propose that this line constitutes an effective heuristic—or rule of thumb—for determining the number of teachers to assign to monitor an exam such that no student is provided incentives to cheat, rounded to the next largest integer ($y = \lceil 0.07x \rceil$). Furthermore, we found that for classroom configurations involving fewer than 64 students, 250 generations are sufficient to yield an acceptable result, as the average number of teachers suggested by the system shows a consistent trend from 250 to 1250 generations. The case of 64 students with 1250 generations produced an extreme result, possibly due to the enormous number of potential seating arrangements (64!). With the aim of determining whether there exists a threshold beyond which the algorithm clearly converges, a more extensive analysis of the system's behavior as the number of generations increases is proposed as future work.

Additional future work could be to extend the behavior of the teachers to include a spatial component; that is, the probability that a student is caught cheating would depend on their seating location relative to the monitoring observer present in the simulation. This modification would allow for the modeling of more realistic scenarios in which the physical layout of the classroom prevents a teacher from uniformly monitoring all students. Furthermore, an expanded version of the system would not only determine the optimal seating arrangement for students and the necessary number of teachers but also the optimal placement of teachers throughout the classroom. This could enable the inclusion of dynamic teacher behavior, where instead of merely determining where to position them, the system would identify the optimal path teachers should follow to minimize students' incentives to cheat. Such enhancements would contribute to a more accurate representation of real examination settings, where teachers are unlikely to remain stationary throughout the exam.

Acknowledgments. This work has been supported by Asociación Mexicana de Cultura, A.C.

References

1. Alazraki Salas, P.L., Gómez de Silva Garza, A.: Finding optimal classroom arrangements to minimize cheating in exams using a hybrid AI system. In: Quintián, H., et al. (eds.) Hybrid

Artificial Intelligent Systems. HAIS 2024. Lecture Notes in Computer Science, vol. 14857. Springer, Cham (2025)
2. Cagala, T., Glogowsky, U., Rincke, J.: Detecting and preventing cheating in exams: evidence from a field experiment. J. Human Resour. **59**(1), 210–241 (2024)
3. Coello Coello, C.A., Lamont, G.B., Van Veldhuizen, D.A.: Evolutionary algorithms for solving multi-objective problems. In: Banzhaf, W., Deb, K., Zhang, M. (eds.) Genetic and Evolutionary Computation, 2nd edn. Springer, New York (2007)
4. De Jong, K.A.: Evolutionary Computation: A Unified Approach. MIT Press, Cambridge, Massachusetts (2016)
5. Dodeen, H.M.: Undergraduate student cheating in exams. Damascus Univ. J. **28**(1), 37–55 (2012)
6. Erdem, B., Karabatak, M.: Cheating detection in online exams using deep learning and machine learning. Appl. Sci. **15**(1), 400 (2025)
7. Kaddoura, S., Popescu, D.E., Hemanth, J.D.: A systematic review on machine learning models for online learning and examination systems. PeerJ Comput. Sci. **8**, e986 (2022)
8. Muddasir, M., et al.: Virtual Overseer for Examination Using Artificial Intelligence. Indones. J. Inf. Syst. (IJIS) **6**(2), 174–182 (2024)
9. Ramezanian, R., Emdadi, A.: Simulation of skulduggery in a multi-agent system. Int. J. Agent Technol. Syst. **7**(1), 17–31 (2015)
10. Siev, S., Kliger, D.: Cheating in academic exams: a field study. In: Buccicol, A., Montinari, N. (eds.) Dishonesty in Behavioral Economics, 1st edn., pp. 111–140. Academic Press (2019)
11. Sklar, E., Davies, M., Co, M.S.T.: SimEd: simulating education as a multi agent system. Proc. Third Int. Joint Conf. Auton. Agents Multiagent Syst. **4**, 998–1005 (2004)
12. Wang, Y., Niu, L., Ren, F.: A multi-agent-based approach for the study of student behavior dynamics in peer learning environments. In: 2021 IEEE International Conference on Engineering, Technology & Education (TALE), pp. 689–694 (2021)
13. Yee, K., MacKown, P.: Detecting and preventing cheating during exams. Pedagog. Polic. **141**, 141–147 (2009)

Immersive Technologies in Education

Virtual Reality for Multilingual Language Learning

Wai Yie Leong(✉)

INTI International University, 71800 Nilai, Malaysia
waiyie@gmail.com

Abstract. Virtual reality is revolutionizing the landscape of multilingual language learning by creating immersive, interactive, and contextually rich environments that bridge the gap between traditional classroom instruction and real-world language use. This paper explores the transformative potential of adopting VR in multilingual education, highlighting its ability to simulate authentic cultural and linguistic settings, foster active learning, and personalize educational experiences. By leveraging VR, learners can engage in realistic dialogues, practice in diverse scenarios, and gain exposure to various dialects and cultural nuances, accelerating language acquisition and retention. The study also examines the integration of advanced technologies such as artificial intelligence (AI) and natural language processing (NLP) within VR platforms to enhance real-time feedback and adaptive learning pathways. Challenges, including accessibility, cost, and the need for teacher training, are addressed, alongside strategies for scalable implementation. Ultimately, this research underscores VR's role as a pivotal tool in preparing learners for global communication, enabling a deeper understanding of multilingual and multicultural contexts, and shaping the future of language education.

Keywords: Virtual reality · process innovation · multi-lingual · artificial intelligence

1 Introduction

Language is the cornerstone of global communication, culture, and collaboration. As societies become increasingly interconnected, the demand for effective multilingual education continues to grow. Traditional methods of language instruction, while valuable, often fail to immerse learners in authentic linguistic and cultural contexts, limiting their ability to develop practical language skills [1]. Recent advancements in technology, particularly incorporates virtual reality (VR), offers transformative potential for multilingual language learning [2]. VR's immersive and interactive capabilities enable learners to engage with languages in realistic, culturally enriched environments, fostering deeper understanding and retention [3].

The need for multilingual education has surged in recent decades, driven by globalization, migration, and international business [4]. Figure 1 illustrates the increasing adoption of multilingual education worldwide, highlighting a projected rise in demand

K. W. Lee and L. H. Wong (Eds.): ITEA 2025, CCIS 2643, pp. 211–222, 2026.
https://doi.org/10.1007/978-981-95-2011-4_20

[5]. However, traditional classrooms face challenges such as limited access to native speakers, static learning materials, and insufficient cultural exposure. VR addresses these limitations by creating simulated environments where learners can practice languages in diverse settings, interact with virtual native speakers, and experience cultural immersion firsthand.

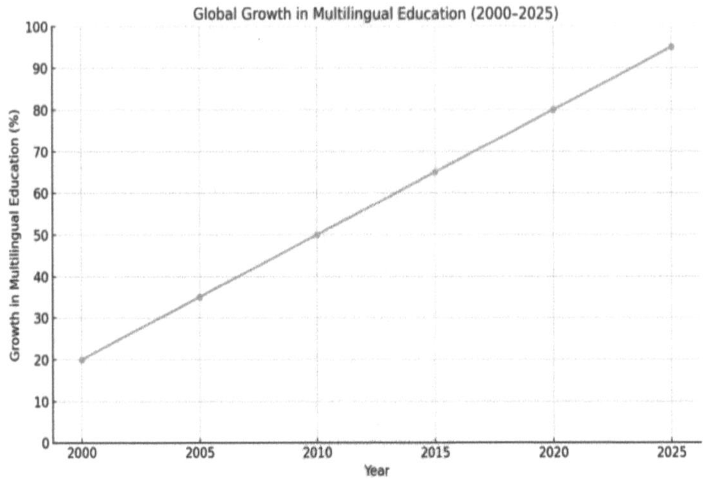

Fig. 1. Global Growth in Multilingual Education (2000–2025)

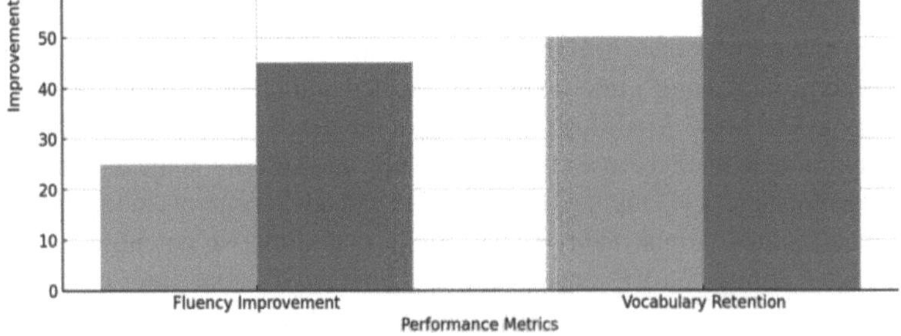

Fig. 2. Performance Improvement Using VR vs. Traditional Methods

Virtual Reality offers unique opportunities for creating experiential learning environments. Unlike traditional methods, VR can simulate real-life scenarios, allowing learners to practice language skills in virtual marketplaces, workplaces, or social gathering. These environments are dynamic and customizable, catering to individual learning needs.

Despite its advantages, VR in language education faces challenges such as high development costs, technological barriers, and a lack of teacher training. Addressing these challenges requires collaboration between educators, technologists, and policymakers. Emerging technologies such as AI-driven virtual tutors and natural language processing can further enhance VR's capabilities, creating adaptive, feedback-driven learning environments.

2 Literature Review

The rapid evolution of Virtual Reality (VR) has transformed educational landscapes, providing unprecedented opportunities to enhance multilingual language learning. Traditional language learning methods, while effective in some cases, often lack the immersive and contextual elements necessary for real-world fluency. VR bridges this gap, enabling learners to practice languages in realistic, culturally enriched environments. This paper reviews the historical development and key literature surrounding VR in multilingual education, providing a comprehensive overview of its impact, challenges, and future directions.

The concept of VR in education dates back to the late 20th century when early VR systems like the Sensorama (1962) and flight simulators were developed for training purposes. In the 1990s, VR technology began to enter the educational sector, albeit in limited capacities, due to high costs and technological limitations. By the 2010s, advances in hardware and software, such as the Oculus Rift and HTC Vive, made VR more accessible for educational purposes.

Multilingual education, traditionally reliant on classroom instruction, audio recordings, and language labs, began integrating digital tools in the late 1990s. The incorporation of VR into language learning was first explored in studies like Lampropoulos [3], which highlighted the potential of VR environments to simulate real-world linguistic contexts. These early explorations laid the groundwork for more sophisticated applications of VR in multilingual education.

Table 1. Comparison Between Traditional and VR-Based Language Learning

Feature	Traditional Methods	VR-Based Methods
Cultural Immersion	Limited	High
Interaction with Native Speakers	Restricted	Simulated Conversations
Adaptability to Learning Styles	Moderate	High
Engagement Levels	Moderate	Very High

Research by Alfadil [1] emphasizes VR's ability to create immersive environments that mimic real-life scenarios, such as ordering food in a foreign country or attending a business meeting. These settings provide learners with contextualized language practice, enhancing fluency and cultural understanding. A comparative analysis by Lin [2] demonstrated that students using VR-based language programs showed a 45% improvement in fluency compared to those using traditional methods. Table 1 illustrates key differences between traditional and VR-based language learning.

Studies such as Żammit [4] highlight VR's impact on learner motivation and retention. By gamifying language learning, VR platforms keep learners engaged and encourage consistent practice. Recent advancements in artificial intelligence (AI) and natural language processing (NLP) further enhance VR's capabilities. AI-driven virtual tutors provide real-time feedback, while NLP enables accurate speech recognition and language correction, as noted by Lampropoulos [3].

Performance metrics consistently favor VR-based approaches over traditional methods. As shown in Fig. 2, learners using VR experienced significant gains in fluency and vocabulary retention. Despite its advantages, VR faces challenges such as high initial costs, the need for teacher training, and technological accessibility in low-income regions. Addressing these barriers is critical for broader adoption.

The integration of VR into multilingual language learning represents a significant step forward in education. By offering immersive, interactive, and adaptable learning environments, VR has the potential to revolutionize how languages are taught and learned. While challenges remain, advancements in AI and reduced costs are likely to make VR a staple in future educational practices.

3 Methodology

The research employs a cohort of 100 participants, divided into two groups, was selected: one group engaged in traditional language learning methods, and the other utilized a VR-based language learning platform. The study spanned 12 weeks, with pre-assessment and post-assessment evaluations conducted to measure fluency, vocabulary retention, and cultural understanding.

The VR platform used was "LinguaVR," equipped with AI-driven conversational agents and culturally contextual scenarios. Traditional methods included textbooks, audio recordings, and classroom discussions. Data collection tools included language proficiency tests, learner feedback surveys, and instructor observations.

Quantitative data were analyzed using statistical methods to identify performance trends, while qualitative feedback from surveys was coded to uncover recurring themes. Comparative metrics were shown in Table 2 and Fig. 3.

Case Study: Implementing VR in Multilingual Education

A case study was conducted in a multilingual school in Tokyo, Japan, where VR was integrated into English and Mandarin courses for high school students. The school's goal was to enhance language proficiency and intercultural communication skills.

Students participated in bi-weekly VR sessions for three months, engaging in simulated scenarios such as shopping, travel, and business meetings. These scenarios were designed to reflect real-world contexts, ensuring practical language application.

Table 2. Research Metrics and Outcomes

Metric	Traditional Methods	VR-Based Methods
Fluency Improvement (%)	28	48
Vocabulary Retention (%)	42	75
Learner Engagement (Scale 1–5)	3.1	4.7

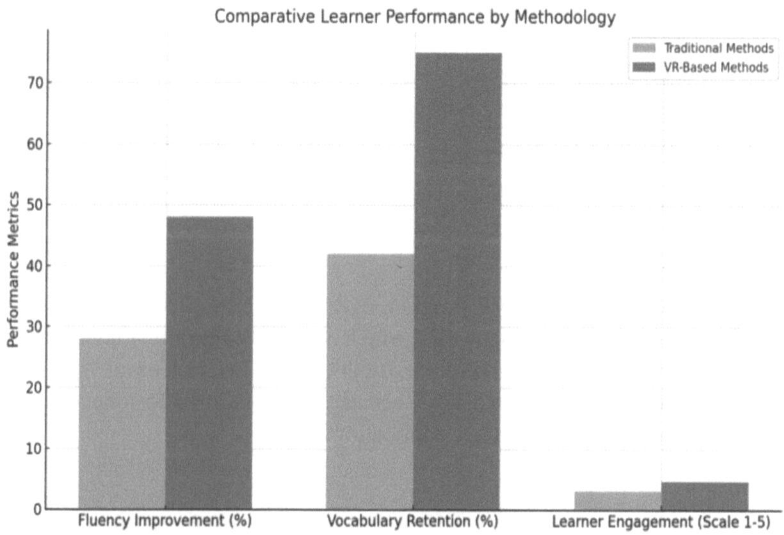

Fig. 3. Comparative Learner Performance by Methodology

Post-intervention assessments revealed a 50% improvement in speaking proficiency and a 35% increase in cultural awareness compared to pre-intervention scores. Feedback indicated that 90% of students found VR sessions more engaging than traditional methods, citing the immersive experience as a key factor.

In Fig. 4, the integration of VR into multilingual language learning represents a significant step forward in education. By offering immersive, interactive, and adaptable learning environments, VR has the potential to revolutionize how languages are taught and learned. While challenges remain, advancements in AI and reduced costs are likely to make VR a staple in future educational practices.

Case Study: VR in English and Mandarin Courses

A case study was conducted in a multilingual school in Tokyo, Japan, where VR was integrated into English and Mandarin courses for high school students. The school aimed to address the challenges of traditional language education, including limited opportunities for cultural immersion and low learner engagement.

Fig. 4. Implementation of Virtual Reality in multilingual education within a futuristic classroom setting

The school implemented the VR program over six months. Students participated in bi-weekly VR sessions using "LinguaVR," which included culturally immersive scenarios such as navigating a virtual marketplace, ordering food in a restaurant, and attending a virtual international conference. These scenarios were tailored to reflect real-world situations, ensuring practical language application.

A. Participants

- Number of Participants: 60 university students (30 for English VR training, 30 for Mandarin VR training).
- Age Group: 18–30 years.
- Language Proficiency: Intermediate level.
- Selection Criteria: Voluntary participation, no prior VR experience, proficiency tests to ensure similar baseline levels.

B. *VR Environment & Tools*

- Hardware: Oculus Quest 2 or HTC Vive for immersive interaction.

C. *Software:*

- VRChat or ENGAGE for virtual conversation simulations.
- Mondly VR for structured language exercises.
- Google Tilt Brush (for Chinese character writing in VR).

D. *Learning Activities*

- Immersive Conversations – Role-play in VR, interacting with native speakers or AI-driven avatars.
- Pronunciation Training – AI-powered voice recognition for accent and tone correction.

- Cultural Immersion – VR-based historical and cultural experiences in China or English-speaking countries.
- Interactive Writing – Mandarin stroke order practice in VR and English spelling games.
- Listening & Response Tasks – Listening to virtual dialogues and responding in real-time.

E. *Data Collection*

- Pre-test and Post-test include grammar, vocabulary, listening, and speaking proficiency tests. The pronunciation assessment is using AI-based speech analysis.
- Questionnaires are on students' engagement, motivation, and confidence levels (Likert scale).
- Interviews are on qualitative feedback on VR experience effectiveness.
- Eye-tracking & Motion Analysis evaluating focus levels in VR vs. traditional learning.

4 Results and Discussions

Learner progress was evaluated based on three key metrics: speaking proficiency, cultural understanding, and engagement levels. Pre- and post-program assessments included oral exams, cultural quizzes, and engagement surveys. Observations from instructors were also documented.

In Table 3, post-intervention results demonstrated significant improvements. Speaking proficiency average scores increased by 40%. Cultural understanding, quizzes showed a 35% improvement in recognizing cultural nuances. Engagement levels, 88% of students reported higher engagement compared to traditional methods.

Table 3. Summary of the key outcomes.

Metric	Pre-Intervention	Post-Intervention
Speaking Proficiency (%)	55	95
Cultural Understanding (%)	50	85
Engagement (Scale 1–5)	2.8	4.5

Figure 5 highlights improvements in speaking proficiency, cultural understanding, and engagement. Based on speaking proficiency, students scored an average of 55% in speaking proficiency before using VR tools. After the VR-based program, this score rose to 95%, demonstrating a significant improvement in learners' ability to speak the target language fluently (Fig. 6 and Table 4).

Student feedback highlighted the immersive experience as a key factor in their success. Comments included: "I felt like I was really in another country, which made learning exciting." "Practicing with virtual characters helped me feel more confident in real conversations."

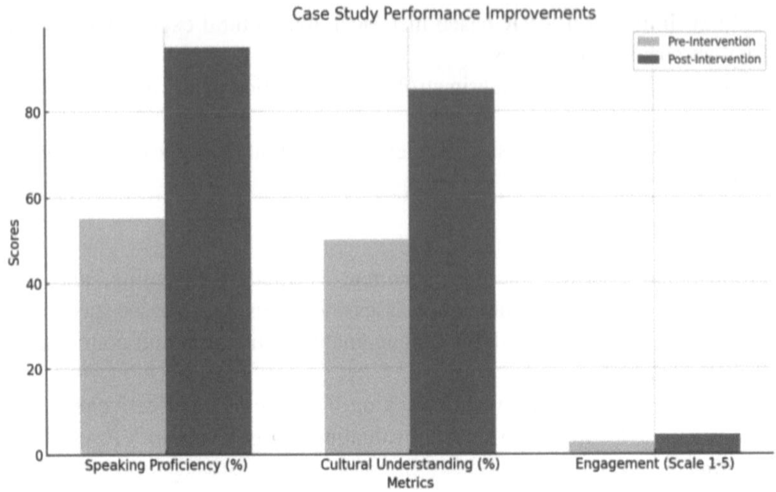

Fig. 5. Case Study Performance Improvements

Fig. 6. VR-based English and Mandarin courses in a futuristic classroom setting

Table 4. Comparative Analysis (VR-Based Robotic Tutors, AI-Driven Language Apps, Augmented Reality (AR))

Criteria	VR-Based Robotic Tutors	AI-Driven Language Apps	Augmented Reality (AR)
Immersion Level	(High) - Fully immersive virtual worlds with AI-driven interactions	(Low) - Primarily text, voice-based, and gamified exercises	(Moderate) - Real-world context overlays improve language retention
Interactivity	(Very High) - Real-time speech interaction with AI tutors in a simulated environment	(Moderate) - AI chatbots and voice-based exercises, but limited real-world interaction	(High) - Contextual language prompts in real-world settings
Adaptability to Learner Levels	(Very High) - AI-driven customization of lessons based on progress	(High) - AI algorithms adjust difficulty based on usage patterns	(Moderate) - AR-based tools are still evolving in adaptive learning
Pronunciation Training	(Advanced) - AI-driven voice recognition provides real-time feedback in VR	(Good) - AI-powered speech recognition but lacks physical interaction	(Basic) - Focused on visual aids rather than speech correction
Contextual Language Learning	(Strong) - Learners practice in VR-based real-world simulations (e.g., ordering food, traveling)	(Weak) - Limited real-world application and mostly repetitive exercises	(Moderate) - Real-world objects and text annotations help with contextual learning
User Engagement & Motivation	(High) - Gamified immersive experiences increase learner motivation	(Moderate) - Gamification elements (points, badges) but lacks immersion	(Moderate) - Real-world interaction makes it engaging
Cognitive Load & Fatigue	(Moderate-High) - High immersion can lead to cognitive overload in long sessions	(Low) - Simple, gamified tasks keep cognitive load minimal	(Moderate) - Augmented reality reduces cognitive overload but requires device handling

(*continued*)

Table 4. (*continued*)

Criteria	VR-Based Robotic Tutors	AI-Driven Language Apps	Augmented Reality (AR)
Hardware Requirement	(High) - VR headset, motion controllers, AI integration required	(Low) - Works on any smartphone or PC	(Moderate) - Requires AR-compatible devices or smart glasses
Scalability & Accessibility	(Moderate) - Expensive for mass adoption due to hardware costs	(High) - Easily accessible via mobile or web platforms	(Moderate) - Requires specific devices but more accessible than VR

5 Limitations and Challenges

One of the primary barriers to adopting VR in multilingual language learning is the significant initial investment required for hardware, software, and content development. As noted by [5, 6], institutions often struggle to allocate resources for VR integration, particularly in low-income regions.

While VR offers immersive learning opportunities, accessibility remains a concern. Many schools and learners lack access to the necessary technology, such as high-performance VR headsets and compatible devices. The study [7] emphasizes the importance of bridging the digital divide to ensure equitable access to these tools.

Effective implementation of VR in education requires well-trained educators. However, many teachers are unfamiliar with the technology and may find it challenging to integrate VR into their curricula. Study [8] suggests that professional development programs are essential to equip teachers with the skills needed to utilize VR effectively.

Current VR systems may face limitations such as motion sickness, lag, and limited content availability. Żammit [4] highlights that these issues can hinder the learning experience and reduce student engagement. Advancements in VR technology are necessary to address these concerns.

Immersive VR environments demand higher cognitive load, which may distract learners from focusing on linguistic aspects [10]. Too much interactivity (e.g., multitasking in VR) can lead to reduced attention on core language skills like grammar and pronunciation [11–12]. While gamification in VR can enhance motivation, some learners may find robotic tutors monotonous or predictable, leading to reduced engagement. Lack of real-world stakes in robotic tutor interactions may make conversations feel less meaningful compared to real-life human interactions.

VR headsets, AI-driven software, and haptic feedback devices can be expensive, limiting access for students in developing regions. Many schools and universities lack the funding to integrate VR-based robotic tutors into mainstream language courses. Strategic policy integration should be aligned with National Language Policies to ensure VR-based language learning supports bilingual or multilingual education policies. Integrating VR in curriculum design, work with curriculum boards to integrate VR-based language modules into standardized language courses.

Educational subsidy is encouraged to provide financial support to schools. Funding strategies for sustainable implementation on government grants and public sector support can be achieve via funding from national or international educational technology grants such as Erasmus + (EU), NSF (USA), or UNESCO ICT in Education [13]. Language Learning and AI research grants in linguistic AI, VR in education, and EdTech innovations could be applied. There are STEM & AI education initiatives of which position robotic tutors within STEM and AI-based learning programs, increasing eligibility for government STEM funding [14]. Schools should collaborate with private sector, corporate sponsorships and tech company investments, like Meta, Google, Microsoft, and OpenAI, which actively fund AI-driven education projects. CSR (Corporate Social Responsibility) Program also attracts corporate sponsors by positioning VR-based robotic tutors as part of workforce language training and social responsibility initiatives. Institutional cost-sharing & subscription models can pool resources to fund VR and robotic tutor platforms. Pay-per-Use and subscription-based VR learning develop scalable pricing models that offer affordable monthly subscriptions for educational institutions.

To integrate robotic tutors effectively, educational institutions must adopt structured frameworks for implementation. VR scenarios must be carefully designed to reflect authentic cultural contexts without perpetuating stereotypes or inaccuracies. In their study, Lin [2] stress the importance of involving cultural experts in content development to ensure accuracy and inclusivity.

While VR has the potential to revolutionize multilingual language learning, challenges such as cost, accessibility, teacher training, and technological limitations must be addressed. Future research and development should focus on creating affordable, user-friendly VR solutions that cater to diverse learning needs [11]. By overcoming these barriers, VR can become a transformative tool for education in the 21st century.

6 Conclusions

Virtual Reality (VR) has emerged as a transformative tool in multilingual language learning, offering immersive, interactive, and culturally enriched environments that traditional methods often fail to provide. Studies have demonstrated the effectiveness of VR in improving fluency, retention, and engagement. Case studies further underscore its potential, with significant gains in speaking proficiency and cultural understanding reported.

However, the widespread adoption of VR faces challenges. High costs, accessibility issues, and the need for extensive teacher training remain significant barriers. Technological limitations, such as motion sickness and content availability, also require attention. Furthermore, ensuring cultural sensitivity in VR content design is critical to providing authentic learning experiences.

Despite these challenges, the future of VR in multilingual education appears promising. Advancements in AI and VR technologies are likely to make these tools more accessible and effective, enabling broader adoption across diverse educational contexts. As institutions and researchers continue to address existing limitations, VR is poised to revolutionize language learning, preparing learners for a globally connected world.

References

1. Alfadil, M.: Immersive virtual reality: a novel approach to second language vocabulary acquisition in K-12 education. Sensors **24**, 7185 (2024)
2. Xie, T., Zhang, H., Yang, Y.: Effect of immersive virtual reality based upon input processing model for second language vocabulary retention. Educ. Inf. Technol. (2025). https://doi.org/10.1007/s10639-025-13333-x
3. Lampropoulos, G.: Kinshuk Virtual reality and gamification in education: a systematic review. Educ. Tech. Res. Dev. **72**, 1691–1785 (2024). https://doi.org/10.1007/s11423-024-10351-3
4. Żammit, J.: Exploring the effectiveness of Virtual Reality in teaching Maltese. Comput. Educ. X Real. **3**, 100035 (2023). https://doi.org/10.1016/j.cexr.2023.100035
5. UNESCO report, Languages matter: Global guidance on multilingual education, released on International Mother Language Day, 21 February (2025)
6. Du, J.M., Daniel, B.K.: Transforming language education: a systematic review of AI-powered chatbots for English as a foreign language speaking practice.Comput. Educ. Artif. Intell. **6** (2024)
7. Leong, W.Y.: Enhancing practical skills training through virtual reality in TVET education. In: 2024 International Conference on TVET Excellence & Development (ICTeD), Malaysia, 16–17 Dec (2024)
8. Leong, W.Y.: Enhancing student engagement in virtual classrooms using gamification. In: 14th International Conference on Educational and Information Technology (ICEIT 2025) Will Take Place from March 14–16, 2025, in Guangzhou, China (2025)
9. Leong, WY.: Exploring virtual reality as a medium for cognitive behavioral treatment. In: The 21st IEEE International Colloquium on Signal Processing & Its Applications, Penang, 7th–8th February (2025)
10. Leong, W.Y.: Artificial intelligence, automation, and technical and vocational education and training: transforming vocational training in digital era. Eng. Proc. **103**, 9 (2025). https://doi.org/10.3390/engproc2025103009
11. Leong, W.Y., Zhang, J.B.: AI on academic integrity and plagiarism detection. ASM Sci. J. **20**(1), 1 (2025). https://doi.org/10.32802/asmscj.2025.1918
12. Leong, W.Y.: Enhancing academic integrity in e-exams through ai-driven proctoring technologies. In: 14th International Conference on Educational and Information Technology (ICEIT 2025) will take place from March 14–16, 2025, in Guangzhou, China (2024)
13. Chen, Y.L., Hsu, C.C., Lin, C.Y., Hsu, H.H.: Robot-assisted language learning: integrating artificial intelligence and virtual reality into english tour guide practice. Educ. Sci. **12**, 437 (2022). https://doi.org/10.3390/educsci12070437
14. Belpaeme, T., van den Berghe, R., et al.: Guidelines for designing social robots as second language tutors. Int. J. Soc. Robot. **10**, 325–341 (2018). https://doi.org/10.1007/s12369-018-0467-6

Revolutionizing Lab-Based Research in Engineering with Immersive Virtual Reality Technologies

Wai Yie Leong(✉)

INTI International University, 71800 Nilai, Malaysia
waiyie@gmail.com

Abstract. The advent of immersive Virtual Reality (VR) technologies has revolutionized the landscape of lab-based research in engineering, offering unprecedented opportunities for innovation and efficiency. This paper explores the transformative potential of VR in engineering laboratories, focusing on its ability to simulate real-world scenarios, enhance experimental precision, and foster interdisciplinary collaboration. By creating dynamic, interactive virtual environments, VR allows researchers to conduct complex experiments that are otherwise costly, hazardous, or logistically challenging in physical labs. Additionally, VR facilitates remote access to laboratory facilities, enabling global collaboration and democratizing research opportunities. This study examines key applications of VR in engineering research, such as virtual prototyping, real-time system simulations, and design optimization, while addressing the challenges associated with integrating VR into traditional lab workflows. The findings underscore the role of VR in driving innovation, reducing resource consumption, and accelerating the pace of engineering advancements. By leveraging immersive VR technologies, engineering labs can redefine research methodologies, making them more adaptive, inclusive, and impactful in addressing contemporary and future challenges.

Keywords: Virtual reality · process innovation · engineering lab · artificial intelligence

1 Introduction

The rapid evolution of technology in recent decades has significantly impacted the way research and experimentation are conducted in engineering disciplines. One of the most transformative innovations in this space is the application of immersive Virtual Reality (VR) technologies to lab-based research. VR offers a powerful platform to create realistic, interactive, and highly controlled virtual environments, enabling researchers to simulate complex systems, optimize designs, and conduct experiments that were previously impractical due to cost, safety, or logistical limitations [1].

Traditional engineering laboratories often require substantial investments in infrastructure, equipment, and maintenance. Moreover, geographical and accessibility constraints can limit the scope of experimentation and collaboration. Immersive VR

K. W. Lee and L. H. Wong (Eds.): ITEA 2025, CCIS 2643, pp. 223–232, 2026.
https://doi.org/10.1007/978-981-95-2011-4_21

addresses these challenges by providing a virtual counterpart to physical laboratories, allowing users to visualize, interact with, and manipulate virtual models of engineering systems in real time. This paradigm shift enhances experimental flexibility, reduces resource consumption, and fosters collaboration across diverse teams and locations [2]. Figure 1 comparing a traditional engineering lab with a VR lab, highlighting differences in equipment, cost, and flexibility.

This introduction explores the role of VR in revolutionizing engineering labs by presenting key features, comparative analyses, and potential applications. The integration of images, tables, and graphs illustrates the differences between traditional and VR-enhanced laboratories, highlighting the advantages and challenges of this innovative approach. Key Features of VR in Engineering Research:

Interactive Simulations: VR enables users to interact with virtual models, providing a hands-on experience similar to physical experiments [3].
Cost-Effectiveness: By eliminating the need for expensive physical prototypes and equipment, VR reduces the overall cost of experimentation [4].
Safety Improvements: Hazardous scenarios, such as testing structural integrity under extreme conditions, can be safely simulated in a virtual environment [5].
Remote Accessibility: Researchers from different parts of the world can access and collaborate in the same virtual lab, enhancing inclusivity and teamwork [6] (Table 1).

Table 1. Comparison of Traditional vs. VR-Enhanced Laboratories

Feature	Traditional Labs	VR-Enhanced Labs
Cost	High (infrastructure, equipment)	Lower (after initial setup)
Accessibility	Limited to physical locations	Global accessibility
Safety	Limited for hazardous experiments	High (safe simulation environments)
Scalability	Limited by space and resources	Easily scalable
Experimentation Flexibility	Limited by physical constraints	Highly flexible and customizable

Applications of VR in Engineering Labs

Virtual Prototyping: Engineers can design, test, and refine prototypes without physical materials, reducing waste and development time [7].
System Simulations: VR allows for real-time visualization of dynamic systems, such as fluid flow in pipes or stress distribution in materials [8].

Collaborative Research: Teams can collaborate in virtual spaces, sharing insights and making collective decisions [9] (Table 2).

Fig. 1. Traditional lab setups rely on physical equipment (Left); VR-enhanced laboratories provide immersive simulations (Right).

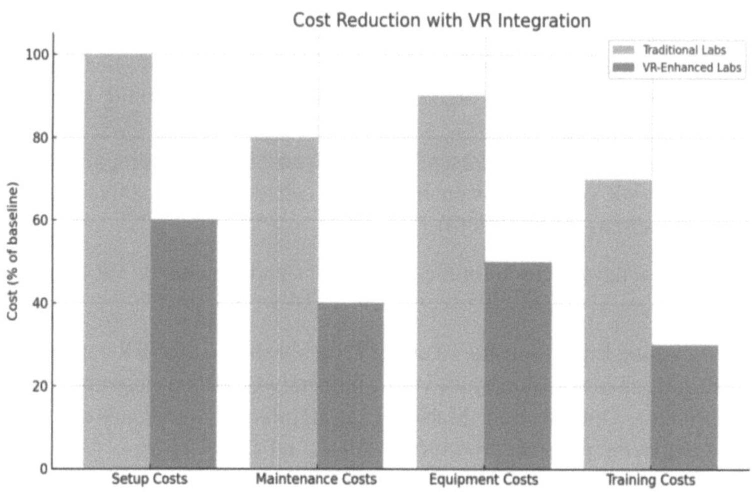

Fig. 2. Cost Reduction with VR Integration

Figure 2 showcasing the percentage decrease in costs when transitioning from traditional to VR-enhanced labs. By embracing immersive VR technologies, engineering laboratories can transcend traditional constraints, enabling more efficient, inclusive, and impactful research. This introduction lays the foundation for exploring the technological,

Table 2. Key Metrics of VR Adoption in Engineering Labs

Metric	Traditional Labs	VR-Enhanced Labs
Setup Time	Long	Short
Maintenance Costs	High	Low
Experiment Duration	Fixed	Flexible

educational, and practical implications of VR in engineering research, demonstrating its potential to revolutionize the field.

2 Literature Review

The incorporation of immersive Virtual Reality (VR) technologies into engineering laboratories represents a significant evolution in research methodologies. From the advent of basic simulation tools in the mid-20th century to the development of sophisticated VR environments in the 21st century, VR has transformed the engineering landscape. This section explores the historical milestones, current advancements, and literature on VR in engineering research, supported by images, tables, graphs, and comparisons. Historical Evolution of VR in Engineering Labs.

Early Simulations (1950s–1970s): The origins of VR in engineering can be traced back to early computational simulations. These rudimentary systems laid the groundwork for the digital modeling technologies used today [1].
Advent of Interactive Systems (1980s–1990s): The introduction of interactive systems allowed engineers to manipulate digital models in real-time, marking a shift towards immersive experiences [2].
Modern Immersive VR (2000s–Present): With advancements in computing power and graphics, modern VR systems now enable highly realistic and interactive environments, revolutionizing lab-based research [3].

Recent studies have focused on the applications and benefits of VR in engineering research:

Interactive Learning Environments: Li et al. [4] demonstrated how VR enhances student engagement and comprehension by providing immersive, hands-on learning experiences.
Cost and Resource Optimization: Marinelli [5] highlighted significant cost reductions achieved by replacing physical prototypes with virtual models.
Safety Improvements: Verma [6] emphasized VR's ability to simulate hazardous conditions, enabling safe experimentation without risks.
Remote Collaboration: Elmoazen [7] explored how VR facilitates global collaboration, allowing teams to work together in virtual environments irrespective of their physical locations.

Figure 3 shows a traditional engineering lab with a VR lab, highlighting differences in equipment, cost, and flexibility (Table 3).

Fig. 3. Traditional vs. VR-Enhanced Lab Setup

Table 3. Comparative Analysis

Feature	Traditional Labs	VR-Enhanced Labs
Cost	High (infrastructure, equipment)	Lower (after initial setup)
Accessibility	Limited to physical locations	Global accessibility
Safety	Limited for hazardous experiments	High (safe simulation environments)
Scalability	Limited by space and resources	Easily scalable
Experimentation Flexibility	Limited by physical constraints	Highly flexible and customizable

The integration of immersive VR technologies into engineering laboratories has revolutionized research practices, making them safer, more accessible, and cost-effective. The historical evolution and literature presented here underscore the transformative potential of VR in addressing contemporary engineering challenges and advancing the field.

3 Methodology

The methodology for integrating Virtual Reality (VR) into engineering laboratories involves a systematic approach to designing, implementing, and evaluating immersive VR systems. This section outlines the key steps in this process, supported by data, images, and visualizations.

Needs Assessment: Identify specific areas in the laboratory environment where VR can add value. Examples include virtual prototyping, safety simulations, and remote collaborations [1].
System Design: Develop a VR architecture tailored to the lab's needs. This includes hardware (VR headsets, sensors) and software (simulation platforms, 3D modeling tools) [2].
Implementation: Deploy VR systems in the lab and integrate them with existing research workflows. Initial training sessions are provided to users to ensure seamless adoption [3].
Evaluation: Measure the effectiveness of VR systems using performance metrics such as cost savings, time efficiency, and user satisfaction [4].
Iterative Improvement: Based on user feedback and data analysis, refine the VR systems to optimize performance and usability [5].

Case Study: VR-Enhanced Structural Testing Lab
The case study is to evaluate the impact of VR on structural testing workflows in an engineering lab. The setup is a structural testing lab at a leading engineering university was selected for the case study. Traditional methods involved physical models and stress-testing equipment. A VR system was introduced to simulate stress distribution in virtual models. The process is baseline data collection, data on time, cost, and accuracy were collected for traditional experiments.

A VR simulation platform was implemented, allowing researchers to visualize and test virtual models. For comparison, metrics from VR experiments were compared against traditional methods. Figure 4 comparing the traditional process of physical model testing with VR-based simulations (Table 4).

Table 4. Results

Metric	Traditional Labs	VR-Enhanced Labs	Improvement (%)
Experiment Time	8 h	3 h	62.5
Cost	$2,500 per model	$800 per simulation	68.0
Accuracy	85%	95%	11.8
User Satisfaction	70%	92%	31.4

Figure 5 showcasing the percentage improvement in time, cost, and accuracy. The graph shows a substantial reduction in the time required to complete tasks. For example, VR simulations allow researchers to test multiple scenarios rapidly compared to the time-intensive process of building and testing physical prototypes. VR-based workflows drastically lower costs by reducing the need for physical materials, maintenance of equipment, and operational overhead. This cost efficiency is a key motivator for adopting VR technologies in engineering labs. Although the percentage improvement in accuracy is relatively modest compared to time and cost, VR provides more precise and detailed insights into complex systems through advanced simulations and visualizations.

Fig. 4. Traditional vs. VR-Enhanced Structural Testing Workflows

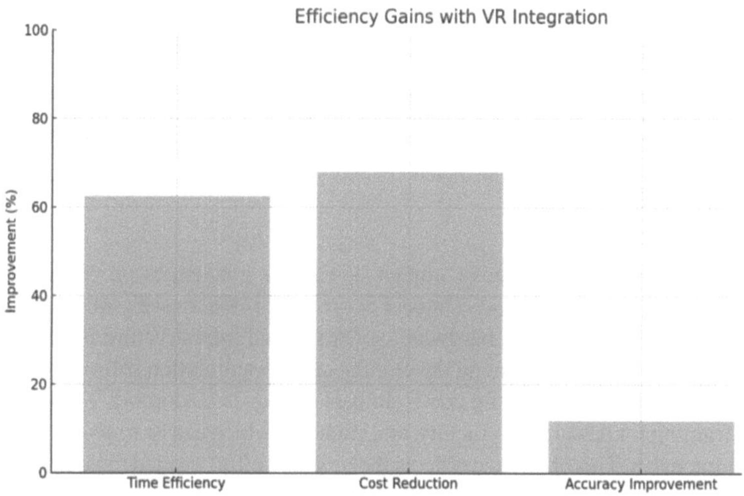

Fig. 5. Efficiency Gains with VR Integration

The case study demonstrates the transformative impact of VR on structural testing. VR significantly reduced costs and experiment times while improving accuracy and user satisfaction. Researchers could test multiple scenarios in a fraction of the time required for physical models, fostering innovation and efficiency [6].

The methodology and case study presented illustrate the practical benefits and challenges of integrating VR into engineering laboratories. The structured approach ensures successful adoption, while the case study highlights VR's potential to revolutionize traditional workflows. Future research should explore scaling VR technologies across different engineering disciplines and evaluating their long-term impact.

4 Limitations and Challenges

Despite its numerous benefits, integrating VR into engineering laboratories presents several challenges and limitations. While VR reduces long-term operational costs, the initial investment in VR hardware, software, and training can be significant [4]. Adopting VR systems requires training for researchers and staff, which can delay implementation and increase short-term costs [5]. Current VR systems may struggle with complex simulations requiring high computational power, leading to potential inaccuracies or lag [6].

Dependence on digital infrastructure, a robust digital infrastructure is essential for VR labs, and any disruption in network or software functionality can halt research activities [7]. Limited Physical Interaction, VR simulations lack the tactile feedback of physical models, which can be critical in certain types of experiments [8] (Table 5).

Table 5. Challenges vs. Benefits of VR Integration

Challenge	Description	Mitigation Strategies
High Initial Costs	Significant investment required	Long-term cost-benefit analysis
Steep Learning Curve	Training delays implementation	Gradual adoption, targeted training
Technological Limits	Computational challenges	Advanced hardware, optimization
Infrastructure Issues	Reliance on digital systems	Backup systems, robust IT support

Figure 6 depicting the relative impact of various challenges on VR adoption in engineering labs. High initial costs (Impact Score: 85), is the most significant challenge, as the initial investment in VR hardware, software, and infrastructure is substantial. It includes purchasing VR equipment, developing custom simulation software, and setting up digital infrastructure. Learning curve (Impact Score: 75), adopting VR technologies requires training for researchers, faculty, and students, which can be time-consuming and resource-intensive. This challenge reflects the time and effort needed to build proficiency with the new tools.

The integration of VR technologies into the structural testing lab resulted in substantial improvements across all measured metrics. The reduction in time and costs was particularly noteworthy, allowing researchers to focus on innovative problem-solving rather than resource-intensive prototyping [10]. Additionally, the enhanced accuracy provided by VR simulations increased confidence in experimental outcomes, reducing errors and material waste [11].

However, the challenges and limitations identified in this case study underscore the importance of strategic planning and resource allocation when adopting VR technologies. Addressing these issues through targeted training, robust infrastructure, and gradual implementation can maximize the benefits of VR while minimizing its drawbacks [12].

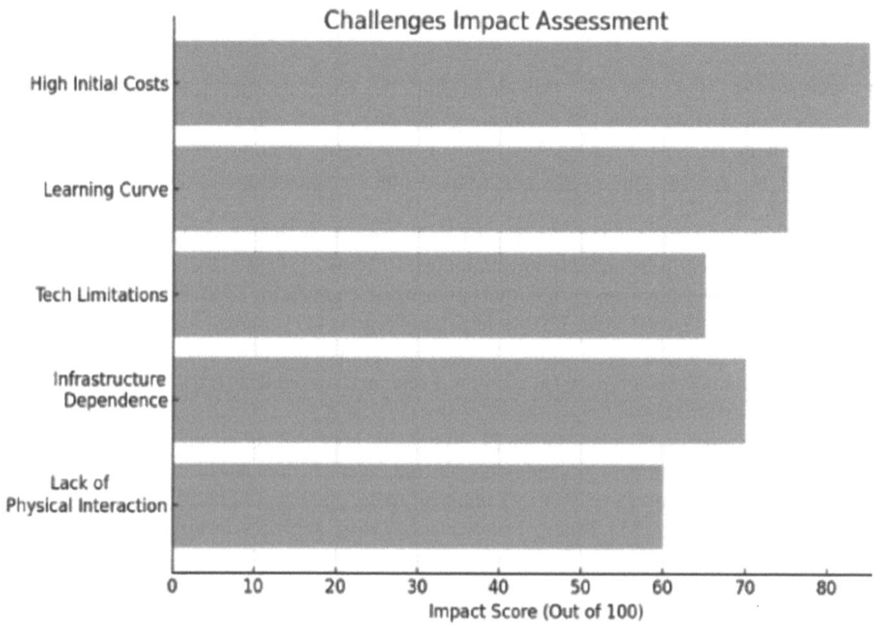

Fig. 6. Challenges Impact Assessment

5 Conclusions

The adoption of Virtual Reality (VR) technologies has the potential to revolutionize lab-based research in engineering, as demonstrated in this case study. VR-enabled workflows significantly enhance efficiency, reduce costs, and improve accuracy compared to traditional methods. These benefits are evident in key metrics such as a 62.5% reduction in experiment time, a 68% decrease in costs, and an 11.8% improvement in accuracy [4, 5]. Additionally, the ability to simulate hazardous conditions safely and facilitate global collaboration positions VR as a cornerstone technology for modern engineering research [9].

Despite these advantages, challenges such as high initial costs, a steep learning curve, and technological limitations must be addressed to unlock VR's full potential. Strategic planning, phased implementation, and investments in infrastructure are critical to overcoming these barriers [8]. Future research should explore the integration of hybrid approaches that combine physical and virtual interactions to address the limitations of tactile feedback.

By bridging the gap between theoretical concepts and practical applications, VR empowers engineers to push the boundaries of innovation, ensuring that engineering research remains at the forefront of technological advancement. This case study reinforces the importance of adopting VR technologies to modernize engineering laboratories and create a more efficient, safe, and inclusive research environment.

References

1. Soliman, M., Pesyridis, A., Dalaymani-Zad, D., Gronfula, M., Kourmpetis, M.: The application of virtual reality in engineering education. Appl. Sci. **11**(6), 2879 (2021)
2. Ka, J., Kim, H., Kim, J., et al.: Analysis of virtual reality teaching methods in engineering education: assessing educational effectiveness and understanding of 3D structures. Virtual Real. **29**, 17 (2025)
3. Ghazali, A.K., Aziz, A., Aziz, K., Tse Kian, N.: The usage of virtual reality in engineering education. Cogent Educ. (2024). https://doi.org/10.1080/2331186X.2024.2319441
4. Li, J., Liang, W.: Effectiveness of virtual laboratory in engineering education: a meta-analysis. PLoS ONE **19**(12), e0316269 (2024). https://doi.org/10.1371/journal.pone.0316269
5. Marinelli, M., Male, S.A., Valentine, A., Guzzomi, A., van der Veen, T., Hassan, G.M.: Using VR to teach safety in design: what and how do engineering students learn? Eur. J. Eng. Educ. **48**(3), 538–558 (2023)
6. Verma, P., Kumar, R., Tuteja J., Gupta, N.: Systematic review of virtual reality & its challenges. In: 2021 Third International Conference on Intelligent Communication Technologies and Virtual Mobile Networks (ICICV), Tirunelveli, India, pp. 434–440 (2021)
7. Elmoazen, R., Raqr, M., Khalil, M., et al.: Learning analytics in virtual laboratories: a systematic literature review of empirical research. Smart Learn. Environ. **10**, 23 (2023)
8. Leong, W.Y., Zhang, J.B.: AI on academic integrity and plagiarism detection. ASM Sci. J. **20**(1) (2025)
9. Leong, W.Y.: Enhancing practical skills training through virtual reality in TVET education. In: 2024 International Conference on TVET Excellence & Development (ICTeD), Malaysia, 16–17 Dec (2024)
10. Leong, W.Y.: Enhancing student engagement in virtual classrooms using gamification. In: 14th International Conference on Educational and Information Technology (ICEIT 2025) will take place from March 14–16, in Guangzhou, China (2025)
11. Leong, W.Y.: Designing for diversity: creating inclusive digital learning environments for global classrooms. Eng. Proc. **103**, 17 (2025). https://doi.org/10.3390/engproc2025103017
12. Leong, W.Y.: Artificial intelligence, automation, and technical and vocational education and training: transforming vocational training in digital era. Eng. Proc. **103**, 9 (2025). https://doi.org/10.3390/engproc2025103009

Content Concept for VR-Based Interactive Breakdance Experien Zone

Xi Ling[1,2] and Yan Huang[2](✉)

[1] Silpakorn University, Nakhon Pathom, Thailand
[2] East China Jiaotong University, Nanchang, Jiangxi, China
linluojun0238@sina.com

Abstract. Since breakdance was selected for the 2024 Olympics in Paris, France, Chinese colleges and universities have been offering breakdance courses. In this context, known for its convenience and live feel, the study of virtual technology in conjunction with breakdance classes is gaining popularity. Within the domain of breakdance instruction and competitions, especially for beginners and breakers, VR applications have gained traction. By recreating the historical backdrop of breakdance and immersing users in a virtual interactive environment, these applications allow for an exploration and learning of breakdance culture in a more engaging way, serving as a platform for cultural experience and learning. This paper proposes a content design concept for breakdance, structured around three key aspects: users' classifying, interactive storytelling, and virtual interaction. Implemented in the Interactive Chinese Breakdance ExperienZone, this approach aims to contribute to the revitalization of breakdance in China.

Keywords: Breakdance · Street dance · VR · Virtual Reality · Content concept · Experien zone

1 Introduction

In the process of rapid modernization and globalization, breakdance, as a powerful form of expressing individual and collective identity, has become a global cultural phenomenon sought after by the public for its dynamic dance style and rich cultural connotation [1]. In recent years, breakdance, as an important element of cultural soft power, has received more and more attention around the world. Breakdance became a competitive sport at the Olympic Games in Paris, France, in 2024 [2], and has become one of the popular sports events in China. Breakdance contributes greatly to a country's economic vitality and international image by attracting talents, businesses and investments in related fields such as entertainment, media and tourism. Breakdance courses offered by Chinese universities and street dance clubs have further promoted the popularity of breakdance [3], giving more people access to this vibrant art form.

Traditional breakdance instruction largely retains the master-apprentice model, relying on oral teaching. Due to the constraints of offline classrooms, students often struggle to fully grasp breakdance's cultural, historical, and competitive aspects [4]. Virtual

K. W. Lee and L. H. Wong (Eds.): ITEA 2025, CCIS 2643, pp. 233–241, 2026.
https://doi.org/10.1007/978-981-95-2011-4_22

Reality (VR) technology addresses these limitations by enabling immersive, interactive learning experiences in a flexible and accessible environment. Through VR, learners can engage with simulated real-world breakdance settings, receive personalized instruction, and interact with virtual instructors or peers [5].

This paper introduced a content design framework for a VR-based interactive breakdance experience zone, currently under development in China as an interdisciplinary collaboration between VR developers and breakdance researchers. The paper outlined the design strategy, including goals, target users, and interactive narratives for the proposed experience.In the subsequent sections, Sect. 2 examined the challenges of offline breakdance instruction and explored digital promotion strategies. Section 3 investigated VR's potential in preserving breakdance cultural heritage. Section 4 detailed the design and implementation of the interactive breakdance experience zone. Finally, Sect. 5 presented conclusions and future research directions.

2 Challenges Faced by Breakdance

2.1 Limitations of Geographic Location and Economic Conditions

Traditional breakdance instruction remains heavily concentrated in urban centers with developed dance infrastructures, creating significant accessibility challenges for those in suburban, rural, or remote areas. Geographic barriers force many enthusiasts to undertake costly travel to access quality training. Furthermore, the combined expenses of course fees, transportation, and accommodation disproportionately exclude lower-income participants, reinforcing socioeconomic disparities in breakdance participation.

2.2 Single Content and Form

Traditional breakdance classes tend to focus on technique training [6]. The judgement of learning outcomes is based on the results of the competition scene as one of the reference indicators for assessment. The consequence of this is that breakdance courses may be obsessed with the pursuit of technical improvement and neglect the cultivation of breakdance humanistic and historical knowledge. It is worth noting that the courses of breakdance humanistic and historical knowledge are often taught orally by teachers with PowerPoint explanations, which makes it difficult for students to obtain a more intuitive and vivid learning experience. This provides an opportunity for this study, and the VR interactive experience area can solve this problem.

2.3 Inconsistent Teaching Quality and Standardization

The quality and consistency of breakdance instruction can vary widely depending on the instructor's background, experience, and teaching methodology [7]. Unlike more formalized dance styles, breakdance lacks a unified curriculum and certification system [8], leading to inconsistencies in how techniques and styles are taught. This can result in learners receiving fragmented or incomplete training, which may hinder their progress and understanding [9]. Additionally, without standardized evaluation criteria, it is challenging to measure and compare the skills and achievements of breakdance practitioners.

2.4 Safety Concerns and Space Limitations

Practicing breakdance, particularly high-intensity moves like power moves and freezes, requires adequate space and safe environments to prevent injuries. Traditional venues may have limitations in terms of floor quality, space dimensions, and protective equipment, increasing the risk of accidents [10]. Additionally, finding suitable practice spaces that accommodate the physical demands of breakdance can be challenging, especially in densely populated urban areas where space is limited and costly.

The challenges outlined above highlight the pressing need for the development of an online interactive breakdance experience zone. Such a digital platform would democratize access to breakdance education and engagement, breaking down geographical and economic barriers. It would provide a safe, standardized learning environment that remains accessible regardless of the COVID-19 pandemic's restrictions. By leveraging VR technology, this experience zone could offer personalized instruction, real-time feedback, and immersive cultural experiences that traditional classes often cannot provide. It would also create a global community where breakdance enthusiasts can connect, share, and grow together, ensuring the art form's continued vitality and reach in an increasingly digital world.

3 Virtual Reality for Breakdance Cultural Heritage

Since the 1980s, VR technology has advanced significantly and is now widely used in cultural heritage preservation and promotion [11]. Its advantage lies in providing immersive experiences [12], enabling users to feel as if they are present at historical sites and thus enhancing their understanding and memory of cultural heritage.

3.1 Interactive Storytelling with VR

VR transforms users from passive observers to active participants through interactive storytelling. As users move and interact within virtual environments, they trigger plot developments. This immersive interaction not only boosts user engagement but also deepens their cognitive and emotional connection with cultural heritage.

3.2 Promoting Breakdance Culture with VR

VR technology shows great potential in promoting breakdance cultural heritage. It can create virtual breakdance scenarios, simulate historical backgrounds, and allow users to learn breakdance skills while experiencing its cultural essence. This offers new avenues for the preservation and development of breakdance culture.

4 Content Modeling for the Interactive Breakdance Experien Zone

While Virtual Reality (VR) technology is recognized as a tool that transcends space and time. The question of how to design breakdance content to enhance the desired performance and user-centered perspective remains a problem to be solved. A key question is whether content created in conjunction with cutting-edge technologies such as VR can motivate users to engage or keep them attached to the product. Although with the help of VR technology, users can experience breakdance at home without time and space constraints, it is of utmost importance that VR content should stimulate users' basic interest and motivation to participate in the breakdance experience through interesting scene settings, storylines, and technical content.

Based on the recognition of this issue, content design should be based on the perspective of collaboration between breakdance researchers and VR developers to enhance the understanding of breakdance and its expressive style. Therefore, in content development for Interactive Breakdance Experien Zone, we suggest designing content that promotes active user participation by setting target users and storytelling; a method that allows users to interact with breakdance in a virtual space.We designed the content framework for the VR-based Interactive Breakdance Experien Zone, as detailed in Table 1.

Table 1. Content framework for the VR-based interactive breakdance experien zone.

Content	Item	Detail
Users' classifying	***Enthusiast mode***	General enthusiasts who are interested in breakdance culture but lack understanding. By providing a fun and educational breakdance learning experience, we help them understand the cultural background, development history and styles of breakdance, and stimulate the interest of general enthusiasts to explore further
	Player Mode	Provide breakdancers with an immersive breakdance practice and creation environment, enabling them to interact with virtual dancers, learn new dance steps and showcase their breakdance skills
Interactive Storytelling	***Cultural narrative mode***	Create virtual scenes set in different cities with breakdance culture, such as Shanghai, New York, Los Angeles, Tokyo, Paris and other cities. Each scene has a unique architectural style, street vibe and cultural elements that make users feel like they are in a real breakdance hot city

(continued)

Table 1. (*continued*)

Content	Item	Detail
	Competition narrative mode	Designed with a rich storyline, the user plays the role of a breakdancer who is new to an unfamiliar city and gradually integrates into the breakdance circle by communicating, learning and cooperating with local dancers. With breakdance competitions as the main theme, users need to complete a series of tasks and challenges to improve their dancing skills and eventually win the competition
	Practice the narrative mode	It includes key scenarios such as breakdance studios, street-end improvisation venues, and underground breakdance arenas. In the breakdance studio, users can follow virtual instructors to learn basic moves and combinations, the street corner improvisation venue provides space for free play and interaction with other users or virtual dancers, and the underground breakdance competition arena is a stage for users to show themselves and challenge their limits
Virtual interaction	***Interactive learning***	Provide diversified interactive learning methods, such as one-on-one teaching by virtual instructors, attending virtual breakdance classes, and practicing movement imitation with virtual dancers. The virtual tutor will give real-time feedback and guidance according to the user's movement performance to help users correct wrong movements and improve their dance level. At the same time, multiple users are online at the same time, and users form study groups to make progress together
	Simulation mechanisms	Design a real breakdance movement simulation mechanism. Through motion capture technology, the user's body movements are transformed into the virtual character's dance movements in real time, and the corresponding visual and tactile feedback is provided. For example, when the user completes a difficult movement, the virtual character will react accordingly

(*continued*)

Table 1. (*continued*)

Content	Item	Detail
	Competition and feedback	Set up virtual breakdance competitions and challenges that users can sign up for to compete with virtual dancers from all over the world. During the competition, virtual judges will score users based on their dance skills, creativity, sense of rhythm, etc. and provide detailed evaluations and suggestions. In addition, users can also view their ranking at the end of the competition and receive appropriate rewards and honors to motivate them to keep challenging themselves
User Feedback	***User Satisfaction Survey***	At the end of each experience, a concise questionnaire pops up to allow users to quickly rate their preference for different breakdance styles, and a text input box is set up to collect user suggestions for new dance steps. The questionnaire also included satisfaction ratings for each functional module in the experience area (e.g. history review, challenge mode, etc.), as well as feedback options for the design of the virtual environment (e.g. scene styles, special effects, etc.), in order to gain a comprehensive understanding of users' needs, and to provide a basis for subsequent optimisation

4.1 Target User

The Breakdance Interactive Experience Zone is designed to offer a range of breakdance experiences targeting the widest range of potential breakdance users and enthusiasts. Hip-hop culture and breakdance combined with advanced virtual technology is the latest trend that can appeal to many people who are reluctant to experience breakdance due to fragmented work or study schedules, lack of transportation to their residences, and financial constraints. By developing virtual breakdance experiences, it is also expected to breathe new life into the systematization of breakdance courses in colleges and universities and the commercialization of breakdance. In fact, as breakdance has gained popularity in Chinese sports competitions, the breakdance audience has increased dramatically, and their interest in and demand for breakdance culture has grown, much like hip-hop and street dance. Breakdance and hip-hop culture were emphasized as key programs to attract new consumers. In addition, breakdance target users are not limited to adolescents and adults, but can also be extended to the older population.

In addition, in the field of education, virtual reality becomes a platform to enhance the learning process and stimulate students' interest in hip-hop culture and breakdance styles. The interactive breakdance experience zone can be used in conjunction with breakdance programs in colleges and breakdance clubs as an effective teaching tool. By learning breakdance in the Breakdance Interactive Experience Zone, students can interactively experience breakdance in a virtual immersive environment to understand the positive mindset and positive energy content embedded in breakdance.

4.2 Storytelling Based on Breakdance

The Interactive Storytelling of the VR-based Interactive Breakdance Experien Zone consists of three interconnected modes that together create a comprehensive narrative experience for users. These modes are carefully designed to guide users through different aspects of breakdance culture, from understanding its historical and cultural context to actively participating in its practice and competition.

1) Cultural narrative mode serves as the foundational element, immersing users in virtual scenes that represent iconic cities known for their breakdance culture. This mode provides users with a rich cultural and historical context, allowing them to appreciate the diversity and roots of breakdance. It acts as the starting point from which users can develop a deeper interest and understanding of the art form.
2) Building upon this cultural foundation, Competition narrative mode introduces users to the dynamic and competitive side of breakdance. By engaging users in a storyline where they gradually integrate into the breakdance community through interaction and learning, this mode motivates users to enhance their skills and knowledge. It simulates the real-world experience of entering a new environment, making friends, learning from others, and ultimately proving oneself through competition.
3) Practice narrative mode then offers users a practical space to apply and refine the skills and knowledge gained from the first two modes. It provides a variety of virtual settings where users can practice, improvise, and showcase their talents. This mode is crucial for skill development and allows users to express their creativity and personal style within the breakdance culture.

In summary, the three modes of Interactive Storytelling work in harmony to offer users a rich and multi-dimensional experience of breakdance. Cultural narrative mode lays the groundwork by providing cultural context, Competition narrative mode drives user engagement and skill development through an engaging storyline, and Practice narrative mode enables users to apply their learning and express themselves creatively. Together, they form a cohesive narrative journey that mirrors the real-world experience of immersing oneself in breakdance culture.

4.3 Creation of Content for Experiencing Breakdance

The VR-based Interactive Breakdance Experien Zone integrated three key components of virtual interaction to create an immersive and engaging experience.

1) Interactive learning forms the foundation of the Breakdance Experien Zone by offering various methods to enhance users' dance skills through virtual instructor tutorials and group learning sessions, fostering skill development and community building
2) The Simulation mechanisms immerse users by converting their physical movements into real-time virtual dance actions via motion capture technology. This creates a seamless connection between real and virtual dance practice, enhancing the authenticity of the experience.
3) Competition and feedback serve as motivational tools by allowing users to engage in virtual breakdance battles and receive evaluations. This encourages continuous improvement and persistence in skill development. Together, these three components create a comprehensive and engaging virtual breakdance experience.

These three components provided a holistic virtual breakdance experience. Interactive learning builds foundational skills, simulation mechanisms create immersion, and competition and feedback drive motivation and improvement. Together, they mirror the real-world breakdance learning and competition experience.

5 Conclusion

Since breakdance entered China in 1984, breakdance has been an important part of street dance because it represents hip-hop and pop culture. However, with the impact of the global epidemic and the development of network technology, offline breakdance teaching and activities have maintained a certain amount of crowd share, but have been in a form that is in urgent need of updating and upgrading. In the field of breakdance, advanced technologies such as virtual reality technology not only promote the interactive experience of the audience in learning and entertainment, but also expand the number of users. In order to enable users to better experience breakdance using VR, we proposed a strategy to design content through users' classifying, interactive storytelling, and virtual interaction. In the Interactive Breakdance Experience Zone development project, which aims to popularize breakdance, we set breakdance enthusiast and breakdancer as the target users to help them understand hip-hop culture while experiencing breakdance. Interacting with the users through the virtual scene, the users are involved in the narrative.

In the future, in addition to refining user needs, breakdance genres can be expanded to other street dance categories, and different styles can be specifically evaluated, with a refined evaluation plan that is conducive to enhancing the user experience.

Acknowledgment. This work was supported by the Jiangxi Provincial Education Science "Fourteenth Five-Year Plan" Project, Project Approval No.: 2021–065.

References

1. Sotiriadou, P., Thrush, A., Hill, B.: The attraction, retention, and transition of elite sport development pathways in surfing in Australia. Managing sport and leisure, 1–18 (2023)
2. Yang, Z, Bai, Y, Wei, M.T.: The Importance of Creativity in the Sportification of Breakdance. Frontiers in Education. Frontiers **112** (2022)

3. Zhi Li, R., Vexler, Y.A.: Breaking for gold: another crossroads in the divergent history of this dance. Int. J. History Sport **36**(4–5) (2019)
4. Ling, X., et al.: Develop a formative assessment protocol to examine the practice of Pop** dance in students online learning. In Frontiers in Education, vol. 8, p. 1207086. Frontiers Media SA, July 2023
5. Lin, X.P., Li, B.B., Yao, Z.N., Yang, Z., Zhang, M.: The impact of virtual reality on student engagement in the classroom–a critical review of the literature. Front. Psychol. **15**, 1360574 (2024)
6. Shimizu, D., Okada, T.: How do creative experts practice new skills? Exploratory practice in breakdancers. Cognitive science **42**(7), 2364–2396 (2018)
7. Ling, X., Chen, Y., Zhao, S., Zheng, D.: What do we know: positive impact of hip-hop pedagogy on student's learning effects. Front. Sports Active Living **6**, 1490432 (2025)
8. Yang, Z., Whatman, S.: Development and validation of standards for evaluating the quality of qualitative research on Olympics breakdance. Humanit. Soc. Sci. Commun. **12**, 471 (2025)
9. Ling, X., Zhang, S.R., Zhu, X.M., Zhao, L.H., Zeng, Z.M.: Scoring criteria of breakdance education according to trivium value system. Open J. Soc. Sci. **12**, 284–294 (2024)
10. Tsiouti, N., Wyon, M.: Injury occurrence in break dance: an online cross-sectional cohort study of breakers. J. Dance Med. Sci. **25**(1), 2–8 (2021)
11. Zhu, X.: Research on the application of establishing VR technology in dance communication. In: 2021 2nd International Conference on Information Science and Education (ICISE-IE), pp. 1463–1466. IEEE, November 2021
12. Claudio, P., Maddalena, P.: Overview: virtual reality in medicine. J. Virtual Worlds Res. **7**(1) (2014)

Development of Augmented Reality Based E-module on Electromagnetic Induction Material to Improve Students' Critical Thinking Skills

Nurul Husna(✉), Sahyar, and Yuni Warty

State University of Medan, Medan, Indonesia
nurulhusna.8236175004@mhs.unimed.ac.id

Abstract. This study aims to develop an Augmented Reality (AR)-based e-module on electromagnetic induction material and examine its validity, practicality, and effectiveness in improving students' critical thinking skills. The research employed the ADDIE development model, consisting of five stages: Analysis, Design, Development, Implementation, and Evaluation. The product was validated by experts in material, instructional design, and media. Practicality was assessed through small- and large-scale trials involving teachers and students, while effectiveness was measured using pretest and posttest data analyzed through normalized gain (N-Gain) and One Sample t-Test.The results showed that the developed e-module is highly valid, with an average expert validation score of 4.57 for content, accuracy, language, presentation, and support for critical thinking. The practicality aspect also received high ratings, with an average score of 4.60 from physics teachers and 85.3% from students, indicating that the e-module is user-friendly, useful, and easy to integrate into classroom learning. In terms of effectiveness, the N-Gain scores across three learning sessions ranged from 0.64 to 0.68 (medium category), and the t-test results confirmed a significant increase in posttest scores compared to the minimum mastery criteria (KKM).

These findings indicate that the AR-based e-module is not only valid and practical but also effective in fostering students' critical thinking. The integration of AR technology enhances visualization and interactivity, making it a valuable tool for 21st-century science education.

Keywords: e-module · augmented reality · electromagnetic induction · critical thinking · ADDIE model

1 Introduction

21st century education demands mastery of critical thinking, collaboration, communication and creativity skills. To fulfill these demands, the integration of technology in learning is crucial. One effective innovation is the use of digital learning media, such as e-modules, which can improve the quality and effectiveness of the teaching-learning process (Redhana, 2024). According to (Kemendikbud, 2017), e-modules are teaching

K. W. Lee and L. H. Wong (Eds.): ITEA 2025, CCIS 2643, pp. 242–251, 2026.
https://doi.org/10.1007/978-981-95-2011-4_23

materials that are systematically organized and presented in electronic format that can be accessed independently by students through links. In addition, with the ability to insert various multimedia elements, e-modules can be more interesting and can improvestudent understanding (Prihastuti & Sukaesih, 2024).

Empirical data based on needs analysis observations at SMAS Darul Ilmi Murni can be concluded that students have a high awareness of the importance of learning physics, especially electromagnetic induction material. However, students' level of understanding of physics material is still low, as seen from the difficulty in remembering the material, working on problems, and achieving the expected average score and still limited time in learning. Although the learning experience has involved digital media, the methods used still need to be more interactive and relevant to motivate students. Most students showed a clear need for teaching materials in the form of interactive modules with attractive displays that can encourage independent learning and critical thinking skills.

AR technology not only facilitates better understanding, but also enables more contextualized and authentic learning. In a study by (Mulyadi & Putra, 2023), the application of AR in physics learning was shown to help students relate abstract concepts to real-world phenomena, thus improving their critical thinking skills. AR also provides a more in-depth learning experience through interactive simulations that support experiment-based learning.

Research from (Zakaria, Wahyuni, Satriawan, Saputra, & Habibbulloh, 2023) on Augmented Reality Digital Book learning media that describes electromagnetic induction physics is feasible to use as new media, the shortcomings of ARDi media have not presented gamification and virtual laboratories that require additional presentation of physics concepts. Although several studies have developed AR-based media for physics materials, including electromagnetic induction, their implementation still has limitations. For example, there is no in-depth virtual laboratory feature and a lack of gamification to increase student engagement.

In addition, previous studies have not systematically explored the development of AR-based e-modules, especially for electromagnetic induction material. Thus, there is a significant research gap related to the development of AR-based physics e-modules integrated with virtual laboratories. Therefore, this research focuses on "Development of Augmented Reality-Based E-Modules on Electromagnetic Induction Material to Improve Students' Critical Thinking Skills" to answer modern learning needs and overcome challenges in understanding complex physics material.

Based on the background that has been described, the problem formulation of this research is obtained, namely:

How is the level of feasibility, practicality, effectiveness of AR-based e-modules on electromagnetic induction material to improve students' critical thinking skills developed. Based on the formulation of the existing problems, the objectives of this study are:To analyze the level of feasibility, practicality, and effectiveness of AR-based e-modules on electromagnetic induction material to improve students' critical thinking skills.

2 Method

2.1 Type of Research

This research is a development research commonly called Research and Development (R&D). The development research conducted aims to produce products in the form of physics teaching materials in the form of AR-based e-modules on Electromagnetic Induction material to improve students' critical thinking skills.

2.2 Research Subject and Variable

The subjects of this study consisted of class XII students who studied Electromagnetic Induction, teachers who implemented the e-module, and the content developed in the e-module. The variable in this study is to ensure that the developed AR e-modules meet the criteria of feasibility, practicality, and effectiveness in the learning context to improve students' critical thinking skills.

2.3 Research Type

1. Analysis involved identifying students' and teachers' needs through questionnaires and interviews, and analyzing the curriculum to ensure alignment with core competencies and learning objectives.
2. Design consisted of structuring the e-module into three learning sessions, integrating AR visualizations, and developing instruments for assessing critical thinking skills.
3. Development included the creation of the e-module and AR content, followed by expert validation by media, material, and instructional design experts. The product was revised based on feedback and tested through a small-scale trial with 9 students.
4. Implementation was carried out through a large-scale trial involving 27 students across three learning sessions. Practicality was measured through user responses from both students and physics teachers, while effectiveness was analyzed through pretest and posttest scores using normalized gain (N-Gain) and One Sample t-Test.
5. Evaluation included formative evaluation during each phase and summative evaluation after the full implementation to determine the overall validity, practicality, and effectiveness of the developed product.

3 Results

The development model used in this research is the ADDIE development model. The process of implementing product development in the form of E-modules goes through several stages starting from analysis, design, development, implementation, and evaluation. The results of all stages of the ADDIE development model are presented in the following description.

3.1 Analyze

The initial phase of this research involved curriculum and student needs analysis. Based on the revised 2013 curriculum, the selected content was Basic Competency 3.11 and 4.11 on Electromagnetic Induction—considered abstract and difficult to understand without visual or interactive media. The results guided the formulation of achievement indicators tailored to the students' learning characteristics.

The student needs analysis revealed that 87.5% required interactive, engaging, and easy-to-understand learning materials. Student interest in learning was categorized as moderate (57.5%), while conceptual understanding was low (37.5%), and teaching methods were predominantly conventional (85%). These findings underscored the urgency for a more contextual, technology-enhanced learning medium.

3.2 Design

At this stage, a prototype of the AR-based e-module was designed systematically, incorporating appropriate media selection, content mapping aligned with the curriculum, communicative language based on BSNP and PUEBI standards, and a visual storyboard. The module was created using Canva and Heyzine Flip Book, while AR features were built using Blender and Unity, integrated into AssemblerEdu. Key components include a cover, usage guide, learning objectives, concept maps, structured content, AR simulations, reflection activities, and HOTS-based assessments.

3.3 Development

The development process involved producing a functional AR-based e-module accessible on Android devices. It combined textual content, learning videos, examples, exercises, and marker-triggered AR simulations to enhance conceptual understanding and critical thinking.

1. Expert Validation

The product was validated by six experts—two in content, two in instructional design, and two in media (Tables 1, 2, 3, 4, 5, 6 and 7).

Table 1. Result of Expert Material Validation

No.	Assesment Aspect	Score		Average	Category
		V1	**V2**		
1.	Content feasibility	4,57	4,71	4,64	Very valid
2.	Material accuracy	4,50	4,33	4,42	Very valid
3.	Language quality	4,40	4,40	4,40	Very valid
4.	Presentation	4,67	4,67	4,67	Very valid
5.	Critical thinking skill support	4,80	4,60	4,70	Very valid
Overall average				**4,57**	Very valid

- **Content Experts** emphasized aligning objectives with critical thinking skills, contextualizing formulas, using implicit problem-solving questions, and providing image explanations. Improvements were made accordingly.

  The overall average score was 4.57, categorized as "very valid".

- **Design Experts** recommended improvements in grammar, visual layout, readability, and consistency.

  The final average score was 4.35, also rated "very valid".

- **Media Experts** highlighted issues with simulation responsiveness and visual overlay placement. These were optimized for smoother access.

  Their assessment resulted in an average score of 4.52, categorized as "very valid".

2. Small-Scale Trial

Table 3. Result of Expert Media Validation

No.	Assesment Aspect	Score		Average Score	Category
		V1	**V2**		
1.	Progamming	4,00	4,00	4,00	Very valid
2.	AR Visual design	4,63	4,88	4,76	Very valid
3.	Software engineering	4,50	4,50	4,50	Very valid
4.	Text	5,00	5,00	5,00	Very valid
5.	Navigation	4,50	4,50	4,50	Very valid
6.	VLab Visuals	4,25	4,75	4,50	Very valid
7.	Animation	4,33	4,33	4,33	Very valid
Overall average				**4,52**	**Very valid**

Table 2. Result of Expert Design Validation

No.	Assesment Aspect	Score		Average Score	Category
		V1	**V2**		
1.	Layout design appearance	4,00	4,50	4,25	Very valid
2.	Ease of use	4,75	4,75	4,75	Very valid
3.	Consistency	4,00	4,33	4,17	Valid
4.	Graphic quality	4,33	4,50	4,42	Very valid
5.	Usefulness	4,00	4,25	4,13	Valid
Overall average				**4,35**	Very valid

A limited trial involving nine students revealed an average rating of 70.7% (good category). While the content was well-received, technical access issues to the virtual lab were initially encountered. A revised access method using a Google Drive download link resolved the problem.

Table 4. Result of Small – Scall Trial

No.	Assesment Aspect	Average	Percentation(%)	Category
1.	Material	3,71	74,2	Good
2.	Language quality	3,63	68,0	Good
3.	Presentation	3,50	70,0	Good
Overall average		**3,61**	**70,7**	**Good**

3.4 Implementation

1. Large-Scale Trial

A large-scale trial was conducted with 27 students over three sessions focusing on different aspects of electromagnetic induction. Using Facione's critical thinking indicators—interpretation, analysis, inference, and evaluation—students engaged with simulations, questions, and reflective tasks. The practicality score from students reached an average of 85.3%, indicating that the e-module was "highly practical" in terms of content clarity, language, and presentation.

Table 5. Result of Large – Scall Trial

No.	Assesment Aspect	Average	Percentation(%)	Category
1.	Material	4,39	79,8	Highly practical
2.	Language quality	4,40	87,9	Highly practical
3.	Presentation	4,42	88,3	Highly practical
Overall average		**4,40**	**85,3**	Highly practical

2. Teacher Practicality Assessment

Two physics teachers rated the product with an average score of 4.60 ("highly practical"), confirming its effectiveness and ease of use in classroom instruction.

3. Effectiveness Testing

Table 6. Practicality Results by Physics Teachers

No.	Assesment Aspect	Score		Average Score	Category
		P1	**P2**		
1.	Learning implementation	4,80	4,80	4,80	Highly practical
2.	Quality	4,40	4,60	4,50	Highly practical
3.	Visual appearance	4,67	4,50	4,59	Highly practical
4.	Usefulness	4,40	4,60	4,50	Highly practical
Overall average				**4,60**	Highly practical

N-Gain Test results showed moderate improvement in critical thinking across three sessions, with the highest gain in the third meeting focused on real-world applications. One Sample t-Test confirmed that student posttest scores significantly exceeded the minimum mastery criteria (KKM = 80), with p-values <0.05 across all sessions.

Table 7. Measurement Results of Students' Critical Thinking Skills Using N-Gain Test

Session	Average		N-Gain Score	Category
	Pretest	*Posttest*		
1.	65	87	0,64	Medium
2.	66	87	0,64	Medium
3.	68	89	0,68	Medium

Facione's five indicators were measured across sessions. "Interpretation" consistently achieved a high category (N-Gain = 0.80), while others like "analysis" and "inference" showed moderate but improving scores, especially in the third session, indicating enhanced conceptual and analytical abilities through visual simulation and reflection activities.

3.5 Evaluation

The final evaluation concluded that the AR-based e-module meets validity (content, design, and media), practicality (from students and teachers), and effectiveness criteria. It significantly enhances students' critical thinking and is well-suited for implementation as an innovative learning medium in physics education.

4 Discussion

4.1 Validity of the E-Module

The developed AR-based e-module was classified as "highly valid" according to evaluations by subject matter experts, instructional design experts, and media experts. Subject matter experts assigned an average score of 4.57 out of 5. Content feasibility scored 4.64, content accuracy 4.42, language clarity 4.40, presentation 4.67, and support for critical thinking skills 4.70. Revisions were made based on expert input, including clarification of learning objectives, insertion of introductory explanations before formulas, refinement of analytical questions, and clearer image captions.

Instructional design experts gave an average score of 4.35. Layout design scored 4.25, ease of use 4.75, consistency 4.17, graphics 4.42, and usefulness 4.13. Suggestions included simplifying sentence structure, enhancing grammar, optimizing image layout, and improving color harmony.

Media experts awarded an average score of 4.52. Programming scored 4.00, AR visual design 4.76, software engineering 4.50, text 5.00, navigation 4.50, VLab visuals 4.50, and animation 4.33. Recommended improvements included optimizing AR simulation loading speed, adjusting content placement, and expanding theoretical depth.

Overall, the high average scores confirmed that the AR-based e-module met strong validity criteria in content, design, and media. These findings support previous studies indicating the positive impact of AR on student engagement and understanding.

4.2 Practicality of the E-Module

The e-module demonstrated a high level of practicality based on evaluations from both students and physics teachers. In a large-scale trial involving 27 students across three independent learning sessions, the average practicality score was 4.40 (85.3%), categorized as very practical. Specifically, content scored 4.39 (79.8%), language 4.40 (87.9%), and presentation 4.42 (88.3%). Students successfully engaged with interactive features such as AR simulations and reflective activities. Initial technical issues were resolved by switching access to Google Drive links, enhancing ease of use.

Teacher evaluations from two physics instructors yielded an average score of 4.60, with instructional value at 4.80, content quality 4.50, visual appeal 4.59, and usefulness 4.50. This affirmed the e-module's relevance, user-friendliness, and contribution to classroom learning. These findings are consistent with prior studies that reported similarly high practicality ratings for AR-based and digital modules.

The effectiveness of the AR-based e-module was assessed through improvements in students' critical thinking skills, measured via One-Sample t-Test and N-Gain analysis based on Facione's critical thinking indicators. In all three sessions, post-test scores significantly exceeded the minimum mastery criteria (80), with p-values <0.05. This confirmed the module's significant effect on student achievement.

N-Gain analysis showed consistent progress in critical thinking indicators. Interpretation showed the highest gains (0.80; high category), with other indicators such as analysis and inference ranging from 0.65 to 0.72 (medium to high). The third session yielded the most optimal results, with multiple indicators approaching or achieving high-level gains. These results align with previous research supporting the effectiveness of AR in improving cognitive engagement and learning outcomes.

5 Conclusion

This study concludes that the AR-based e-module on Electromagnetic Induction is highly valid, practical, and effective in enhancing students' critical thinking skills. The module achieved high validation scores from content experts (4.57), design experts (4.35), and media experts (4.52), indicating strong alignment with instructional and technological standards. Practicality assessments from 27 students (85.3%) and two physics teachers (4.60/5) confirmed the module's ease of use, engaging presentation, and relevance to classroom needs. Effectiveness was demonstrated through consistent improvements in students' critical thinking across three sessions, with the highest N-Gain score reaching 0.67 and posttest scores exceeding the minimum mastery threshold. Overall, the AR-based e-module is a promising instructional tool for 21st-century science education.

6 Recommendations

To further enhance the effectiveness and reach of the AR-based e-module, it is recommended to increase interactivity by incorporating quizzes, gamification, and adaptive learning pathways to improve engagement. Regular updates should be carried out to refine the module based on user feedback and technological advancements. Expanding its implementation to different schools and physics topics will help assess its broader effectiveness. Additionally, providing educators with training on integrating AR-based e-modules into their teaching methods will ensure optimal utilization. Lastly, further research should be conducted to investigate long-term knowledge retention and cognitive impacts, optimizing the module's educational value.

Acknowledgements or Notes. The author would like to express his sincere thanks to BPI (Indonesian Education Scholarship, PPAPT (*Center for Higher Education Funding and Assessment*) and LPDP (*Indonesian Endowment Fund for Education*), Ministry of Higher Education, Science, and Technology of Republic Indonesia for financial support for the publication of this article.

References

Aliyah, S.: Entrepreneurship-based biotechnology E-module development to improve critical and creative thinking skills. Biosaintifika **14**(1), 45–57 (2022)

Amalia, N., Ksani, I., Suprapto, N.: Development of learning media based augmented reality electromagnetic induction subject matter. Stud. Philos. Sci. Educ. **3**(2), 82–92 (2022). https://doi.org/10.46627/sipose.v3i2.312

Handayani, D.: Development of guided discovery based electronic module for chemical lessons in redox reaction materials. Int. J. Interact. Mob. Technol. **15**(3), 45–56 (2021)

Kebudayaan, D.P.: Panduan pengembangan modul pembelajaran. Jakarta: Kementerian Pendidikan dan Kebudayaan.(2017)

Mulyadi, A., Putra, Y.A.: Utilization of augmented reality in education: a study on learning outcomes in physics. J. Pendidikan Fisika **8**(2), 120–130 (2023)

Rahman, I., Setiawan, J., Rina, S.: Pengembangan E-modul berbasis augmented reality (AR) pada Sistem Kearsipan di kelas X SMK Negeri 1 Penukal. J. Pendidikan dan Teknologi **15**(2), 100–110 (2024)

Rahmawati, Y., Kusuma, H.S.: Efektifitas penggunaan E-Modul berbasis augmented reality dalam pembelajaran sains untuk meningkatkan pemahaman konsep dan keterlibatan Siswa. EDUKASIA J. Pendidikan dan Pembelajaran **4**(1), 1–12 (2023)

Rahmayani, F., Kuswanto, H., Rahmat, A.D.: Development of E-book integrated augmented reality based on STEM approaches to improve critical thinking and multiple representation skills in learning physics. Int. J. Inf. Educ. Technol. **14**(1), 80–90 (2024)

Zakaria, A., Wahyuni, I.S., Satriawan, M., Saputra, O., Habibbulloh, M.: Development of ARDI learning media (AR-Digital Book) based on augmented reality 3D animated on electromagnetic induction material. IPF Inovasi Pendidikan Fisika **12**(2), 54–64 (2023)

Factors Shaping Instructors' Augmented Reality Adoption: An Extended UTAUT2 Using a Mixed-Method Approach

Baraa Albishri[1,2](✉) and Karen L. Blackmore[1]

[1] School of Information and Physical Sciences, University of Newcastle, Newcastle, Australia
Baraa.Albishri@uon.edu.au

[2] College of Computing and Information Technology at Khulais, University of Jeddah, Jeddah, Saudi Arabia

Abstract. Higher education institutions are exploring Augmented Reality (AR) for its potential to enhance teaching and learning, yet instructor adoption remains limited. This study investigates the factors influencing higher education instructors' behavioural intention to use AR, employing a sequential explanatory mixed-methods approach. An extended Unified Theory of Acceptance and Use of Technology 2 (UTAUT2) model, incorporating Content Quality (CQ) and Resistance to Change (RC), was tested quantitatively using survey data from 436 instructors globally (analysed via PLS-SEM). Findings revealed Performance Expectancy (PE), Effort Expectancy (EE), Social Influence (SI), CQ, and Hedonic Motivation (HM) significantly predicted instructors' intention. Facilitating Conditions (FC) and RC indirectly influenced intention by impacting perceptions of performance and effort expectancy. Age moderated the relationship between FC and intention. Subsequent qualitative two focus groups corroborated AR's perceived benefits (aligning with quantitative predictors) but highlighted critical barriers, primarily insufficient institutional support, lack of training, and resistance, providing context for FC's and RC's indirect roles. The study concludes that while perceived value drives instructors' initial intentions, overcoming practical barriers through robust institutional support and training is crucial for successful AR integration in higher education.

Keywords: Augmented Reality · Higher Education · UTAUT2 · Academics

1 Introduction

Higher education institutions are increasingly investing in innovative technologies to meet the growing demands for enhanced student learning and the development of workplace-relevant skills. Augmented Reality (AR), with its capacity to create immersive and hands-on learning experiences by overlaying digital assets onto the real world, is recognised as a potentially powerful educational tool [1]. The limitations of traditional classroom methods, particularly highlighted during the COVID-19 pandemic, have further accelerated interest in technologies like AR, with many institutions now investing

K. W. Lee and L. H. Wong (Eds.): ITEA 2025, CCIS 2643, pp. 252–271, 2026.
https://doi.org/10.1007/978-981-95-2011-4_24

in it for laboratory and practical training purposes [2]. While research on the educational benefits of AR continues to emerge, particularly in higher education, understanding user perceptions (specifically those of university instructors) is crucial to support widespread adoption and achieve desired learning outcomes [3]. This paper, therefore, focuses on investigating university instructors' attitudes toward integrating AR into their teaching practices.

AR is widely recognised for its potential to revolutionise education. Scholars suggest that AR can significantly improve students' learning experiences and academic achievements by providing authentic, experiential learning opportunities [4]. This potential aligns well with the goals of higher education, where instructors are tasked with equipping students with career-relevant knowledge and skills. AR bridges the gap between theoretical concepts and practical application by overlaying digital information onto real-world settings, facilitating interaction and immersion, creating dynamic and adaptive teaching spaces [5]. This allows educators to teach authentic industry skills without the constraints of limited access to specialised tools or environments. Furthermore, AR's immersive features support the development of essential 21st-century skills, such as problem-solving and digital literacy, which are highly valued in today's workforce [6].

Despite these advantages, AR adoption in higher education remains limited compared to more established educational technologies [7]. This gap may be attributed to factors such as instructors' awareness of AR's capabilities [8], the level of institutional support provided [9], and perceptions of its ease of use and effectiveness in diverse teaching contexts [10]. While some research exists on educators' attitudes toward AR, often indicating generally positive perceptions, there is a gap in research that comprehensively explores the specific factors influencing acceptance among higher education instructors. Previous research, often employing models like the Technology Acceptance Model (TAM) and the Unified Theory of Acceptance and Use of Technology (UTAUT), identified factors like "perceived ease of use", "perceived usefulness", and "resistance to change" [3]. Despite student-centred AR studies, instructor perspectives, especially post-COVID-19, remain underexplored. This study addresses this gap by applying and extending the extended Unified Theory of Acceptance and Use of Technology 2 (UTAUT2) to specifically investigate the factors influencing university instructors' intention to use AR.

This study adopts a sequential explanatory mixed-methods design to:

1. Identify the key factors, within the extended UTAUT2 framework, that influence higher education instructors' behavioural intention to use AR as a teaching tool.
2. Identify and analyse the moderating effects of gender, age, educational technologies experience (ETE), and awareness on the relationships between Performance Expectancy, Effort Expectancy, and Facilitating Condition constructs and instructors' intention to use AR in teaching. This will reveal how these individual differences influence the previously established relationships.
3. Gain deeper, qualitative insights into instructors' perceptions, experiences, and concerns related to AR adoption, providing a nuanced understanding that complements the quantitative data. This qualitative phase, using focus groups, will explore why

certain factors are influential, uncover unforeseen challenges, and generate practical recommendations for promoting AR adoption in higher education.

2 Literature Review

2.1 Introduction to Augmented Reality in Education

AR has emerged as a transformative educational tool, enhancing learning experiences across education levels. By combining digital content with physical spaces, AR aims to increase student engagement and comprehension [11]. Studies show positive impacts in language learning [12], multimedia design [13], physics visualisation [14], and medical training [15]. The COVID-19 pandemic highlighted AR's utility in remote learning [16].

AR supports students with learning and intellectual disabilities [17] and facilitates understanding of complex STEM concepts through simulations [18]. In construction education, it aids practical skill development. AR promotes ubiquitous learning and interactive engagement [19], and studies emphasise positive achievement and attitude in science courses in distance education [4]. However, some studies highlighted AR adoption challenges, including technical limitations, cost, and the need for instructor training [20].

While the empirical evidence highlights AR's potential benefits and ongoing implementation challenges, understanding why and how educators adopt (or resist) this technology requires a robust theoretical lens to examine the underlying factors influencing their decisions.

2.2 Theoretical Framework for AR Adoption in Education

Understanding the adoption of new technologies like AR within educational settings is crucial for successful integration. Various theoretical models have been developed and applied to explain user acceptance, evolving over time to capture more nuanced factors.

The TAM proposes that technology adoption intention is determined by perceived usefulness (belief that technology enhances job performance) and perceived ease of use (belief that technology requires minimal effort) [21]. Studies applying TAM to AR in education confirm these factors' importance [22]. Research shows positive relationships between PU, PEoU, and AR adoption intention among instructors [23] and students [16]. Researchers extended TAM by adding variables like perceived enjoyment and behavioural control [24]. While valuable, TAM's focus on usefulness and ease of use may not fully capture adoption complexity, especially in voluntary contexts.

Venkatesh et al. [25] developed the UTAUT, integrating constructs from TAM and other models. UTAUT proposes four key determinants: Performance Expectancy (PE), Effort Expectancy (EE), Social Influence (SI), and Facilitating Conditions (FC). The model includes moderators like age, gender, experience, and voluntariness. Studies applying UTAUT to AR in education found that PE, EE, FC, and SI influenced adoption intentions among nursing students [26] and teachers [27]. Alvi [28] found PE, EE, and SI influenced college students' reception of social networking tools for learning.

Venkatesh et al. [29] extended UTAUT to UTAUT2 to better predict technology acceptance in consumer settings. UTAUT2 adds three determinants to UTAUT's core constructs: Hedonic Motivation (HM), Price Value (PV), and Habit (H). This model helps understand instructors' voluntary decisions to integrate AR in teaching. Studies using UTAUT2 have validated its relevance in AR contexts. Faqih and Jaradat [30] found Task-Technology Fit (TTF), PE, EE, SI, FC, and HM influenced students' AR adoption during the pandemic. Sunardi et al. [31] showed PE, HM, and H impacted AR acceptance in video conferencing, while Ameri et al. [32] confirmed PE, H, and SI's roles in mobile-based educational application.

However, a critical analysis of this literature reveals several gaps. Firstly, much of the existing UTAUT2 research in AR focuses predominantly on student populations [30, 32] or primary teachers [27]. While studies involving instructors or academic staff exist [23], they often rely on earlier models like TAM, potentially overlooking factors like hedonic motivation or habit captured by UTAUT2. While Alahmari [23] confirm PU's importance among instructors using TAM, Ibrahim and Abdullah [33] explicitly identifies resource constraints as a barrier, suggesting context specific moderating effects of institutional support that UTAUT/UTAUT2 constructs like FC might capture more directly.

Secondly, few studies apply the comprehensive UTAUT2 framework specifically to higher education instructors, particularly examining their perspectives in the post-COVID educational landscape. Methodologically, many studies rely solely on quantitative surveys [30], limiting the depth of understanding regarding instructors' experiences and the context-specific reasons behind their acceptance or resistance. Furthermore, the prevalent use of cross-sectional designs restricts the ability to infer causality regarding AR adoption drivers.

Thirdly, existing models may not fully capture all relevant factors influencing instructor adoption. This study proposes extending UTAUT2 by incorporating two additional constructs deemed particularly relevant for instructors evaluating AR:

- Content Quality (CQ): Refers to the perceived accuracy, relevance, appropriateness, and comprehensiveness of the educational content delivered via the AR system [34]. For instructors, the pedagogical accuracy and relevance of the content itself are paramount.
- Resistance to Change (RC): Represents an instructor's tendency to oppose or avoid adopting AR due to factors like adherence to existing routines, perceived threats to autonomy, or discomfort with new technological demands, distinct from simple effort expectancy [3].

This study aims to address these gaps by applying an extended UTAUT2 model to understand AR adoption among higher education instructors using a sequential explanatory mixed-methods design.

2.3 Proposed Research Model and Hypotheses

Building upon the UTAUT2 framework and addressing the identified gaps, this study proposes an extended model to investigate the factors influencing AR adoption intention among higher education instructors. UTAUT2 has been widely adopted in technology acceptance research, offering a robust foundation [29]. While UTAUT2 provides a strong base, adding contextually relevant elements like CQ and RC aims to enhance its explanatory power for this specific population and technology (Fig. 1).

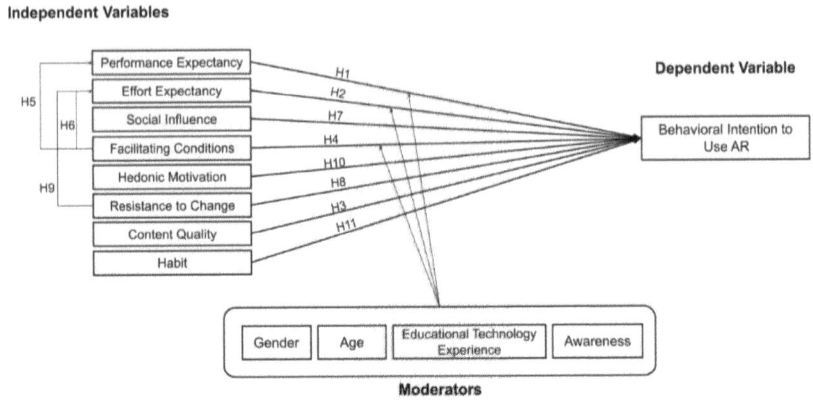

Fig. 1. Revised proposed research model (UTAUT2-ARHE)

The model excludes the original UTAUT2 variable 'Price Value'. This decision is based on the typical higher education context where AR technologies are often procured and provided by the institution, meaning individual instructors usually do not bear the direct financial cost. Therefore, the perceived trade-off between benefits and personal monetary expense is considered less relevant to their individual adoption decisions compared to factors like institutional support (FC) or perceived usefulness (PE).

The following constructs and hypotheses form the core of the proposed model Table 1:

Moderating Factors. The literature shows mixed results on gender differences in technology acceptance (Binyamin et al., 2020). While some AR studies found no gender effect [38], others reported differences [39], justifying investigation of gender as a UTAUT2 moderator for instructor AR adoption.

Age commonly moderates technology adoption in UTAUT studies [25]. Younger users adapt faster, while older users weigh effort expectancy differently [40]. Age moderation analysis will inform targeted support strategies.

Experience with educational technologies influences self-efficacy with new tools like AR [41]. UTAUT2 research indicates experience moderates adoption [42]. This moderation explores how digital comfort affects AR adoption.

Limited AR awareness affects higher education adoption [20] and relates to perceived usefulness [43]. Examining awareness as moderator can indicate if awareness campaigns are needed. So, we hypothesise age, gender, educational technologies experience, and awareness moderate relationships between (PE, EE, FC) and BI.

Table 1. Model Constructs.

Constructs	Definition / Hypothesis	Resources
Performance Expectancy (PE)	The degree to which an instructor believes using AR will help them achieve gains in teaching performance **H1:** Performance expectancy positively influences instructors' behavioural intention to adopt AR	[25, 29]
Effort Expectancy (EE)	The degree of ease associated with the use of AR technology **H2:** Effort expectancy positively influences instructors' behavioural intention to adopt AR	[25, 29]
Content Quality (CQ)	The instructor's perception of the accuracy, relevance, and suitability of the educational content delivered through the AR system **H3:** Content quality positively influences instructors' behavioural intention to adopt AR	[35, 36]
Facilitating Conditions (FC)	An instructor's perception of the available resources and support (e.g., technical assistance, training, infrastructure) to use AR **H4:** Facilitating conditions positively influence instructors' behavioural intention to adopt AR **H5:** Facilitating conditions positively influence instructors' perceptions of performance expectancy **H6:** Facilitating conditions positively influence instructors' perceptions of effort expectancy	[25, 29]
Social Influence (SI)	The extent to which an instructor perceives that important others (e.g., colleagues, administrators) believe they should use AR **H7:** Social influence positively influences instructors' behavioural intention to adopt AR	[25, 29]
Resistance to Change (RC)	An instructor's psychological or emotional opposition towards adopting AR, potentially stemming from comfort with existing methods or perceived disruption **H8:** Resistance to change negatively influences instructors' behavioural intention to adopt AR **H9:** Resistance to change negatively influences instructors' perceptions of effort expectancy	[37]

(continued)

Table 1. (*continued*)

Constructs	Definition / Hypothesis	Resources
Hedonic Motivation (HM)	The novelty, fun or pleasure derived from using AR technology in teaching **H10:** Hedonic motivation positively influences instructors' behavioural intention to adopt AR	[29]
Habit (H)	The extent to which an instructor performs the behaviour of using AR (or similar technologies) automatically due to learned experience **H11:** Habit positively influences instructors' behavioural intention to adopt AR	[29]

3 Methodology

This mixed-methods research follows the explanatory sequential design, which involves the collection of quantitative data, followed by qualitative data [44]. This design method allows for a comprehensive examination of quantitative findings through subsequent qualitative data collection, providing the opportunity to elaborate on perspectives that may not have been fully captured by quantitative methods alone. For this study, quantitative data were gathered via an online questionnaire, while qualitative insights were obtained through a focus group.

This study builds on our earlier work but differs in two key ways: first, we extend UTAUT2 with theoretically grounded links (FC→PE, FC→EE, RC→EE) to explore new indirect mechanisms; second, we integrate mixed-methods analysis.

3.1 Quantitative Study

Participants. A total of 436 instructors from universities worldwide participated in this study. Participants were recruited using purposive sampling. As detailed in Table 2, the sample comprised 52.7% male, 45.9% female, and 1.4% other faculty members. The participants represented diverse academic disciplines, employment levels, and years of experience.

Questionnaire Design. To identify factors influencing instructors' acceptance of AR in higher education, an online survey questionnaire was utilised. Following a pilot study to ensure validity and reliability, the final survey was structured into three sections: (1) demographics, (2) classroom technology use and experience, and (3) factors influencing AR acceptance. The third section included 37 questions covering various aspects. Responses in this section used a five-point Likert scale, ranging from 'strongly disagree' (1) to 'strongly agree' (5).

Data Collection and Analysis. Data were collected using a multi-pronged recruitment strategy targeting academics at various universities worldwide. This involved disseminating the survey link via social media platforms (Facebook, WhatsApp, Reddit, X) and direct email invitations. The online survey remained accessible from August to November 2023. Ethical approval for this study was granted by The University of Newcastle Human Research Ethics Committee (HREC) under approval number H-2023-0143.

Data analysis used PLS-SEM with SmartPLS software for prediction analysis and SPSS for descriptive statistics. Dataset cleaning involved removing partial responses and outliers (identified using z-scores >3), with missing data handled through linear interpolation, yielding 436 valid responses. Exploratory factor analysis identified eight factors explaining 75% of the variance, with the 'Habit' construct excluded due to overlap with Behavioural Intention. This resulted in the deletion of H11. Common method bias assessment using Harmon's test and VIF calculations (ranging from 1.000–2.234 Table 3) indicated no significant bias concerns.

Results. PLS-SEM analysis validated measurement constructs and assessed the hypothesised structural model for AR acceptance factors. PLS-SEM evaluates complex variable relationships and establishes measurement reliability and validity [45]. PLS-SEM does not require normal data distribution, making it suitable for fields like management, marketing, and education, especially for non-normal data or small samples [45]. Its effectiveness in emerging technology topics made PLS-SEM appropriate for this study on augmented reality adoption in higher education.

Measurement Model. The measurement model evaluated construct reliability and validity of the revised UTAUT2-ARHE. Internal consistency was assessed using Cronbach's alpha and composite reliability (CR), with all constructs showing CR values above 0.7 [45] (Table 3). Convergent validity was confirmed with Average Variance Extracted (AVE) above 0.5 (Table 3) and most item outer loadings exceeding 0.6. RC3 fell below 0.6 (0.537) but was retained as it improved the construct's metrics [45]. Discriminant validity was confirmed using Heterotrait-Monotrait ratio (HTMT), with values below 0.9 [45], affirming the measurement model's validity and reliability (Table 4).

Structural Model. Following the confirmation of the measurement model's validity and reliability, the structural model was assessed. This involved examining the coefficient of determination (R2) and the significance of the path coefficients (β) to test the hypothesised relationships [45]. Prior to path analysis, collinearity diagnostics were checked; all constructs exhibited VIF values below the threshold of 3, indicating no multicollinearity issues within the structural model.

The path coefficients were then analysed to evaluate the hypothesised relationships (Table 5, Fig. 2). The PLS-SEM results indicated that performance expectancy ($\beta = 0.291$, $p < 0.001$), effort expectancy ($\beta = 0.169$, $p < 0.001$), social influence ($\beta = 0.181$, $p < 0.001$), content quality ($\beta = 0.186$, $p < 0.01$), and hedonic motivation ($\beta = 0.191$, $p < 0.001$) were all significant positive predictors of behavioural intention to adopt AR. Consequently, hypotheses H1, H2, H7, H3, and H10 were supported. Though facilitating conditions ($\beta = -0.048$, $p = 0.188$) and resistance to change ($\beta = 0.012$, $p = 0.599$) were not found to be significant predictors of BI, leading to the rejection of hypotheses H4 and H8, facilitating conditions positively impacted instructors' perceptions of performance expectancy ($\beta = 0.199$, $p < 0.001$) and effort expectancy ($\beta = 0.175$, $p < 0.001$), and resistance to change negatively influenced instructors' perceptions of effort expectancy

Table 2. Demographic Data

		n	%
Gender	Male	230	52.7
	Female	200	45.9
	Other/Prefer not to say	6	1.4
Age	<25	2	0.5
	25–34	95	21.8
	35–44	155	35.6
	45–54	110	25.2
	>55	74	17.0
Academic Major	ART	35	8.0
	Science	72	16.5
	Engineering	34	7.8
	Health	70	16.1
	IT/CS	38	8.7
	Social Sciences	95	21.8
	Other	92	21.1
Employment Level	Professor	47	10.8
	Associate Professor	66	15.1
	Assistant Professor	96	22.0
	Lecturer	168	38.5
	Teaching Assistant	19	4.4
	Other	40	9.2
Experience	<3 years	36	8.3
	3–5 years	81	18.6
	6–10 years	110	25.2
	11–20 years	125	28.7
	>20 years	84	19.3

(β = -0.110, $p < 0.05$). Consequently, hypotheses H5, H6, and H9 were supported. The model explained 58.4% of the variance in Behavioural Intention (R2 = 0.584).

Moderators Effects. The study examined four potential moderating variables (age, gender, educational technologies experience, and awareness) on the relationships between (PE, EE, FC) and behavioural intention (BI) to adopt AR in higher education. The analysis, including moderators, improved the explained variance in BI to 61.2% (R2 = 0.612), a modest increase of 2.8% compared to the model without moderators. One significant moderating effect was identified, as detailed in the following paragraph.

Table 3. Constructs' reliability and validity

Construct	α	CR	AVE	VIF
BI	0.913	0.913	0.851	-
CQ	0.939	0.940	0.804	2.234
EE	0.912	0.921	0.738	1.661
FC-> BI	0.791	0.827	0.604	1.449
FC-> EE				1.315
FC-> PE				1.000
HM	0.953	0.959	0.914	1.377
PE	0.917	0.921	0.801	1.942
RC-> BI	0.736	0.901	0.604	1.387
RC-> EE				1.315
SI	0.839	0.855	0.604	1.563

Table 4. Heterotrait-Monotrait Ratio (HTMT)

	BI	CQ	EE	FC	HM	PE	RC
BI							
CQ	0.683						
EE	0.607	0.613					
FC	0.176	0.301	0.252				
HM	0.542	0.485	0.431	0.125			
PE	0.713	0.676	0.561	0.213	0.467		
RC	0.098	0.167	0.187	0.661	0.213	0.212	
SI	0.567	0.574	0.417	0.335	0.257	0.515	0.118

Age was found to significantly moderate the relationship between facilitating conditions and behavioural intention ($\beta = -0.142$, $p < 0.05$). Simple slope analysis revealed that for younger faculty members, there is a slight positive association between FC and BI, suggesting that enhanced support might somewhat increase their intention to use AR. Conversely, for older faculty members, the relationship becomes negative, indicating that as facilitating conditions improve, their behavioural intention tends to decrease. Age did not significantly moderate the effects of EE or PE on BI.

Finally, none of the moderators—gender, awareness, and educational technology experience—showed significant moderating effects on the relationships between the independent constructs (PE, EE, FC) and behavioural intention in this study.

Table 5. Structural Model Path Coefficients

Hypothesis	PLS-SEM				
	R^2	β	*t*-test	p-value	Result
CQ -> BI	0.584	0.186	3.395	<0.01	Accepted
EE -> BI		0.169	3.835	<0.001	Accepted
FC -> BI		-0.048	1.193	0.233	Rejected
FC -> EE		0.175	3.356	<0.010	Accepted
FC -> PE		0.199	3.795	<0.001	Accepted
HM -> BI		0.191	5.363	<0.001	Accepted
PE -> BI		0.291	5.061	<0.001	Accepted
RC -> BI		0.028	0.673	0.501	Rejected
RC -> EE		-0.110	2.109	<0.05	Accepted
SI -> BI		0.181	3.888	<0.001	Accepted

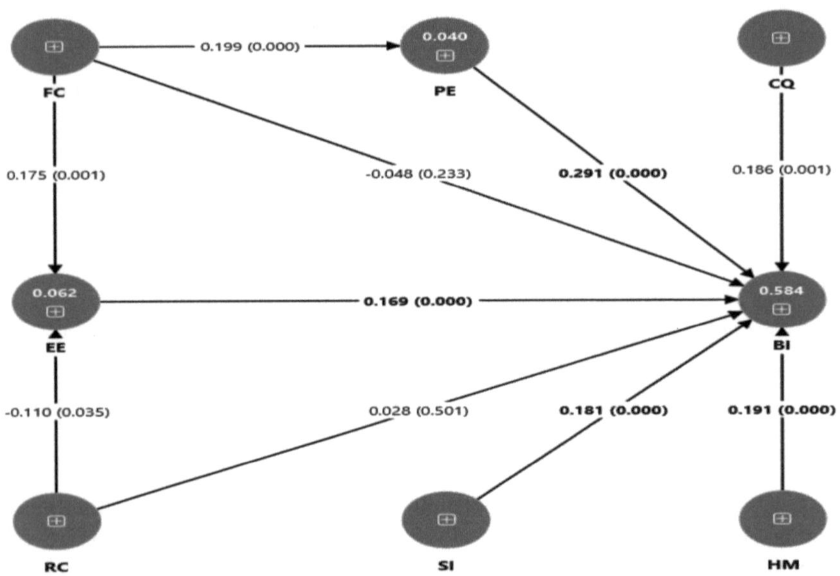

Fig. 2. Path analysis results

3.2 Qualitative Study

The aim of the second phase of this study was to investigate faculty members' perceptions of augmented reality as a teaching tool in higher education, understand the factors influencing these perceptions, and gather additional insights that may not have been captured in the questionnaire. The focus groups interview questions were structured around a main question:

RQ1: What reasons do higher education academics give for their attitudes and beliefs towards the acceptance and adoption of AR technology in the classrooms?

Participants. Twelve faculty members from various universities in Australia and Saudi Arabia, who had previously participated in the quantitative phase, participated in two focus group interviews, seven participants in the first session and five participants second session.

Data Collection and Analysis. Each group participated in a one-hour focus group interview via Zoom, using a semi-structured format [44]. With ethical approval and participants' consent, the interviews were recorded, producing video/audio recordings and transcripts. For analysis, the automatically generated transcripts were reviewed against recordings and corrected. Responses were analysed using thematic analysis within Nvivo 12 software.

Results. The analysis revealed five themes:

Theme 1: Familiarity and Current Usage of AR. The analysis revealed varying levels of AR familiarity among participants, with most showing limited direct experience. This theme emerged from both groups, with only a few participants having hands-on experience with AR technology in educational settings. The half of participants (6 out of 12) expressed awareness of AR but acknowledged their limited practical experience, indicating a significant gap between awareness and actual implementation in educational settings. This limited familiarity aligns with the quantitative findings where Awareness emerged as a significant moderator. Specifically, Awareness strengthened the positive relationship between PE and BI. Participants from both groups often compared AR to VR, showing some confusion between the technologies:

> *"...I have a simple insight about augmented reality and virtual reality. I think they are different from each other..."*
>
> *"...I have looked into VR more than AR, but I can see that VR is just a lot more complicated..."*

Those with direct experience expressed more positive attitudes and could articulate specific use cases:

> *"...I'm familiar with augmented reality where you kind of look through a camera and new representations are put over..."*
>
> *"...I watched a video once about augmented education in medicine. It was a beautiful experience..."*

Notably, there was a clear distinction between theoretical knowledge and practical experience, with most participants falling into the former category:

> *"...but specifically as applications in education, frankly, I did not hear the people say we can apply it in education..."*

Theme 2: Perceived Benefits of AR in Education. Participants across both groups recognised numerous potential benefits of AR in education, particularly in specific disciplines like medicine. The benefits identified included enhanced learning experiences, cost efficiency, and increased student engagement. This positive perception strongly corresponds with the quantitative results, where several constructs representing these benefits were significant positive predictors of BI. Notably, PE, reflecting perceived usefulness and enhanced learning, was the strongest predictor. HM is representing enjoyment and engagement, and CQ is related to the value of AR learning materials, were also significant positive drivers of adoption intention. This theme was strongly supported by 7 out of 12 participants, suggesting a generally positive outlook toward AR's potential in education. Several key benefits were highlighted:

1. Enhanced Learning Experience: "*...I imagine that it will be useful in terms of giving a good experience to the student...*"
2. Cost Effectiveness: "*... it can be used in medicine, which saves a lot of money for universities because it uses the augmented reality instead of buying bodies...*"
3. Increased Accessibility: "*...there are some great things about teaching people who can't come to campus regularly...*"
4. Student Engagement: "*...so, I see the augmented reality as very useful; it excites them...*"

Practical applications were particularly emphasised in specific fields:

"...for example there is a presentation of the body how to describe and so on this helps students in developing their skills for example in the examination of the patient's body..."

Theme 3: Challenges and Barriers to AR Adoption. Despite recognising the benefits, instructors also highlighted significant obstacles to adopting AR. These barriers included technical difficulties, the high cost associated with AR technology and implementation, a lack of adequate training and institutional resources, and resistance to change among faculty. Concerns about the expense and potential security issues like hacking were raised. A major recurring point was the lack of institutional support and training:

"...the university is not providing opportunities to explore those technologies..."

"...there are no courses or trainings or anything towards the augmented reality..."

Instructor readiness and resistance to deviating from established teaching methods were also identified as significant hurdles. One participant remarked:

"...sometimes, you know, everyone's very comfortable sitting and doing the same thing they've been doing for 20 years..."

while another noted the difficulty of implementing change within institutions:

"...it's not supported by the university after that trial..."

Theme 4: Impact of COVID-19 on Technology Adoption. The COVID-19 pandemic emerged as a significant factor influencing instructors' attitudes towards educational technology. The forced shift to remote and online teaching during the pandemic increased instructors' openness to adopting new technologies. participants felt that the experience changed their perspective on teaching methods and made them more receptive to digital tools:

"...to be honest, the COVID-19 situation has changed the way we think about our teaching methods..."

This period led to greater familiarity and trust in online teaching, fostering an environment where innovative tools like AR might be more readily considered. The pandemic also intensified competition among educators to utilise technology effectively to reach students.

Theme 5: Support and Training Needs. This theme underscored the critical role of institutional support and targeted training for the successful integration of AR. Participants emphasised that effective adoption hinges on several factors: university endorsement of new technologies, the availability of comprehensive training programs, and ensuring access to the necessary tools and resources for all faculty members. the need for personal development and training was strongly felt: with one participant expressing:

"...but to be honest, I feel I need to learn so much, and I don't know how to learn. I don't know where to go..."

While some instructors felt ready to adopt AR:

"...for me, as a teacher... I can use it 100%. I will accept it..."

Others pointed out the difficulty in accessing the required technology and developing the necessary skills without dedicated institutional backing. The perceived effort required to learn and use AR remains a significant barrier if adequate support and training are not provided.

4 Discussion and Conclusion

This research aimed to identify the key factors influencing higher education instructors' behavioural intentions to adopt augmented reality as a teaching tool, using an extended UTAUT2 framework. It also sought to analyse the moderating effects of individual differences (age, gender, educational technology experience, awareness) and gain deeper qualitative insights into instructors' perspectives. This study builds upon existing technology acceptance research by specifically focusing on higher education instructors in the post-COVID landscape, incorporating contextually relevant constructs (content quality, resistance to change), and employing a sequential explanatory mixed-methods design to provide a richer understanding than quantitative or qualitative methods alone could offer.

The results of the quantitative data analysis indicate that several factors significantly predict instructors' behavioural intention (BI) to use AR. Performance Expectancy (PE), Effort Expectancy (EE), Social Influence (SI), the newly introduced Content Quality (CQ), and Hedonic Motivation (HM) were all found to have a statistically significant positive influence on instructors' intentions. This suggests that instructors are more likely to intend to use AR if they perceive it as useful for improving their teaching performance (PE), easy to use (EE), supported by important others (SI), delivering high-quality educational content (CQ), and enjoyable or engaging (HM). These findings align with previous UTAUT/UTAUT2 studies in various educational contexts, which often highlight the importance of perceived usefulness and ease of use [26, 27] and increasingly recognise the role of enjoyment or hedonic motivation, particularly with engaging technologies like AR [31]. The significance of CQ underscores the paramount importance instructors place on the pedagogical value and relevance of the technology's content, consistent with discussions by Salloum et al. [46].

Interestingly, Facilitating Conditions (FC) and the added construct Resistance to Change (RC) were not found to directly influence Behavioural Intention. This is somewhat contrary to some UTAUT/UTAUT2 findings where FC often predicts BI [26, 27, 30]. However, the qualitative findings provide crucial context here. While direct support (FC) might not be the primary driver of initial intention, its critical role was heavily emphasised in the focus groups (Theme 5: Support and Training Needs), aligning with the quantitative finding that FC significantly and positively influenced both PE and EE. This suggests that while instructors might form intentions based on perceived benefits and ease, the availability of support directly impacts their perception of AR's usefulness and ease of use, indirectly shaping adoption likelihood, as noted by Tsai [47]. Similarly, while RC did not directly deter intention, it significantly negatively influenced perceptions of Effort Expectancy, suggesting resistance manifests as a belief that the technology will be harder to use, aligning with qualitative Theme 3 (Challenges and Barriers), which highlighted comfort with existing methods as an obstacle. The model explained a substantial 58.4% of the variance in BI, increasing slightly to 61.2% with moderators, indicating good explanatory power.

The moderator analysis revealed that age significantly moderated the relationship between FC and BI. For younger instructors, better facilitating conditions showed a slight positive association with intention, whereas for older instructors, the relationship was negative. This complex finding might suggest that while younger faculty may see support as enabling, older faculty might perceive increased institutional resources (FC) for AR as pressure to adopt a technology they are less comfortable with or see less need for, potentially linking back to the qualitative theme of resistance (Theme 3), as supported by insights from [40]. No significant moderation effects were found for gender, educational technology experience, or awareness on the core relationships examined, suggesting these factors might play less of a role than anticipated in this specific context, or that their influence operates differently than hypothesised.

The findings of the qualitative study largely corroborated and elaborated upon the quantitative results. Instructors expressed positive perceptions regarding AR's potential benefits (Theme 2), including enhanced learning, cost-effectiveness, accessibility, and engagement, directly mirroring the significance of PE, CQ, and HM in the quantitative model. Participant quotes emphasised AR's value in providing experiences (*"giving a good experience to the student"*) and its engaging nature (*"it excites them"*), consistent with observations by Sharma et al. [48]. However, the qualitative data also illuminated significant barriers (Theme 3), such as technical difficulties, cost, lack of training, and institutional support, explaining why FC, despite being crucial indirectly, might not be a primary direct driver of intention itself, aligning with insights from Alvi [28]. The strong emphasis on the need for institutional support and training (Theme 5: *"I feel I need to learn so much, and I don't know how to learn"*) reinforces the importance of FC's indirect role via PE and EE, as highlighted by Tsai [47]. The theme of low familiarity and limited direct experience (Theme 1) also highlights a potential reason why factors like perceived benefits (PE, HM, CQ) might currently outweigh practical considerations (FC) in forming initial intentions instructors are judging potential more than practicality, consistent with Weilage and Stumpfegger [48] discussion. Furthermore, the impact of COVID-19 (Theme 4) was seen as increasing general openness to technology, potentially creating a more receptive environment for AR adoption than might have existed previously, supporting findings by Al-Absy [49].

These findings have implications for practice and future research. For institutions and educational technologists seeking to promote AR adoption, efforts should focus not only on showcasing AR's benefits (addressing PE, HM, CQ) and usability (addressing EE) but critically on providing robust facilitating conditions (training, technical support, resources) to positively influence PE and EE and mitigate RC's negative impact on EE, aligning with suggestions by Nav and Ye [50]. Targeted support might be needed based on age, acknowledging the different ways support (FC) impacts intention across age groups, as indicated by findings from Buentello-Montoya et al. [40]. The qualitative data strongly suggests that without adequate support and training, adoption will likely remain limited despite positive intentions, corroborating insights by Sharma et al. [48]. For researchers, this study highlights the value of mixed-methods approaches and context-specific model extensions (like CQ and RC for instructors), consistent with recommendations by Salloum et al. [46] and Alkhattabi [3]. Future research could explore the evolution of these factors as instructor familiarity grows, investigate the impact of specific types of institutional support, and further explore the complex interplay of age, resistance, and facilitating conditions. Developing longitudinal studies could also track the transition from intention to actual use.

This study has limitations. The quantitative data relies on self-reported intentions and perceptions via convenience sampling across diverse international universities, potentially limiting generalisability. The qualitative data comes from a smaller group predominantly from two countries (Australia and Saudi Arabia), which might not capture the full range of global perspectives. Future studies could benefit from larger, probabilistically sampled quantitative data and broader qualitative participation across more institutions and geographical regions to enhance generalisability. Despite these limitations, this study provides valuable insights into the multifaceted factors shaping higher education instructors' adoption of AR, offering a robust foundation for future research and practice.

References

1. Rusli, R., Nalanda, D.A., Tarmidi, A.D.V., Suryaningrum, K.M., Yunanda, R.: Augmented reality for studying hands on the human body for elementary school students. Procedia Comput. Sci. **216**, 237–244 (2023). https://doi.org/10.1016/j.procs.2022.12.132
2. Cai, S., Zhou, Y., Shen, J., Guo, J., Xiong, X., Jiang, X.: Augmented Reality Based Surgical Training and Education System for Neurosurgery. In: 2022 International Conference on Advanced Robotics and Mechatronics (ICARM). pp. 678–681. IEEE, Guilin, China (2022). https://doi.org/10.1109/ICARM54641.2022.9959349
3. Alkhattabi, M.: Augmented reality as E-learning tool in primary schools' education: barriers to teachers' adoption. Int. J. Emerg. Technol. Learn. **12** (2017). https://doi.org/10.3991/ijet.v12i02.6158
4. Çetin, H., Türkan, A.: The Effect of Augmented Reality based applications on achievement and attitude towards science course in distance education process. Educ. Inf. Technol. **27**, 1397–1415 (2022). https://doi.org/10.1007/s10639-021-10625-w
5. Ahmad, N., Junaini, S.: Augmented reality for learning mathematics: a systematic literature review. Int. J. Emerg. Technol. Learn. IJET. **15**, 106–122 (2020)
6. Al-Ansi, A.M., Jaboob, M., Garad, A., Al-Ansi, A.: Analyzing augmented reality (AR) and virtual reality (VR) recent development in education. Soc. Sci. Humanit. Open. **8**, 100532 (2023)
7. Cheng, S., Xiao, J.: Research on the application of virtual reality and augmented reality technologies in higher education. In: Proceedings of the 2024 10th International Conference on Frontiers of Educational Technologies, pp. 6–11. Association for Computing Machinery, New York (2024). https://doi.org/10.1145/3678392.3686396
8. Al-Okaily, M., Alqudah, H., Al-Qudah, A.A., Al-Qadi, N.S., Elrehail, H., Al-Okaily, A.: Does financial awareness increase the acceptance rate for financial inclusion? an empirical examination in the era of digital transformation. Kybernetes **52**, 4876–4896 (2023). https://doi.org/10.1108/K-08-2021-0710
9. Che Hashim, N., Abd Majid, N.A., Arshad, H., Khalid Obeidy, W., Mäkilä, T.: User satisfaction for an augmented reality application to support productive vocabulary using speech recognition. Adv. Multimed. 2018 (2018). https://doi.org/10.1155/2018/9753979
10. Aburub, F., Alnawas, I.: A new integrated model to explore factors that influence adoption of mobile learning in higher education: An empirical investigation. Educ. Inf. Technol. **24**, 2145–2158 (2019). https://doi.org/10.1007/s10639-019-09862-x
11. Rahman, M.M., Ahmed, A., Jubair, M.A.A., Amin, M.R., Bondhon, R.H.: AR Lab/Practical Simulation Book for Physics Chemistry & Computer Science. In: Proceedings of the 2nd International Conference on Computing Advancements. pp. 97–102. Association for Computing Machinery, New York (2022). https://doi.org/10.1145/3542954.3542969
12. Belda-Medina, J., Calvo-Ferrer, J.R.: Integrating augmented reality in language learning: pre-service teachers' digital competence and attitudes through the TPACK framework. Educ. Inf. Technol. **27**, 12123–12146 (2022). https://doi.org/10.1007/s10639-022-11123-3
13. Hanafi, H.F., Wahab, M.H.A., Selamat, A.Z., Masnan, A.H., Huda, M.: A systematic review of augmented reality in multimedia learning outcomes in education. In: Intelligent Human Computer Interaction: 12th International Conference, IHCI 2020, Daegu, South Korea, November 24–26, 2020, Proceedings, Part II, pp. 63–72. Springer, Heidelberg (2020). https://doi.org/10.1007/978-3-030-68452-5_7
14. Campisi, C.A., Li, E.H., Jimenez, D.E., Milanaik, R.L.: Augmented reality in medical education and training: from physicians to patients. Augment. Real. Educ. New Technol. Teach. Learn., 111–138 (2020). https://doi.org/10.1007/978-3-030-42156-4_7

15. Dhar, P., Rocks, T., Samarasinghe, R.M., Stephenson, G., Smith, C.: Augmented reality in medical education: students' experiences and learning outcomes. Med. Educ. Online **26**, 1953953 (2021). https://doi.org/10.1080/10872981.2021.1953953
16. Huang, H., Liu, G.: Evaluating students' behavioral intention and system usability of augmented reality-aided distance design learning during the COVID-19 pandemic. Univers. Access Inf. Soc. **23**, 1217–1231 (2024). https://doi.org/10.1007/s10209-022-00920-9
17. Mokmin, N.A.M., Rassy, R.P.: Review of the trends in the use of augmented reality technology for students with disabilities when learning physical education. Educ. Inf. Technol. **29**, 1251–1277 (2022). https://doi.org/10.1007/s10639-022-11550-2
18. Ajit, G., Lucas, T., Kanyan, R.: A Systematic Review of Augmented Reality in STEM Education. Stud. Appl. Econ. **39** (2021). https://doi.org/10.25115/eea.v39i1.4280
19. Velarde-Camaqui, D., Sanabria-Z, J.: Augmented Reality as a Driver to Enhance Engagement in High School Students. In: Proceedings of TEEM 2023: The Eleventh International Conference on Technological Ecosystems for Enhancing Multiculturality, pp. 1414–1421. Springer, Heidelberg (2024). https://doi.org/10.1007/978-981-97-1814-6_140
20. Alzahrani, N.M.: Augmented reality: a systematic review of its benefits and challenges in e-learning contexts. Appl. Sci. **10**, 5660 (2020). https://doi.org/10.3390/app10165660
21. Davis, F.D.: Perceived usefulness, perceived ease of use, and user acceptance of information technology. MIS Q. **13**, 319 (1989). https://doi.org/10.2307/249008
22. Abd Majid, F., Mohd Shamsudin, N.: Identifying factors affecting acceptance of virtual reality in classrooms based on technology acceptance model (TAM). Asian J. Univ. Educ. **15**, 1–10 (2019)
23. Alahmari, M.: Exploring the influential factors affecting staff willingness to adopt augmented reality. Int. J. Inf. Educ. Technol. **13**, 1078–1084 (2023). https://doi.org/10.18178/ijiet.2023.13.7.1907
24. Alalwan, A.A., Baabdullah, A.M., Rana, N.P., Tamilmani, K., Dwivedi, Y.K.: Examining adoption of mobile internet in Saudi Arabia: extending TAM with perceived enjoyment, innovativeness and trust. Technol. Soc. **55**, 100–110 (2018). https://doi.org/10.1016/j.techsoc.2018.06.007
25. Venkatesh, V., Morris, M.G., Davis, G.B., Davis, F.D.: User acceptance of information technology: toward a unified view. MIS Q. **27**, 425–478 (2003). https://doi.org/10.2307/30036540
26. Mengying, L., et al.: Pathway analysis of clinical nurse educator's intention to use virtual reality technology based on the UTAUT model. Front. Public Health **12**, 1437699 (2024). https://doi.org/10.3389/fpubh.2024.1437699
27. Ateş, H., Garzón, J.: An integrated model for examining teachers' intentions to use augmented reality in science courses. Educ. Inf. Technol. **28**, 1299–1321 (2023). https://doi.org/10.1007/s10639-022-11239-6
28. Alvi, I.: College students' reception of social networking tools for learning in India: an extended UTAUT model. Smart Learn. Environ. **8**, 19 (2021). https://doi.org/10.1186/s40561-021-00164-9
29. Venkatesh, V., Thong, J.Y.L., Xu, X.: Consumer acceptance and use of information technology: extending the unified theory of acceptance and use of technology. MIS Q. **36**, 157–178 (2012). https://doi.org/10.2307/41410412
30. Faqih, K.M.S., Jaradat, M.-I.R.M.: Integrating TTF and UTAUT2 theories to investigate the adoption of augmented reality technology in education: Perspective from a developing country. Technol. Soc. **67**, 101787 (2021). https://doi.org/10.1016/j.techsoc.2021.101787
31. Sunardi, S., Ramadhan, A., Abdurachman, E., Trisetyarso, A., Zarlis, M.: Acceptance of augmented reality in video conference based learning during COVID-19 pandemic in higher education. Bull. Electr. Eng. Inform. **11**, 3598–3608 (2022). https://doi.org/10.11591/eei.v11i6.4035

32. Ameri, A., Khajouei, R., Ameri, A., Jahani, Y.: Acceptance of a mobile-based educational application (LabSafety) by pharmacy students: an application of the UTAUT2 model. Educ. Inf. Technol. **25**, 419–435 (2020). https://doi.org/10.1007/s10639-019-09965-5
33. Ibrahim, S., Abdullah, S.: Student-Centered Method in the Higher Education System of the Kurdistan Region: Soran University as an Example. J. Educ. Teach. JET. **5**, 248–270 (2024). https://doi.org/10.51454/jet.v5i2.422
34. Xue, H., Sharma, P., Wild, F.: User satisfaction in augmented reality-based training using microsoft HoloLens. Computers. **8**, 9 (2019). https://doi.org/10.3390/computers8010009
35. Lee, B.C., Yoon, J.-O., Lee, I.: Learners' acceptance of e-learning in South Korea: theories and results. Comput. Educ. **53**, 1320–1329 (2009). https://doi.org/10.1016/j.compedu.2009.06.014
36. Almaiah, M.A., Jalil, M.A., Man, M.: Extending the TAM to examine the effects of quality features on mobile learning acceptance. J. Comput. Educ. **3**, 453–485 (2016). https://doi.org/10.1007/s40692-016-0074-1
37. Alroqi, T.M.: An investigation into the acceptance of augmented reality in Saudi Arabian schools (2021)
38. Cabero-Almenara, J., Fernández-Batanero, J.M., Barroso-Osuna, J.: Adoption of augmented reality technology by university students. Heliyon. **5**, e01597 (2019). https://doi.org/10.1016/j.heliyon.2019.e01597
39. Aboudahr, S.M.F., Govindarajoo, M.V., Olowoselu, A., Sani, R.: Investigating moderating influence of gender on augmented reality and students satisfaction: experiences in cultures and linguistic diversity. Asian J. Univ. Educ. **19**, 447–461 (2023). https://doi.org/10.24191/ajue.v19i3.23328
40. Buentello-Montoya, D.A., Lomelí-Plascencia, M.G., Medina-Herrera, L.M.: The role of reality enhancing technologies in teaching and learning of mathematics. Comput. Electr. Eng. **94** (2021). https://doi.org/10.1016/j.compeleceng.2021.107287
41. Alamäki, A., Dirin, A., Suomala, J.: Students' expectations and social media sharing in adopting augmented reality. Int. J. Inf. Learn. Technol. **38**, 196–208 (2021). https://doi.org/10.1108/IJILT-05-2020-0072
42. Schomakers, E.-M., Lidynia, C., Vervier, L.S., Calero Valdez, A., Ziefle, M.: Applying an extended UTAUT2 model to explain user acceptance of lifestyle and therapy mobile health apps: survey study. JMIR MHealth UHealth. **10**, e27095 (2022). https://doi.org/10.2196/27095
43. Alahmari, M.: Students' Awareness of Augmented Reality Adoption in Saudi Arabia Universities (2019)
44. Creswell, J.W.: Controversies in mixed methods research. The SAGE. (2011)
45. Hair, J.F., Risher, J.J., Sarstedt, M., Ringle, C.M.: When to use and how to report the results of PLS-SEM. Eur. Bus. Rev. **31**, 2–24 (2019). https://doi.org/10.1108/EBR-11-2018-0203
46. Salloum, S.A., Al-Emran, M., Shaalan, K., Tarhini, A.: Factors affecting the E-learning acceptance: a case study from UAE. Educ. Inf. Technol. **24**, 509–530 (2019)
47. Tsai, L.L.: Evaluating the effects of facilitating conditions and usage experience on mobile payment: Int. J. Inf. Syst. Serv. Sect. **13**, 88–106 (2021). https://doi.org/10.4018/IJISSS.2021100105
48. Sharma, S., Bodempudi, S.T., Scribner, D., Grazaitis, P.: Active Shooter response training environment for a building evacuation in a collaborative virtual environment. Electron. Imaging. **32**, 223–1–223–7 (2020). https://doi.org/10.2352/ISSN.2470-1173.2020.13.ERVR-223

49. Al-Absy, M.S.M.: Effects of COVID-19 Pandemic on Accounting Students' Capability to Use Technology. Int. J. Learn. Teach. Educ. Res. **22**, 247–267 (2023). https://doi.org/10.26803/ijlter.22.1.14
50. Nov, O., Ye, C.: Resistance to change and the adoption of digital libraries: an integrative model. J. Am. Soc. Inf. Sci. Technol. **60**, 1702–1708 (2009). https://doi.org/10.1002/asi.21068

Innovative Pedagogical Approaches and Multimedia Integration

Development of STEAM-Based Electronic Student Worksheets (E-LKPD) for Science Learning

Vivi Sebastiani Pandiangan(✉), K. Abdul Hamid, and Samsidar Tanjung

Medan State University, Medan, Indonesia
vivisebastianipandianganbio@gmail.com

Abstract. The objective of this research is to develop STEAM-based E-LKPD (Electronic Student Worksheets) that is feasible, practical, and effective for use in enhacing students' learning outcomes in science learning. This study utilized development research with the Borg & Gall development model. The instruments used in this research included learning needs observation sheets, validation sheets for media, content, and design, feedback sheets for teacher and student response, and learning outcome assesment sheets. The research results show: (1) material validation scored an average of 98.06%, categorized as very feasible, (2) media validation scored an average of 84.18%, categorized as very feasible, (3) design validation scored an average of 97.11%, categorized as very feasible, (4) individual trial scored 91.50% and small group trials 97.75%, categorized as very feasible, (5) field trial scored 97.75% categorized as very feasible. Furthermore, the experimental results using STEAM-based E-LKPD in the experimental class obtained an average learning outcome of 83, while the control class using LKPD published by Kemdikbud obtained learning outcomes of 78.5. Normality and homogeneity tests showed that the research data has been declared normal and homogeneous. Independent samples t-test result showed a significance value of $t < 0.05$ ($0.024 < 0.05$), therefore H_0 was rejected and H_1 was accepted. This means that the STEAM-based E-LKPD product developed is effective for improving student learning outcomes in science learning. Thus, the STEAM-based E-LKPD is very feasible, practical, and effective for improving science learning outcomes.

Keywords: E-LKPD · STEAM · Science Learning

1 Introduction

The 21st century is characterized by rapid developments in science and technology, globalization, and economic growth. Education needs to prepare students to face global challenges, social realities, and future employment. In 21st century education, everyone must possess three skills: (1) life and professional skills, (2) learning and innovation skills, and (3) information media and technology skills. Regarding learning and innovation skills, students must develop four capabilities: Communication, Collaboration, Critical Thinking, and Creativity, known as the 4Cs [1].

K. W. Lee and L. H. Wong (Eds.): ITEA 2025, CCIS 2643, pp. 275–285, 2026.
https://doi.org/10.1007/978-981-95-2011-4_25

The 21st century emphasizes student-centered learning to enhance skills (Patresia et al., 2020). According to The Assessment and Teaching of 21st Century Skills (ATC21S) Project, the framework of thinking skills that constitutes competencies required in the 21st century comprises problem-solving, creativity and innovation, critical thinking, and decision-making. The demands of 21st century work require workers to possess various related skills such as creative thinking, problem-solving, and communication [2]. Thinking skills are cognitive abilities to generate and develop new ideas, new concepts as an extension of previously conceived ideas, and skills to solve problems divergently [3]. Creativity is a necessary skill that involves mental processes to produce original ideas [4]. Students are trained to have high levels of creativity to develop, enrich, and elaborate ideas and solve problems from different perspectives [5].

Natural Science is one of the subjects consistently present in schools, comprising two components: process and product. As a product, Natural Science consists of a body of knowledge including facts, concepts, principles, and laws about natural phenomena. As a process, Natural Science is a structured and systematic sequence conducted to discover concepts, principles, and laws about natural phenomena [6].

Natural Science learning in junior high schools plays a crucial role in developing students' critical, creative, and innovative thinking abilities. Science learning provides direct experiences to students, thereby enhancing their ability to construct, understand, and apply concepts they have learned. Students are trained to discover themselves through various concepts in a holistic, meaningful, authentic, and applicable manner for problem-solving purposes [7]. This aligns with constructivist theory, which states that students can build knowledge based on personal experiences. These experiences are based on what they have encountered with others and their environment. Science learning emphasizes not only conceptual mastery but also science process skills and their application in daily life.

The specific characteristic of Natural Science material is studying factual natural phenomena, whether in the form of realities, events, and cause-effect relationships [8]. Natural Science is closely related to nature; sometimes the subject becomes difficult for students because of its abstract nature. Therefore, understanding Natural Science requires a positive attitude from within students. However, besides instilling positive attitudes in students, it is also necessary to cultivate the character value of student learning creativity, as learning creativity is an important factor that can help students understand concepts in Natural Science [9]. Creativity involves a range of attributes (such as confidence, achievement drive, sensitivity) and thinking skills (such as fluency, mental flexibility, imagination) [10]. That is why learning creativity is needed to support students in understanding Natural Science concepts.

Based on interviews conducted at SMP Negeri 2 Satu Atap Batang Serangan, the creative thinking abilities of students are still classified as very low. Students' fluency thinking skills remain very limited, as evidenced by their lack of habit in generating multiple ideas, answers, problem solutions, or questions. When presented with questions, students can typically provide only a single answer and are unable to adequately explain their reasoning. Similarly, regarding asking questions, students are not accustomed to raising inquiries about material that actually represents real-world problems related to daily life.

Likewise, with flexibility thinking skills, students are unable to generate varied ideas, answers, or questions, or view a problem from different perspectives. Students only answer questions according to explanations found in textbooks. They are not habituated to seeking various literature or knowledge sources that could enrich their understanding. Despite the rapid advancement of technology today, students could search for materials or sources from applications downloadable from the Play Store, YouTube, or other digital sources and compare them to gain multiple perspectives that would broaden their knowledge. These limitations affect student learning outcomes across several core topics in Science education.

The researcher suspects that students' generally low learning outcomes occur due to several factors, including teachers' use of inappropriate strategies and approaches for the learning material. Additionally, Science education, which is closely related to daily life, actually requires integration with other disciplines such as technology, engineering, art, and mathematics. Therefore, a learning approach that can integrate various disciplines and connect them to real-world problems is necessary. Furthermore, Science learning also demands mastery of concepts and natural laws through conceptual understanding via analysis and practical activities. These activities require teaching materials or guides containing systematic work steps, often referred to as Student Worksheets (LKPD), naturally with appropriate approaches as well.

One learning approach relevant to21st century demands in Science education is the STEAM (Science, Technology, Engineering, Arts, and Mathematics) approach. The STEAM approach represents an evolution of the STEM (Science, Technology, Engineering, Mathematics) approach with the addition of Arts. In implementing the STEAM approach, teaching materials that can facilitate students to explore and integrate various disciplines in an integrated manner are required. One such teaching material that can be utilized is STEAM-based Student Worksheets (LKPD). Student Worksheets, as written teaching materials, play an important role as teacher agents in effective teaching practices to achieve learning outcomes [11, 12].

Student Worksheets (LKPD) have been used in teaching practices for a long time. Therefore, Student Worksheets must also evolve dynamically to meet current learning demands. Contemporary learning must provide students with the skills and knowledge needed to thrive in the21st century (Darling-Hammond, 2014; Greenstein, 2012; Osborne, 2013). Since the COVID-19 pandemic, many electronic Student Worksheets, abbreviated as E-LKPD, have been developed. In the process of adapting to new learning habits during the Covid-19 pandemic, one of the necessities for adaptation in learning is the availability of teaching materials and online learning tools that use interesting media easily accessible to students. Educators are required to design learning tools and media as innovations by utilizing online learning devices and media [13]. Although the Covid-19 Pandemic has now ended, presenting Student Worksheets in electronic form (E-LKPD) needs to be developed, considering that these E-LKPDs will be easily accessible via laptops, computers, and smartphones, making their use more effective and efficient.

The use of Student Worksheets that are not yet STEAM-based likely contributes to the low student learning outcomes in Science education. Therefore, the development of STEA-based E-LKPD for Science subjects needs to be conducted. STEAM-based

Student Worksheets in this research are expected to contribute to resolving problems that still emerge in Science learning.

2 Method

The objective of this research is to develop a STEAM-based E-LKPD (Electronic Student Worksheet) product that is feasible, practical, and effective in improving science learning outcomes. The research will be conducted at SMP Negeri 2 Satu Atap Batang Serangan. The population and sample in this study are students from classes VIII-1 and VIII-2 of SMP Negeri 2 Satu Atap Batang Serangan. Class VIII-1 serves as the experimental group comprising 30 students, while class VIII-2 serves as the control group comprising 30 students. Sample selection in this study employs Cluster Random Sampling, where sample determination is based on the researcher's considerations, provided that the samples meet the criteria required for the research and align with the research objectives.

The research and development of this learning media use the Research and Develop ment model, approach following the Borg & Gall development model. The instruments used in this research include learning needs observation sheets, material validation sheets, media and design validation sheets, teacher and student response forms, and learning outcome test sheets.

3 Result and Discussion

This research uses a Research and Development (R&D) approach. The study resulted in the development of a STEAM-based Electronic Student Worksheet (E-LKPD) using the Borg & Gall development steps.

3.1 Need Assesment

Based on needs analysis, information was obtained that the development of STEAM-based E-LKPD is highly needed by teachers in the learning process. Interview results with subject teachers and students indicated that STEAM-based E-LKPD is required to support the learning process. Survey and interview results showed that 50% of teachers concluded that their current teaching practices have not met expectations. This occurs because some students still lack seriousness in following the learning process, have low learning motivation, and the teaching materials used are still limited to a single source. Survey results also revealed that some teachers have not prepared their lessons thoroughly and structurally, nor have they prepared teaching modules properly according to the curriculum. However, teachers agree that using E-LKPD would be beneficial for delivering learning materials, practicum activities, and assignments. Additionally, teachers do not experience difficulties in using digital learning media/teaching materials. Teachers also estimate that learning using E-LKPD can improve student learning outcomes.

In addition to teachers, students were also given questionnaires to determine whether they need E-LKPD in science learning. Needs analysis results showed that 100% of students agree that the science learning process should also utilize mobile phones in addition to printed books. Students feel that E-LKPD is needed in science learning, and they agree if teachers use E-LKPD in the delivery process of learning materials, practicum, and assignments. Furthermore, 47% of students experience difficulties in learning or understanding material from printed books. Additionally, 83% do not frequently use the internet to view the material being discussed.

3.2 Design

Design phase was conducted, which is a design phase dealing with learning objects, research instruments, exercises and content, subject analysis, lesson plans, and selection of learning media. At this stage, the researcher designed the developed media by utilizing the Canva application, beginning with creating a storyboard. During this stage, the E-LKPD display was arranged using the Canva application, with its flow organized according to STEAM learning syntax while adapting to the characteristics of food and food substances material. This research involved activities of compiling teaching modules, E-LKPD, concept delivery and material organization, evaluation questions, images, and STEAM elements (see Fig. 1).

Fig. 1. The display of STEAM-based E-LKPD

3.3 Validation and Evaluation

The feasibility of this STEAM-based E-LKPD was validated by expert lecturers consisting of two material expert validators, two media expert validators, and two design expert validators. Validation was carried out by sending the link to the developed STEAM-based E-LKPD to the validators along with the validation sheets for examination, assessment, and suggestions for further improvement of the E-LKPD. If there were still inconsistencies, material misconceptions, errors, or incompatibilities, the validators provided suggestions and returned them to the researcher to be revised according to these improvement suggestions. After making revisions and being re-examined by expert validators, the validators provided assessments which were then calculated by the researcher to obtain percentages for each aspect to get the average total validation value.

For the material aspect, validation was carried out on assessment aspects including content, presentation, display, and language. The results of the material expert validation showed an average of 98.06%, categorized very feasible. Validation was carried out twice against two material expert validators, where in the first assessment there were still some shortcomings such as in the aspects of the accuracy of STEAM (Science, Technology, Arts, and Mathematics) procedures in E-LKPD and providing opportunities for students to carry out STEAM activities. After revisions, there was an increase in validation results from the previous 97.37% for validator 1 to 100% and 95.07% to 100% for validator 2, with the category being very feasible to be field-tested.

For the media aspect, media expert lecturers conducted validation twice each. The assessment aspects in media expert validation included display, user convenience, graphics, presentation, and E-LKPD content design. The results of media expert validation showed an average of 84.18. Material expert categorized very feasible. Validation was carried out twice against two material expert validators, where in the first assessment there were still some shortcomings in aspects of display, user convenience, graphics, presentation, and E-LKPD content design. After revisions, there was an increase in validation results from the previous 68.41% for validator 1 to 95.41% and 87.91% to 88.74% for validator 2, with the category being very feasible to be field-tested.

For the design aspect, design expert lecturers conducted validation twice each. The assessment aspects in media expert validation included learning design and E-LKPD characteristics. The results of design expert validation showed an average of 97.11%. Categorized very feasible. Validation was carried out twice against two material expert validators, where in the first assessment there were still some shortcomings in the learning design aspect. After revisions, there was an increase in validation results from the previous 94.23% to 100% for validator 1 and validator 2, categorized very feasible to be field-tested.

This is in line with research Martatiyana, Nasbey, and Utami [14] which found that student responses to STEM-PjBL-based Science e-LKPD (electronic Student Worksheet) in fourth-grade students showed an average percentage of 84% in the one-to-one trial phase, which falls into the excellent category. Subsequently, in the small group trial phase, the average percentage increased to 95% within the same category, which is excellent. Teacher responses to this e-LKPD also demonstrated highly positive assessments with a percentage reaching 93%. Based on these data, it can be concluded that the developed e-LKPD is classified as highly suitable for use in learning and has advantages in various important aspects of education.

Similarly, research conducted by Haifaturrahmah, that showed an average expert rating of 4.28, categorized as excellent. Meanwhile, user responses (from teachers and students) averaged 4.55, also categorized as excellent [15]. Based on the results of this data analysis, it can be concluded that the STEAM-based e-LKPD that was developed is appropriate for use as a supporting learning resource in the implementation of integrated thematic learning.

Overall, the validation results from material, media, and learning design expert validators on the development of STEAM-based E-LKPD stated that it has met the eligibility requirements and can be tested in science learning. The recapitulation of the final validation results by expert lecturers can be seen in Table 1.

Table 1. Recapitulation of Validation Results by Expert

No	Validator	Percentage (%)	Categori
1	Material Expert	98,06%	Very Feasible
2	Media Expert	84,18%	Very Feasible
3	Design Expert	97,11%	Very Feasible
Average		**93,11%**	**Very Feasible**

Table 1 above shows that the average validation result of STEAM-based E-LKPD that has been carried out by expert lecturers in material, media, and learning design is 93.11%, categorized as very feasible overall.

The practicality test of STEAM-based E-LKPD was conducted by science subject teachers, consisting of 3 assessment aspects, namely content and benefits, presentation, display, and language. Based on teacher assessment, the developed STEAM-based E-LKPD is very feasible to be used in science learning with a percentage of 100%. After the developed STEAM-based E-LKPD was declared valid by material experts, media experts, design experts, and practitioners (teachers) who utilize E-LKPD in learning, the next stage was to conduct trials that would be carried out individually, small group trials, and then the final stage of conducting field trials in the class that was used as the research subject, namely VIII-1 class. Individual trials were conducted to identify deficiencies in the developed STEAM-based E-LKPD, as well as to determine student responses to the developed media. This individual trial was conducted by including 3 students as samples with the consideration that the selected students have the same characteristics as the target research class. Information obtained from the individual trial results from 3 student samples showed an average of 91.50%, categorized "very feasible". Based on these trial results, it can be concluded that the STEAM-based E-LKPD development product categorized "very feasible", although there are still things that need to be improved to be used more effectively and efficiently in the process of field trial II.

Small group trials on the STEAM-based E-LKPD development product were conducted on 10 students. Samples were taken randomly consisting of 4 students with high learning achievement, 3 students with medium learning achievement, and 3 students with low learning achievement. The purpose of this small group trial was to identify deficiencies in the developed STEAM-based E-LKPD product. The assessment from this small group trial was about the practicality of the product developed from the user's point of view, which includes several aspects of content and benefits, presentation, display, and language. From the results of the small group trial from 10 student samples, an average of 97.75% was obtained with the category "very feasible". Based on these trial results, it can be concluded that the STEAM-based E-LKPD development product categorized "very feasible". Thus, the STEAM-based E-LKPD development product is suitable for use in science learning.

Field trials were conducted on 30 students of VIII-1 class as research subjects. The purpose of conducting this field trial was to identify deficiencies in the developed

STEAM-based E-LKPD after the validation stage from the experts. The average value of the field trial results is 97.75% with very feasible criteria. With this, it can be concluded that the developed STEAM-based E-LKPD has met the eligibility requirements to be applied in science learning in the classroom. After the developed STEAM-based E-LKPD was validated by several sources related to media development and users of this E-LKPD, the recapitulation results of the STEAM-based E-LKPD validation can be seen in Table 2 below:

Table 2. Recapitulation of Trial Results

No	Respondent/Validator	Percentage (%)	Criteria
1	Practicality Test (Teacher)	100%	Very Feasible
2	Individual Trial	91,50%	Very Feasible
3	Small Group Trial	97,75%	Very Feasible
4	Field Trial	97,75%	Very Feasible
Jumlah		**96,75%**	**Very Feasible**

3.4 Results of Product Effectiveness Test Research

The effectiveness of STEAM-based E-LKPD in science learning that was developed can be measured by analyzing student learning outcome data. Student learning outcomes were obtained from two stages, namely pretest before using STEAM-based E-LKPD and posttest after utilizing STEAM-based E-LKPD.

The acquisition of student learning outcome data using STEAM-based E-LKPD in science learning obtained the lowest score of 70, the highest score of 95, the mean value of 83, mode of 84.5, median of 83.07, and standard deviation of 7.92. From the student learning outcome data using STEAM-based E-LKPD, there were 7 people at the average value, namely 23%, 10 people (33%) below the average learning outcome value, and 13 people (43%) above the average learning outcome value.

While the learning outcomes of students using LKPDs in printed books and E-books published by Kemdikbud, from 30 students, obtained the highest learning outcomes of 90 and the lowest of 65, with an average value of 78.5, mode 83.17, median 79.5, and standard deviation of 6.96. The learning outcomes of students using printed books and E-books published by Kemdikbud, there were 7 people who were at the average value, namely 23%, 8 people (27%) were below the average value of learning outcomes, and 15 people (50%) were above the average value of learning outcomes.

The effectiveness test of the E-LKPD based on the STEAM Approach developed was carried out by comparing the average value of the learning outcomes of the experimental class using the E-LKPD based on the STEAM Approach and the control class which only used LKPD from printed books and E-Books published by Kemdikbud. The acquisition of learning outcomes for the experimental class and for the control class on food and food substances. Furthermore, from the t test results, obtained tcount and ttable with a significance level of $\alpha = 0.05$, the results obtained t count > t table. It can be interpreted that H_0 is rejected and H_1 is accepted. This means that the STEAM Approach-based E-LKPD product developed is effective in improving student learning outcomes in science subjects.

The effectiveness of E-LKPD based on the STEAM Approach was found to be able to improve student learning outcomes and improve collaboration. This is in line with research conducted by Mariyana, Syahri, and Haryanto who identified the creative thinking skills of students at SMAN 2 Muaro Jambi which showed an unoptimal level, which was indicated by low interest in learning chemistry subjects. To overcome these problems, the development of Electronic Learner Worksheets (E-LKPD) integrated with the Problem Based Learning approach was carried out to increase the creative thinking capacity of students on the acid-base concept. The results showed the significance of differences in learning outcomes between conditions without E-LKPD and with E-LKPD, with a difference of 11.56 points. There was a progressive increase in the average score by 5–7 points at each stage of learning, which confirmed that the E-LKPD developed was effective in improving students' creative thinking skills and learning outcomes [16].

Likewise, research conducted by Herlina, Ramlawati, and Hasri that conducted at SMAN 6 Enrekang. Based on the pretest and posttest data, the n-gain value was 0.71 with a high category. The average posttest score was 82.73 and the percentage of class completeness was 84.85%. Based on data analysis, it shows that the use of STEAM-based e-modules and E-LKPD is proven to be effective in improving student learning outcomes on colloidal system material with a high effectiveness category [17].

Likewise, research conducted by Annisa, Effendi and Damris at SMAN 11 Jambi City which shows the results of the correlation of pretest-postest values 0.263 > 0.05, meaning that there is no relationship between pretest-postest values. The 2- tailed significance value of 0.000 < 0.05, it can be concluded that there is a real difference in creative thinking ability and student learning outcomes in pretest and posttest data. Based on the results of the study, it can be concluded that there is a real difference in the ability of student learning outcomes with STEAM-based E-LKPD at SMAN 11 Jambi City [18].

The ideal Student Worksheet must meet the requirements of validity, practicality, and effectiveness [19–21]. Based on the results of the research that has been conducted and supported by theories from various literatures above, the E-LKPD based on the STEAM approach is effectively used in science learning.

Acknowledgements. The authors gratefully acknowledge the financial support from BPI *(Indonesian Education Scholarship)*, PPAT *(Centre for Higher Education Funding and Assessment)* dan LPDP *(Indonesian Endowment Fund for Education)*.

References

1. Putra, T. T., Irwan, and Viononda, D.: Meningkatkan Kemampuan Berpikir Kreatif Siswa dengan Pembelajaran Berbasis Masalah. J. Pendidik. Mat. **1**(1), 22–26 (2012). https://adoc.pub/meningkatkan-kemampuan-berpikir-kreatif-siswa-dengan-pembela.html#google_vignette
2. Mu'minah, I.H., Suryaningsih, Y.: Implementasi STEAM (science, Technology, Engineering, Arts and Mathematics) dalam Pembelajaran Abad 21, 5(1), 65–73 (2020). https://www.jurnal.unma.ac.id/index.php/BE/article/view/2105

3. Salfina, A.H., Pasaribu, M.: Pengaruh Metode Mind Map terhadap Ketrampilan Berfikir Kreatif dan Kemampuan berkomunikasi tentang Fisika Siswa Kelas Vii SMP Negeri 1 Biromaru. e-Jurnal Mitra Sains **3**(2), 1–8, chromeextension://kdpelmjpfafjppnhbloffcjpeomlnpah/https://media.neliti.com/media/publications/152769-ID-pengaruh-metode-mind-map-terhadap-ketram.pdf (2015)
4. Dinantika, H.K., Suyanto, E., Dewa, I., Nyeneng, P.: Pengaruh Penerapan Model Pembelajaran Project Based Learning Terhadap Kreativitas Siswa Pada Materi Energi Terbarukan," 11(2), 73–80 (2019). https://doi.org/10.30599/jti.v11i2.473
5. Harizah, D.T.D., Sumarmi, Bachri, S.: Pengaruh model pembelajaran project based learning terhadap kreativitas dan hasil belajar geografi siswa. J. Pendidik. Teor. Penelitian, dan Pengemb. **6**(5), 015–2019. http://journal.um.ac.id/index.php/jptpp/EISSN: 2502-471X DOAJ-SHERPA/RoMEO-Google Scholar-IPI Jurnal (2021)
6. Rati, N.W., Kusmaryatni, N., Rediani, N.: Model Pembelajaran Berbasis Proyek, Kreativitas dan Hasil Belajar Mahasiswa. J. Pendidik. Indones **6**(1), 60–71 (2017). https://adoc.pub/model-pembelajaran-berbasis-proyek-kreativitas-dan-hasil-bel.html
7. Taufik, M., Sukmadinata, N.S., Abdulhak, I., Tumbelaka, B.Y.: Model Meningkatkan Kemampuan Pemecahan Masalah Dalam Pembelajaran IPA (FISIKA) sekolah menengah pertama di kota. Berk. Fis. **13**(2), 31–44 (2010). https://www.researchgate.net/publication/277787205
8. Wisudawati, A.W., Sulistyowati, E.: Metodologi pembelajaran IPA. Jakarta: Bumi Aksara (2022)
9. Harahap, S.: Identifikasi Kreativitas Siswa Terhadap Mata Pelajaran IPA. Integr. Sci. Educ. J. **1**(1), 16–22 (2020). https://doi.org/10.37251/isej.v1i1.21
10. Dewanti, B.A.: Comparing student creativity skills in experiment-based and project- based science learning. Prism. Sains J. Pengkaj. Ilmu dan Pembelajaran Mat. dan IPA IKIP Mataram 10(3), 786–794 (2022). https://ejournal.undikma.ac.id/index.php/prismasains/article/download/5348/3594
11. Lee, C.: Worksheet Usage, Reading Achievement, Classes' Lack of Readiness, and Science Achievement : A Cross-Country Comparison. Int. J. Educ. Math. Sci. Technol. **2**(2), 96–106 (2014). chrome-extension://kdpelmjpfafjppnhbloffcjpeomlnpah/https://files.eric.ed.gov/fulltext/EJ1066356.pdf, (2014)
12. Nyamupangedengu, E., Lelliott, A.D.: An exploration of learners ' use of worksheets during a science museum visit An exploration of learners' use of worksheets during a science museum visit. African. J. Res. Math. Sci. Technol. Education **16**(1), 85–99 (2015). https://doi.org/10.1080/10288457.2012.10740731
13. Ghufron, S.: Development of Electronic Student Worksheets (E-LKPD) Based on Stad-Type Cooperative Learning on Writing Materials **10**(5), 128–135 (2023). https://doi.org/10.51244/IJRSI
14. Martatiyana, D. R., Nasbey, H., Utami, N.C.M.: Praktikalitas E-LKPD Berbasis STEM-PjBL dalam Pembelajaran IPA Fase B **10**(1), 57–66 (2024). https://doi.org/10.31602/muallimuna.v10i1.15771
15. Haifaturrahmah, Hidayatullah, R., Maryani, S., Nurmiwati: Pengembangan Lembar Kerja Siswa Berbasis STEAM untuk Siswa Sekolah Dasar **6**(2), 310–318 (2020). http://ojs.ikipmataram.ac.id/index.php/jurnalkependidikan/index Juli
16. Mariyana, W.S., Haryanto: Based E-LKPD development based problem based learning to improve students' Creative Thinking Skills on Acid-Base Material **15**(2), 163–169 (2023). https://doi.org/10.24114/jpkim.v15i2.48264
17. Herlina, R., Hasri: Efektivitas Penggunaan e- Modul Berbasis STEAM Pada Materi Sistem Koloid untuk Meningkatkan Hasil Belajar Peserta Didik Kelas XI SMAN 6 Enrekang. Pros. Semin. Nas. Pendidik. IPA II "Optimalisasi Literasi Digit. melalui Pendekatan STEM **1**(1), 63–70 (2021). https://doi.org/10.26858/semnaspendipa.v1i1.30546

18. Annisa, R., Effendi, M.H., Damris, D.: Peningkatan Kemampuan Berpikir Kreatif Siswa Dengan Menggunakan Model Project Based Learning Berbasis Steam (Science, Technology, Engineering, Arts Dan Mathematic) Pada Materi Asam Dan Basa Di Sman 11 Kota Jambi. J. Indones. Soc. Integr. Chemistry **10**(2), 14–22 (2019). https://doi.org/10.22437/jisic.v10i2.6517,
19. Ayva, O.: Developing Students' Ability to Read, Understand, and Analyze Scientific Data through the Use of Worksheet that Focus on Studing Historical Documents. **46**(2012), 5128–5132 (2012). https://doi.org/10.1016/j.sbspro.2012.06.395
20. Saputro, R., Setiawan, D., Saragih, D.: The Development of Students Worksheet (SW) based on Inquiry to Improve Activity and Learning Outcomes in Civic Lesson of Students Grade VII. Proc. 1st Int. Conf. Soc. Sci. Interdiscip. Stud. (ICSSIS 2018) **208**(1), 299–304. https://doi.org/10.2991/icssis-18.2019.62, (2019)
21. Subhan, M., Oktolita, N.: Developing Worksheet (LKS) Base on Process Skills in Curriculum 2013 at Elementary School Developing Worksheet (LKS) Base on Process Skills in Curriculum 2013 at Elementary School Grade IV, V, VI. IOP Conf. Ser. Mater. Sci. Eng. **335**(2018), 1–8 (2018). https://doi.org/10.1088/1757-899X/335/1/012108

The Effect of Interactive Learning Multimedia on Learning Motivation and Student Achievement

Dewi Bernike Tampubolon(✉) and Yenji Betaria Sonata Tampubolon

Universitas Negeri Medan, North Sumatra, Indonesia
ibernike7@gmail.com

Abstract. This study aims to evaluate the effectiveness of interactive learning multimedia on students' learning motivation and achievement. By involving 42 junior high school teachers as respondents, this study analyzed five main aspects: (1) students' learning motivation, (2) students' involvement in learning, (3) material understanding and learning achievement, (4) teachers' perception of interactive multimedia, and (5) the impact of multimedia on students. Data were obtained through interviews and questionnaires, which were then analyzed descriptively qualitatively. The results showed that 80% of teachers reported an increase in student learning motivation with multimedia, while 85% of teachers observed an increase in student involvement during learning. A total of 78% of teachers also reported an increase in students' understanding of the material, with 70% of teachers noting an increase in learning achievement. Perceptions of the interactive multimedia were very positive, with 90% of teachers rating it as effective in creating engaging learning. Overall, 80% of teachers saw a positive influence of multimedia on students' learning attitudes. These findings confirm that interactive multimedia can improve the quality of learning and student learning outcomes, although a balanced approach is needed to optimize its effectiveness without creating dependency, and of course it must also adapt the learning model used and the learning environment.

Keywords: Interactive multimedia · Learning motivation · Student engagement · Material understanding · Learning achievement

1 Introduction

In this digital era, educational technology has developed rapidly and it is changing the way teaching and learning is done. The use of interactive multimedia, including videos, animations, simulations and educational games in learning allows students to interact with the material through various media, which has proven to be effective in increasing student engagement and understanding. According to Mayer (2009), interactive multimedia has great potential to facilitate better information processing, as it involves students' visual and auditory channels at once. This is in line with the cognitive processing theory of multimedia which states that learning will be more effective when students receive information through multiple sensory pathways.

K. W. Lee and L. H. Wong (Eds.): ITEA 2025, CCIS 2643, pp. 286–293, 2026.
https://doi.org/10.1007/978-981-95-2011-4_26

Learning motivation has an important role in the success of student learning. Motivation, both intrinsic and extrinsic, affects student engagement in learning and increases the desire to achieve better academic performance (Deci & Ryan, 2000). Research conducted by Schunk, Pintrich, and Meece (2008) shows that technology-based learning, especially interactive multimedia, can increase students' learning motivation through a more engaging and personalized learning experience. Technology-based learning provides experiences that facilitate deeper student engagement and reduce boredom that often occurs in conventional learning methods (Selwyn, 2011).

In terms of learning achievement, research shows that learning with interactive multimedia not only helps students understand the material better but also improves critical thinking and analysis skills (Clark & Mayer, 2016). Students who learn with interactive multimedia tend to get better academic results compared to students who learn with traditional methods, because this media allows them to learn according to their own style and rhythm (Alessi & Trollip, 2001). With interactive features, multimedia allows students to construct their own understanding through active exploration.

This research focuses on "The Effectiveness of Interactive Learning Multimedia on Students' Learning Motivation and Learning Achievement." The purpose of this study is to examine the impact of using interactive multimedia on students' motivation and learning achievement, hoping to contribute to the educational technology literature and offer practical insights for classroom application. Based on this study, it is expected that the application of interactive multimedia can be used as an effective strategy in improving the quality of education in the digital era.

2 Methods

2.1 Research Design

This study used a qualitative approach with interview techniques. This technique is considered to help the researchers to obtain information about perspective in-depth and comprehensively. The interview questions were divided into two parts, in which the first part focuses on the demographic information of the respondents, while the second part focuses on answering the following 5 research aspects: 1) learning motivation, 2) student engagement in learning, 3) material understanding and learning achievement, 4) perception of Interactive Multimedia, and 5) the effect of multimedia on students.

2.2 Data Collection

From November September - October 2024, we invited junior high school teachers to participate in the current research through social media. A total of 42 early childhood teachers from Indonesia were accepted to be interviewed. The information about respondents can be seen in Table 1. The interview process was carried out online with a duration of about 20-30 min using Google Forms to record the answers.

Table 1. Profiles of respondents.

Personal Details	Category	Number	Percentage
Age	<25 years 25 - 33 years 34 - 42 years 43 - 51 years >51 years	1 22 15 3 1	2.38 52.38 35.71 7.14 2.38
Years of teaching experiences	1–5 years 6–10 years 11–15 years >15 years	5 25 9 3	11.90 59.52 21.42 7.14
Gender	Male Female	6 36	14.28 85.71
Geographic location	Medan Deli Serdang Karo District Langkat Toba District	11 20 5 4 2	26.19 47.61 11.90 9.52 4.76

2.3 Data Analysis

The data were analyzed using thematic coding techniques. This analysis process focused on determining the main themes from all respondents' answers. First, all interview transcripts were grouped based on the five main aspects. From these aspects, the main themes will be organized to provide an overview of the effect of interactive multimedia on student motivation and learning achievement. Then second, the results of the answers that have been grouped were then read many times to determine the theme category (each respondent may provide one response, more than one response, or no response at all). Third, the connection between each respondents' answers was further checked. These three processes were done manually by all authors to minimize subjectivity. Validity in this research was done through data triangulation, by comparing the results of interviews and observations. Reliability is done by member-checking, which involves participants to reconfirm the results of the interview to ensure the data obtained is accurate and represents their views.

3 Results

3.1 Learning Motivation

The results indicate that 80% of the teachers observed an improvement in students' motivation when interactive multimedia was incorporated into lessons, as shown in Table 2. These teachers noted that students displayed increased enthusiasm, particularly for subjects that were previously challenging or less engaging for them. However, 20% of teachers felt that while multimedia could enhance motivation for some students, others required additional support to remain engaged.

Table 2. Learning Motivation

Question	Mean Score	% of Agree (4 & 5)
How often do students show increased interest in learning when interactive multimedia is used?	4.3	80%
Does the multimedia content make students feel more motivated to complete their assignments?	4.1	75%
Do students seem more enthusiastic about attending class when multimedia is included?	4.3	80%

The data for each question uses a 5-point Likert scale (1 = Strongly Disagree, 5 = Strongly Agree).

3.2 Student Engagement in Learning

Among the respondents, 85% reported higher student engagement levels when using interactive multimedia as shown in Table 3. Teachers observed that students were more active in class discussions and willing to collaborate with peers when lessons included multimedia elements. The remaining 15% reported mixed results, mentioning that a few students could be distracted by the multimedia itself rather than focusing on the content.

Table 3. Student engagement in learning

Question	Mean Score	% of Agree (4 & 5)
Do students participate more actively in class discussions with multimedia?	4.4	85%
Does multimedia encourage students to collaborate more with peers?	4.0	70%
Are students more focused on tasks when using interactive multimedia?	4.3	82%

The data for each question uses a 5-point Likert scale (1 = Strongly Disagree, 5 = Strongly Agree).

3.3 Material Understanding and Learning Achievement

A total of 78% of teachers reported that interactive multimedia facilitated a clearer understanding of complex material among students as shown in Table 4. Many teachers observed improvements in students' abilities to grasp abstract concepts and remember content more effectively. Regarding learning achievement, 70% of teachers noted increased scores on assessments following multimedia use, whereas 30% indicated no significant changes, highlighting a need for consistent alignment of multimedia with assessment goals.

Table 4. Material Understanding and Learning Achievement

Question	Mean Score	% of Agree (4 & 5)
Does multimedia improve students' understanding of difficult concepts?	4.3	78%
Have you observed an increase in test scores after using multimedia in teaching?	4.0	70%
Do students retain information better when taught with interactive multimedia?	4.2	76%

The data for each question uses a 5-point Likert scale (1 = Strongly Disagree, 5 = Strongly Agree).

3.4 Perception of Interactive Multimedia

A strong majority of teachers (90%), as shown in Table 5, held positive perceptions of interactive multimedia, viewing it as a valuable tool that makes learning more dynamic and reduces monotony. Teachers found multimedia particularly effective in breaking down complex topics and promoting visual learning. However, 10% expressed concerns about students' potential over-reliance on multimedia, cautioning that it may weaken traditional learning skills, such as reading comprehension and independent analysis.

Table 5. Perception of Interactive Multimedia

Question	Mean Score	% of Agree (4 & 5)
Do you feel that interactive multimedia is an effective tool for improving learning experiences?	4.5	90%
Does multimedia make it easier to explain complex topics?	4.6	88%
Do you find multimedia beneficial for creating a more dynamic learning environment?	4.6	90%

The data for each question uses a 5-point Likert scale (1 = Strongly Disagree, 5 = Strongly Agree).

3.5 The Effect of Multimedia on Students

The majority (80%) of teachers as shown in Table 6, reported that multimedia had a positive influence on students' attitudes toward learning. Teachers noted that students exhibited increased confidence, participation, and autonomy when multimedia was incorporated. However, 20% of teachers observed that some students became dependent on multimedia presentations and struggled to engage in lessons without it, suggesting a potential need to balance multimedia use with other teaching approaches.

Table 6. The Effect of Multimedia on Students

Question	Mean Score	% of Agree (4 & 5)
Do students show greater confidence in their learning after using multimedia?	4.0	70
Do you think multimedia positively influences students' attitudes toward learning?	4.2	80
Do students become more independent learners with the use of multimedia?	4.1	75

The data for each question uses a 5-point Likert scale (1 = Strongly Disagree, 5 = Strongly Agree).

4 Discussion

4.1 Learning Motivation

The findings reveal a significant correlation between the use of interactive multimedia and enhanced learning motivation among students. This aligns with motivational theories that suggest visually engaging materials can boost intrinsic interest. The 80% of teachers who observed positive outcomes emphasize that multimedia adds an element of novelty and excitement, making learning more appealing. For students who did not respond as positively, it may indicate that personalized approaches and scaffolding could further support motivation alongside multimedia use.

4.2 Student Engagement in Learning

The substantial increase in engagement noted by 85% of teachers underscores the potential of multimedia to facilitate active learning environments. These findings support the theory of active engagement, which posits that interactive elements can enhance participation and attention. However, the 15% who noted potential distractions suggest that multimedia should be carefully curated to ensure that it supports, rather than distracts from, the core learning objectives. Integrating interactive elements in a structured manner could mitigate potential issues with focus.

4.3 Material Understanding and Learning Achievement

The use of multimedia in simplifying complex concepts proved beneficial, as reflected in the 78% of teachers who reported enhanced material comprehension among students. According to cognitive theory, multimedia can help in dual coding by providing both visual and verbal representations, thereby aiding memory retention. The observed improvement in learning achievement for 70% of students highlights the potential of multimedia to reinforce learning outcomes. However, the 30% without notable improvement suggests the importance of aligning multimedia with assessment objectives to ensure that knowledge is both retained and demonstrable in tests or evaluations.

4.4 Perception of Interactive Multimedia

The overwhelmingly positive perception (90%) among teachers indicates that multimedia is broadly accepted as an effective teaching tool that makes learning enjoyable and varied. This high approval is consistent with research suggesting that multimedia can enhance teacher satisfaction by enabling diverse instructional strategies. The concerns from the remaining 10% about over-reliance highlight the importance of balanced multimedia use, so that students develop well-rounded skills in traditional areas such as reading and critical thinking.

4.5 The Effect of Multimedia on Students

The findings in this category reveal that the majority (80%) of teachers observed a positive shift in students' learning attitudes due to multimedia use, including increased confidence and independence. This aligns with self-determination theory, which suggests that autonomy-supportive tools like multimedia can empower students to take greater ownership of their learning. Conversely, the 20% who noted dependency concerns underscore the need for instructional balance. Integrating multimedia with other teaching techniques can ensure students remain adaptable, capable of engaging across various learning formats.

5 Conclusion

This study concludes that interactive learning multimedia has a positive impact on multiple facets of the learning process, including student motivation, engagement, understanding of material, and overall achievement. Feedback from 42 teachers highlights that multimedia enhances the learning experience by making content more engaging and accessible, with 80% observing increased motivation and 85% noting higher student engagement levels. Additionally, 78% of teachers reported that multimedia supported students in understanding complex topics, and 70% observed improvements in student achievement. Teachers overwhelmingly perceived interactive multimedia as an effective tool for modernizing and enriching classroom instruction. However, they also highlighted the importance of balancing multimedia use with other instructional methods to foster a well-rounded skill set in students, preventing dependency on digital tools alone.

Overall, this research suggests that integrating interactive multimedia can significantly enhance learning outcomes. To maximize its effectiveness, educators should ensure that multimedia is aligned with curriculum objectives and paired with various instructional approaches to cultivate both digital and critical thinking skills. Further research could explore specific multimedia elements that most effectively contribute to these positive outcomes and how multimedia can be tailored to meet diverse student needs in various learning contexts.

Acknowledgments. The authors gratefully acknowledge the financial support from Lembaga Pengelola Dana Pendidikan (LPDP), Ministry of Finance, Republic of Indonesia.

References

Alessi, S.M., Trollip, S.R.: Multimedia for learning: Methods and development. Allyn and Bacon, Boston (2001)

Aloraini, S.I.: The impact of using multimedia on students' academic achievement in the College of Education at King Saud University. J. King Saud Univ. – Lang. Translation **24**(2), 75–82 (2012)

Astleitner, H., Wiesner, C.: An integrated model of multimedia learning and motivation. J. Educ. Multimed. Hypermedia **13**(1), 3–21 (2004)

Clark, R.C., Mayer, R.E.: E-Learning and the Science of Instruction: Proven Guidelines for Consumers and Designers of Multimedia Learning. Wiley, Hoboken, NJ (2016)

Deci, E.L., Ryan, R.M.: Intrinsic and extrinsic motivations: classic definitions and new directions. Contemp. Educ. Psychol. **25**(1), 54–67 (2000)

Doolittle, P.E.: Multimedia learning: Empirical results and practical applications. TechTrends **46**(5), 38–43 (2002)

Fredricks, J.A., Blumenfeld, P.C., Paris, A.H.: School engagement: Potential of the concept, state of the evidence. Rev. Educ. Res. **74**(1), 59–109 (2004)

Hattie, J., Yates, G.C.: Visible Learning and the Science of How We Learn. Routledge (2014)

Creswell, J.W.: Research design: Qualitative, quantitative, and mixed methods approaches. SAGE Publications, Thousand Oaks (2003)

Liu, Y., Szabo, Z.: Teachers' attitudes toward technology integration in schools: a four-year study. Teachers and Teaching: Theory and Practice **15**(1), 5–23 (2009)

Mayer, R.E.: Multimedia Learning. Cambridge University Press (2009)

Moreno, R., Mayer, R.E.: Interactive multimodal learning environments: Special issue on interactive learning environments: contemporary issues and trends. Educ. Psychol. Rev. **19**(3), 309–326 (2007)

Reeve, J.: A Self-determination Theory Perspective on Student Engagement. In: Christenson, S.L., Reschly, A.L., Wylie, C. (eds.) Handbook of Research on Student Engagement, pp. 149–172. Springer (2012)

Boyatzis, R.E.: Transforming qualitative information: Thematic analysis and code development. Thousand Oaks, CA: SAGE (1998)

Schunk, D.H., Pintrich, P.R., Meece, J.L.: Motivation in Education: Theory, Research, and Applications. Pearson Education (2008)

Selwyn, N.: Education and Technology: Key Issues and Debates. Continuum International Publishing Group (2011)

Zimmerman, B.J.: Attaining self-regulation: A social cognitive perspective. In: Boekaerts, M., Pintrich, P.R., Zeidner, M. (eds.) Handbook of Self-Regulation, pp. 13–39. Academic Press (2000)

Application of Learning Media Using Google Site in the Subject of Al-Qur'an Hadith at Madrasah Aliyah Negeri 1 Medan

Rika Lasmini Ritonga(✉), Abdul Hamid K, and Dewi Endriani

Universitas Negeri Medan, Medan, Indonesia
rikalasminiritonga@gmail.com

Abstract. This study explores the implementation of Google Site as a digital learning medium to enhance students' learning outcomes and motivation in the Qur'an and Hadith subject at Madrasah Aliyah Negeri (MAN) 1 Medan. Employing a quasi-experimental design with a nonequivalent control group, the research involved 37 eleventh-grade students in the experimental group. The data were collected through pre-tests and post-tests, motivation questionnaires, and observations. Findings revealed a significant increase in both cognitive achievement and learning motivation. The average motivation score improved from 68.4 (moderate) to 87.6 (high), while the average achievement score rose from 72.1 to 89.0, surpassing the school's Minimum Mastery Criteria. The normalized gain score (N-Gain) of 0.61 for both variables indicates a high level of improvement. The results suggest that Google Site, with its interactive features and multimedia integration, provides an effective platform for student-centered learning, contributing positively to student engagement and academic performance.

Keywords: Google Site · Learning Media · Qur'an and Hadith · Student · Motivation · Learning Achievement

1 Introduction

The advancement of technology in the era of the Industrial Revolution 5.0 has brought significant changes across various sectors, including the field of education. Technology now functions not merely as a supporting tool but as an integral part of creating a more engaging, adaptive learning environment that aligns with the characteristics of the digital native generation. In modern educational approaches, student- centered learning is increasingly prioritized, where learners are encouraged to actively construct their own understanding and knowledge (Sevtia et al., 2022).

Madrasah Aliyah Negeri (MAN) 1 Medan, as one of the leading Islamic senior high schools in Medan City, has demonstrated a strong commitment to delivering interactive and contemporary education. Teachers at the school have utilized learning media such as PowerPoint presentations and YouTube videos to support the delivery of material in a more systematic and visual manner. Nevertheless, the integration of digital technology

K. W. Lee and L. H. Wong (Eds.): ITEA 2025, CCIS 2643, pp. 294–301, 2026.
https://doi.org/10.1007/978-981-95-2011-4_27

in the learning process still holds considerable potential for further development, particularly in terms of creating learning media that promote two-way interaction and greater student engagement.

Preliminary observations in the Qur'an and Hadith subject, specifically in class XI Science B-2, revealed that most students have not yet achieved optimal learning outcomes. Out of 36 students, only 25% met the Minimum Mastery Criteria (KKM) of 78. In addition, students' learning motivation was found to be relatively low, as indicated by their limited participation during lessons. This suggests that the existing learning media need to be enhanced to better capture students' interest and cater to their learning preferences.

One innovative alternative that can be adopted is the use of Google Sites as a digital learning platform. This platform enables teachers to present content in various formats text, images, videos, and even interactive quizzes that students can access anytime and anywhere. Besides improving flexibility, Google Sites also supports integration with other Google services such as Google Drive, Docs, and Forms, thereby enriching learning resources and activities.

Previous studies have shown that web-based media like Google Sites can significantly enhance students' motivation, understanding, and active participation in the learning process (Nurliswati & Nurlizawati, 2022; Munawaroh & Indah, 2022). Given the adequate technological infrastructure and the digital-native characteristics of students at MAN 1 Medan, the implementation of Google Sites holds great potential to support a more effective and enjoyable learning experience.

Based on this background, this article aims to explore the implementation of Google Sites as a learning medium to improve students' comprehension and academic performance in the Qur'an and Hadith subject at MAN 1 Medan.

2 Methods

2.1 Research Design

This study applied a quantitative research approach using a quasi-experimental design, specifically the Nonequivalent Control Group Design. This type of design was chosen because the sample groups were not randomly assigned but selected based on specific considerations and similarities in academic background.

The research was conducted at Madrasah Aliyah Negeri (MAN) 1 Medan, with the population consisting of five eleventh-grade classes (Grade XI). From this population, one class XI Science B-2 was purposively selected to serve as the experimental group, comprising 37 students. This group received instruction using Google Site-based learning media, while another class (not detailed in this design) was designated as the control group using conventional teaching methods.

The learning process was carried out over four meetings. Both the experimental and control groups were given a pre-test prior to the treatment and a post-test after the instructional period to assess students' cognitive learning outcomes. In addition to the tests, a learning motivation questionnaire was administered before and after the intervention to measure changes in student motivation. Observations were also conducted during the teaching sessions to record student engagement and participation.

The structure of the research design is represented as follows:

Group	Pre-test	Treatment	Post-test
Experimental	O_1	X (Google Site-based instruction)	O_2

Legend:
O_1 = Pre-test
O_2 = Post-test
X = Learning intervention using Google Site

This design enabled the researcher to measure the effectiveness of Google Site as a learning medium by comparing students' performance before and after the implementation. The pre-test and post-test results, along with questionnaire responses and observational data, were analyzed to evaluate the impact of the digital learning media on students' achievement and motivation in the subject of Qur'an and Hadith.

2.2 Data Collection

The data collection process in this study was conducted through test-ing, questionnaires, and observation. The primary objective was to gather data on students' learning outcomes and learning motivation before and after the implementation of the Google Site-based learning media.

The population of this study consisted of five classes of eleventh-grade students (Grade XI) at Madrasah Aliyah Negeri (MAN) 1 Medan. From this population, one class was selected as the sample using a purposive sampling technique. The selected class, XI Science B-2, consisted of 37 students, who participated in the research as the experimental group.

The data collection instruments used in this study included:

a. A pre-test and post-test, which were administered to measure students' cognitiv learning outcomes before and after the learning intervention.
b. A learning motivation questionnaire, distributed at both the beginning and end of the learning cycle to evaluate any changes in students' motivation levels.
c. An observation sheet, used by the researcher to monitor students' engagement, participation, and interaction during the implementation of the learning activities.

All instruments were developed based on relevant theoretical frameworks and validated by educational experts to ensure their reliability and appropriateness for the study. The data collected were then analyzed to determine the effectiveness of the Google Site-based learning media in improving both student achievement and motivation.

2.3 Data Analysis

The data analysis in this study involved a systematic process to ensure the validity, reliability, and accuracy of the research results. All instruments used including the pre-test, post-test, motivation questionnaire, and observation sheet were first validated through expert judgment to establish content validity. Experts in Islamic education and instructional design reviewed the items to ensure that they aligned with the learning objectives and effectively measured students' cognitive outcomes and motivation. Revisions were made based on their feedback to improve clarity and relevance. For the cognitive test, item analysis was conducted to determine the level of difficulty and discrimination power of each item. The results of this analysis were used to select the most appropriate items for measuring student performance accurately.

To establish instrument reliability, internal consistency was tested using statistical formulas appropriate for each instrument. The reliability of the motivation questionnaire was calculated using Cronbach's Alpha, while the reliability of the multiple-choice cognitive test was assessed using the Kuder-Richardson Formula 20 (KR-20). Both coefficients met the acceptable threshold of 0.70, indicating that the instruments were statistically reliable. After the instruments were validated and proven reliable, quantitative data were analyzed using inferential and descriptive statistics. A normality and homogeneity test was performed to determine whether the data met parametric assumptions, followed by an independent sample t-test to assess significant differences between pre-test and post-test scores. In addition, gain score analysis was used to measure the extent of improvement in learning outcomes, while descriptive statistics were used to analyze changes in students' learning motivation. This comprehensive approach allowed the researcher to draw valid conclusions regarding the effectiveness of Google Site as a learning medium.

3 Results

This study aimed to investigate the effectiveness of using Google Site as a digital learning medium in improving students' learning outcomes and motivation in the Qur'an and Hadith subject. Data were collected through pre-test and post-test scores, learning motivation questionnaires, and observations. The results demonstrated a notable improvement in both cognitive achievement and motivational levels among the students who participated in the learning intervention using Google Site.

Learning Motivation. Learning motivation was assessed through a structured questionnaire distributed before and after the learning intervention. The pre-test average score of students' motivation was 68.4, indicating a moderate level of motivation. After the implementation of Google Site-based learning, the post-test average increased significantly to 87.6, which falls into the high motivation category. The improvement in students' motivation can be attributed to the interactive elements available on Google Site, such as embedded videos, visual materials, self-paced navigation, and digital quizzes. These features created a more engaging and student-centered learning environment, increasing students' enthusiasm and active participation during the learning process.

Learning Achievement. The improvement in students' cognitive learning outcomes was measured using a multiple-choice test administered before and after the intervention. The average pre-test score was 72.1, which is below the school's Minimum Mastery Criteria (KKM) of 78. After the learning process using Google Site, students achieved an average post-test score of 89.0, surpassing the expected competency level. This significant increase indicates that Google Site provided an effective platform for delivering learning materials in a format that students found accessible, interactive, and easy to understand.

Gain Score Analysis. To measure the effectiveness of the learning media, a normalized gain (N-Gain) score was calculated for both variables. As shown in Table 1, the gain score for learning motivation and learning achievement was 0.61, categorized as a high level of improvement based on Hake's classification. This reinforces the conclusion that Google Site was not only beneficial in enhancing students' academic performance but also in fostering a more motivated and active learning attitude.

Table 1. Summary of Students' Learning Motivation and Learning Achievement (Experimental Group)

No	Variable	Pre-Test Mean	Post-Test Mean	Gain Score	Category
1	Learning Motivation	68.4	87.6	0.61	Increased (High)
2	Learning Achievement	72.1	89.0	0.61	Increased (High)

Here is the visual comparison of pre-test and post-test scores for both learning motivation and learning achievement. The graph clearly illustrates the significant improvement in both variables after the implementation of Google Site-based learning.

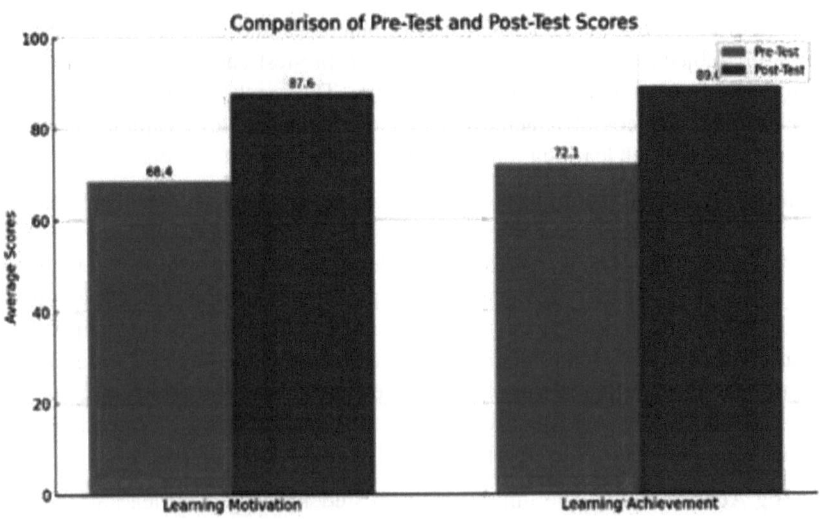

4 Discussion

The results of this study indicate that the use of Google Site as a learning medium significantly influenced both students' learning motivation and academic achievement in the Qur'an and Hadith subject. This section discusses the implications of these findings in relation to existing theories and previous research.

Learning Motivation

The notable increase in students' learning motivation after the implementation of Google Site reflects the effectiveness of digital plat-forms in creating engaging learning environments. Prior to the inter-vention, students showed moderate levels of motivation, with some exhibiting boredom or lack of focus during traditional classroom sessions. However, the use of Google Site introduced interactive components such as videos, images, hyperlinks, and self-paced quizzes that allowed students to take more control over their learning experience. This aligns with the concept of student-centered learning, where learners are actively involved and have autonomy in how they engage with educational content. The findings also support the study by Munawaroh & Indah (2022), which showed that students' motivation increased when web-based media were integrated into classroom activities. The increase in motivation observed in this study suggests that the visual and navigational interactivity of Google Site played a key role in capturing students' attention, sustaining their interest, and promoting more meaningful participation.

Learning Achievement

In addition to improving motivation, the use of Google Site contributed to a significant enhancement in students' cognitive learning outcomes. The rise in the average post-test score from 72.1 to 89.0 demonstrates that students not only became more motivated but also developed a deeper understanding of the material. The platform's ability to combine textual explanations with audiovisual resources made it easier for students to grasp complex religious concepts presented in the Qur'an and Hadith. Furthermore, the flexibility offered by Google Site—allowing students to revisit materials and engage with learning content at their own pace—may have contributed to better retention and comprehension. This is consistent with the findings of Nurliswati & Nurlizawati (2022), who emphasized the pedagogical advantages of integrating multimedia in digital learning environments. From a theoretical perspective, the improvement in learning outcomes supports constructivist views that emphasize active knowledge construction through exploration and interaction with digital content. Therefore, the use of Google Site not only served as a delivery tool but also functioned as a catalyst for deeper and more effective learning.

5 Conclusion

This study aimed to explore the effectiveness of using Google Site as a digital learning medium to enhance students' learning motivation and achievement in the Qur'an and Hadith subject at Madrasah Aliyah Negeri (MAN) 1 Medan. The findings indicate that the integration of Google Site significantly improved both students' motivation and academic performance. Students showed a notable increase in their motivation, with the average motivation score rising from 68.4 to 87.6, reflecting a shift from moderate to high motivation levels. This can be attributed to the interactive features of Google Site, which made learning more engaging, flexible, and accessible.

Furthermore, students' learning achievement also improved, with the average post-test score increasing from 72.1 to 89.0, surpassing the Minimum Mastery Criteria (KKM) of 78. The positive impact on learning outcomes suggests that the interactive, multimedia elements of Google Site facilitated deeper understanding and retention of the material. The results of this study confirm that digital learning plat-forms, such as Google Site, are effective tools for fostering active learning environments that not only engage students but also enhance their academic performance.

The findings of this research contribute to the growing body of literature on the use of digital media in education, highlighting the potential of Google Site to improve both student motivation and learning achievement. As educational technology continues to evolve, it is crucial to explore and implement innovative learning tools that cater to the needs and preferences of digital-native students. This study also emphasizes the importance of integrating technology into educational practices to create a more interactive, student-centered learning experience.

Acknowledgments. The authors gratefully acknowledge the financial support from BPI (*Indonesian Education Scholarship)* PPAPT (*Center for Higher Education Funding and Assessment*) dan LPDP (*Indonesian Endowment Fund for Education*).

References

Barkati, H., Cahyadi, D.: Penggunaan media dalam proses pembelajaran di era digital. Jakarta: Literasi Nusantara (2024)
Munawaroh, S., Indah, F.: Efektivitas pengembangan media pembelajaran berbasis Google Site pada materi pendidikan agama Islam. Jurnal Teknologi Pendidikan **10**(1), 45–55 (2022)
Nurliswati, N., Nurlizawati, L.: Penerapan Google Site dalam pembelajaran interaktif: Studi kasus pada mata pelajaran Pendidikan Agama. Jurnal Inovasi Pendidikan Islam **8**(2), 132–141 (2022)
Sevtia, A., Rahayu, D., Yuliana, T.: Peran student-centered learning dalam meningkatkan keterlibatan siswa di kelas digital. Jurnal Pendidikan dan Teknologi **5**(3), 210–219 (2022)
Trianto, D.: Model pembelajaran terpadu: Konsep, strategi dan implementasinya dalam kurikulum tingkat satuan pendidikan (KTSP). Jakarta: Prestasi Pustaka (2018)
Azhar, A.S.: Revolusi digital dalam pendidikan: Tantangan dan peluang, 1st edn. Medan: Pustaka Mandiri (2021)
Chandra, M., Manoppo, P.: Enhancing student engagement through interactive media. J. Educ. Technol. **15**(3), 223–234 (2019)
Cohen, L., Manion, L., Morrison, K.: Research Methods in Education, 8th edn. Routledge, London (2018)
Conole, G.: Designing for Learning in an Open World. Springer (2020)
Keller, J.M.: Motivational Design for Learning and Performance: The ARCS Model Approach. Springer (2017)
Leedy, P.D., Ormrod, J.E.: Practical Research: Planning and Design, 12th edn. Pearson (2018)

Mayer, R.E.: Multimedia Learning (3rd ed.). Cambridge University Press (2019)
Moore, M.G., Kearsley, G.: Distance Education: A Systems View of Online Learning, 4th edn. Cengage Learning, Belmont (2020)
Roblyer, M.D., Doering, A.H.: Integrating Educational Technology into Teaching (7th ed.). Pearson (2020)
Smith, P.L., Ragan, T.J.: Instructional Design (5th ed.). Wiley (2021)
Wang, M.: Exploring the use of digital tools for educational improvement in high schools. J. Educ. Innov. **13**(2), 101–112 (2021)
Zimmerman, B.J.: Self-Regulated Learning and Academic Achievement: Theoretical Perspectives. Routledge (2020)

Image Processing Analysis of Preview Behavior of Average Students in Junior High School Mathematics Under the Remote Education Environment

Yuqi Wang(✉)

Shijiazhuang Yingteng Education Consulting Co., Ltd, Shijiazhuang 050000, Hebei, China
nuonuo567@126.com

Abstract. The purpose of this article is to explore the preview behavior of junior high school mathematics average students in the distance education environment, and make an in-depth analysis by using image processing technology. Aiming at the problem that students' learning behavior in distance education is difficult to observe directly, a preview behavior analysis method based on image processing is proposed. In this study, a data set containing the preview behavior images of junior high school mathematics average students is constructed, and then the convolutional neural network (CNN) is used for feature extraction and behavior classification to identify students' different preview behaviors. The results show that CNN model can accurately identify students' preview behavior categories and achieve high classification accuracy. Recurrent neural network (RNN) model also successfully predicted the students' future preview behavior trend, showing good prediction performance. By comparing different feature extraction methods, the advantages of CNN feature extraction are verified. The preview behavior analysis method based on image processing is feasible, which provides a new perspective for students' behavior analysis in the distance education environment.

Keywords: Distance education · Junior high school mathematics · Average students · Image processing

1 Introduction

As a new model in the field of education, distance education is changing the traditional teaching methods and students' study habits. As an important part of basic education, junior high school mathematics bears the task of imparting basic mathematics knowledge, and shoulders the important mission of cultivating students' logical thinking, abstract thinking and problem-solving ability [1]. In the actual teaching process, average students often face many difficulties in mathematics learning, such as lack of learning motivation, improper learning methods and weak self-monitoring ability [2]. These problems are particularly prominent in the distance education environment. The rise of distance education provides the possibility for the balanced distribution of educational resources, enabling more students to enjoy high-quality educational resources [3].

K. W. Lee and L. H. Wong (Eds.): ITEA 2025, CCIS 2643, pp. 302–312, 2026.
https://doi.org/10.1007/978-981-95-2011-4_28

Learning in the distance education environment has also brought new problems, such as the challenge of students' autonomous learning ability, the lack of teacher-student interaction and the lag of learning feedback [4]. For junior high school mathematics average students, these problems may further aggravate their difficulties in learning [5]. Distance education requires students to have higher autonomous learning ability, and average students often fail to perform well in this respect. The decrease of teacher-student interaction in distance education makes it difficult for average students to get help in time when they encounter learning difficulties, thus affecting their learning effect [6].

In the distance education environment, the preview behavior of average students often lacks effective supervision, which leads to poor preview effect. For this reason, how to improve the preview behavior of junior high school mathematics average students in the distance education environment has become an urgent problem to be solved. The purpose of this study is to analyze the preview behavior of junior high school mathematics average students in the distance education environment with the help of image processing technology, and to reveal the characteristics and patterns of their preview behavior.

2 Present Situation of Average Students' Preview Behavior

In the distance education environment, the learning characteristics of junior high school mathematics average students show a diversified trend. They are not only different from the top students, but also different from the below average students. They are in a relatively middle position, with a certain learning foundation and many challenges.

Preview before class is an important part of mathematics learning, which helps students to better understand and master knowledge in classroom learning. The data in Table 1 shows that students of different levels have significant differences in the completion of preview before class.

Table 1. Pre-class Preview Completion Rate

Group	100%	80%-99%	50%-79%	Below 50%
Top Students	18 (24%)	35 (46.67%)	15 (20%)	7 (9.33%)
Average Students	16 (21.33%)	25 (33.33%)	18 (24%)	16 (21.33%)
Below Average Students	7 (9.33%)	15 (20%)	22 (29.33%)	31 (41.33%)

Top students have a high degree of preparation before class, with 24% students being able to complete 100% preparation, while average students and below average students have a relatively low degree of preparation. Among average students, only 21.33% students can complete 100% preview, and more than 20% students' preview completion is less than 50%. Average students have obvious shortcomings in preview before class, so it is necessary to further strengthen the cultivation of preview habits.

Furthermore, the data reveals that a considerable portion of average students—over 45%—complete less than 80% of their pre-class preview. This inconsistent preparation behavior may be linked to several factors: lack of external motivation, limited self-discipline, unclear preview strategies, or low confidence in mathematical ability. Since average students are often overlooked in differentiated instruction strategies, they tend to drift without sufficient support or targeted guidance. Their preview habits are easily disrupted in the online learning environment due to distractions, insufficient supervision, and poor time management.

In addition, some average students reported in follow-up interviews that they do not understand how to preview effectively, treating it as a simple reading process rather than active learning. They often skip key steps such as attempting example problems or identifying difficult concepts before class. Therefore, to improve their mathematical performance, educators should provide explicit training on preview methods, integrate preview tasks into learning management systems, and offer timely feedback. By cultivating structured preview habits, average students can gradually improve their comprehension and participation in class, ultimately narrowing the achievement gap between them and top students.

Pre-class test is an important means to test students' preview effect. Table 2 also provides the distribution of pre-class test accuracy of different groups of students.

Table 2. Pre-class Quiz Accuracy

Group	100%	80%-99%	50%-79%	Below 50%
Top Students	20 (26.67%)	35 (46.67%)	12 (16%)	8 (10.67%)
Average Students	18 (24%)	23 (30.67%)	20 (26.67%)	14 (18.67%)
Below Average Students	7 (9.33%)	13 (17.33%)	16 (21.33%)	39 (52%)

The data shows that top students performed well in the pre-class test, with 26.67% students achieving 100% test accuracy, while average students and below average students had relatively low test accuracy. Among average students, only 24% students have a test accuracy of 100%, and more than 50% students have a test accuracy of less than 80%. The performance of below average students is even worse. Only 9.33% students have a test accuracy of 100%, and more than half of them have a test accuracy of less than 50%. This further confirms the shortcomings of average students in preview effect and their difficulties in mastering knowledge.

In addition, the data implies a clear correlation between students' academic performance level and their preview efficiency. Top students not only demonstrate a stronger ability to understand the pre-class content independently but also appear to engage more actively in the preview process. In contrast, the majority of below average students struggle to comprehend the material prior to class, which may hinder their in-class performance and overall academic progress. These findings highlight the necessity of differentiated instructional strategies. For example, providing additional preview guidance or scaffolding resources such as guided reading questions or short video explanations could help improve the preview effectiveness of average and below average students, thereby narrowing the performance gap and fostering a more inclusive learning environment.

Homework after class is an important link to consolidate classroom knowledge. Tables 3 and 4 also provide the distribution of the completion and accuracy of homework for different groups of students.

Table 3. Post-class Homework Completion Rate

Group	100%	80%-99%	50%-79%	Below 50%
Top Students	35 (46.67%)	30 (40%)	8 (10.67%)	2 (2.67%)
Average Students	12 (16%)	35 (46.67%)	16 (21.33%)	12 (16%)
Below Average Students	5 (6.67%)	10 (13.33%)	35 (46.67%)	25 (33.33%)

Table 4. Post-class Homework Accuracy

Group	100%	80%-99%	50%-79%	Below 50%
Top Students	17 (22.67%)	45 (60%)	8 (10.67%)	5 (6.67%)
Average Students	12 (16%)	32 (42.67%)	18 (24%)	13 (17.33%)
Below Average Students	5 (6.67%)	11 (14.67%)	20 (26.67%)	39 (52%)

In the completion of after-school homework, the performance of top students is still ahead, with 46.67% students being able to complete 100% homework. Average students' homework completion degree is relatively low, only 16% of students can complete 100% of their homework, and more than 15% of students' homework completion degree is less than 50%. Below average students have the lowest degree of homework completion, with only 6.67% of the students being able to complete 100% of their homework, and more than one third of the students having less than 50% of their homework completion.

In terms of the accuracy of homework after class, top students performed equally well, with 22.67% students' homework accuracy being 100%. Average students' homework accuracy is slightly lower than top students', but more than 40% students' homework accuracy is between 80% and 99%. Below average students' homework accuracy is the lowest, only 6.67% students' homework accuracy is 100%, and more than half students' homework accuracy is less than 50%.

Based on the above analysis, there are obvious deficiencies in the preview behavior of junior high school mathematics average students in the distance education environment. They are lower than top students in the completion of preview before class, the accuracy of test before class, the completion of homework after class and the accuracy of homework after class, and some indicators are even lower than below average students. Although the overall performance of below average students is worse, in some aspects, such as the low completion rate of after-school homework, below average students is not high because of its small base. This does not change the relative weakness of average students in preview behavior. Average students need to pay more attention to the preview link in the distance education environment to improve the preview effect.

3 Analysis Model of Average Students' Preview Behavior in Middle School Mathematics Based on Image Processing

In the distance education environment, analyzing the preview behavior of junior high school mathematics average students is helpful to understand students' learning habits and learning status, and can also provide strong support for teaching improvement [7]. In the distance education environment, students' preview behavior is often difficult to observe directly, but it can be analyzed indirectly with the help of the image data left by students in the preview process. For example, when students use electronic textbooks, watch teaching videos or finish preview homework, they will produce a lot of image data [8]. These data contain a wealth of preview behavior information. Image processing technology can effectively extract and analyze these data, thus revealing the characteristics of students' preview behavior [9]. As an advanced algorithm in the field of image processing, CNN has become an important tool to build a preview behavior analysis model with its excellent feature extraction and pattern recognition capabilities.

In the distance education environment, students' preview behavior data mainly comes from electronic textbooks, teaching videos and preview assignments. In the study, these data are collected by screen recording, camera monitoring or homework images submitted by students. The collected data should reflect students' preview behavior as comprehensively and accurately as possible. Pre-processing is the preliminary processing of collected image data to improve the accuracy and efficiency of subsequent feature extraction and behavior analysis. The preprocessing steps include image denoising, image enhancement, image segmentation and so on. In feature extraction, the key features that can reflect students' preview behavior are extracted from the preprocessed image data. These characteristics may include students' reading speed, concentration, operating frequency and so on.

CNN effectively reduces the number of network parameters by means of local connection and weight sharing, and can capture the local features in the data [10]. In the preview behavior analysis model, CNN is used to extract the features of the preprocessed image data. The convolution layer of CNN can capture the local features of the image, such as edges, corners and textures, by applying a series of learned filters directly to the input image [11]. These local features will further reduce the dimension and the number of parameters of the feature map, while maintaining the most important features. The fully connected layer combines the extracted features and outputs the final feature vector with the help of activation function.

Figure 1 shows the learning behavior image feature fusion mode. In this mode, firstly, the image data generated by students in the preview process are obtained by means of data collection steps. Then, the collected image data is preprocessed to improve the accuracy of subsequent feature extraction. In the feature extraction stage, the key features that can reflect students' preview behavior are extracted from the image by using the powerful feature extraction ability of CNN. These characteristics may include students' reading speed, page turning frequency, fixation point distribution and so on. In order to describe students' preview behavior more comprehensively, these features are fused to form a feature vector.

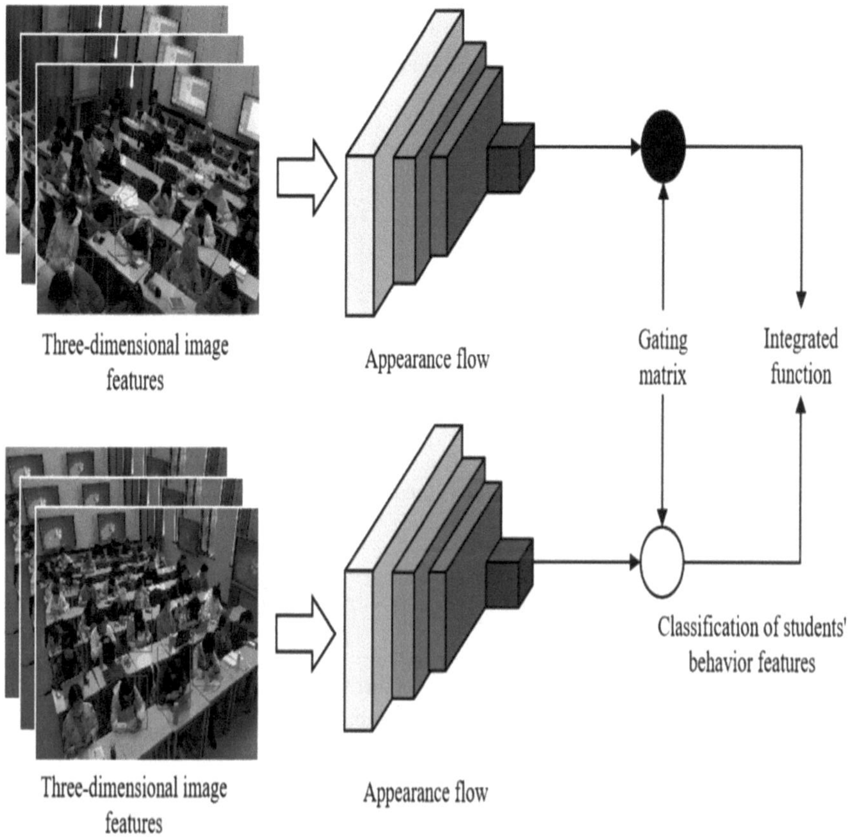

Fig. 1. Learning behavior image feature fusion mode

$$z = \sum_{i=1}^{n} w_i x_i + b \tag{1}$$

$$a = f(z) \tag{2}$$

Here, w_i represents the weight, x_i denotes the input, b stands for the bias, f is the activation function, z signifies the weighted input, and a is the neuron's output.

Figure 2 shows the principle of image enhancement based on CNN. In the distance education environment, due to the limitation of network transmission, equipment performance and other factors, the preview homework images submitted by students may have poor quality problems, such as blur and noise. In order to solve this problem, the image enhancement technology based on CNN is introduced. With the help of convolution layer, pooling layer and fully connected layer, CNN can learn the deep features in the image and enhance the image. After the input original image is processed by CNN, the enhanced image is output. The enhanced image has higher definition and contrast, which can better reflect the characteristics of students' preview behavior.

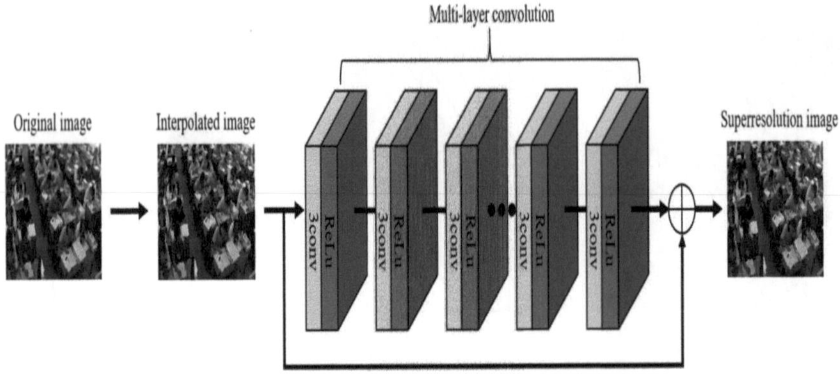

Fig. 2. Image enhancement based on CNN

If $x_i(t)$ is the input at time $o_j(t)$ and t is the output at time j, the state of neuron j can be expressed as:

$$o_j(t) = f\left\{\left[\sum_{i=1}^{n} \omega_{ij} x_i\left(t - \tau_{ij}\right)\right] - T_j\right\} \tag{3}$$

τ_{ij} denotes the synaptic delay, T_j the neuron threshold, ω_{ij} the weight from i to j, and $f(\cdot)$ the transfer function. Given τ_{ij} as the unit time, then:

$$o_j(t+1) = f\left\{\left[\sum_{i=1}^{n} \omega_{ij} x_i(t)\right] - T_j\right\} \tag{4}$$

The subscripts of input and output reflect the variety of modes for the neuron model's inputs and outputs, allowing us to leverage this model characteristic to address learning behavior recognition tailored to different needs. The neuron inputs at time t are given by the following formula:

$$net_{j'}(t) = \sum_{i=1}^{n} \omega_{ij} x_i(t) \tag{5}$$

The formula is only effective for $net_{j'}(t) > T_j$ neurons. Upon simplification, the neuron model transforms into:

$$o_j = f\left(net_j\right) = f\left(W_j^T X\right) \tag{6}$$

Finally, the model will output the analysis results. These results include students' preview behavior categories, preview behavior feature vectors, preview behavior prediction results and so on. Teachers can use these results to understand students' preview and adjust teaching strategies in time.

The convolution layer of CNN applies a series of learned filters, which can capture local features of images, such as edges, corners and textures. With the help of local connection and weight sharing, CNN reduces the number of network parameters, reduces the complexity of the model and improves the computational efficiency. In the training process, CNN also uses the back propagation algorithm to optimize the model parameters and learn the deep features in the input data, which has good generalization ability.

4 Experimental Results and Analysis

In order to verify the validity of the analysis model of junior high school mathematics average students' preview behavior based on image processing, we have carried out detailed simulation experiments. This section will systematically introduce the design idea, implementation process and simulation results of the experiment, and conduct in-depth analysis and discussion on the results.

4.1 Experimental Design

The preview behavior image data covering 200 junior high school mathematics average students were collected from a distance education platform. The data sources are extensive, including electronic textbook browsing, teaching video viewing, preview homework completion and other scenes, and the diversity of samples is ensured, covering students of different genders, grades and learning styles, so as to enhance the universality and representativeness of the experiment. The experiment was conducted on a high-performance computing server equipped with GPU acceleration, and TensorFlow was used to build, train and evaluate the CNN model. The data set is divided into training set (70%), verification set (15%) and test set (15%) to ensure the generalization ability of the model, and the performance of CNN model is optimized by careful hyperparameter tuning, including adjusting the number of convolution layers, filter size and learning rate.

4.2 Simulation Process

In the data preprocessing stage, the original image data is denoised, enhanced, cropped and normalized to improve the accuracy and stability of feature extraction. In the stage of feature extraction and behavior classification, the trained CNN model is used to extract features from the preprocessed image data to generate high-dimensional feature vectors, and SVM classifier is used to classify these feature vectors to identify students' preview behavior categories, such as careful preview, perfunctory preview and no preview. In the stage of behavior trend prediction, RNN model is trained based on historical preview behavior data to predict students' future preview behavior trend, and the parameters such as the number of hidden layers and units of RNN are adjusted to optimize the prediction performance. Finally, in the stage of result output and evaluation, the classification recognition and prediction results are output and compared with the actual data.

4.3 Experimental Results

It is not difficult to find from Table 5 that CNN model has achieved high accuracy, recall and F1 score in the classification and recognition of various preview behaviors, and the overall accuracy rate has reached 91.7%. This shows that the model can effectively identify students' preview behavior categories.

Table 5. CNN Model Classification Performance

Classification Category	Accuracy	Recall	F1 Score	Sample Size
Diligent Preview	95.0%	93.8%	94.4%	70
Perfunctory Preview	90.0%	88.5%	89.2%	60
No Preview	87.5%	86.0%	86.7%	50
Overall Accuracy	91.7%	-	-	180

It is not difficult to find from Table 6 that with the extension of the prediction time window, the accuracy of RNN model gradually decreases and the mean square error gradually increases. However, under the three-week forecast time window, the accuracy of the model still reached 80.0%. This shows that the model has a certain long-term forecasting ability.

Table 6. RNN Model Prediction Performance

Prediction Time Window	Accuracy	Mean Squared Error (MSE)	Sample Size
1 Week	88.0%	0.035	120
2 Weeks	84.0%	0.050	100
3 Weeks	80.0%	0.065	80

It is not difficult to find from Table 7 that CNN feature extraction method improves the classification accuracy and prediction accuracy of the model compared with manual feature extraction method. Although the training time is a little longer, the performance improvement is remarkable.

Table 7. Comparison of Different Feature Extraction Methods

Feature Extraction Method	Classification Accuracy	Prediction Accuracy	Training Time (Hours)
Handcrafted Features	75.0%	70.0%	2
CNN Features	91.7%	88.0%	4

This study focuses on the preview behavior of junior high school mathematics average students in the distance education environment, and analyzes it with the help of image processing technology. However, due to the limitations of research conditions and time, this study has certain limitations. There may be some deviation in the selection of samples, which cannot fully represent the average students in all distance education environments. The application of image processing technology may have limitations, which can not completely and accurately reflect students' preview behavior. Despite the above limitations, this study still has certain practical value. This article studies the preview behavior of junior high school mathematics average students under the distance education environment, hoping to provide useful reference for improving the distance education mode and improving the teaching effect.

5 Conclusions

Aiming at the preview behavior of junior high school mathematics average students in the distance education environment, this article proposes an analysis method based on image processing. With the help of constructing a data set containing rich and diverse preview behavior images, and using CNN to extract features and classify behaviors, this article studies students' preview behavior patterns.

The experimental results show that CNN model performs well in the task of classification and recognition of preview behavior, and achieves high accuracy, recall and F1 score. RNN model has also achieved good performance in previewing behavior trend prediction. By comparing different feature extraction methods, the superiority of CNN feature extraction method is further verified. It significantly improves the classification accuracy and prediction accuracy of the model. However, the experiment also has some limitations, such as the data set size can be further expanded and the classification category can be further refined.

In the future, we will continue to optimize the model, expand the application fields, and make greater contributions to the development of distance education and the in-depth study of students' behavior.

References

1. Liu, Z.W., Cui, N.P.: Strategies for improving the quality of learning support services at off-campus learning centers in modern distance education. Vocational Techn. Educ. **40**(20), 10–15 (2019)
2. Wu, Y., Shi, H.Y., Wang, Q., et al.: Analysis of AI image recognition method for monitoring outdoor activity time of primary school students. Chin. J. School Health **44**(8), 1178–1181 (2023)
3. Zeng, Y.Q., Liu, B., Zhong, B.C., et al.: Student classroom behavior detection algorithm based on improved YOLOv8 in smart education. Comput. Eng. **50**(9), 344–355 (2024)
4. Tan, S.Q., Tang, G.F., Tu, Y.Y., et al.: Student abnormal behavior detection system in classroom monitoring. Comput. Eng. Appl. **58**(7), 176–184 (2022)
5. Gao, X.D., Hao, X.K.: Machine vision-based student psychological intervention treatment and behavior monitoring system. Modern Electron. Technol. **43**(24), 63–66 (2020)

6. Xu, X.L., Zhang, J.Y.: Student classroom behavior recognition based on improved YOWO algorithm. Comput. Syst. Appl. **33**(4), 113–122 (2024)
7. Su, C., Wang, G.Z.: Research on student behavior recognition based on improved OpenPose. Appl. Res. Comput. **38**(10), 3183–3188 (2021)
8. Chen, C., Bao, W.X., Chen, X., et al.: DMS-YOLOv8: an improved YOLOv8 algorithm for student classroom behavior recognition. Comput. Eng. Appl. **60**(24), 222–234 (2024)
9. Zhu, X., Li, M.X., Zhang, X.F.: Research on student classroom behavior recognition based on deep neural networks. J. Jiangsu Univ. Sci. Technol. (Natural Science Edition) **37**(6), 72–76 (2023)
10. Huang, Y.K., Liang, M.Y., Wang, X.X., et al.: Multi-person classroom behavior recognition in teaching videos based on deep spatio-temporal residual convolutional neural networks. Comput. Appl. **42**(3), 736–742 (2022)
11. Liu, Z.G., Han, P.J.: Research and application of student classroom state recognition methods in teaching scenarios. Electron. Des. Eng. **31**(21), 180–185 (2023)

Bridging Tradition and Innovation the Cognitive and Emotional Impact of Randomness in AI-Generated Chinese Calligraphy

Kai Wang and Dongxing Yu(✉)

School of Education, Sanda University, Shanghai, China
yudongxing@sandau.edu.cn

Abstract. The study digs out the revolutionary impact introduced by AI randomness, especially focus on Chinese calligraphy influencing by models like Stable Diffusion. Though rooted by Confucianism, Taoism, and Buddhism, Chinese calligraphy philosophical principles of harmony and balance are changing a lot by AI integrating. The study shows that how this randomness affects traditional aesthetic values while produces creative possibilities,, thereby altering the cognitive and emotional engagement of viewers. Through a comparasion of traditional and AI-generated calligraphy, the study points out the popularity of calligraphy, making it more reachable to a global audience, including young generation. It also concerns the historical evolution of calligraphic aesthetics criteria, the role of cultural implicit meanings, and cross-cultural perceptions of AI-generated Chinese calligraphy. Key findings suggest that AI brings a deeper understanding of Chinese calligraphy skills rather than only introduces innovative ways of calligraphy producing,. The study underscores a balance between preserving cultural heritage and embracing technological innovation, proposing future research to explore the global implications of AI-generated art in connecting tradition and innovation.

Keywords: AI-Generated Calligraphy · Randomness in Art · Stable Diffusion Models · Cognitive-Emotional Aesthetics · Cross-Cultural Artistic Innovation

1 Introduction

1.1 Research Background and Significance

Under the strong impact of digital technology, the luster of handwritten calligraphy art has gradually faded, and Chinese calligraphy is no exception. The fast - paced modern life and the rapid rise of design software have led to the gradual forgetting of traditional calligraphy techniques as they fail to meet the needs of the times [1]. Computer fonts, which highly imitate handwritten calligraphy, blur the line between handwritten and digital calligraphy [2]. Coupled with the shift in public aesthetic tastes, the inheritance and development of calligraphy art and its philosophical connotations are facing unprecedented challenges [3].

K. W. Lee and L. H. Wong (Eds.): ITEA 2025, CCIS 2643, pp. 313–325, 2026.
https://doi.org/10.1007/978-981-95-2011-4_30

The advent of artificial intelligence has brought new hope to calligraphy art. Take Nullification as an example; it breaks the stroke rules of traditional calligraphy. By introducing random changes, it endows each calligraphy work with a unique visual effect [4]. Digital calligraphy exhibitions have broken the time - and space - bound limitations of traditional calligraphy dissemination and appreciation [5]. At the same time, the VR technology provides realistic creation scenes, stroke movements, and tactile sensations of paper. The application of Metaverse Intelligent Education Technology (MIET) has injected new vitality into the calligraphy teaching model, while tactile feedback technology makes the calligraphy learning experience more real and three - dimensional [6]. The deep integration of MIET technology and calligraphy not only provides new means for cultural heritage protection and global cross - cultural cooperation but also enhances students' learning interest, motivation, and cultural participation, enabling calligraphy art to adapt to the development needs of modern education [8, 9].

1.2 Research Objectives and Core Problem Statement

In the era of rapid development of artificial intelligence, the information dissemination mode of Chinese calligraphy has broken the norm. The randomness in AI - generated calligraphy works breaks the principles of harmony and balance that traditional calligraphy aesthetics follows, profoundly changing the audience's perception and emotional experience of calligraphy art [5, 10]. This study focuses on the randomness in computer - generated calligraphy, aiming to deeply explore its impact on traditional visual norms and how it shapes new psychological feelings, thereby uncovering the infinite possibilities of calligraphy creation at the intersection of AI thinking and human imagination.

By integrating the precision of computers with human instincts, we attempt to explore the subtleties behind these works. Uncertainty can trigger strong emotions and reshape the ways of creative expression and art appreciation. Exploring the convergence of AI thinking and human imagination can also inject new vitality into calligraphy through random creation. The study also finds that uncertain strokes not only challenge but can also enhance classic visuals and bring new perspectives to art creation in the Internet age.

1.3 Structure of the Study

This study will deeply analyze the impact of randomness in AI - generated Chinese calligraphy from multiple dimensions, including historical, psychological, and cross - cultural aspects. By tracing the development history of calligraphy aesthetics, comparing the cognitive differences between the East and the West regarding AI calligraphy, analyzing the relationship between psychological and emotional responses and randomness, this study reveals how randomness challenges and innovates traditional aesthetics. Finally, based on the research results, future research directions are proposed, aiming to deepen the understanding of AI - generated art in the context of global society and reveal the dynamic relationship among social expression, creativity, and technology.

2 Historical Evolution of Calligraphy Aesthetics

2.1 Aesthetic Traditions in Chinese Calligraphy

The aesthetic connotations of Chinese calligraphy have gradually formed four main styles in the long history: image - oriented, charm - oriented, rule - oriented, and intention - oriented. Image - oriented aesthetics originated from The Book of Changes. Oracle bone inscriptions imitate natural forms, full of the simple beauty of primitive art [11]. Charm - oriented aesthetics are deeply influenced by Zhuangzi's thoughts, pursuing a state of natural spontaneity. The Lanting Collection of Prefaces by Wang Xizhi is an excellent example of this style, with its soothing writing rhythm and natural and smooth brushwork fully demonstrating the elegance of literati [12, 13]. Rule - oriented aesthetics reached their peak in the creation of regular script in the Tang Dynasty, which was closely related to the imperial examination system at that time. It emphasized norms and preciseness, and Thirty - six Methods by Ouyang Xun became a classic work of this period [14]. Intention - oriented aesthetics prevailed in the Song Dynasty, with literati becoming the dominant force in creation. They pursued individual expression, and the works of calligraphers such as Su Shi and Huang Tingjian each had their own unique charm [14]. These styles are interrelated and have a continuous inheritance, fully demonstrating the strong adaptability and inheritance of Chinese calligraphy.

2.2 Cultural Connotations of Calligraphy

Calligraphy art is closely intertwined with the philosophical thoughts of Confucianism, Taoism, and Buddhism. It is not only an artistic expression but also a symbol of culture and spirit. Confucianism endows calligraphy with the meaning of self - cultivation. The rigorous structural aesthetics of regular script in the Tang Dynasty vividly reflects this concept. Taoism advocates nature, and the cursive scripts of Zhang Xu and Huai Su fully demonstrate the beauty of "inaction" [15]. Buddhist steles and Zen calligraphy have played an important role in the inheritance and development of calligraphy. In the Song Dynasty, literati integrated Zen thoughts into calligraphy creation, forming the unique "intention - oriented" style [16].

2.3 Evolution of Calligraphic Tools and Techniques

Traditional calligraphy creation depends on four major elements: the brush (毛笔, Máobǐ), ink(墨, Mò), paper (纸, Zhǐ), and inkstone (砚, Yàn). These elements work together to determine the final effect of the work. Calligraphy techniques include brushwork, character formation, and composition, and their evolution is closely related to the development of tools. From the early rough and simple fonts to the later delicate and smooth running and cursive scripts, each change in font reflects the innovation of tools and the transformation of aesthetic concepts. Today, new technologies represented by Stable Diffusion integrate traditional calligraphy with high - tech, expanding the boundaries of calligraphy creation and achieving a perfect combination of tradition and innovation.

3 Modern Aesthetic Psychology and Changes in SD Calligraphy

3.1 Trends in Modern Aesthetic Psychology

The development of digital technology has profoundly changed people's aesthetic psychology. Audiences are no longer satisfied with a single art form. They seek to gain pleasure from "the eyes and ears," "the heart," and "the will" [17], and instead pursue diverse experiences and personalized expressions [18]. After artificial intelligence is integrated into artistic creation, the works it generates challenge traditional aesthetics in new forms and meet people's pursuit of self - creation. Through interactive and immersive experiences, these works can attract audiences from multiple sensory levels and trigger strong emotional resonances [19, 20].

3.2 Mechanism of Aesthetic Reshaping via SD Calligraphy

Stable Diffusion is a professional algorithm model that creates with controllable random parameters. By fine - tuning the parameters, it deconstructs and reconstructs aspects such as the stroke shapes, ink distribution, and structural layout of traditional calligraphy, creating a new visual order and artistic style. This new kind of deliberate randomness not only challenges traditional norms but also stimulates creative inspiration, giving rise to a unique style that deviates from traditional forms, broadening the aesthetic vision of this art from a more comprehensive and in - depth level [5].

Fig. 1.

Fig. 2.

These images demonstrate how randomness enhances the visual and emotional expressions of calligraphy works. In Fig. 1, the starting strokes vary with "exposed tip," "hidden tip," and "side tip." The overlapping strokes bring unexpected ink blending, conveying the natural artistic conception of Taoism's "inaction." In Fig. 2, the turning

Fig. 3.

points of the strokes are full of subtle changes. The stable and gradual pen movements and ink colors not only show smooth writing but also reveal a peaceful state of mind. Figure 3 combines traditional brushwork with abstract elements. The combination of thick and thin ink and blank spaces, with vigorous and swift strokes, creates a strong visual impact and emotional tension. These cases show that randomness enriches the aesthetic experience and builds a new emotional and cognitive bond between art and the audience.

Fig. 4.

Fig. 5.

However, the application of randomness in AI - generated calligraphy is not always successful. Figures 4 and 5 reveal the related challenges and limitations. In Fig. 4, excessive ink blending and inconsistent stroke structures, such as the abrupt "flying white" in the "pie" stroke, make the work chaotic and weaken its aesthetic appeal and emotional resonance. In Fig. 5, the random scribbles at the starting and ending points of strokes disrupt the emotional connection of the creative intention, and the confusing visual experience fails to evoke the expected response. These indicate that to create excellent calligraphy works, it is necessary to balance randomness with traditional aesthetic principles.

Fig. 6.

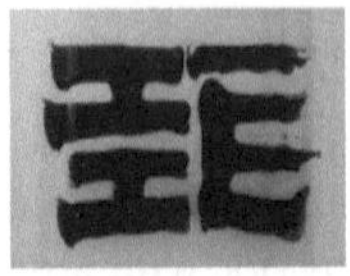

Fig. 7.

Taking Figs. 6 and 7 as examples, they show how randomness can transform calligraphy into abstract art, even without meaningful content. In Fig. 6, the chaotic ink diffusion and unconventional strokes form an abstract picture that is visually striking. In Fig. 7, the random changes in stroke thickness and ink distribution create an aesthetically pleasing abstract form. Both show that randomness drives traditional calligraphy to break through boundaries and bring new aesthetic experiences.

Tools Facilitating Calligraphy Randomness: In terms of tools, advanced tools like ControlNet and specialized small models assist in the random creation of calligraphy. ControlNet can precisely regulate the randomness of brushstrokes, structures, etc., between the generated image and the reference image, enabling artists to incorporate changes while grasping the creative direction [21]. Small models trained on rich datasets can inject subtle innovative elements into works and stimulate creative potential [20].

Mathematical Representation of Aesthetic Randomness: The process of generating aesthetically pleasing randomness in SD calligraphy can be represented mathematically as follows:

$$C = \sum_{i=1}^{n} (P_i \cdot R_i) + \epsilon$$

where:

- C_{output}: Final calligraphy composition
- P_i: Predefined aesthetic parameters (e.g., stroke weight, ink density)
- Ri: Random variables introduced by SD algorithms
- ϵ: Controlled noise for stylistic variation

This formula encapsulates the interplay between traditional constraints (P_i) and modern randomness (R_i) in creating innovative calligraphy.

3.3 Comparative Analysis with Traditional Calligraphy

To comprehensively explore the cognitive and emotional connotations of calligraphy, a comparative analysis reveals the differences between traditional and AI - generated (SD) calligraphy. Traditional calligraphy attracts audiences with precise techniques, artistic skills, and adherence to aesthetic principles, evoking emotions at the cultural and philosophical levels, such as a sense of openness and reverence. In contrast, SD calligraphy, as shown in Figs. 1, 2, and 3, brings about a paradigm shift through randomness and technological innovation, creating an exhibition experience full of unpredictability, curiosity, and intellectual stimulation. The two present a sharp contrast in aesthetic experiences.

3.4 Implications for Calligraphy Education and Appreciation

Traditional calligraphy allows people to appreciate the inheritance of techniques and historical backgrounds in contemplation, while AI - generated (SD) calligraphy prompts the audience to actively interpret works that break the norm. Figures 6 and 7 are examples of this paradigm shift, breaking through the boundaries of traditional calligraphy and expanding the dimensions of emotional experience. This contrast highlights the dynamic nature of artistic perception and demonstrates how technological intervention fundamentally changes the cognitive and emotional interaction between people and art, blurring the line between human creation and algorithm - generated works.

4 Interactive Effects of Randomness, Culture, and Cognition

4.1 Cultural Connotations as Bridges

The audience's familiarity with traditional calligraphy aesthetics is the key to accepting Stable Diffusion (SD) - generated calligraphy. Traditional aesthetics provide a framework for the audience to understand new art forms [22]. The visual elements of SD - generated calligraphy echo the principles of classic works such as The Lanting Collection of Prefaces by Wang Xizhi, facilitating audience acceptance [5].

The randomness of SD calligraphy introduces novel visual elements, stimulating the audience's curiosity and imagination, which is in line with aesthetic preference theory. The random ink 晕染 creates a moderately complex visual object, preventing the audience from being bored by simplicity or overwhelmed by complexity. The sense of difference attracts the audience to explore the details of the works.

However, Figs. 4 and 5 reveal the problems of excessive randomness. In Fig. 4, excessive ink diffusion makes the picture chaotic, and in Fig. 5, the disordered stroke and ink distribution weaken the beauty and resonance of the works. This shows that only by integrating innovation with traditional aesthetics can harmonious and appealing calligraphy works be created.

4.2 Impact on Calligraphy Heritage and Innovation

SD calligraphy significantly lowers the threshold for participating in calligraphy art, allowing more people to access calligraphy [23]. Randomness helps non - professionals create personalized works, especially attracting the attention of young people, effectively promoting the inheritance and innovation of calligraphy art and enhancing people's cultural sense of belonging and identity [1, 6].

4.3 Cultural Influences on Perception

There are significant differences in the cognition of SD calligraphy between the East and the West. The East tends to interpret it from a philosophical perspective [24], while the West mostly focuses on visual, creative, aesthetic, and creative processes from a formalist perspective [25]. Although cultural differences affect the audience's understanding, the shared aesthetic principles of humanity help bridge cultural barriers, making SD calligraphy an important medium for cultural exchange [26].

4.4 Case Studies and Examples

AI calligraphy works in exhibitions such as "Eternal Ink" and the "Random Harmony" series fully demonstrate the unique charm of the integration of technological innovation and traditional calligraphy, attracting the attention of audiences from both the East and the West. They enable people from different fields to gather and explore new creative paths [27]. In SD calligraphy creation, various factors are intertwined, creating a favorable environment for artistic development. However, problems such as cultural misunderstandings also need to be solved through strengthened education and communication [28–30].

5 Cross-cultural Aesthetics and Cognitive Emotion

5.1 Cultural Background and Aesthetic Cognition

Eastern and Western Perceptions of SD Calligraphy Aesthetics: The aesthetic concepts of SD calligraphy in the East and the West are quite different. The East, based on traditional philosophy, focuses on the expression of the spiritual connotations of works [10], while the West, influenced by ancient Greek philosophy, pays more attention to formal analysis. In addition, there are differences in the acceptance of SD calligraphy among different generations in the East. The older generation values traditional aesthetic rules, but the randomness of algorithm - generated calligraphy severs the spiritual connection between the work and the creator, so they question the "spirit and vitality" of such works [1]. The younger generation is more adaptable to the integration of digital and art and is willing to appreciate works that combine tradition and innovation. The novel creation methods of SD calligraphy enable them to quickly obtain traditional cultural knowledge and inspiration [31]. Western audiences may misunderstand or underestimate this art form due to their lack of understanding of the cultural philosophy behind SD - generated calligraphy, such as elements like blank space, density, and "flying white" [31] (Table 1).

Table 1. Comparative Analysis of Eastern and Western Perceptions of SD Calligraphy Aesthetics

Aspect	Eastern Perspective	Western Perspective
Philosophical Foundation	Rooted in Daoist and Confucian ideals; emphasizes spiritual expression and moral integrity [23]	Lacks traditional philosophical context; focuses on visual impact and design elements[31]
Artistic Evaluation Criteria	Values brushwork precision, structural balance, and adherence to traditional forms [23]	Prioritizes creativity, abstraction, and novelty in artistic expression [31]
Interpretation of Randomness	May view randomness as a deviation from disciplined practice and intentionality [23]	Often perceives randomness as a form of artistic experimentation and freedom [31]

5.2 Opportunities and Challenges in Cross-cultural Communication

Strategies such as establishing multilingual interpretation libraries and customizing cultural packages can effectively promote the cross - cultural dissemination of SD calligraphy, attracting global attention and integrating it into the education system. However, this process also faces challenges such as insufficient background interpretation and high technical barriers, urgently requiring the improvement of the dissemination system [31].

5.3 Strategies for Cross-cultural Communication

To promote the global appreciation of SD - generated calligraphy, it is necessary to integrate technological, cultural, and strategic means. Develop interpretation materials such as multimedia resources and interactive tutorials to explain the cultural background of works and reduce cultural barriers [6].Customized cultural projects and cutting - edge technologies can strengthen the connection between culture and SD calligraphy. Integrating calligraphy into exhibitions, digital media, and creating immersive experiences with VR/AR can enhance interactivity. Through forums, exhibitions, and AI - personalized experiences, people from different backgrounds can be encouraged to participate in appreciation and discussion, narrowing cross - cultural differences and strengthening exchanges [34].VR and AR technologies allow audiences to interact and create in virtual spaces, presenting the characteristics and connotations of SD calligraphy in innovative ways and promoting it to become a global cross - cultural art form [6, 33]. In the final part, we will summarize the research results and look into its future in the global culture.

6 Conclusion and Outlook

6.1 Research Summary

This study explores the transformative role of randomness in SD - generated calligraphy. Although it challenges traditional calligraphy norms, it has become a powerful tool for aesthetic innovation, stimulating people's curiosity, creativity, and emotional resonance, and connecting traditional philosophy with contemporary digital art [5, 23].

SD calligraphy integrates the concepts of the East and the West, making calligraphy more accessible to the public. It helps global audiences access and create calligraphy through the Internet [1, 31], protecting cultural heritage, breaking cultural barriers, and reshaping the value of calligraphy in modern society.

6.2 Implications for Calligraphy Preservation and Innovation

The combination of artificial intelligence and randomness has opened up a new path for the protection and innovation of calligraphy art. On the basis of inheriting the essence of tradition, it attracts different cultural groups to participate in appreciation and creation. It realizes innovation with modern technology, prevents calligraphy from becoming stagnant, and enables calligraphy to maintain its importance and artistic vitality in the digital wave.

6.3 Future Research Directions

Although relevant research and creation have made continuous progress, there is still a huge gap in the comprehensive understanding of how SD generated calligraphy affects cross-cultural aesthetics and emotional response mechanism. In order to make up for these deficiencies, future research should adopt empirical methods and combine cutting-edge technologies to provide solutions.

Empirical Cross-Cultural Studies: Follow - up research should combine quantitative methods such as eye - tracking and questionnaires to explore how audiences from different cultural backgrounds interpret SD calligraphy [17], and compare generational differences within specific cultures [22].

Aesthetic Measurement Methods: Establish an effective framework to evaluate the impact of randomness on cognition and emotion. Research on brain activities during aesthetic experiences from a neuroscience perspective may provide key insights [10, 23].

Expanding the SD Model's Capacity: Model improvement should focus on fine customization, allowing users to control random parameters, incorporate traditional calligraphy styles and cultural elements, and strengthen the connection with historical art [5]. In addition, integrating multimodal features such as interactive and auditory elements can enhance user experience and the effects of works.

6.4 Practical Applications and Recommendations

In the era of global multicultural exchanges, a multi - dimensional strategy that integrates technological innovation, education, and cross - cultural cooperation is crucial for Chinese calligraphy to maintain its global influence and continue to develop. AI - generated calligraphy can be incorporated into the educational curriculum system, digital communication platforms can be built, and a variety of cultural activities can be organized to create a diversified development ecosystem. Meanwhile, by lowering the threshold for participation, calligraphy can transform from a niche art form into a global mass art medium, bridging the gaps between different fields and promoting communication and innovation.

6.5 Final Thoughts

Encouraging diverse participation from the fields of art, academia, and technology is at the core of reshaping calligraphy for future generations. The cross - disciplinary collaboration among computer scientists, traditional artists, cultural historians, and others explores new dimensions for the evolution of calligraphy. Technology broadens the boundaries of aesthetics, while tradition imparts cultural depth. Cross - cultural cooperation helps calligraphy break through geographical limitations, evolving into a global form of artistic expression and achieving a deep integration of tradition and modernity.

The integration of randomness into Chinese calligraphy creation marks a milestone change. Traditional calligraphy embodies philosophy and emotion through rigorous techniques. The random introduction of digital elements breaks the boundaries of creation, and machine learning and algorithms endow works with new meanings, reconstructing the creative relationship. The dual commitment to inheritance and innovation injects contemporary vitality into calligraphy, establishing a cross - cultural and cross - disciplinary communication platform and enriching the global art ecosystem. Practitioners and scholars can consolidate the historical foundation of calligraphy and drive its innovative development, ensuring that this thousand - year - old art tradition remains vibrant in the future and moves towards a more inclusive and diverse new realm of global art.

Acknowledgements. This work was supported by the 2023 General Project of Shanghai Educational Science Research C2023262 Theoretical Construction and Exploratory Application Research of Educational Metauniverse. This study is a part of the 2023 Shanghai Key Curriculum Construction project on "Chinese Calligraphy Art."

References

1. Zhao, L.: Decline of handwriting in the digital age. Chinese J. Cultural Preservation **12**(1), 45–52 (2021)
2. Wang, Y., Li, J.: Generational shifts in calligraphy appreciation. Chinese Cultural Stud. Quarterly **15**(4), 112–126 (2019)
3. Guo, Y. : Chinese calligraphy and aesthetic principles. Hebei Fine Arts Press (2020)
4. Chen, Z.: The philosophical roots of Chinese calligraphy. J. Chinese Stud. **25**(3), 32–45 (2018)

5. Liao, Q., Xia, G., & Wang, Z.: Calliffusion: Chinese calligraphy generation and style transfer with diffusion modeling. arXiv preprint arXiv:2305.19124 (2023). https://arxiv.org/abs/2305.19124
6. Ma, N., Yu, D.: How do VR applications address the challenges of conveying the tactile feedback crucial to traditional calligraphy practice? In: Proceedings of the International Conference on Artificial Intelligence and VR (2024)
7. McCosker, A., Wilken, R.: AI and creativity: Art in the age of algorithms. Springer (2020)
8. Yu, D., Ma, N.: Enhancing Chinese Character Education and Calligraphy Through Metaverse Intelligent Technology: Integration and Impact. In International Conference on Computer Science and Education, pp. 181–193. Singapore: Springer Nature Singapore (2023, December)
9. Dongxing, Y., et al.: Unleashing the tactile dimension: exploring VR technologies for authentic calligraphy training. PriMera Sci. Eng. **4**(4), 36–54 (2024)
10. Berlyne, D.E.: Aesthetics and psychobiology. Journal of Aesthetics and Art Criticism, 31(4) (1973)
11. Zhao, T.: A historical study on Chinese classical imagery Doctoral dissertation, Southwest University Doctoral dissertation, Southwest University. (Original work in Chinese) (2012)
12. Yin, N. :A comparison between "Jin shang yun" and "Song shang yi." Journal of Luoyang Normal University, (6), 124–126. (Original work in Chinese) (2004)
13. Chen, R.: Observing the Wei-Jin literati's attitude toward life from Lanting Xu. Modern Communication, (4), 91–92. (Original work in Chinese)(2011)
14. Zhang, J. :The concept of poetry-painting unity and the Song Dynasty's pursuit of "shang yi." Chinese Literature Studies, (9), 18–22. (Original work in Chinese)(2003)
15. Zhou, L.: The origins of calligraphy art and Chinese life philosophy. Social Science Forum, (1), 65–70. (Original work in Chinese) (2011)
16. Hu, J.: A study on the ink works of Song Dynasty Chan masters transmitted to Japan Master'sthesis,NanjingUniversityoftheArtsMaster's thesis, Nanjing University of the Arts. (Original work in Chinese) (2006)
17. Han, D.: The issue of aesthetic education in Li Zehou's "subjectivity" aesthetic thought. Literature & Art Studies, (11), 11. (Original work in Chinese) (2005)
18. Crimaldi, F., Leonelli, M. :AI and the creative realm: A short review of current and future applications(2023). arXiv preprint arXiv:2306.01795. https://arxiv.org/abs/2306.01795
19. Bidgoli, A., Kang, E., Llach, D.C.: Machinic surrogates: Human-machine relationships in computational creativity (2019). arXiv preprint arXiv:1908.01133. https://arxiv.org/abs/1908.01133
20. Yang, Z., et al.: PaCaNet: a study on CycleGAN with transfer learning for diversifying fused Chinese painting and calligraphy (2023). arXiv preprint arXiv:2301.13082. https://arxiv.org/abs/2301.13082
21. Zhang, W., et al.: CultiVerse: Towards cross-cultural understanding for paintings with large language model (2024). arXiv preprint arXiv:2405.00435. https://arxiv.org/abs/2405.00435
22. Tang, Y.: Confucianism, Buddhism, Daoism. Springer, Christianity and Chinese culture (2015)
23. Shi, X.: Chinese calligraphy as "force-form." J Aesthetic Educ. **53**(4), 98–110 (2019)
24. Xiong, P. :A study of the intersection of traditional calligraphy and digital media art. Applied Mathematics and Nonlinear Sciences (2024)
25. Guo, J., Li, J., Linghu, K., Gao, B., Xia, Z. : CCST-GAN: generative adversarial networks for Chinese calligraphy style transfer. In: 3rd International Conference on Image Processing and Media Computing (ICIPMC)(2024)
26. Wang, Y., Lyu, R.: Characteristics of visual complexity: Calligraphic fonts vs. printed fonts. In: 2024 IEEE International Conference on Multimedia and Expo Workshops (ICMEW) (2024)

27. Kopecka, H., Such, J., Luck, M.: Preferences for AI explanations based on cognitive style and socio-cultural factors. In: Proceedings of the ACM on Human-Computer Interaction (2024)
28. Zhang, W., Sun, Z., Wu, X.: An end-to-end generation model for Chinese calligraphy characters based on dense blocks and capsule network. Electronics (2024)
29. Zhao, R.: Exploring the functions of calligraphy in contemporary cultural perspective. Journal of Global Humanities and Social Sciences (2024)
30. Yan, F., Lan, X., Zhang, H., Li, L.: Intelligent evaluation of Chinese hard-pen calligraphy using a Siamese transformer network. Appl. Sci. (2024)
31. Xu, Y., Shen, R.: Aesthetic evaluation of Chinese calligraphy: a cross-cultural comparative study. Curr. Psychol. **42**, 23096–23109 (2022). https://doi.org/10.1007/s12144-022-03390-7
32. Bi, H., & Mohd Nasir, N. B. : Innovative approaches to preserving intangible cultural heritage through AI-driven interactive experiences. Academic Journal of Science and Technology(2024)
33. Zheng, R. : Virtual reality (VR) innovative communication strategies for Chinese traditional arts in the digital age. Applied Mathematics and Nonlinear Sciences(2024)
34. Shum, P. Y. S., & Klein, T. : VR calligraphy transposing Chinese calligraphy as choreographed movements into whole-body performances in VR. ISEA2023 Proceedings(2024)

E-Exams and Academic Integrity: Combating Cheating with Advanced Proctoring Solutions

Wai Yie Leong(✉)

INTI International University, 71800 Nilai, Malaysia
waiyie@gmail.com

Abstract. The rapid adoption of e-exams has transformed the landscape of education, enabling greater accessibility, flexibility, and scalability in assessments. However, the rise of digital testing has brought significant challenges, particularly concerning academic integrity and the potential for cheating. This paper explores the integration of advanced proctoring solutions to safeguard the credibility of e-exams and ensure fair assessments. Techniques such as AI-powered monitoring, biometric verification, and secure browser technologies are analyzed for their effectiveness in detecting and preventing malpractice. Additionally, the ethical implications of surveillance and privacy concerns are addressed, emphasizing the importance of striking a balance between security and student rights. Case studies of successful implementations highlight best practices and the impact of these technologies on enhancing trust in online education systems. By examining the evolving landscape of e-exams and the role of cutting-edge proctoring tools, this study provides actionable insights for educators, institutions, and policymakers aiming to uphold academic integrity.

Keywords: E-Exam · AI-powered monitoring · ethical implication · process innovation

1 Introduction

The transition from traditional paper-based exams to electronic examinations (e-exams) has been a pivotal development in education. E-exams offer numerous advantages, such as scalability, environmental sustainability, and accessibility for remote learners. With the digital transformation of education accelerating due to global crises like the COVID-19 pandemic, the adoption of e-exams has been further solidified as a core component of modern education systems [1]. However, as these technologies advance, so do the complexities surrounding their implementation, particularly with respect to maintaining academic integrity [2].

E-exams are increasingly replacing conventional examination methods in schools, universities, and professional certification bodies worldwide. This shift is driven by technological innovations that enable automated grading, instant feedback, and adaptive testing tailored to individual learners [3]. Moreover, e-exams align with broader digital

K. W. Lee and L. H. Wong (Eds.): ITEA 2025, CCIS 2643, pp. 326–338, 2026.
https://doi.org/10.1007/978-981-95-2011-4_31

transformation initiatives, such as smart classrooms, online degrees, and lifelong learning platforms, offering seamless integration into an interconnected educational ecosystem.

Despite these advancements, e-exams are not without challenges. Academic dishonesty has long been a concern in traditional educational settings, and its prevalence is exacerbated in online environments where the lack of physical oversight creates opportunities for misconduct. Incidents of impersonation, unauthorized collaboration, and access to prohibited resources during exams threaten the credibility of digital assessment frameworks.

Academic integrity is foundational to the credibility and effectiveness of any assessment system. It ensures that grades and certifications reflect a learner's true abilities and knowledge, thereby upholding the value of educational qualifications in the job market and society at large [4]. Breaches of academic integrity undermine trust in educational institutions and devalue credentials, creating far-reaching consequences for both individuals and systems.

The online nature of e-exams introduces unique challenges to maintaining academic integrity. Unlike traditional exams conducted in invigilated classrooms, e-exams are often taken in unsupervised environments where students can exploit technological vulnerabilities to gain unfair advantages [5]. For example, sharing answers via social media, using unauthorized software tools, or having proxies complete exams are common methods of cheating in e-exams.

To address these challenges, institutions have increasingly turned to advanced proctoring solutions that leverage artificial intelligence (AI), biometrics, and secure browsers. These technologies aim to replicate or even surpass the invigilation capabilities of physical exam settings, enabling robust monitoring and deterrence mechanisms in virtual environments.

The history of e-exams dates back to the advent of computer-based testing in the 1990s, with pioneers such as the Graduate Record Examination (GRE) transitioning from paper-based formats to digital platforms. Over the decades, technological advancements have expanded the scope and sophistication of e-exams. Initially confined to multiple-choice questions on standalone computers, modern e-exams now support complex problem-solving, interactive simulations, and multimedia-rich assessments delivered via cloud-based platforms.

Key milestones in the evolution of e-exams include:

1990s: Emergence of computer-based testing systems like GRE and TOEFL, which introduced features such as adaptive testing and instant score reporting.

2000s: Widespread adoption of secure online testing platforms by professional certification bodies, enabling global access to standardized exams.

2010s: Integration of e-exams into massive open online courses (MOOCs) and learning management systems (LMS), democratizing access to education.

2020s: Accelerated adoption of e-exams during the COVID-19 pandemic, coupled with innovations in AI-driven proctoring technologies to address security concerns.

This evolution highlights the growing reliance on e-exams as a cornerstone of digital education, necessitating robust frameworks to ensure their credibility and fairness.

Fig. 1. E-exam proctoring technologies

E-exams are underpinned by a combination of software, hardware, and network technologies that collectively enable secure and scalable assessment solutions (Fig. 1). The technical infrastructure for e-exams typically includes:

Exam Delivery Platforms: Cloud-based systems that facilitate the creation, deployment, and management of digital exams. These platforms often integrate question banks, grading tools, and analytics dashboards.

Proctoring Technologies: AI-powered tools for real-time monitoring and anomaly detection. These include webcam-based surveillance, eye-tracking systems, and keystroke pattern analysis.

Secure Browsers: Specialized software that restricts access to unauthorized applications, websites, and resources during exams.

Biometric Authentication: Techniques such as facial recognition, fingerprint scanning, and voice verification to ensure candidate identity and prevent impersonation.

Encryption and Data Security: Robust encryption protocols to protect sensitive exam content and student data from breaches.

These technologies are critical in addressing the dual imperatives of scalability and security in e-exams. However, their implementation must be carefully managed to avoid technical failures, usability issues, and ethical controversies.

The use of advanced proctoring solutions in e-exams raises significant ethical and privacy considerations. Continuous video monitoring, for instance, can make students feel surveilled, leading to heightened stress and discomfort. Moreover, the collection and storage of biometric data introduce risks of data misuse and breaches, underscoring the need for stringent data protection policies.

Balancing the need for security with respect for student privacy is a pressing challenge for institutions. Transparent communication about the purpose, scope, and limitations of proctoring technologies is essential to building trust among students. Additionally, institutions must ensure compliance with legal frameworks such as the General Data Protection Regulation (GDPR) to safeguard user rights.

This paper seeks to address the following objectives, to analyze the effectiveness of advanced proctoring technologies in combating cheating in e-exams. Explore the technical, ethical, and operational challenges associated with the implementation of these solutions. Provide actionable recommendations for educational institutions to enhance academic integrity in digital assessments. By examining the intersection of technology, pedagogy, and ethics, this study aims to contribute to the development of secure and equitable e-exam frameworks that align with the evolving needs of the education sector.

This comprehensive exploration of e-exams and academic integrity aims to provide a holistic understanding of the opportunities and challenges associated with digital assessments, paving the way for future innovations in this critical domain.

2 Literature Review

The history of e-exams reflects the broader evolution of educational technology, from simple digital tools to sophisticated platforms capable of delivering highly secure and scalable assessments [5]. Understanding this evolution provides context for the challenges and innovations associated with e-exams today.

Early Developments: The Foundation of E-Exams The concept of digital examinations emerged in the late 20th century with the introduction of computer-based testing (CBT). Early adopters, such as standardized tests like the GRE and TOEFL, capitalized on advancements in computing power to transition from traditional paper-based formats to CBT platforms [6]. These systems offered numerous advantages, including automated grading and reduced logistical costs.

In the 1990s, standalone computer systems equipped with proprietary software facilitated localized CBT sessions. While innovative, these systems faced limitations such as restricted scalability and the need for dedicated hardware. As internet connectivity improved, online testing emerged as a viable alternative, allowing institutions to administer exams remotely and on a larger scale [7].

The Rise of Internet-Based Testing Platforms: The 2000s marked a turning point with the proliferation of web-based testing platforms. These systems integrated learning management systems (LMS) and expanded the functionality of e-exams to include multimedia content, adaptive testing, and real-time feedback [8]. The launch of certification exams by organizations like Microsoft and Cisco further validated the reliability of internet-based assessments.

Integration with Massive Open Online Courses (MOOCs)

The 2010s saw the advent of MOOCs, which democratized access to education globally. Platforms such as Coursera, edX, and Udemy incorporated e-exams as a core component of their credentialing processes. Innovations in user authentication and secure browsers addressed concerns about exam integrity, enabling these platforms to award certificates with confidence.

Impact of the COVID-19 Pandemic

The global shift to remote learning during the COVID-19 pandemic significantly accelerated the adoption of e-exams. Institutions faced unprecedented challenges in transitioning assessments online, prompting rapid advancements in proctoring technologies [9]. AI-driven tools capable of analyzing video feeds, detecting anomalies, and verifying identities became essential in ensuring the credibility of digital exams.

Emerging Trends in E-Exams

Today, e-exams are characterized by their scalability, interactivity, and integration with advanced technologies. Emerging trends include blockchain for credential verification, ensuring the authenticity of certificates issued through e-exams. Augmented Reality (AR) in assessments enabling immersive and interactive exam experiences. Data Analytics providing actionable insights into student performance and behavior.

The history of e-exams underscores the dynamic interplay between technology and education, highlighting the ongoing need for innovation to address emerging challenges. The body of literature on e-exams and academic integrity is extensive, encompassing studies on technological, pedagogical, and ethical dimensions. This section synthesizes key findings to contextualize the challenges and opportunities in e-exam implementation.

In Table 1, numerous studies emphasize the efficiency and accessibility of e-exams. For example, the study [1] found that automated grading systems significantly reduced administrative overhead, allowing educators to focus on pedagogy. Additionally, e-exams expand access to learners in remote and underserved regions, aligning with global educational equity goals.

Table 1. Comparative Analysis of Paper-Based and E-Exams

Feature	Paper-Based Exams	E-Exams
Accessibility	Limited	High
Grading Efficiency	Manual	Automated
Environmental Impact	High (Paper Use)	Low (Digital Format)

The transition to e-exams has exacerbated concerns about academic dishonesty. The analysis [2] identified common cheating methods in online assessments, including impersonation, unauthorized collaboration, and digital resource misuse. These challenges necessitate robust proctoring solutions to safeguard exam integrity.

Recent advancements in proctoring technologies have focused on enhancing detection capabilities while minimizing intrusiveness. AI-powered solutions, such as facial recognition and keystroke analysis, have demonstrated high accuracy in identifying suspicious behaviors [4]. However, their implementation raises ethical and technical concerns, including false positives and student privacy violations.

Student perceptions play a critical role in the success of e-exam implementations. Research by [3] indicates that while students recognize the importance of proctoring for fairness, many express discomfort with intrusive surveillance methods. Addressing these concerns requires a balance between robust security measures and respect for privacy.

In Table 2, the use of proctoring technologies introduces ethical dilemmas and legal considerations. For instance, continuous video monitoring may violate privacy laws such as the General Data Protection Regulation (GDPR). Ethical frameworks must guide the deployment of these technologies to ensure compliance and maintain student trust [10].

Table 2. Key Ethical Considerations in Proctoring

Ethical Issue	Description	Mitigation Strategy
Privacy Invasion	Continuous surveillance may feel intrusive	Transparency and informed consent
Data Security	Risk of breaches and misuse of sensitive data	Encryption and access controls
Bias in AI Algorithms	Potential discrimination in detection systems	Regular audits and bias testing

The literature identifies best practices for implementing e-exams, including training for educators and students, ensuring familiarity with e-exam platforms and proctoring tools. Regular audits and monitoring the performance and fairness of proctoring systems. Stakeholder engagement, involving students and educators in decision-making processes to build trust.

Despite the extensive body of literature, several gaps remain. Limited studies on the long-term effectiveness of proctoring technologies. Insufficient exploration of cultural and regional differences in e-exam adoption. Need for frameworks to address ethical dilemmas systematically. By addressing these gaps, future research can contribute to the development of secure, equitable, and widely accepted e-exam solutions.

3 Methodology

The research methodology for this study incorporates a mixed-methods approach to provide a comprehensive understanding of the effectiveness and challenges associated with advanced proctoring solutions in e-exams. Both quantitative and qualitative data were collected and analyzed to evaluate the performance of these technologies and their impact on academic integrity. The study follows an exploratory research design to address the complex interplay of technical, ethical, and operational factors influencing the adoption of proctoring technologies.

The primary research objectives include assessing the effectiveness of AI-driven proctoring systems in detecting and preventing cheating. Evaluating student and instructor perceptions of proctoring technologies. Identifying technical, ethical, and logistical challenges in implementation.

Data was collected from multiple sources to ensure a robust analysis.

- Surveys: Administered to 500 students and 200 instructors across five universities. Questions focused on experiences, perceptions, and concerns related to proctoring technologies.
- System Logs: Analyzed logs from three proctoring systems to measure detection accuracy, false positive rates, and performance metrics.
- Interviews: Conducted in-depth interviews with 20 stakeholders, including IT administrators, faculty, and students.
- Case Studies: Detailed investigations of institutions that have implemented AI-based proctoring and biometric authentication technologies.
- Literature Review: Secondary data from journals, white papers, and industry reports provided additional insights.
- Data was analyzed using:

Quantitative Analysis: Statistical tools such as SPSS and Python for numerical data analysis, including correlation and regression analyses.

Qualitative Analysis: NVivo software for coding and thematic analysis of interview transcripts and open-ended survey responses.

- Performance Metrics: System performance metrics, including precision, recall, and detection accuracy, were computed to evaluate proctoring tools.

To ensure reliability and validity, triangulation was used by cross-referencing survey results with interview data and system logs. Pilot testing of survey instruments ensured clarity and relevance. Peer review of findings minimized bias and improved robustness.

The three proctoring systems demonstrated average detection accuracy of 90% for cheating incidents. False positives averaged 10%, primarily influenced by environmental variables (e.g., lighting conditions). 70% of instructors found AI-based proctoring tools effective in reducing cheating. 55% of students reported increased exam-related stress due to perceived surveillance. Implementation costs ranged between $25 and $50 per exam session, depending on the technology stack and scale.

In Table 3, the case studies provide a detailed analysis of the implementation and outcomes of advanced proctoring technologies in educational institutions. These real-world examples highlight both successes and challenges, offering valuable insights for future applications.

Table 3. Features E-exam Technologies

Feature	AI-Driven Proctoring	Biometric Authentication	Secure Browsers
Cheating Prevention	High	High	Moderate
User Experience	Moderate	Moderate	High
Implementation Cost	High	Moderate	Low
Data Security	Strong	Strong	Moderate
Ease of Use	Moderate	Moderate	High
Scalability	High	Moderate	High

A) Case Study: AI-Driven Proctoring

University adopted an AI-based proctoring solution to conduct high-stakes remote exams for its undergraduate programs. The technology stack includes real-time video monitoring with facial recognition. AI algorithms for behavioral anomaly detection (e.g., eye movement, head position). Integration with the university's learning management system (LMS). The implementation process was conducted with 500 students in a controlled environment to assess system performance. Feedback was collected to refine the system and address technical issues. The full deployment was rolled out across all undergraduate courses, affecting approximately 10,000 students.

Detection accuracy referes to 92% of cheating attempts were identified. False positives are 8%, primarily due to technical glitches or environmental factors. 65% of students reported moderate to high levels of stress due to surveillance.

Operational efficiency is with reduced instructor workload for invigilation by 75%. The most common anomalies included background noise and multiple faces on the screen.

The challenges were resistance from students citing privacy concerns. Technical issues, such as unstable internet connections leading to exam interruptions. The impacts were significant reduction in cheating incidents compared to previous years. Enhanced trust among faculty members regarding exam integrity.

B) Case Study: Biometric Authentication

University implemented a biometric authentication system to verify student identities during online exams. The technology stack involves facial recognition for login authentication. During the pre-exam preparation, students were required to register biometric data (e.g., facial images, typing samples) prior to exams.

Exam monitoring involves continuous authentication during exams to detect impersonation attempts. The results shown impersonation detection and reduced incidents by 85% compared to the previous year. System reliability was 95% uptime, with occasional failures in facial recognition due to lighting conditions. User acceptance was 80% of students found biometric authentication minimally intrusive compared to live proctoring.

Further Findings were on data security implemented encryption protocols ensured zero breaches during the study period. Performance metrics showns average login time was reduced by 30% due to streamlined biometric authentication.

The challenges were student apprehension about sharing biometric data and need for robust data encryption to prevent security breaches. In Fig. 2, the impacts were improved fairness and trust in online assessments, strengthened institutional reputation for academic integrity.

C) Case Study: Secure Browsers

University adopted a secure browser technology to restrict access to unauthorized resources during exams. The technology stack was browser-based lockdown system with real-time monitoring of system activity. The Features included disabling copy-paste functions, blocking external websites, and restricting application switching. The implementation process was deployment and installation on university-managed devices and made available as a downloadable application for personal devices. Logs of student activity were reviewed post-exam to identify suspicious patterns.

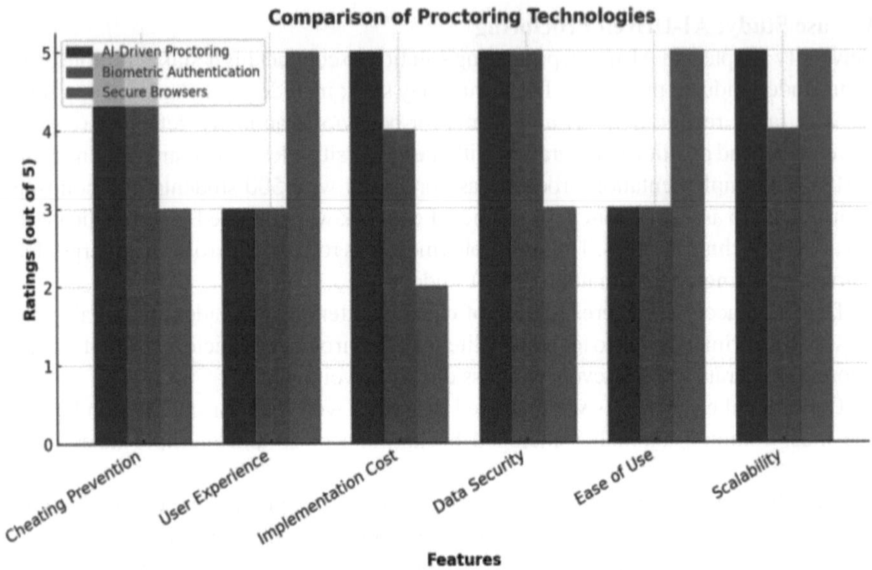

Fig. 2. Comparison of proctoring technologies

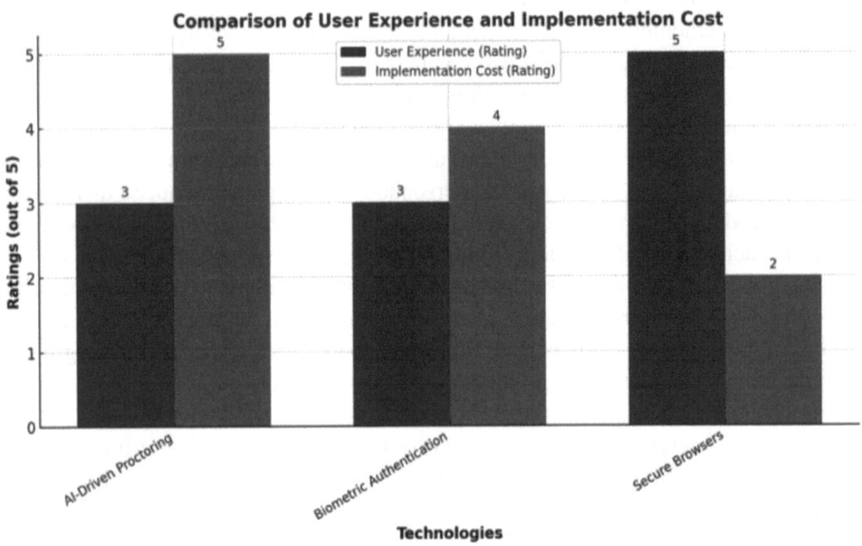

Fig. 3. Comparison of user experience and implementation cost.

Results were on cheating incidents reduced by 60% compared to open-access online exams. Student experience was 80% reported minimal disruption, although 10% faced compatibility issues. Instructor efficiency was reduced manual oversight requirements by 50%.

The Further Findings on compliance was adhered to regional data protection laws, ensuring minimal legal risk. User support shown an average of 3 technical support tickets per 100 users were reported, highlighting manageable operational overhead.

The challenges were compatibility with different operating systems and devices, and technical support demands during exams. The impact was on enhanced exam security with minimal intrusion into student privacy. High levels of satisfaction among faculty and administrators.

4 Limitations and Challenges

The implementation of e-exams and advanced proctoring solutions, while offering numerous benefits, presents a range of challenges and limitations that must be addressed to ensure their effectiveness and acceptance. These challenges span technical, ethical, operational, and user-related domains [11].

Reliable internet connectivity is a critical requirement for the success of e-exams. However, inconsistent bandwidth, network outages, and latency issues can disrupt the exam process. These challenges are particularly prevalent in remote and rural areas where technological infrastructure is underdeveloped.

E-exam platforms often face compatibility issues with various devices, operating systems, and browsers. Additionally, software bugs or server downtimes can lead to disruptions, undermining trust in the system [12]. Continuous updates and compatibility testing are required to address these concerns. Managing large-scale deployments, especially during peak exam periods, can overwhelm system resources, resulting in crashes or delays. Ensuring scalability through cloud-based solutions and load balancing mechanisms is essential but can be costly.

In Fig. 4, the use of advanced proctoring technologies such as facial recognition, video monitoring, and behavioral analysis raises significant privacy concerns. Students often feel uncomfortable being constantly surveilled, and the storage of biometric data increases the risk of misuse or breaches. AI-driven proctoring tools may exhibit biases in detecting anomalies, leading to false accusations of cheating [13]. For example, variations in lighting, facial features, or background noise can disproportionately affect certain demographic groups.

Continuous surveillance during exams can elevate stress and anxiety levels among students, potentially affecting their performance. Transparent communication and measures to reduce stress, such as practice sessions, can help alleviate these concerns.

Educators and administrative staff require training to effectively use proctoring tools. The lack of technical expertise can lead to mismanagement and errors during exams. Additionally, providing timely technical support to students is crucial for minimizing disruptions. In Fig. 3, the adoption of advanced proctoring solutions involves significant costs, including software licensing, infrastructure upgrades, and maintenance. These costs can be prohibitive for institutions with limited budgets.

Resistance from stakeholders, including students, faculty, and parents, can hinder the adoption of proctoring technologies. Addressing concerns through stakeholder engagement and education is essential for building trust.

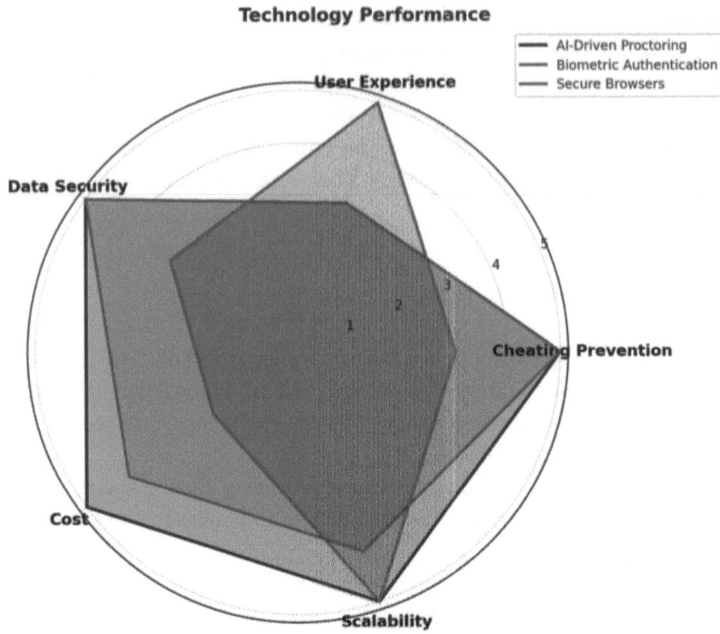

Fig. 4. Technology performance

No proctoring system is infallible. False positives (flagging legitimate behavior as cheating) and false negatives (failing to detect cheating) can occur, leading to disputes and a loss of credibility in the system [14]. The heavy reliance on technology makes e-exams vulnerable to failures caused by hardware malfunctions, software glitches, or cyberattacks. Backup plans and contingency measures are necessary to mitigate these risks. While advanced proctoring tools can detect many forms of cheating, they are not foolproof. For example, covert collaboration or the use of undetectable devices may still bypass detection mechanisms.

The storage and transmission of sensitive data, such as biometric information and exam content, are susceptible to breaches. Ensuring robust encryption and compliance with data protection regulations, such as GDPR, is critical. Institutions must navigate complex legal frameworks governing data privacy and surveillance. Non-compliance can result in legal penalties and damage to institutional reputation.

Addressing these challenges are possible via enhancing infrastructure. Invest in reliable internet infrastructure and cloud-based platforms to ensure uninterrupted connectivity and scalability. Bias Mitigation in AI could be reduced via conducting regular audits of AI algorithms to identify and rectify biases. Include diverse datasets during training to improve fairness.

Transparent communication is need to educate stakeholders about the purpose, functionality, and limitations of proctoring technologies to build trust and reduce resistance. Implement stringent data protection measures, including anonymization and secure storage protocols, to address privacy concerns. Develop contingency protocols, such as alternative exam formats, to handle technical failures effectively. The implementation should be user-centric design, prioritize user experience in system design to minimize stress and enhance usability.

5 Conclusions

The adoption of e-exams and advanced proctoring technologies has redefined the landscape of education, offering unparalleled flexibility and scalability in assessments. However, their integration is not without challenges, requiring careful consideration of technical, ethical, and operational factors to ensure success. AI-driven proctoring, biometric authentication, and secure browser technologies have proven effective in reducing incidents of academic dishonesty. They offer robust frameworks for ensuring fairness and maintaining the credibility of digital assessments. The dual imperative of safeguarding academic integrity and respecting student privacy is central to the success of e-exams. Transparent communication and stringent data protection measures can bridge this gap, fostering trust among stakeholders.

While the costs of implementation may be prohibitive for some institutions, the scalability and long-term benefits of e-exams make them a worthwhile investment. Leveraging cloud-based solutions and open-source platforms can reduce financial barriers. Prioritizing ease of use and minimizing exam-related stress are crucial for increasing acceptance and effectiveness. Features like practice sessions, clear guidelines, and real-time support can enhance user experience significantly.

Future iterations of AI in proctoring systems should focus on reducing biases, improving detection accuracy, and addressing edge cases, such as complex environmental conditions and diverse user demographics. The integration of blockchain for credential verification and augmented reality (AR) for immersive exam environments can further strengthen the credibility and engagement of e-exams. Developing global standards for e-exam technologies and practices will ensure consistency, fairness, and compliance across institutions. Institutions must collaborate with policymakers and ethicists to establish robust guidelines that balance innovation with ethical considerations.

The journey toward fully digitalized assessments is both exciting and challenging. Advanced proctoring solutions are at the forefront of this transformation, enabling institutions to uphold academic integrity in a rapidly evolving educational ecosystem. By addressing the challenges and building on the successes outlined in this study, stakeholders can unlock the full potential of e-exams, creating a secure, equitable, and technologically advanced future for education.

References

1. Jurāne-Brēmane, A.: Digital assessment in technology-enriched education: thematic review. Educ. Sci. **13**(5), 522 (2023)
2. Tsigaros, T., Fesakis, G.: E-assessment and academic integrity: a literature review. In: Reis, A., Barroso, J., Lopes, J.B., Mikropoulos, T., Fan, C.W. (eds.) Technology and Innovation in Learning, Teaching and Education. TECH-EDU 2020. Communications in Computer and Information Science, vol. 1384. Springer, Cham (2021)
3. Hernandez-de-Menendez, M., Morales- Menendez, R., Escobar. R.A., et al.: Biometric applications in education. Int. J. Interact. Des Manuf. **15**, 365–380 (2021)

4. Nigam, A., Pasricha, R., Singh, T., et al.: A systematic review on AI-based proctoring systems: past, present and future. Educ. Inf. Technol. **26**, 6421–6445 (2021)
5. Diarsini, M.S., Artini, L.P., Padmadewi, N.N., Ratminingsih, N.M., Utami, I.G.A.L.P., Marsakawati, N.P.E.: Challenges and opportunities of online assessment implementation during covid-19 pandemic in Indonesia based on recent studies. Europ. J. Educ. Pedagogy **3**(6), 82–88 (2022)
6. Bommireddy, L.R., Marasu, R.T., Karanam, R.P., Sri, K.S.: Smart proctoring system using AI. In: 2023 3rd International Conference on Pervasive Computing and Social Networking (ICPCSN), Salem, India, pp. 591–593 (2023)
7. Alnasser, F., Elrashidi, A.: Improving the security of E-exam systems. In: 2023 International Conference on IT Innovation and Knowledge Discovery (ITIKD), Manama, Bahrain, pp. 1–7 (2023)
8. Han, S.N., ikou, S.N., Ayele, W.Y.: Digital proctoring in higher education: a systematic literature review. Int. J. Educ. Manage. **38**(1), 265–285 (2023)
9. Noshi, Xu, Y.: Development of blockchain-based academic credential verification system. Open Access Library J. **11**, 1–19 (2024)
10. Leong, W.Y.: Beyond exams: alternative evaluation techniques to measure engineering competency. In: 2025 IEEE 8th Eurasian Conference on Educational Innovation (IEEE ECEI 2025), 6–8 Feb 2025, Bali, Indonesia (2025)
11. Leong, W.Y.: Enhancing practical skills training through virtual reality in TVET education. In: 2024 International Conference on TVET Excellence & Development (ICTeD), Malaysia, 16–17 Dec (2024)
12. Leong, W.Y., Zhang, J.B.: Revolution in University Ranking System. ASM Sci. J. **19** (2024)
13. Leong, W.Y.: Industry 5.0: Design, standards, techniques and applications for manufacturing. Institution of Engineering and Technology (2024)
14. Leong, W.Y.: TVET for all: fostering social equity through inclusive skills education. In: 2024 International Conference on TVET Excellence & Development (ICTeD), Malaysia, 16–17 Dec (2024)

Implementation of E-ATCM (Accounting Trading Company's Module) to Enhance Accounting Students' Level of Understanding

Betanika Nila Nirbita(✉), Muhammad Roy Aziz Haryana, Syahida Norviana, and Lu'lu'ul Jannah

Business and Accounting Department, Universitas Negeri Yogyakarta, Yogyakarta, Indonesia
nbetanika@uny.ac.id

Abstract. The purpose of the research is to examine the effectiveness of the E-ATCM (Accounting Trading Company's Module) in improving students' cognitive learning outcomes. This research uses an experimental approach to evaluate the efficacy of the E-ATCM learning media. The experiment involved 77 students from the 2023 cohort at Yogyakarta State University. The researcher highlights the phenomenon of E-ATCM media development, which has rarely been investigated. A pre-post experimental design with a control group is employed in the research. This study compares an experimental group receiving the E-ATCM media intervention with a control group receiving material via PowerPoint. Hypothesis testing using an independent t-test demonstrated a notable difference between the experimental and control classes. Specifically, the E-ATCM media was found to be effective and significant in the learning process of Accounting students in the Basic Financial Accounting course. This study has implications for the use of E-ATCM as an independent learning medium to deepen material comprehension. Furthermore, students are expected to optimize their learning time by uttilizing the ease of access offered by E-ATCM, which can be accessed anytime and anywhere.

Keywords: E-Modules · Accounting · Learning Media

1 Introduction

The development of technology in learning media demands interactivity for media optimization [1, 2]. Researchers highlight the development of interactive learning media to enhance the learning process [3, 4]. Specifically, the use of e-module learning media is still rarely developed, particularly in the field of accounting [5, 6] Moreover, the development of e-learning modules specifically for basic financial accounting remains limited. In other words, the urgency of this research focuses on the development and testing of accounting e-modules in learning [6, 7].

Educational institutions have developed various learning media, particularly those based on technology [8–10] However, concerns about the efficacy of the created educational materials continue to surface on a regular basis [11, 12]. This study has identified that the development of specific learning media can improve the learning process for

K. W. Lee and L. H. Wong (Eds.): ITEA 2025, CCIS 2643, pp. 339–350, 2026.
https://doi.org/10.1007/978-981-95-2011-4_32

students ([13, 14]). However, issues related to cost, regulations, and curriculum continue to be attached to the development of learning media [10, 15]. These issues are further emphasized by the lack of effectiveness testing for technology-based learning media developed for specific purposes [16, 17].

The researcher focuses on the development of a specific e-module tested for its effectiveness through experimentation. Experimental research has the advantage of intervening in treatments to provide evidence of changes or differences with the control group [18, 19]. The experimental method supports representative testing for the development of specific learning media [20, 21] In other words, using the experimental method is appropriate for examination the efficiency of educational media. Furthermore, experimental methods offer a research approach that is still rarely applied in examination the efficiency of educational media, particularly in accounting [20, 22]. The success of this method is inseparable from the precise procedures, interventions, and participant control within the research [19, 23].

This study directs the expansion of e-module learning media development in the field of accounting. Specifically, this study develops E-ATCM (Accounting Trading Company's Module). A specific e-module supports a more effective learning process [24–26]. In other words, this research addresses the practical gap in developing effective learning media in the accounting field [27, 28]. The development of E-ATCM media supports research in accounting, particularly in technology-based learning media [29]. Initial observations related to the need for interactive learning media provide an alternative solution in the development of accounting research (Eka Chandra et al., 2023; Faizahain, 2024).

Previous research has examined the development and feasibility of using E-ATCM learning media [29] This study provides direction for further research on the effectiveness of E-ATCM. Therefore, this study responds to previous research developments by conducting experimental testing. This study notes that effectiveness testing is crucial in the development of educational media. The continuation of development research involves the application of product feasibility and the dissemination or mass production of the product [30, 32, 33]. Researchers recognize that competitive advantages in product effectiveness testing will support the dissemination and mass production of subsequent products [34, 35] Therefore, this study is be expected to contribute methodologically and practically to the effectiveness testing of E-ATCM.

This study is based on several underlying assumptions. First, it emphasizes the optimization of learning media through the application of Media Richness Theory [2, 36]. The optimization process categorizes instructional design into different levels of learning media, ranging from low to high. The fundamental distinction between learning media levels is their potential to enhance learning effectiveness sitasi [37, 38]. Specifically, higher levels of learning media are expected to improve the learning process more significantly than lower levels [3, 4] This study argues that E-ATCM represents a higher level of learning media compared to PowerPoint. Consequently, according to Media Richness Theory, E-ATCM is anticipated to enhance learning effectiveness more effectively than PowerPoint.

Second, this study aims to develop a specialized learning medium for accounting education. The E-ATCM learning media is designed in alignment with Indonesia's national curriculum standards, reinforcing the need for standardized instructional media in accounting education. The effectiveness of E-ATCM contributes to government policies on optimizing learning media and supports national education standards.

Finally, this research employs an experimental method to examine the effectiveness of learning media. Experimental approaches are seldom utilized in accounting education due to the complexity of accounting material [6, 22, 39], which presents challenges in both development and testing [40, 41]. However, this study conducts a preliminary experimental investigation based on recommendations from previous research [29].

In conclusion, this research aims to answer the following main research question: Is there difference substansial in learning outcomes between students using E-ATCM learning media and those using PowerPoint learning media?

2 Research Methods

2.1 Participants

This study had employed a number of participants as required to ensure the data validity along with its conclusion (Libby, Bloomfield and Nelson, 2002). The participants of this study were accounting students Faculty of vocational State University of Yogyakarta, Indonesia. There were 77 participants who were chosen randomly by applying a lottery system. Accounting students were eligible to become the research's participants because they were the daily users of computer-based learning media. Meanwhile, the faculty were selected for whether they had computer learning facilities accompanied by an internet network. This study was carried out in an experimental duration that was sufficient for both the instructors and the students to get involved in a teaching and learning process.

2.2 The Experimental Design

This study utilized an experimental study employing the pre-post control group design. This research compared two groups with E-ATCM learning media and ordinary learning media treatment (ppt). Learning materials used were one of an introductory accounting subject that had never been taught in class. The equipment used in this study was provided in the computer and internet laboratories. To make the two groups equivalent, they were assigned randomly by using a lottery ticket in which number 1 is E-ATCM learning media, number 2 is the ordinary learning media treatment (ppt).

E-ATCM learning media were represented by interactive media. Ordinary learning media treatment (ppt) were represented by only learning text and picture. This experiment was conducted during the schedules of the class. The experiment was also done in the class and computer laboratories as provided by the class. The rooms were facilitated with proper lighting, fans, and AC. The experiment was done in the morning to avoid potential problems such as fatigue, information leakage, and decreasing numbers of participants.

2.3 Procedures

In this research, the participants are arbitrarily split into two groups. Group 1 used a E-ATCM learning media, Group 2 used a ordinary learning media treatment (ppt). After that the participants were exposed to the learning process. The participants then filled out questionnaires concerning student intentions of using the media.

Ethical procedures in this study were carried out by conducting a debriefing method on all the subjects shortly after the experiment was conducted. This was feasible since the subjects got different treatment so that they have the potential to experience psychological pressure or other losses. Debriefing contains an elaboration of the research objectives and procedures which had been experienced by the subjects. Ethically the purpose of debriefing was to help the subjects to restore their normal conditions. The subjects also were given privilege to decide whether they join the experiment or not.

2.4 Instrument Development

This study developed questions for measure the student intentions of using the media based on previous research. The instruments used a Likert scale ranging from 1 to 4. Each statement item in this questionnaire had been reviewed by some experts in order to ensure the face and content validities. Moreover, this study also conducted a pilot test. Specifically, learning media were designed and evaluated according to research objectives and verified by professionals in the educational field.

2.5 Hypotheses Testing

This study tested the hypothesis using independent-sample t-test, which compared users' student intentions within various types of learning media. The test showed the relationship between learning media. It explained the effectiveness learning media and the student student intentions of using the media.

3 Results and Discussion

3.1 Research Instrument Validation

Validation of research tools, such as pre-test and post-test questions and student response questionnaires, is conducted to ascertain the validity of the instruments used in the study. Once the validity test has been carried out, it is followed by a reliability test to ensure that the data obtained accurately reflects the actual conditions.

3.2 Testing the Validity and Reliability of Survey Items

Twenty-seven students were given the questionnaire to complete in order to verify its validity and reliability. The following are the findings of the validity and reliability tests (Table 1):

The calculated r-value (r_{hitung}) and the table r-value (r_{tabel},) are compared in order to examine the questionnaire items. If r_hitung > r_{tabel}, the item is considered valid, whereas

Table 1. Validity Test Analysis Results for the E-ATCM (Accounting Trading Company's Module) Media Assessment Questionnaire for Students

No	r_{hitung}	r_{tabel}	Conclusion	Description
1.	0,518	0,381	$r_{hitung} > r_{tabel}$	Valid
2.	0,116	0,381	$r_{hitung} < r_{tabel}$	Not valid
3.	0,608	0,381	$r_{hitung} > r_{tabel}$	Valid
4.	0,588	0,381	$r_{hitung} > r_{tabel}$	Valid
5.	0,571	0,381	$r_{hitung} > r_{tabel}$	Valid
6.	0,488	0,381	$r_{hitung} > r_{tabel}$	Valid
7.	0,555	0,381	$r_{hitung} > r_{tabel}$	Valid
8.	0,514	0,381	$r_{hitung} > r_{tabel}$	Valid
9.	0,384	0,381	$r_{hitung} > r_{tabel}$	Valid
10.	0,488	0,381	$r_{hitung} > r_{tabel}$	Valid
11.	0,402	0,381	$r_{hitung} > r_{tabel}$	Valid
12.	0,387	0,381	$r_{hitung} > r_{tabel}$	Valid
13.	0,563	0,381	$r_{hitung} > r_{tabel}$	Valid
14.	0,518	0,381	$r_{hitung} > r_{tabel}$	Valid
15.	0,444	0,381	$r_{hitung} > r_{tabel}$	Valid
16.	0,465	0,381	$r_{hitung} > r_{tabel}$	Valid
17.	0,438	0,381	$r_{hitung} > r_{tabel}$	Valid
18.	0,438	0,381	$r_{hitung} > r_{tabel}$	Valid
19.	0,419	0,381	$r_{hitung} > r_{tabel}$	Valid
20.	0,466	0,381	$r_{hitung} > r_{tabel}$	Valid

Source: Processed Data, 2024

if r_{hitung}, $< r_{tabel}$, l, the item is invalid. To ascertain the consistency or dependability of the measurement data, the questionnaire results must also be checked for reliability. The reliability test is conducted by comparing the Cronbach's alpha value. If the Cronbach's $r_{tabel} <$ alpha value, the instrument is considered consistent or reliable, and vice versa. Below is the reliability test table for the questionnaire, conducted with 27 students and 20 statements (Table 2):

Considering the table of Reliability Test Analysis Results, the Cronbach's alpha value is 0.836, which is greater than the table r_{tabel} of 0.3739. This means the questionnaire items are consistent.

3.3 Participants' Characteristics

77 accounting students from Yogyakarta State University's Vocational Faculty, Class of 2023, participated in the experimental study. 38 students from Class B served as

Table 2. Reliability Test Analysis Results for the E-ATCM (Accounting Trading Company's Module) Media Assessment Questionnaire for Students

Cronbach's alpha	r_{tabel}	Conclusion	Description
0,804	0,381	*cronbach's alpha* > r_{tabel}	Reliabel

Source: Processed Data, 2024

the control group, and 39 students from Class A served as the experimental group. To evaluate their starting skills, a pre-test was administered to both the experimental and control groups. The E-ATCM (Accounting Trading Company's Module) media was then employed to treat the experimental group, whereas PowerPoint was used as the learning tool for the control group. Students in the experimental and control groups were given a post-test to gauge their final skills at the conclusion of the session, more precisely during the second meeting.

3.4 Experiment Results

The appendix provides a summary of the learning objectives for the experimental and control groups from the pre-test and post-test. It is known from the learning data recap that the experimental and control groups' pre-test outcomes were quite comparable. The control group's average pre-test score was 62.53, 0.50 points higher than the experimental group's average score of 62.03. The experimental and control groups' average post-test results, however, differed significantly. The experimental group's average post-test score was 85.58, 9.75 points higher than the control group's average score of 75.83. Nevertheless, when compared to the post-test, the average pre-test scores for both the experimental and control groups increased.

3.5 Assumption Test Results

Assumption tests are the steps that must be taken before conducting the independent t-test.

3.5.1 Pre-test Scores Using an Independent T-Test

To ascertain the differences between the experimental group and the control group, the independent t-test is used. The efficacy of E-ATCM (Accounting Trading Company's Module) is also evaluated using the independent t-test. The following are the assumptions for the independent t-test:

H_0: The experimental group and the control group do not significantly differ in their learning outcomes.

H_1: The experimental group and the control group's learning outcomes differ significantly.

The null hypothesis (H_0), which states that there is no significant difference between the experimental and control groups, is accepted if the significance value (sig) > 0.05.

Table 3. Descriptive Statistics Table for Pre-test Scores of Experimental and Control Groups

Group Statistics					
	Kelas	N	Mean	Std. Dev	Std. Error Mean
Pre-test score	Control	40	62.5250	7.26420	1.14857
	Experimen	40	62.0250	5.31320	.84009

Source: Processed Data, 2024

The following are the descriptive statistics for the experimental and control groups' pre-test results (Table 3):

The experimental group's average pre-test score was 62.03, which was lower than the control group's average pre-test score of 62.53, according to the descriptive statistics table. This suggests that the experimental group did not do as well as the control group did. However, an independent t-test needs to be performed to see whether the pre-test results of the experimental and control groups differ significantly. The findings are shown as follows (Table 4):

Table 4. Independent t-Test Results for Pre-test Scores of Experimental and Control Groups

Paired Samples Test								
	Mean	Std.Dev	Std. Error Mean	95% Confidence interval of the Difference		t	df	Sig.(2-tailed)
				Lower	Upper			
Pre1-pre2	.500000	4.59654	.72678	-.97005	1.97005	.688	39	.496

Source: Processed Data, 2024

Based on the independent t-test table, H_0 is approved, indicating that there is no significant difference between the experimental and control groups' pre-test scores, according to the independent t-test table, where the significance value (sig) > 0.05 (Table 5).

3.5.2 Independent t-Test for Post-test Scores

The experimental group's average post-test score was 85.58, while the control group's was 75.83, according to the independent t-test table. The experimental group outperformed the control group in terms of average post-test scores. According to this, the experimental group outperformed the control group. However, in order to verify this, the following independent t-test needs to be performed (Table 6):

Based on the independent t-test table, the significance value (sig) (2-tailed) < 0.05, so H_0 is rejected, meaning there is a significant difference between the post-test scores of the experimental and control groups. This result is further supported by the t-value of 0.000 and the significance level $\alpha = 0.05$.

Table 5. Descriptive Statistics Table for Post-test Scores of Experimental and Control Group

Group Statistics					
	Kelas	N	Mean	Std.Dev	Std.Error Mean
Post-test score	Control	40	75.8250	7.56811	1.19662
	Experimen	40	85.5750	5.87204	1.08657

Source: Processed Data, 2024

Table 6. Independent t-Test Results for Post-test Scores of Experimental and Control Groups

Paired Samples Test								
	Mean	Std.Dev	Std. Error Mean	95% Confidence interval of the Difference		t	df	Sig.(2-tailed)
				Lower	Upper			
Post1-post2	-9.7500	10.12676	1.60118	-12.98870	-6.5113	-6.089	39	.000

Source: Processed Data, 2024

3.6 Effectiveness of E-ATCM (Accounting Trading Company's Module)

The effectiveness of the E-ATCM (Accounting Trading Company's Module) was tested using an independent t-test on the pre-test and post-test data obtained from the field trial. The field trial was conducted with students from class A and B of the 2023 batch of the Applied Accounting Bachelor's degree program (Table 7).

Table 7. Independent t-test Results

Jenis Tes	Kelas	X	Uji Independent t test
Pre-test	Experimen	62.03	0,726
	Control	62.53	
Post-test	Experimen	85.58	0,000
	Control	75.83	

Source: Processed Data, 2024

The independent t-test findings showed that the significance value (sig) (2-tailed) was 0.000 < 0.05, rejecting H_0, indicating that the experimental and control groups differed significantly. The experimental group fared better than the control group, according to the post-test results. The post-test independent t-test result, which shows a significant difference between the two groups, supports this.

4 Conclusion, Contribution, and Limitations

The findings of the independent t-test showed that the experimental and control groups' learning outcomes differed, with a significant value (sig) (2-tailed) of $0.000 < 0.05$. Additionally, the comparison of post-test average scores shows a difference of 6.88 points between the control and experimental groups. Therefore, it can be determined that the E-ATCM (Accounting Trading Company's Module) is effective and significantly improves cognitive learning outcomes for accounting students in the Basic Financial Accounting course.

Based on the conclusions of the study and the development of the E-ATCM (Accounting Trading Company's Module), several recommendations for improvement in the quality of learning are as follows: Effective usage of the Accounting Trading Company's Module (E-ATCM) as a stand-alone learning resource can help students grasp the subject matter more thoroughly. Furthermore, students should optimize their time by taking advantage of the easy access that the E-ATCM media provides, which can be accessed anytime and anywhere. Lecturers are encouraged to use the E-ATCM (Accounting Trading Company's Module) as a variation in accounting learning media, making it a more enjoyable learning experience so that students can better understand and engage with the material. Lecturers should also combine the E-ATCM media with methods such as Problem-Based Learning (PBL) or case studies to make the learning experience more interesting. Additionally, lecturers should encourage students to install the E-ATCM (Accounting Trading Company's Module) as a supplementary learning tool.

Based on the findings and the development of the E-ATCM (Accounting Trading Company's Module), future research is recommended to explore several key areas. First, further studies could examine the effectiveness of E-ATCM across different learning environments, such as online, hybrid, and face-to-face settings. In addition, research could investigate the integration of E-ATCM with various active learning tactics, encompassing Problem-Based Learning (PBL), case studies, and flipped classroom models, to enhance students' engagement and critical thinking. Future studies may also focus on evaluating user experiences and identifying factors that influence the adoption and sustained use of E-ATCM among both students and lecturers. Longitudinal research could evaluate the long-term effects of E-ATCM on students' learning outcomes and preparedness for professional practice. Furthermore, comparative studies between conventional learning modules and E-ATCM-based learning could provide valuable insights into their relative effectiveness. Lastly, future research could consider the development of adaptive features within E-ATCM to accommodate diverse learning styles and extend its implementation across various educational institutions and cultural contexts.

References

1. Tjiptady, B.C., Rohman, M., Rahman, R.Z., Elmunsyah, H.: Exploring Masterweb's Effectiveness in Optimizing Digital Based Learning and Education Management. Ultima Infosys : Jurnal Ilmu Sistem Informasi, vol. 15, no. 2 (2024)
2. Haryana, M.R.A., Warsono, S., Achjari, D., Nahartyo, E.: Virtual reality learning media with innovative learning materials to enhance individual learning outcomes based on cognitive load theory. Int. J. Manage. Educ. **20**(3), November 2022. https://doi.org/10.1016/j.ijme.2022.100657

3. Fitria, T.N.: Augmented Reality (AR) and Virtual Reality (VR) Technology in Education: Media of Teaching and Learning: A Review," 2023. [Online]. Available: https://ijcis.net/index.php/ijcis/index
4. Dahlan, T., Darhim, D., Juandi, D.: How digital applications as mathematics learning media in the automation era (2021). http://journalppw.com
5. Eva Hoerunisa Nur, Z., Raharjo, H., Wahid, S., Syekh Nurjati Cirebon, I.: Development of Quizizz Application E-Module-Based Teaching Materials on Student Mathematics Learning Outcomes, vol. 1, no. 1 (2023). https://doi.org/10.58557/eduinsights.vxix
6. Fahrurrozi, M., Mohzana, M., Mispandi, M., Murcahyanto, H.: Developing Basic Accounting E-Module Based on Scientific Approach in Vocational High Schools. Jurnal Kependidikan: Jurnal Hasil Penelitian dan Kajian Kepustakaan di Bidang Pendidikan, Pengajaran dan Pembelajaran **9**(1), 356 (2023). https://doi.org/10.33394/jk.v9i1.7117
7. Arcadio, R.D., et al.: European Journal of Innovation in Nonformal Education Simplified Modular Instruction for Grade 2 Learners in Technology and Livelihood Education: A Qualitative Inquiry (2023). http://innovatus.es/index.php/ejine
8. Laurensius Setyabudhi, A.: Application of video-based learning media with applications to improve learning activities of vocational high school students vol. 3, no. 1, pp. 2721–9798, 2023, 10.556442
9. Nemorin, S., Vlachidis, A., Ayerakwa, H.M., Andriotis, P.: AI hyped? A horizon scan of discourse on artificial intelligence in education (AIED) and development. Learn. Media Technol. **48**(1), 38–51 (2023). https://doi.org/10.1080/17439884.2022.2095568
10. Hoerudin, C.W., Syafruddin, S., Mayasari, A., Arifudin, O., Lestari, S.: E-Learning as A Learning Media Innovation Islamic Education. QALAMUNA: Jurnal Pendidikan. Sosial, dan Agama **15**(1), 723–734 (2023). https://doi.org/10.37680/qalamuna.v15i1.4466
11. Hennessy, S., et al.: Technology use for teacher professional development in low- and middle-income countries: a systematic review. Comput. Educ. Open **3**, 100080 (2022). https://doi.org/10.1016/j.caeo.2022.100080
12. Hikmah, D., Petoukhoff, G., Papaioannou, J.: The utilization of the animiz application as a media for arabic language learning on students. J. Int. Lingua Technol. **1**(2), 157–171 (2022). https://doi.org/10.55849/jiltech.v1i2.84
13. Bulkani, M.F., Adella, H., Andi Setiawan, M.: Development of animation learning media based on local wisdom to improve student learning outcomes in elementary schools. Int. J. Inst. **15**(1), 55–72 (2022). https://doi.org/10.29333/iji.2022.1514a
14. Sanulita, H., et al.: Analysis of the effectiveness of audio visual learning media based on macromedia flash usage on school program of increasing student learning motivation. J. Educ. **06**(02), 12641–12650 (2024)
15. Verawati, A., Agustito, D., Pusporini, W., Utami, W.B., Widodo, S.A.: Designing Android learning media to improve problem-solving skills of ratio. Adv. Mob. Learn. Educ. Res. **2**(1), 216–224 (2022). https://doi.org/10.25082/AMLER.2022.01.005
16. Sari, H.P., Afriliani, S., Sutanti, N.: Website Based 'BUSWORLD' vocabulary learning media for marketing students of vocational school. Educatio: Journal of Education, vol. 8, no. 2 (2023). www.busworld.id
17. Mursyida, L., Dewi, I.P., Samala, A.D., Ranuharja, F.: E-modules for computer network practicum based on problem-based learning and peer tutoring: a practical solution to develop 21st-century skills. J. Educ. Technol. **8**(1), 77–85 (2024). https://doi.org/10.23887/jet.v8i1.63568
18. Cowan, S., et al.: Lifestyle management in polycystic ovary syndrome – beyond diet and physical activity," Dec. 01, 2023, BioMed Central Ltd. https://doi.org/10.1186/s12902-022-01208-y
19. Diener, E., Northcott, R., Zyphur, M.J., West, S.G.: Beyond experiments. Perspect. Psychol. Sci. **17**(4), 1101–1119 (2022). https://doi.org/10.1177/17456916211037670

20. Tong, D.H., Uyen, B.P., Ngan, L.K.: The effectiveness of blended learning on students' academic achievement, self-study skills and learning attitudes: a quasi-experiment study in teaching the conventions for coordinates in the plane. Heliyon, vol. 8, no. 12, Dec. 2022. https://doi.org/10.1016/j.heliyon.2022.e12657
21. Schneider, S., Beege, M., Nebel, S., Schnaubert, L., Rey, G.D.: The Cognitive-Affective-Social Theory of Learning in digital Environments (CASTLE) Mar. 01, 2022. Springer. https://doi.org/10.1007/s10648-021-09626-5
22. Armstrong, C., Kepler, J.D., Samuels, D., Taylor, D.: Causality redux: the evolution of empirical methods in accounting research and the growth of quasi-experiments. J. Accounting Econ. **74**(2–3), November 2022. https://doi.org/10.1016/j.jacceco.2022.101521
23. Andersson, E.M., Johansson, H., Nordin, S., Lindvall, K.: Cognitive and emotional reactions to pictorial-based risk communication on subclinical atherosclerosis: a qualitative study within the VIPVIZA trial. Scand. J. Prim. Health Care **41**(1), 69–80 (2023). https://doi.org/10.1080/02813432.2023.2178850
24. Asih, T.L.B., Prayitno, B.A., Ariani, S.R.D.: Improving the problem-solving skill of students using problem-based learning-based E-modules. Jurnal Penelitian Pendidikan IPA **8**(3), 1447–1452 (Jul.2022). https://doi.org/10.29303/jppipa.v8i3.1696
25. Mauliana, M.I., et al.: Acitya: Journal of Teaching & education practicum E-module development to improve distance learning efficiency in basic physics courses in the pandemic period (2022). http://journals.umkt.ac.id/index.php/acitya
26. Suryana, D., Lina, L., Sari, N.E.: E-module to assist early childhood learning. Int. J. Early Childhood Learn. **31**(2), 55–76 (2024). https://doi.org/10.18848/2327-7939/cgp/v31i02/55-76
27. Tavares, M.C., Azevedo, G., Marques, R.P., Bastos, M.A.: Challenges of education in the accounting profession in the Era 5.0: A systematic review. (2023). *Cogent OA*. https://doi.org/10.1080/23311975.2023.2220198
28. Mardini, G.H., Mah'd, O.A.: Distance learning as emergency remote teaching vs. traditional learning for accounting students during the COVID-19 pandemic: Cross-country evidence. J. Accounting Educ. vol. 61, December 2022. https://doi.org/10.1016/j.jaccedu.2022.100814
29. Nirbita, B.N., Sartika, S.H.: Development of E-ATCM (Accounting Trading Company Module) as an Interactive Digital Learning Media During the Covid-19 Pandemic. Jurnal Kependidikan: Jurnal Hasil Penelitian dan Kajian Kepustakaan di Bidang Pendidikan, Pengajaran dan Pembelajaran **7**(4), 924 (Dec.2021). https://doi.org/10.33394/jk.v7i4.4317
30. Faizahain, N.: Development of Articulate Storyline Interactive Learning Media to Support Basic Accounting Learning For Class X," Jurnal Pendidikan Ilmu Sosial, vol. 34, no. 2 (2024)
31. Eka Chandra, N., Rizky, M., Bariroh, L., Irvan Arista, A.: Development of accounting learning media based on wetland environment for high school students in South Kalimantan. Econ. Bus. Accounting Soc. Rev. **2**(1), 1–9 (2023). https://doi.org/10.55980/ebasr.v2i1.44
32. Veldkamp, T., et al.: Overcoming technical and market barriers to enable sustainable large-scale production and consumption of insect proteins in Europe: A SUSINCHAIN Perspective. Insects **13**(3), March 2022. https://doi.org/10.3390/insects13030281
33. Birhanu, M.Y., et al.: Beyond diffusion to sustained adoption of innovation: A case of smallholder poultry development in sub-Saharan Africa. Int. J. Agric. Sustain. **20**(6), 1028–1046 (2022). https://doi.org/10.1080/14735903.2022.2041235
34. Hossain, M.A., Agnihotri, R., Rushan, M.R.I., Rahman, M.S., Sumi, S.F.: Marketing analytics capability, artificial intelligence adoption, and firms' competitive advantage: evidence from the manufacturing industry. Ind. Mark. Manage. **106**, 240–255 (Oct.2022). https://doi.org/10.1016/j.indmarman.2022.08.017
35. Rachman Putra, A., Darmawan, D.: Competitive advantage of MSMEs in terms of technology orientation and entrepreneurship competence (2022)

36. Tseng, F.C., Huang, T.L., Pham, T.T.L., Cheng, T.C.E., Teng, C.I.: How does media richness foster online gamer loyalty? Int. J. Inf. Manage. **62**, Feb 2022. https://doi.org/10.1016/j.ijinfomgt.2021.102439
37. Zhang, R., Zou, D.: Types, purposes, and effectiveness of state-of-the-art technologies for second and foreign language learning. Routledge (2022). https://doi.org/10.1080/09588221.2020.1744666
38. Amin, F., A. Y. & Wahyudin: "Age of Empires II" toward Students' Reading Comprehension on Narrative Text (2022). http://jim.teknokrat.ac.id/index.php/english-language-teaching/index
39. Apostolou, B., Dorminey, J.W., Hassell, J.M.: Accounting education literature review. J. Accounting Educ. **59**, June 2022. https://doi.org/10.1016/j.jaccedu.2022.100781
40. Li, Z., et al.: Machine learning in concrete science: applications, challenges, and best practices. Nature Research, Dec. 01, 2022. https://doi.org/10.1038/s41524-022-00810-x
41. Mize, T.D., Manago, B.: The past, present, and future of experimental methods in the social sciences. Soc. Sci. Res. 108, Nov. 2022. https://doi.org/10.1016/j.ssresearch.2022.102799

Research on the Implementation Path and Development Strategy of Artificial Intelligence Technology Enabling Higher Education

Shousen Zhao[1,2] and Zhaolin Liu[1,2(✉)]

[1] College of Textile and Garment, Hebei University of Science and Technology, Shijiazhuang 050018, China
liuzhaolin0508@163.com

[2] Textile and Garment Technology Innovation Center of Hebei Province, Hebei University of Science and Technology, Shijiazhuang 050018, China

Abstract. The current situation and challenges faced by the application of AI technology in higher education teaching, management and science and technology innovation is analyzed on the implementation path of AI technology in enhancing the quality of teaching, optimizing the allocation of resources and improving the learning experience is elaborated. The challenges faced by the application of AI technology in the process of technology, education equity and other dimensions are explored. Then the sustainable development strategies is proposed, including the construction of AI education ecosystem, the integration of technological research and development with educational scenarios, the formulation of standards and norms, and the promotion of international exchanges and cooperation. The aim is to provide a reference for the innovative development of higher education driven by AI technology, and to facilitate the cultivation of talents meeting the needs of the intelligent era.

Keywords: Artificial Intelligence · Higher Education · Innovative Development. Intelligence Literacy

1 Opportunities Brought by Artificial Intelligence Technology to Higher Education

1.1 Deep Changes in Teaching and Learning Process

With the powerful data analysis capabilities of artificial intelligence technology, today's online learning platforms can meticulously track students' learning behaviors and then plan an exclusive learning path for each student through intelligent algorithms. For example, when the system finds that students have difficulty understanding a certain knowledge point and have a high error rate in answering questions, AI will automatically recommend relevant basic consolidation courses, practice questions and easy-to-understand explanatory videos, and then gradually guide them to the next stage of

K. W. Lee and L. H. Wong (Eds.): ITEA 2025, CCIS 2643, pp. 351–361, 2026.
https://doi.org/10.1007/978-981-95-2011-4_33

learning content of moderate difficulty to ensure that students steadily improve their knowledge level according to their own learning ability and the pace of progress [1].

Virtual Reality (VR), Augmented Reality (AR) and other artificial intelligence-related technologies are widely used to create immersive virtual teaching environments. Taking the textile profession as an example, students can enter the virtual textile processing laboratory through VR equipment, as if they are in a real textile production site, and intuitively observe the process of yarn interweaving, fabric organization and the impact of different processing parameters on the finished product. This immersive learning experience helps to improve learning outcomes. Similarly, in history, geography and other disciplines, the use of AR technology can vividly present historical scenes and geographic landscapes in the real environment, helping students better understand abstract historical events and complex geographic concepts [2, 3].

The intelligent teaching assistant has become a powerful helper for teachers in the classroom, not only answering simple questions from students in real time, but also in classroom management. In terms of after-class homework correction and learning effect assessment, the AI-driven automatic correction system can quickly and accurately grade objective questions, and give preliminary correction suggestions and feedback on subjective questions through natural language processing technology, helping teachers save time and focus more energy on in-depth analysis of students' learning and personalized guidance.

1.2 Efficient Optimization of Educational Management

In college admissions, artificial intelligence technology can achieve a more accurate and comprehensive assessment by mining and analyzing massive amounts of candidate data. In addition to the traditional factor of academic performance, artificial intelligence can also comprehensively consider students' interests, social practice experience, competition awards and other aspects of information. Therefore, admissions staff can obtain a more objective, three-dimensional portrait of the candidates, assisting in the development of scientific and reasonable admissions strategy, improving the probability of selection of students who fit the characteristics of the school and the professional needs of the students, so as to make the admissions process more comprehensive and efficient.

In terms of campus resource management, artificial intelligence technology plays an important role in the aspects from classroom and laboratory scheduling to intelligent recommendation and inventory management of library books. Intelligent scheduling system can quickly generate the optimal course scheduling plan based on many factors such as course characteristics, teachers' time and number of students, so as to avoid resource conflicts and idle waste [4].

For the management of students' daily affairs, artificial intelligence technology can create a convenient intelligent customer service system, which provides real-time answers to students' frequently asked questions about course scheduling, campus living facilities, scholarship applications, etc. with 24-h uninterrupted service. In addition, through the analysis of students' behavioral data on campus, such as consumption records and social activities participation, possible academic difficulties and psychological problems of the students can be detected in advance. Therefore, timely intervention and support can be provided to ensure healthy growth and good development of the students in an all-round way.

1.3 Strong Impetus for Scientific and Technological Innovation

In the field of scientific research, artificial intelligence technology can help researchers quickly extract valuable information, discover potential patterns and new research directions from the huge ocean of data. For example, in the field of biology, artificial intelligence technology helps researchers to explore the association between genes and diseases by gene sequence data analysis, which can speed up the research process and improve the output efficiency.

The AI-based research collaboration platform can break the geographical and disciplinary boundaries. Artificial intelligence technology facilitates real-time communication and exchange among researchers from different universities and research institutions, the sharing of research resources, and the collaborative implementation of scientific research projects [5]. The AI-based platform can intelligently match researchers with similar research interests and professional skills, push the latest research results, cutting-edge information and project cooperation opportunities in related fields, promote cross-disciplinary and cross-regional scientific research cooperation and innovation, and provide strong support for solving complex scientific problems.

2 Implementation Path of Artificial Intelligence Technology in Higher Education

2.1 To Enhance the Quality of Education and Teaching

Teaching quality is one of the core objectives of higher education modernization. Artificial intelligence technology significantly contributes to the overall improvement of teaching quality by optimizing course design, supporting personalized teaching and improving assessment and feedback.

Artificial intelligence plays an important role in course design. By analyzing and summarizing massive academic resources, AI technology can generate high-quality course content, handouts, case studies, and achieve precise alignment with course objectives [6]. At the same time, artificial intelligence technology can dynamically adjust the teaching content according to the characteristics of different disciplines and students' learning needs, which makes teaching more flexible and adaptable. On the other hand, artificial intelligence technology supports more diversified and personalized teaching methods. The application of intelligent virtual teaching environments and intelligent teaching assistants prompts teachers to constantly explore and try new teaching methods. These teaching methods not only enrich the form of classroom teaching, make the learning process more lively and interesting, stimulate students' interest and enthusiasm for learning, but also help to cultivate innovative thinking of the students and the ability to solve complex problems, which is in line with the requirements of modern education for the cultivation of innovative talents.

By analyzing students' learning behaviors and cognitive levels, artificial intelligence technology can provide tailor-made learning resources and learning suggestions for each student. A personalized learning system based on AI helps to improve students' ability to master complex knowledge points and learning efficiency.

In addition, artificial intelligence technology has irreplaceable advantages in assessment and feedback. AI technology can quickly analyze the content of students' assignments, essays and exams, provide detailed feedback suggestions and point out problems. This real-time, accurate assessment not only improves teaching efficiency, but also provides students with a clearer direction for learning improvement. The improvement of educational and teaching quality by artificial intelligence technology is shown in Fig. 1.

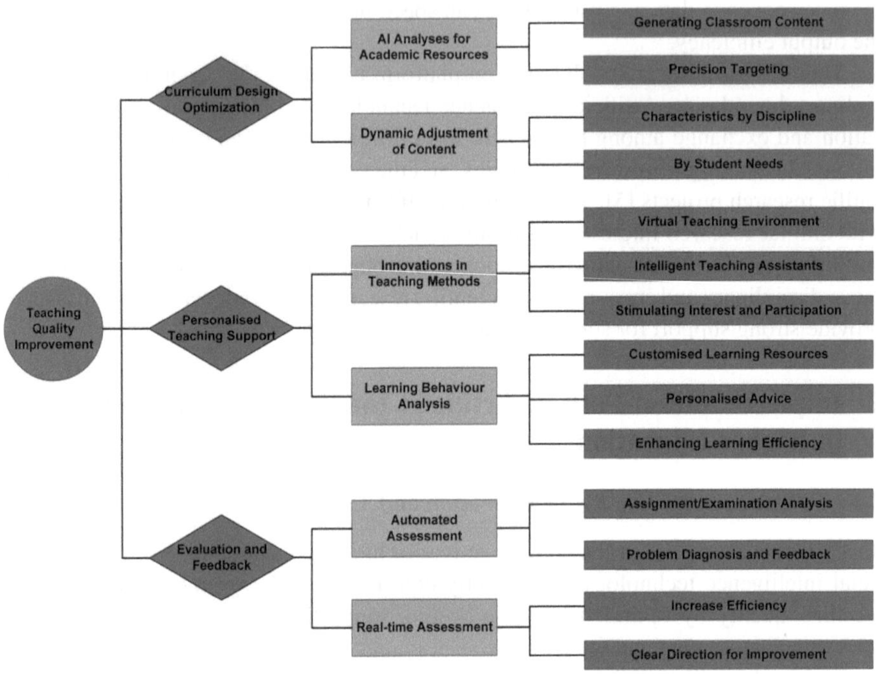

Fig. 1. The improvement of educational and teaching quality by artificial intelligence technology

2.2 To Optimize the Allocation of Educational Resources

Artificial intelligence technology can maximize the efficiency of the use of educational resources, ensure that all types of educational resources can be reasonably allocated and efficiently used according to actual needs. For example, classroom resources can be fully utilized at different times through the intelligent scheduling system to meet the needs of teaching more courses. Library books can accurately flow to the hands of readers who have a real need to read, improving the circulation rate of books and the efficiency of knowledge dissemination, and overall improving the efficiency of the use of educational resources [7].

Artificial intelligence can also promote the sharing and expansion of high-quality resources. Colleges and universities are able to break down barriers and achieve the extensive sharing and dissemination of curriculum resources, scientific research results and teaching experience with the help of the intelligent collaboration and exchange platform built by artificial intelligence. Teachers and students in different regions and at different levels can conveniently access the high-quality educational resources of other universities through the network, which promotes the fair development and construction of education. Artificial intelligence technology provides teachers and students with a broader space for learning and development, and also promotes the optimal allocation of higher education resources and synergistic development on a wider scale.

2.3 To Improve Learning Experience of Students

In the modernization of higher education, the learner experience is increasingly becoming an important criterion for education quality assessment. Artificial intelligence technology has greatly enhanced the quality of the learner experience by providing intelligent learning assistants, generating diverse learning resources and supporting multilingual learning.

The intelligent learning assistant feature is based on natural language generation technology. AI is able to answer learning questions of the students, provide course tutoring suggestions and create personalized learning plans. This virtual assistant provides strong support for students' independent learning. In terms of learning resource generation, artificial intelligence technology is able to provide students with more intuitive and vivid learning materials through multimodal generation technology. Dynamic courseware, virtual experiment videos, and interactive learning content generation not only make the learning process more attractive, but also deepen students' understanding of complex concepts. Cross-language support is also another important manifestation of artificial intelligence technology to optimize the learning experience. Through real-time translation and the generation of multilingual learning resources, AI technology eliminates language barriers, making it easier for international students to access high-quality educational resources, while also helping local students broaden their horizons and enhance their internationalization [8].

2.4 To Cultivate Talents Meeting Demands of the AI Era

By integrating the application of artificial intelligence technology in the daily teaching process, students are able to familiarize themselves with relevant knowledge and skills of intelligent technology in a subtle manner, and enhance their AI literacy, including the understanding of AI principles, the ability to apply AI technology, and the ability to think critically. Meanwhile, the curriculum content and practical teaching of most professional disciplines can be updated in conjunction with artificial intelligence technology. It is of vital importance to cultivate students' ability to apply artificial intelligence to solve practical problems, so that students can quickly adapt to the demands of career development in the intelligent era after graduation, and have strong competitiveness in employment.

The diverse teaching and research environments created by artificial intelligence, such as virtual experiment platforms and intelligent collaborative research projects, provide students with rich opportunities for innovative practice and teamwork scenarios [9]. In the process of participating in the above activities, students need to constantly put forward new ideas, try out new technologies, and work closely with team members, thus their innovation ability, teamwork spirit, and interdisciplinary comprehensive literacy are effectively exercised, which will lay a solid foundation for their future foothold and development in the complex and changing social environment.

2.5 To Accelerate the Modernization of Education Management

Efficient management is an important pillar of the modernization of higher education. Artificial intelligence technology provides intelligent solutions for the modernization of university management in terms of teaching management system optimization, data-driven decision support and teaching quality monitoring.

In terms of teaching management, artificial intelligence technology can optimize course scheduling, enrolment planning and academic resource allocation by building intelligent management systems. For example, AI systems can quickly analyze students' course selection preferences and faculty status, then automatically generates reasonable course scheduling plans, improves management efficiency and reduces resource waste. Data-driven decision support is another important application of artificial intelligence technology in education management, which provides a scientific basis for formulating discipline development plans and talent cultivation strategies by the analysis of multi-dimensional data such as university academic achievements, student performance and social needs. AI-based data analysis can significantly improve the precision and foresight of university management decisions [10]. In addition, teaching quality monitoring is an important part of higher education management. Artificial Intelligence generates dynamic reports through real-time monitoring of classroom data, student feedback and the application of teaching resources. This instant feedback mechanism helps colleges and universities identify problems in teaching and make timely adjustments to continuously optimize teaching quality.

3 Challenges Faced by Artificial Intelligence Technology in Higher Education

3.1 Accuracy and Reliability of Content

Artificial intelligence content generation is based on large amounts of data and complex models, but the results are not always reliable. AI models may generate content with ambiguous semantics, confusing logic, or even incorrect content, which may cause students to misunderstand knowledge or disseminate misinformation. For example, text generation models may generate superficially correct but inaccurate answers to complex academic questions, thus affecting learning outcomes of the students and the credibility of academic research [11]. In addition, AI-generated content lacks a validation mechanism, especially when it faces to multidisciplinary or cross-disciplinary issues. Besides, AI-generated content may exhibit knowledge faults or bias. This shortcoming is particularly prominent in higher education, which requires validated and authoritative knowledge rather than unscreened generated content.

3.2 Resource Consumption of Simulation Training

Large-scale training of artificial intelligence requires massive data and computational resources. The training of large-scale language models usually requires high-performance computing infrastructure and huge energy consumption. This resource-intensive demand makes the widespread application of the artificial intelligence technology limited, especially in resource-limited universities and developing countries, where the popularization of AI faces a high threshold. At the same time, the availability and diversity of data resources is a key issue. Specialized data in many areas of higher education are scarce or difficult to access, which directly limits the effectiveness of the application for artificial intelligence technology in specific disciplines [12].

3.3 Data Privacy and Security Risks

The performance of artificial intelligence technology relies on the training of large-scale data, which may contain personal information and sensitive educational data. For example, learning records of the students, behavioral data and exam results may be used as AI training data, however, if the data protection mechanism is not perfect, it may lead to privacy leakage or malicious use. In addition, as artificial intelligence technology becomes more prevalent in higher education, the system may become a target for cyber-attacks, such as data leakage, falsification of academic documents, or misuse of generative technologies [13]. These potential risks need to be addressed through sound technical solutions and regulatory mechanisms.

3.4 Academic Integrity and Cheating Risks

Artificial intelligence can generate high-quality articles, assignments and code, which may also facilitates academic misconduct [14]. Students may use generative AI to complete assignments or write papers without engaging in learning and research, which would undermine the fundamental value of education. At the same time, it is difficult for teachers to distinguish between content generated by AI and original student content. The existing academic integrity detection tools may not be sufficient to meet the new challenges posed by generative AI, which puts new demands on the evaluation mechanism and integrity culture of higher education.

3.5 Algorithmic Bias in Artificial Intelligence

The performance and output of artificial intelligence is highly dependent on the quality of the training data. However, training data may have inherent biases, such as gender, racial, geographical and cultural biases. These biases may be reflected in the generated results of the models, which lead to unfair distribution of educational resources or disadvantages of specific groups. In higher education, biases may manifest themselves in subtle but harmful ways. For example, generated content may be more biased in favor of the dominant language and culture at the expense of smaller languages or minority cultures, which is detrimental to the achievement of the goals of diversity and inclusion in education [15].

3.6 Attenuation of the Teacher's Role

The widespread application of artificial intelligence technology in teaching and learning may lead to a weakening of the teacher's role. Some educators may rely on artificial intelligence technologies for teaching and assessment tasks, whereas reducing direct interaction with students. It is worth noting that the educational responsibility of teachers is not only to impart knowledge, but also to shape thinking skills and social values of the students. These tasks cannot be completely replace by the artificial intelligence technology [16]. In addition, over-reliance of teachers on AI-generated content may lead to the instrumentalization of educational values and a deviation from the purpose of education, thus violating the human-centered ethical principle of education.

4 Sustainable Development Strategies of Artificial Intelligence Technology in Higher Education

4.1 To Establish an Open, Dynamic and Synergistic Artificial Intelligence Education Ecosystem

The ecosystem theory emphasizes the system's characteristics of wholeness, relatedness, balance, adaptability and openness, which is compatible with the multidimensional and synergistic promotion characteristics required for the transformation of AI education

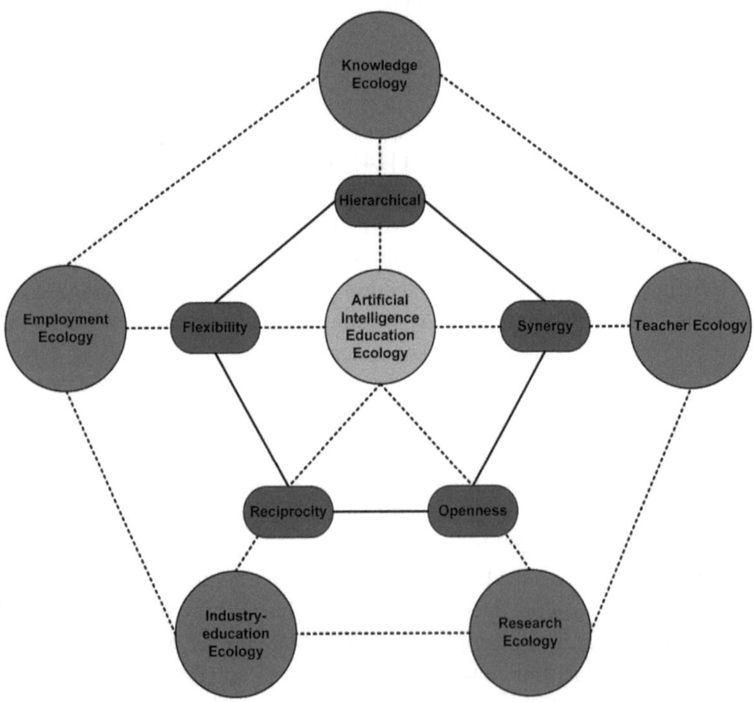

Fig. 2. Construction of an artificial intelligence education ecosystem

[17]. Based on this the above features, the artificial intelligence education transformation practice is constructed into five interrelated ecological subsystems. The curriculum ecosystem is characterized by a three-level progression, the faculty ecosystem is characterized by a two-track approach, the scientific research ecosystem is characterized by a two-dimensional linkage, the industry-education ecosystem is characterized by a co-construction and sharing approach, and the employment ecosystem is characterized by a two-way integration, as shown in Fig. 2. These five sub-ecosystems are both relatively independent and mutually supportive, together constituting an open, dynamic and synergistic artificial intelligence education ecosystem.

4.2 To Promote the Integration of Technological Research and Development with Educational Scenarios

The in-depth integration of artificial intelligence and education requires the construction of a system adapted to the characteristics of educational scenarios. Universities and technology companies need to establish a long-term collaborative mechanism to promote the iterative upgrading of artificial intelligence technology from general-purpose models to specialized education models, which should focus on the special needs of educational scenarios. For example, the dialogue generation model with multilingual interaction capabilities needs to be built for language teaching. The problem solving assistance system that supports formula derivation and logical deduction needs to be developed for mathematics education. Intelligent teaching tools that integrate image generation and creative logic analysis should be built for art disciplines. Through the formation of cross-disciplinary research teams, the laws of educational psychology, subject knowledge systems and natural language processing technology are combined in depth. Special models that can understand teaching goals, identify learning scenarios, and adapt to the needs of teachers and students are developed, so as to realize the transition from "universal adaptation of technology" to "precise empowerment of education". [18].

At the quality control level of technology development, a standardized guarantee system should be established throughout the entire process of AI content generation. In view of the stringent requirements for knowledge accuracy in educational scenarios, it is necessary to introduce authoritative educational resource libraries for data calibration in the model training stage, such as integrating standardized content of professional course syllabi and textbooks to build domain knowledge maps. Furthermore, a dual verification mechanism should be applied in the generation process, both through logical consistency calibration by algorithmic models and manual review and calibration of subject experts. For example, when developing an intelligent homework correction system, knowledge mapping can be used to ensure that the problem-solving steps are in line with the specifications of the syllabus. The accuracy of the answers can be verified by comparing with the authoritative question bank. Meanwhile, a closed loop of user feedback can be established to continuously optimize the model parameters according to the corrective suggestions made by teachers in actual application. This deep coupling of technology development and educational standards can not only guarantee the scientific and authoritative nature of the AI generated content, but also enhance the trust of educators in intelligent technology through a traceable quality control system, laying a solid foundation for large-scale application of artificial intelligence technology in the education field.

4.3 To Formulate Norms and Standards for the Application of Artificial Intelligence Technology

To ensure the regulated application of artificial intelligence technology in universities, it is imperative to develop clear standards and ethical codes. These norms can meticulously delineate the boundaries of the use of artificial intelligence technology in different scenarios, so that the application of artificial intelligence technology can be governed by rules and regulations. Ethical disputes and legal disputes arising from the misuse of the artificial intelligence technology can be avoided.

On one hand, the development of AI content review standards is very critical. Ensure that the content produced by the AI technology is in line with educational goals and mainstream values through strict controls [19]. On the other hand, the establishment of a perfect responsibility tracking mechanism is also indispensable. Ensure that the accuracy and legality of AI-generated content are comprehensively regulated, effectively reduced the potential risks, and help artificial intelligence technology to achieve healthy and orderly development in colleges and universities.

4.4 To Strengthen International Exchanges and Cooperation

The deep integration of artificial intelligence and higher education requires the absorption of global advanced experience [20]. Universities should establish a regular international exchange mechanism, actively participate in academic activities, and share practical experience in areas such as the development of intelligent teaching systems and the analysis of academic data with universities in Europe, the United States, and the Asia-Pacific region through cross-country joint seminars. The two-way interactive internationalization path can not only accelerate the absorption of international cutting-edge technologies, but also gradually transform from an experience receiver to an important participant in the governance of education science and technology through the output of educational application solutions integrating the characteristics of Chinese culture, contributing Chinese wisdom to the digital transformation of global higher education.

5 Conclusion

The application of artificial intelligence technology in higher education has made significant progress and has brought many opportunities to higher education. Artificial intelligence technology plays a positive role in enhancing teaching quality, optimizing resource allocation, improving the learning experience and promoting the modernization of education management. Meanwhile, it is also necessary to clearly recognize the technical, educational equity and ethical challenges in the application of artificial intelligence technology. By adopting corresponding strategies, such as optimizing technological protection, strengthening teacher development, promoting educational equity and regulating ethical behavior, artificial intelligence technology can be better applied in the field of higher education, achieve high-quality and sustainable development.

Acknowledgements. This work is supported by the Higher Education Teaching Reform Research and Practice Project of Hebei Province (No. 2023GJJG198).

References

1. Zhao, X.: Research on artificial intelligence enabled college student mental health education in colleges and universities. PR World **10**, 36–38 (2025)
2. Su, D.: A study on artificial intelligence enabling the development of adult education in the context of digital education - insights based on the application of artificial intelligence in education in Europe and America. Continuing Educ. Res. **6**, 83–89 (2025)
3. Hashmi, N., Bal, A.S.: Generative AI in higher education and beyond. Bus. Horiz. **67**(5), 607–614 (2024)
4. Zheng, Y.: Artificial intelligence enabled high quality development path exploration for universities. Beijing Education **5**, 49–51 (2025)
5. Li, Z.M.: Artificial intelligence enabling higher education: boundary breaking, Reconfiguration and Future Paths. Education International Exchange (3), 1 (2025)
6. Wang, J.Q., Song, J.: Artificial intelligence education in the UK: policy-driven innovation practices in universities. Educ. Int. Exchange **3**, 31–36 (2025)
7. Liu, X.F.: A study of generative artificial intelligence in education. PR World **9**, 154–156 (2025)
8. Aler, T.A., Mora-Cantallops, M., Nieves, J.C.: How to teach responsible AI in higher education: challenges and opportunities. Ethics and Information Technology (1), 26 (2023)
9. He, X.S.: Information dissemination risks and governance paths in artificial intelligence enabled education. Editors' J. **3**, 25–29 (2025)
10. Liang, J.: Reflections on artificial intelligence to promote deep changes in teaching and learning in vocational education. Continuing Educ. Res. **6**, 77–82 (2025)
11. Butson, R., Spronken-Smith, R.: AI and its implications for research in higher education: a critical dialogue. High. Educ. Res. Dev. **43**(3), 563–577 (2024)
12. Pang, Q.L., Tan, T.Y., Wei, Y.F.: Exploration on the optimization path of adaptation of law education in local colleges and universities under the background of artificial intelligence. University Education **9**, 88–92 (2025)
13. Tan, T.Y., Huang, L.A., Pang, Q.L.: Research on the intelligent transformation path of legal education in the age of artificial intelligence. Western Quality Education **11**(8), 124–127 (2025)
14. Cai, J.T.: Generative artificial intelligence technology enables modernization of higher education. China Univ. Sci. Technol. **4**, 43–48 (2025)
15. O'Dea, X.: Generative AI: is it a paradigm shift for higher education? Stud. High. Educ. **49**(5), 811–816 (2024)
16. Sun, Q.S.: Realistic issues and realization path of artificial intelligence enabling ideological and political education in colleges and universities. J. Fujian Inst. Educ. **26**(4), 9–14+102+129 (2025)
17. Wang, B.W., Fu, S.Y.: Ethical risks in the educational application of artificial intelligence and their response. Acad. Res. **4**, 1–9 (2025)
18. Wang, X.M., Zhou, G.L., Zhou, X.: Analysis of higher education research papers in national universities and colleges, 2024 - statistics of publications based on the 23 most influential journals in the field of education. China High. Educ. Res. **4**, 42–54 (2025)
19. Miao, F.C.: Reconfiguring higher education in the post-artificial intelligence era. Open Educ. Res. **31**(2), 4–13 (2025)
20. Akgun, S., Greenhow, C.: Artificial intelligence in education: addressing ethical challenges in K-12 settings. AI Ethics **2**(3), 431–440 (2022)

Innovation and Practice in Computing Education in the Context of Big Models

Jun Hu(✉), Yahui Hu, Fuqiang Peng, Ling He, Zi Wang, and Sheng Tang

Air Force Early Warning College, Wuhan, China
249479274@qq.com

Abstract. Advances in AI and large language models have transformed fields like natural language processing and coding. These changes bring both opportunities and challenges for computer education. While these powerful tools can enhance teaching and personalize learning, they also raise concerns about over-reliance and academic honesty. This paper presents practical ways to use big models effectively in computer education while managing potential risks. We focus on three key areas: (1) customized learning with AI assistance, (2) smart teaching tools, and (3) combining different subjects. Our approach helps students learn better while developing strong computational thinking skills.

Keywords: big models · computer education · educational innovation · personalized learning · intelligent assisted instruction

1 Introduction

In recent years, the rapid development of AI technology, especially the breakthroughs of big models (e.g., GPT, ChatGPT, etc.) in the fields of natural language processing, knowledge reasoning, and code generation, as Fig. 1shown, is profoundly changing the education ecology. Computer education, as an important way to cultivate students' digital literacy and computational thinking, has ushered in new opportunities brought about by intelligent teaching tools, but also faces new challenges such as technology abuse and academic ethics, etc. How to rationally use big models to optimize the teaching mode, while avoiding their potential risks, has become a key issue in current educational research.

2 The Impact of Big Models on Computing Education

The rise of big models of artificial intelligence has brought unprecedented opportunities for change in computer education. At the level of knowledge acquisition, big models can instantly generate high-quality teaching cases, programming examples, and interactive Q&A, which greatly enriches the learning resources; at the level of teaching methodology, its natural language interaction capability makes personalized tutoring possible, and it can provide self-adaptive learning

K. W. Lee and L. H. Wong (Eds.): ITEA 2025, CCIS 2643, pp. 362–373, 2026.
https://doi.org/10.1007/978-981-95-2011-4_34

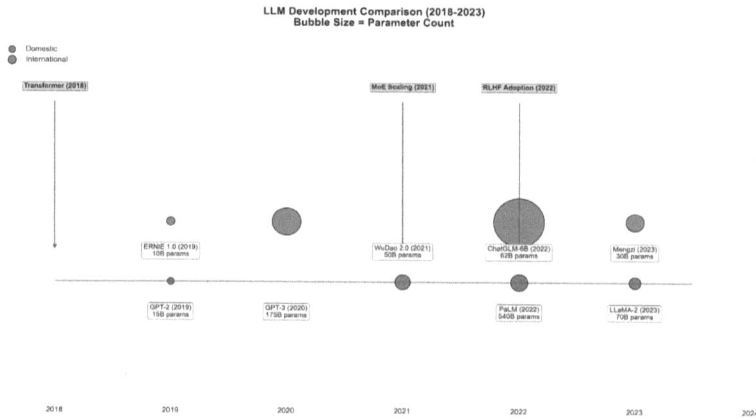

Fig. 1. LLM development

paths for different students; at the level of discipline integration, big models can help build cross-domain knowledge connections and promote the organic integration of computational thinking and humanities and social sciences knowledge. In terms of disciplinary integration, the multimodal processing capability of the model helps to build cross-domain knowledge links and promote the organic integration of computational thinking and knowledge in humanities and social sciences.

However, technological innovation is also accompanied by serious challenges. Over-reliance on model output may lead to the degradation of students' critical thinking skills, automatically generated code and assignments carry academic integrity risks, and the inherent biases and errors of models may be misleading to beginners. In the era of big models, computer education will face the core proposition of how to balance technological innovation and the essence of education.

2.1 Innovation and Opportunity

The combination of big model technology and computer education has a natural fit. The characteristics of the computer discipline of solving real-world problems through programming language and algorithmic logic form a deep fit with the powerful data processing capability of big models, as shown in Fig. 2 , which makes big models able to directly understand and generate code, algorithms, and other core teaching content, and realize accurate knowledge transfer and real-time feedback. This technical feature perfectly matches the essential demand of computer education that emphasizes practicality, and provides learners with personalized practical guidance through innovative forms such as intelligent programming assistants and virtual experimental environments, which significantly improves learning efficiency. More importantly, this in-depth integration is promoting a fundamental shift in the paradigm of computer education, from traditional knowledge transfer to a new model that pays more attention to the cultivation of capabilities. With the technical advantages of AI collaborators, not only does it more effectively cultivate the core literacy of students in computational thinking and system design, but it also provides an innovative technological path to promote educational fairness and realize the universality of high-quality resources, which shows a broad prospect for the integration of technology and education. It also provides an innovative technical path for promoting educational equity and realizing the universalization of quality resources, showing a broad prospect for the integration of technology and education.

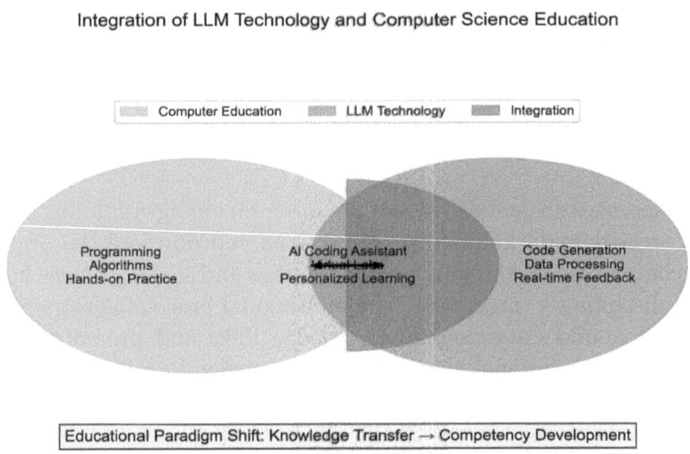

Fig. 2. LLM development

2.2 Negative Impact

Big model technology in the traditional computer teaching mode to bring opportunities and development at the same time, its rapid development of the traditional computer teaching mode has brought many aspects of the negative impact, such as Table 1 shown. Table 1 Impact of the Big Model on the traditional model of computer teaching and learning. Transitional use of large models is prone to weakening students' critical thinking and deep learning ability, leading to overreliance on AI-generated code and solutions, resulting in a lack of solid mastery of basic skills and a decline in active learning motivation. Secondly, the teaching evaluation system faces serious challenges, traditional assessment methods are difficult to detect assignments completed with AI assistance, and academic misconduct is more hidden and difficult to screen.

Big model to the traditional mode of teaching and learning has brought about a revolutionary change, with the help of big model, the ubiquity and convenience of learning relying on big model technology continues to extend and develop, a

Table 1. Impact of the Big Model on the traditional model of computer teaching and learning

No.	Dimension	Negative Impact	Concrete Expression
1	Learning Ability	Weakens critical thinking	Over-reliance on AI reduces independent analysis
2	Academic Integrity	Increases plagiarism risk	Direct submission of AI-generated work
3	Skill Mastery	Declines practical skills	Less hands-on programming/writing practice
4	Teachers' Roles	Challenges authority	Students may prefer AI over teacher guidance
5	Course Content	Knowledge update lag	Models may propagate outdated information

dialogue-based Q&A can achieve multi-dimensional knowledge fast sieve, the sense of experience of the students will even be stronger than the traditional online classroom, how to teach better than the big model, the content is deeper than the model output, forcing the role of the teacher in the era of big models Transformation, the need to redesign the course content and teaching methods.

The big model is based on the autoregressive prediction mechanism of the Transformer architecture, the essence is to learn the probability distribution of words through massive text data, rather than understanding semantic logic, which is easy to form the "AI illusion", and at the same time, the big model is essentially a statistical projection of social cognition, and the quality of the answer will be strongly correlated with the training data, which will easily cause the deviation of the training data to form the answer bias of the big model, which in turn will bring cognitive bias to students in learning. At the same time, the nature of the big model is a statistical projection of social cognition, and the quality of the answer will be strongly correlated with the training data, and it is easy to form the answer bias of the big model due to the bias of the training data, which will bring cognitive bias to the students' learning.

These effects together constitute the core problem that constrains big model technology to better land practice in computer education, which needs to be solved urgently, and requires the establishment of effective preventive and guiding mechanisms while utilizing the advantages of technology in computer teaching.

3 Innovative Practices of Big Modeling Technology in Computing Education

3.1 Constructing an Exclusive Grand Model of Computer Education

To realize the in-depth application of big model technology in the field of education, it is necessary to break through the limitations of the general model and develop proprietary big model technology for educational scenarios. The construction of this proprietary model is by no means simply fine-tuning and optimizing the general model, but rather needs to be based on the fundamental goal of reshaping the future ecology of education, based on the open algorithmic architecture system, and carry out systematic innovations around the core needs of education and teaching. The research and development of the education proprietary model should not only inherit the basic ability of the general model, but also carry out in-depth reconstruction in the dimensions of knowledge representation, interaction mode, evaluation and feedback for the specificity of education scenarios, in order to truly meet the needs of intelligent education.

To address the special needs of the computer education field, we designed a layered education model architecture system: the bottom layer is the basic competency layer (L0), which provides general language comprehension and generation capabilities; the middle layer is the computer professional competency layer (L1), which specializes in strengthening the core skills of programming language processing, algorithmic reasoning, etc.; and the top layer is the education application service layer (L2), which is oriented to the specific teaching scenarios for the development of intelligent programming The top layer is the education application service layer (L2), which develops intelligent programming, tutoring, automatic assessment and other functional modules for specific teaching scenarios. This layered architecture design not only ensures the universality of basic AI capabilities, but also deeply adapts to the specialized needs of computer education, and its specific implementation framework is shown in Fig. 3.

3.2 Big Model-Enabled Changes in Teaching Models for Computer Science Courses

To realize the real value of the educational big model, it is not enough to build a proprietary big model in the field of computer education, and it is even more necessary to deeply integrate the big model technology with the innovative teaching mode, which is not a simple superimposition of technology, but rather a systematic pedagogical design, so that the ability of the big model and the laws of teaching and learning to form an organic fit, so as to ensure a substantial improvement in the quality of education.

In-Depth Construction of an Interactive Generation System for Learning Spaces. With the intelligent support of the Great Model of Education, the learning space is undergoing a revolutionary reconfiguration, where learners are

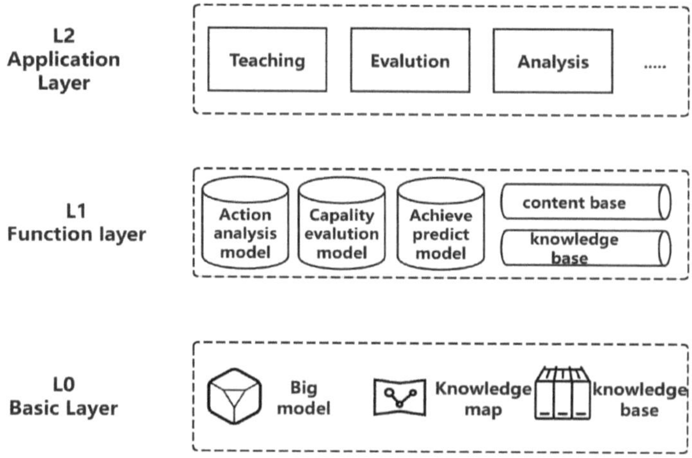

Fig. 3. Education Model Architecture

provided with dynamic learning support through new human-computer interaction methods such as natural language interaction and real-time collaboration of codes, as shown in Fig. 4, which is not only manifested in the level of knowledge acquisition, but also extends to the process of creative generation of learning outcomes.

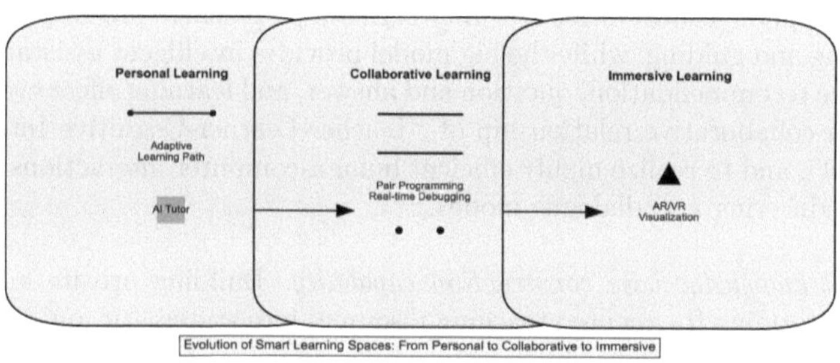

Fig. 4. Smart Learning Evolution

Efficient cognitive diagnosis grand model based on multi-source heterogeneous data, realizing accurate diagnosis and analysis of knowledge mastery, constructing intelligent knowledge tracking grand model, realizing multi-level in-depth cognitive diagnosis driven by multi-source heterogeneous data, expanding individual learning to collaborative innovation in collective learning space on this basis, supporting collaborative learning of multi-learners to form distributed cognitive network, fully utilizing AR/VR technology to abstract computing concepts visualized presentation, to achieve a seamless connection between the computer knowledge system and digital simulation.

Accurate Matching of Learning Resources Supply and Demand System. The educational big model needs to analyze the cognitive characteristics of learners, differentiate the learning content push, and build an exclusive learning environment that fits the individual cognitive development law. Taking the computer network course as an example, the system analyzes the intrinsic correlation relationship between knowledge, extracts the main features, and builds the knowledge map, and builds the student learning path based on the knowledge map, and finally builds the student competence mapping, transforming the abstract behavioral trajectories into quantifiable cognitive ability dimensions.

Paradigm Shift in Teacher Professional Development. The big model of education is reshaping the professional development path of teachers and promoting the intelligent upgrading of the teaching competency system. The role of teachers has changed from a single knowledge transmitter to a composite education designer, and they need to focus on cultivating the following core competencies:

Intelligent curriculum design capability. Using large model technology to analyze students' learning needs, interests, abilities and knowledge base, and customize suitable learning paths for them, not only focusing on their current learning status, but also taking into account their long-term development goals, so as to realize the education concept of "tailor-made education".

Human-computer collaborative teaching capability. Teachers are responsible for supervising and guiding, while the big model provides intelligent assistance, such as resource recommendation, question and answer, and learning effect evaluation, to build a collaborative relationship of "Teacher-Learner-Cognitive Intelligence Big Model", and to realize highly efficient human-computer interactions through cueing engineering and dialogue modes.

Intelligent knowledge base construction capability. Building private knowledge base, transforming fragmented teaching resources into systematic and structured knowledge points, continuously updating and optimizing them, quickly retrieving teaching materials based on the knowledge base, intelligently associating related

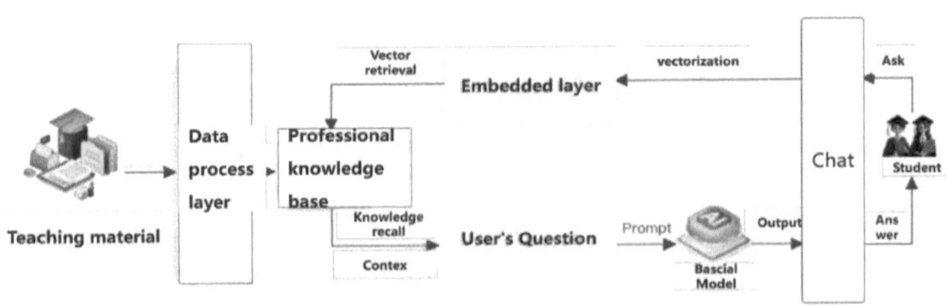

Fig. 5. Construction of Knowledge Base

knowledge points, and automatically generating teaching cases and assessment questions, so as to realize the digital precipitation and intelligent application of teaching resources, the construct of knowledge base is shown in Fig. 5 .

4 Notes on the Integration of Big Models Into Computer Education

4.1 Consistency and Balance in the Essence of Education

Core purpose of using big models to aid teaching and learning is to improve the quality of teaching and learning through technology. So there are two key points to pay particular attention to when using big model technology in education: the technology should serve the teaching and not be anti-climactic. For example, in the use of large model technology to design animation demonstration of sorting algorithm, the core and focus of the design is not to make a cool effect, but the decomposition of the steps, the abstract process of visualization, will be obscure concepts visualization, to allow students to truly understand the core idea of "divided and ruled by" in the classroom, always bearing in mind that technology is only a tool, mastery of knowledge is the purpose. Knowledge is the goal.

Learning requires appropriate "brainstorming". In the daily teaching process, often prone to the problem is that students do not think about the use of large models to generate results, this process completely omitted the most important step in the study of thinking in the computer education learning process to retain some of the links must be done by their own hands, for example, the provisions of certain basic algorithms must be written by hand pseudo-code can not be directly generated by the large model. This deliberate "inconvenience" on the contrary, can exercise the real skills, to prevent students from encountering problems in the search for large models, their own brain does not move.

4.2 Differentiation of Responsibilities in the Teaching-Learning Process

In the intelligent transformation of education, human-computer collaboration requires the establishment of clear "responsibility boundaries", to deal with repetitive work: automatically checking code syntax errors, providing 24/7 answers to basic conceptual questions, batch generation of basic practice questions based on the learning situation of the students, the teacher focuses on the development of the summary of the condensation and enhancement of the expansion of the quality of the content generated by the AI to control the quality of the content, to grasp the classroom progress, to computer Python program teaching process, for example, the big model and value of the specific division of labor tasks as shown in Table 2.

Table 2. AI-Assisted Teaching Role Distribution

Type of Mission	Big Model' s Roles	Teachers' Roles
Basic Grammar Q&A	Major undertaking	Oversight and corrections
System Design Guidance	Provision of reference programs	Lead review and optimization
Code Debugging	Automated error detection	Conceptual explanation and best practices
Project Evaluation	Preliminary assessment	Final grading and feedback
Curriculum Adaptation	Personalized content recommendation	Syllabus design and adjustment

4.3 Realistic Constraints on Implementation

The application of big model technology has put forward brand new requirements for teachers' digital literacy, which are mainly reflected in the two dimensions of ability transformation and cognitive load. In terms of ability transformation, teachers need to systematically master prompt engineering technology, be able to accurately design education-specific prompt templates, and need to cultivate the ability to identify and correct AI-generated content, including the identification of potential errors, correction of knowledge bias, and optimization of expression; more importantly, they must reconfigure the traditional instructional design methodology and develop a new type of teaching mode that is adapted to the synergy between humans and machines, and in order to avoid adaptation barriers in the process of transformation. In order to avoid adaptation barriers during the transformation process, it is recommended to adopt a gradual tiered training strategy: firstly, focus on cultivating backbone teachers with technical foundation, accumulating experience through the construction of demonstration courses, and then gradually expanding the program by "passing on the experience to others", and avoiding adopting the mandatory "one-size-fits-all" promotion mode, so as to ensure that the teachers' group can smoothly complete the digital transformation.

The training and reasoning process of the big model requires a lot of arithmetic, data and human resources input, which is a huge cost, and must be reasonably configured according to the actual teaching needs, and the recommended hardware configuration of the application scenarios is shown in Table 3 of, so as to avoid the waste of resources caused by blindly pursuing high performance. The principle of "three steps" can be referred to: first use the existing equipment → verify the value of teaching → additional investment as needed.

Table 3. AI Infrastructure Configuration for Educational Scenarios

Scenario	Hardware	Cost	Scale
Experimental Apps	1 × RTX 4090	\$20–30K	≤30 students
Course Support	4 × A100	\$300–500K	200 students
School-wide	A100 Cluster	\$2M+	Cross-discipline
Research Lab	8 × H100 HGX	\$1–1.5M	50 researchers
University-wide	Multi-GPU	\$5M+	Campus-wide

5 Big Models Empower Future Trends in Computer Education

5.1 Deeper Integration of Technologies Drives Learning Paradigm Innovation

The big model is poised to revolutionize the field of computer education by breaking through the traditional boundaries of knowledge transfer. Through advanced multimodal interaction and cognitive externalization tools, it will enable visual debugging of code generation and seamless natural language translation of algorithmic logic. This transformative approach shifts the focus of computer education from mere "skill training" to a more profound "thinking embodiment," where learners can intuitively grasp complex concepts and internalize problem-solving methodologies. By bridging the gap between abstract theory and practical application, the big model lays the foundation for a more holistic and immersive learning experience.

Moreover, this paradigm shift will empower learners to achieve a dual leap in both technical thinking and engineering practice capabilities. On one hand, it fosters higher-order cognitive skills, such as logical reasoning, algorithmic design, and system-level understanding. On the other hand, it enhances hands-on engineering abilities by providing real-time feedback, interactive code visualization, and contextualized debugging support. As a result, learners can seamlessly transition from conceptual understanding to practical implementation, cultivating a new generation of innovators who excel in both theoretical depth and technical proficiency. This dual advancement ensures that computer education keeps pace with the rapidly evolving demands of the digital age.

5.2 Intelligent Scene Penetration Reconfigures the Whole Teaching Chain

In the future, as big model technology continues to advance, computer teaching will undergo a fundamental transformation by leveraging dynamic knowledge mapping and generative resource engines. These technologies will reshape the traditional closed-loop structure of curriculum implementation—encompassing curriculum design, experimental guidance, and competency assessment—into a more adaptive and intelligent system. For instance, by employing code style analysis, educators can diagnose students' programming habits in real time, identifying strengths, weaknesses, and individual learning patterns. This shift moves education away from a one-size-fits-all "standardized output" model and toward a more responsive framework that tailors instruction to each learner's unique needs.

Furthermore, the integration of big model technology will enable a deeper level of personalized growth in computer education. Dynamic knowledge mapping ensures that learning resources evolve alongside student progress, while generative engines provide customized exercises, feedback, and assessments. This approach not only enhances comprehension and retention but also fosters creativity and problem-solving skills by adapting to different learning paces and styles. As a result, education becomes more student-centric, empowering learners to develop their technical abilities in alignment with their individual cognitive trajectories. Ultimately, this evolution from standardization to personalization will cultivate a more innovative and capable generation of computer science professionals.

5.3 Industrial Ecological Synergy Accelerates the Iteration of Technical Education

The big model will break down the long-standing data barriers between the education chain and industrial chain, creating a seamless connection between academic training and real-world needs. By integrating enterprise project cases and industry technology trend prediction models, it will establish an agile "demand perception - resource supply - result transformation" response system. This system enables educational institutions to dynamically adjust curricula based on real-time industry developments, ensuring students acquire skills that match current and future market demands. Through this integration, computer education shifts from passively following industry trends to actively anticipating and shaping them, marking a fundamental change in how talent is cultivated.

This transformation represents a strategic evolution from traditional "lagging cultivation" where education struggles to keep pace with rapid technological changes to a model of "forward-looking empowerment." The big model's analytical capabilities allow educators to identify emerging skill requirements early, while its generative functions facilitate rapid development of targeted training materials. Students benefit from exposure to authentic enterprise challenges and cutting-edge technologies during their education, giving them a competitive edge upon entering the workforce. Ultimately, this proactive approach bridges the gap between classroom learning and industrial application, producing graduates who are not just job-ready but innovation-capable, thereby driving both educational and economic advancement.

6 Concludtion

The rapid development of big model technology has brought unprecedented opportunities and challenges for computer education. In the future, computer education will develop in the direction of "human-computer collaboration and intelligent enhancement", and realize the deep integration of technology and education by constructing an exclusive big model for education, optimizing the teaching mode, and clarifying the boundary of responsibility. The future of computer education needs to embrace technological innovation while always keeping in mind the core mission of educating people, balancing the relationship between efficiency and quality, convenience and depth, intelligence and ethics, reasonably planning the path of technology application, establishing a scientific evaluation and adjustment mechanism, and truly giving full play to the empowering role of the big model, so as to cultivate new-age computer talents with solid professional skills, critical thinking and innovation ability.

References

1. Wang, F., Liu, W., Li, W., et al.: Paths and challenges of educational change empowered by big models. Comput. Educ. **2023**(5), 1–10 (2023)
2. Zhang, H., Li, M.: Research on the Construction Method of Educational Big Model Based on Transformer. Tsinghua University, Beijing (2023)
3. Chen, G., Wang, X., Liu, Y., et al.: Application of human-computer collaborative teaching model in computer courses. In: Proceedings of the National Conference on Artificial Intelligence Education, pp. 45–52. Zhejiang University Press, Hangzhou (2023)
4. Department of Science and Technology, Ministry of Education: Artificial Intelligence Helps Modernize Education. China Educ. News (2023-03-15)
5. Stanford HAI: AI in Education: Opportunities and Challenges (2023). https://hai.stanford.edu/research/ai-education
6. Brown, T.B., Mann, B., Ryder, N., et al.: Language models are few-shot learners. Adv. Neural. Inf. Process. Syst. **33**, 1877–1901 (2020)
7. Google AI Education Team: Responsible AI Practices for Educators (2023). https://ai.google/education/responsible-ai

Author Index

K. W. Lee and L. H. Wong (Eds.): ITEA 2025, CCIS 2643, pp. 375–376, 2026.
https://doi.org/10.1007/978-981-95-2011-4

MIX
Papier aus verantwortungsvollen Quellen
Paper from responsible sources
FSC® C105338

If you have any concerns about our products,
you can contact us on
ProductSafety@springernature.com

In case Publisher is established outside the EU,
the EU authorized representative is:
Springer Nature Customer Service Center GmbH
Europaplatz 3, 69115 Heidelberg, Germany

Printed by Libri Plureos GmbH
in Hamburg, Germany